Blockchain, Law and Governance

Benedetta Cappiello • Gherardo Carullo
Editors

Blockchain, Law and Governance

Springer

Editors
Benedetta Cappiello
Department of Italian
and Supranational Public Law
University of Milan
Milan, Italy

Gherardo Carullo
Department of Italian
and Supranational Public Law
University of Milan
Milan, Italy

ISBN 978-3-030-52721-1 ISBN 978-3-030-52722-8 (eBook)
https://doi.org/10.1007/978-3-030-52722-8

This Springer imprint is published by the registered company Springer Nature Switzerland AG.
The registered company address is: Gewerbestrasse 11, 6330 Cham, Switzerland

Foreword

Among the various characteristics generally attributed to blockchain (and DLTs), it can be firmly held that blockchain is a transactional technology. The fact has become widely accepted, and regardless of the qualification that should be given to it (and the importance of semantic), a consensus is emerging on the necessity to study its impact.

That is fortunate. Indeed, blockchain modifies the quadriptych introduced by Lawrence Lessig in his book *Code* as regards the constraints exercised on all subjects when they engage with the rest of society: *architecture*, *social norms*, *the market* and *the law*. Many challenges arise from the new dynamism it creates.

Of course, blockchain central characteristics (such as immutability) is a primary reason why it is being used. It allows interactions in a given framework, making the *architectural* constraint more preeminent. In the meantime, *social norms* and *markets* are coming into greater conflict. On the one hand, blockchain interactions are guided by the values conveyed by each ecosystem, while on the other hand, all exchanges are strongly influenced by economic incentives. Giving a closer look at blockchain forks provides evidence of this. The *law*, at last, is finding a new balance. Blockchain makes specific enforcement mechanisms less efficient while also allowing for reinforcing the law in given situations.

The present book deals precisely with blockchain impact on the legal constraint.

One will find different perspectives in it, making this book utterly valuable. They can be represented as follows:

Cooperation (Law and Blockchain)	⟷	Competition (Law vs. Blockchain)

On the left, the legal constraint and blockchain form alliances to achieve a given objective. On the right, they compete with each other, either to achieve the same objective or because blockchain seeks to reach a different one (sometimes opposite) from the law. Each contribution tends more or less to one side of the spectrum. There are two reasons for this.

The *first* is the subject matter.

Certain subjects lead by nature to discuss the means of a collaboration between the law and blockchain. It is the case, for example, in the literature explaining how blockchain could help to ensure the rights of refugees, where international law is not effective enough. It is also the case with writings dealing with alternative disruptive resolutions, as these are complementary systems.

Other topics deal *per se* with a confrontation between law and technology. One may find all discussions regarding blockchain applications designed to evade the rule of law on this side of the spectrum. Contributions addressing the substitution of current legal systems by technological solutions also fall on this side.

Finally, some other issues exhibit mixed analyses. The issue of protecting personal data is, I believe, a great example of that. Blockchain can indeed preserve the real-life identity of participants in certain exchanges, but it also raises critical issues regarding the right to be forgotten.

The *second* reason is related to the author's very own perspective.

Some are naturally tempted to point out the existence of a dominant strategy resulting in a confrontation between law and technology. To be schematic, the tenants of "West Coast code" tend to consider that technology must always be developed outside the legal constraint because it is restrictive. The advocates of "East Coast law" tend to point to the absolute supremacy of the rule of law, liberating in nature.

Others highlight the necessity for law and technology to work together to achieve a given objective. It involves concessions. For the law, it means that one should not use the full enforcement arsenal in all circumstances. The legal constraints should also be adapted to technology, for example, by creating legal comfort zones with regulatory sandboxes and safe harbors. For technology, it implies that it must be law-oriented, differently put, that architectural choices must be made toward legal uses.

Each of these approaches is necessary to enrich the field of blockchain study. This book is a real tour de force as it brings many substantial contributions representing the entire spectrum in a single place.

If you wish, I invite you to reproduce the above graph on a sheet of paper (or in a digital format. . .) and have fun placing these contributions on one side or the other. If you do so, you will find out that in that some cases, all the writings dealing with one subject are on the same side of the spectrum, probably because the issue imposes it. For other topic matters, you will find the contributions on different sides of the spectrum.

This exercise is particularly insightful considering the breadth and precision of the topics covered. It allows us to create a clear map of academic research advancement on many important issues. They are distributed as follows.

The first part of the book relates to the internationalist discussion. Benedetta Cappiello's article argues that "no blockchain-based organization can rid itself of neither the national provisions nor the principles of international law," and that the interaction of the rules of law with on-chain and off-chain rules should be considered as a major issue. Gherardo Carullo follows up by pointing out that "DLTs could have some utility in complex procedures, that is, where multiple administrations have to interact to exercise a certain public power, especially in cases where this occurs supra-state level, for example in cases of European co-administration."

For Jean Lassègue, there is "a conflict between two forms of legality in today's rule of law: the first one is based on legal texts written in technical but natural languages that are the expression of political sovereignty; the second one is based on unreadable pieces of software the authority." The interaction between the two must be carefully thought of as it would "be illusory to think that legal institutions could be replaced one day by decidable processes that can be written in advance." Lastly, Clemente Biondi Santi and Vincenzo Vespri explore mining activity, which is essential to blockchain functioning, or in other words, to the new legal order described in the three previous contributions.

The second part of the book takes us to the land of governance and regulatory issues. Andrej Zwitter and Jilles Hazenberg turn their attention to blockchain governance principles. They defend the necessity "to see technologies as tools that have effects on our governance structures." It implies understanding it and keeping control over its functioning, "else, we will be living with laws comprised of code inaccessible to our legal understanding or influence."

For Gino Giambelluca, financial authorities should deal with the digital innovation without further ado as it affects "the efficiency and the reliability of payment systems, the smooth functioning of financial market infrastructures, the soundness of the intermediaries, the consumer protection." Martina Tambucci also offers to protect investors and consumers "against frauds through determining a correct use of technology and through the imposition of transparency targeted requirements."

Michele Ferrari goes on argues for creating a "new block" to the chain of the VAT Directive provisions, the goal being to provide legal certainty as to how blockchain operations will be submitted to VAT. Additionally, Cristina Poncibò suggests that regulatory flexibility is also essential to "converge toward forms of accountability to protect fundamental rights within these global private regimes of the digital environment."

The third part of this book deals with smart contracts and dispute resolution. Giesela Rühl introduces the topic by explaining that smart contracts do not escape legal systems as "the applicable choice of law rules of the Rome I Regulation resort to connecting factors, namely party choice and habitual residence, which work reasonably well in a decentralized virtual environment." Paolo Bertoli underlines that not only is the law applicable, but that it is also necessary to blockchain ecosystems. There is indeed "a fundamental methodological flaw in the assertion according to which the code is the law. This assertion, indeed, is based on a reversal of the proper legal methodology: an automated code or computer protocol can have legally binding effects only if and the extent the applicable law so prescribes or allows. So, before one looks at the code, one needs to look at the law."

Oliver R. Goodenough concludes that although "some proponents of digital contracting have argued that the automaticity of machine execution will remove such agreements from legal review, the more realistic view is that interaction with the legacy legal system is likely to remain a feature of contracting." However, it does not mean that the law should take precedence without adapting itself. "To make that interaction productive, the law must integrate itself with the new formats and challenges of computational contracting."

For Amedeo Santosuosso, the priority is first and foremost to improve blockchain. "The conclusion is that blockchain has gained a position among the technological innovation tools and that its real success will depend to a large extent on the ability of establishing efficient and reliable systems of dispute resolution." Furthermore, Pietro Ortolani underlines that the blockchain may avoid specific conflicts, but that "a blockchain-based escrow system may not prevent the *de novo* rehearing of the case, at a later stage." Michele Nastri raises other limits. "Blockchain could indeed improve the notarial activity," but it would be "unrealistic to think about changing the land registry system into a system that does not involve central authorities and does not allow any judicial authority to modify the registers."

The fourth and last part is dedicated to the subject of sustainable blockchain applications. For Giulio Coppi, "distributed technologies can be used together with other solutions to accomplish important and previously unattainable goals" in the humanitarian and development sectors. The author explains the path toward such accomplishment. Anna Burzykowska then focuses on "blockchain-based land registries and data value chains for natural resources management," analyzing how Earth Observation technology and blockchain could be better integrated.

Alessandro Palombo and Raffaele Battaglini go on to explain that "new tool to solve disputes that otherwise may remain with no affordable dispute resolution mechanism" is becoming available. They take part in solving "the problem of inefficient and expensive management of micro-claims." And according to Marco Tullio Giordano, "more and more blockchain-based solutions will be offered on the market, thus raising new questions which will need to be answered. Instead of transposing to decentralized environment concepts and rules specifically designed for a centralized framework, the intimate nature of this new technology should be understood so as to ensure the effective implementation of the GDPR principles."

Tony Lai concludes by stressing that one of the main issues for "computational law (…) of which blockchain technologies are a subset" is to "offer a path toward embedding considered, ethical oversight of these complex data-driven, human–machine systems and platforms, on which increasingly large portions of social and economic activity operate."

These selected excerpts do not pay homage to the scope of each contribution. Here, I simply wanted to highlight the general dynamics of the book. By exploring the entire spectrum, any reader can approach the subject with maximum height despite the very topical nature of the matter. It is, for that very reason, a structuring book to put in all (curious) hands.

Utrecht Law School, Utrecht,
The Netherlands

Harvard University's Berkman Klein
Center, Cambridge, MA, USA

Thibault Schrepel

Contents

Introduction: The Challenges and Opportunities of Blockchain Technologies

Benedetta Cappiello and Gherardo Carullo

Contents

Both from a private and a public perspective, distributed ledger technologies in general, and blockchain in particular, can introduce significant opportunities in national and international legal systems, while at the same time posing new and unexplored challenges. Lawyers, economist, sociologist and market operators are faced with complex issues that require a deep and technical understanding of distributed ledger technologies to go beyond the state-of-the-art and fully grasp the potential of these new tools.

A multidisciplinary approach is therefore quintessential. To this end, the contributions of the distinguished Authors that have written the several chapters of this book represent a fundamental milestone in the process of unravelling the complexities of blockchain and therefore enabling its full potential.

A general overview of legal, economical and sociological issues raised by blockchain is of utmost importance. Particularly, it is of interest to understand how legislators have to tackle this new technology. So far, two possible approaches seem available: regulatory self-restraint or regulatory presence.

As for now, it seems that at all levels, both national and supranational, there has been a broad regulatory self-restraint. Accordingly, legislators have either enacted legal provisions having more a descriptive than a prescriptive nature (see as art. 8 *ter* of the Italian law decree 135/2019). Or, following the so-called principle of technological neutrality, the legislators have been relying on the use of old legislative frameworks, adapted to the new juridical tools (see the use of the UETA). As such, legislators have limited their activity in the way deemed sufficient to preserve and to

B. Cappiello (✉) · G. Carullo
Department of Italian and Supranational Public Law, University of Milan, Milan, Italy
e-mail: benedetta.cappiello@unimi.it; gherardo.carullo@unimi.it

B. Cappiello, G. Carullo (eds.), *Blockchain, Law and Governance*,
https://doi.org/10.1007/978-3-030-52722-8_1

protect technological development, without impairing any user or third parties. To reach this end, legislators have also adopted the so-called sandboxes. These are meant to be experimental area in which operators are free to exploit the new technological instruments, abiding only by the rule of conduct enacted within the sandbox.

Given the current state-of-the-art, coordination among States is therefore desirable to promote a uniform and coherent legislative panorama at both the national and the supranational level.

The present book is divided in four parts. Each one deals with a specific field of law affected, or potentially affected, by distributed ledger technologies in general, and blockchain in particular. Each part shares the same *fil rouge*: it questions whether and how these new technologies impact on the society as a whole. For this reason, legal, economic and sociological issues are approached with the aim of finding a common ground between what is new and what is old.

1 Part I. Understanding Blockchain: The Legal Perspective

The first part deals with the fundamentals of distributed ledger technologies, and blockchain in particular, assessing their possible use and the potential effect of such technologies in daily life. The underlying questions are therefore: what is changing and how this change in fostered by these new technologies.

As regard the what, a first important subject is the role of the so-called Decentralized Autonomous Organizations (DAOs) in our societies: one may wonder whether or not they will replace social groups, as traditionally understood. Particularly, DAOs seem to put at stake the role of State, as traditionally known. The question is then if, and how, a DAO may substitute the State or reduce its power within the society.

It is still to be seen whether this new way of gathering people can significantly impact on how societies are organised and administered. A derived issue concerns how legal reasoning might be affected by the use of blockchain and new technologies.

Under a private law perspective, many interesting questions arise in relation to distributed ledger technologies, in particular under the regulatory perspective. One should ask if each blockchain corresponds to an autonomous legal order, and so if such systems can self-regulate without the need of central (public) authority. To this end it is important to recall the theory of contract governance of the blockchain, which is based on the idea that human relations can be regulated by provisions registered on the blockchain (so-called the rule of codes). Because contract law is flexible, and because contract law is based on the principle of party autonomy, regulating the blockchain through private agreements can be more rapid than relying on rules adopted by public bodies.

In this regard, blockchain technology seems also apt at changing the way through which the participants of a social group—blockchain—trust each other. With blockchain we witness a shift in from a context in which trust is conferred upon another party because of who he/she is, and what he/she guarantees, to a no-party trust. As such, no matter who is the counterpart, technology in itself can guarantee the transactions carried out on the blockchain.

As regarding the how, Distributed Ledger Technologies in general and blockchain in particular are developed through "mining". But what mining actually means in practice is not always easy to grasp.

In a nutshell, mining is the process by which transactions are verified and added to the blockchain, for example to the Bitcoin public ledger. As a result, the blockchain is a chain of blocks which contains data, and the transactions that are verified in it.

Each blockchain works as a peer-to-peer network, made of nodes. A single node is basically a machine combination of the hardware and software and every node is able, at least to some degree, to store, create, send and receive data.

For the creation of each new block a special node called the miner has to solve a specific task, the cryptographic puzzle. There are many different ways in which such cryptographic puzzle can be structured. A common and popular one is the so-called proof-of-work. All the miners are competing to make this block. But only the miner who is firstly able to successfully construct the block and to add it to the blockchain, gets a reward for his job. Because doing so requires a big computational power, which means a lot of electricity is dispended, the miner is incentivized by the system to add the block, so keeping the blockchain alive, with a reward, which usually consists in coins (e.g. Bitcoin). This, at the cost to put at stake the goal to reducing environmental pollution.

2 Part II. Governance and Regulatory Issues

This part focuses on issues raised by the advent of new economic and financial instruments, developed thank to the new technologies. Particularly, this part will deal with the numerous legal questions posed by the increasingly widespread use of cryptocurrencies. In particular, it is necessary to qualify them in order then to understand the legislation that can regulate their collection, their transfer or their simple management. In this perspective, it is important to define the level of financial privacy guaranteed by some "privacy coin" or by cryptocurrencies in general, in particular in relation to traditional banking processes.

At this regard, it will be interesting to see whether financial privacy is, or will become, a money laundering problem. Accordingly, one should question if the most recent computer forensic techniques can support the local or the international authorities in the fight against money laundering. Once the reference framework has been clarified, it becomes interesting to relate cryptocurrencies and the most recent initiatives of some Central Banks now active in the "coinage" of stablecoin (i.e. e-Krona in Sweden).

The ever-growing use of traditional crypto coins raises the problem of understanding whether, and to what extent, they can be used to replace traditional currencies. The question concerns, in particular, the use of crypto in real estate sales, as well as in the case of capital contribution or capital increase in companies.

Moreover, the issue of blockchain and its applications is particularly important in relation to the regulation of payment systems and the role of national central banks in monitoring and regulating the market. First decentralized system imposes a shift in the way in which regulators think of the market, and also in the way in which they intend to intervene in the financial sector. Second, new cryptocurrencies and stable coins might also challenge the role of the State as the sole money printing authority, as the Libra project by Facebook has demonstrated.

The absence of a regulatory framework as well as the volatility of the instrument require the use of legal and non-legal provisions that can give certainty to the parties of the transaction as well as stability to binding agreements. Consequently, the role of legal operators changes, in the sense that an effort is required to subsume the new instruments within the traditional legal categories.

A particular application of the blockchain technology in the financial sector is that of the so-called Initial Coin Offerings (ICOs). The total funds raised by ICOs since 2016 amount to 31.6 billion dollars, 21.6 of which was raised in 2018, while in 2019 total funds raised around 3.1 billion. It is therefore important to assess what is the role of national regulatory authorities, such as CONSOB in Italy, in this context. A primary role that comes into play is the one of enforcing current regulations. The Togacoin case is probably already the most known Italian case, but there have been many other cases that were discovered to be merely frauds. Some of them have been qualified as offers of financial products and in that case, they have been subjected to the applicable provisions.

At this regard it should be noted that the development and diffusion of distributed systems implies the passage from a context in which the identity of the parties is public, while the transactions remain private, to one in which the transactions are public, but the operators can remain anonymous. This requires a change in the legal protection logic of the parties involved, directly or indirectly. This paradigm shift is favouring the development of new credit protection programs; the use of blockchain seems in fact to make it possible to guarantee, in terms other than traditional ones, the transactions concerning the assignment of credits or their custody in portfolios registered on blockchain platforms.

Ultimately, the possibility of guaranteeing the traceability of all operations concerning a crypto asset, understood as a credit instrument, could profoundly innovate the traditional methods of exchange of the latter. And also, the transfer of such new instruments requires some understanding regarding the applicable taxation regulatory system. Particularly, it is doubtful whether and how cryptocurrencies transfer and exploitation either to buy goods, or to pay for services, will be object of VAT. The analysis will focus on the European area, thus analysing the pro and cons of applying European VAT system.

3 Part III. Smart Contracts and Dispute Resolution

The second part of the book deals with how traditional legal instruments are being (supposedly) changed or anyhow affected by distributed ledger technologies.

Particularly, this part focuses on smart (legal) contracts and dispute resolution mechanism platforms based on blockchain. The second section questions how new instruments, such as cryptocurrencies and crypto asset, are to be qualified and how they should be regulated.

As per the smart (legal) contracts, their nature and functioning is deeply scrutinized. At this date, smart legal contracts represent a new label: it seems that every new (supposedly) contractual relationship can be carried out through a smart contract. However, this new tool represents an instrument still surrounded by a lot of uncertainty.

Smart contracts can be loosely defined as computer programs, namely software developed through blockchain; as such, they normally store data, certified and immutable. However, it is doubtful whether or not relations signed through smart (legal) contracts have any legal validity and produce any legal effect. A comparative analysis between a smart contract and a traditional contract is therefore essential. Namely, it is of particular interest to understand at what conditions smart contracts, within civil and common law system, can be deemed valid contracts. This can also clarify if, and how, smart contracts can produce any legal effect.

To understand the legal implications of smart contracts it is mandatory to focus on the technical language in which they are written along with the content within each contract enacted. Following this line of reasoning, a change of perspective is then required. To this end, it is necessary to understand whether informatic language can mirror the complexity of human relations or if informatic language has to be combined with natural languages (as is the case for the so-called Ricardian contract).

An appropriate qualification of smart contracts is important given that any uncertainty can have negative impacts at the supranational level. Particularly within the European union, it is still not clear whether or not EU Regulation Rome I and Bruxelles I *bis* might apply to smart (legal) contracts in order to find the *lex* applicable and the legitimate forum.

To answer this question, it is first necessary to have a uniform definition—preferably at EU level—of smart contracts. Contrarily, in case the EU legislator remains silent, the multiple approaches among the Member States will raise the problem of *forum and lex shopping*. The same incertitude in applying old normative provisions to new instrument, holds true with regard to some international private law regulations on legal contract; namely, the Vienna convention on Contracts for the international sales of good of 1980.

Given the above, it is legitimate to wonder about the state of the art with regard to smart (legal) contracts qualification. Some legislators at both, national and supranational levels, have already tackled the issue by providing some definitions. Recent attempts come from some US federal States (California, Vermont, Tennessee), along with some UE member States (Italy, Malta).

At the international level there have been some initial proposals too, by international organizations such as IncoTerms 20.

Additionally, some attempts to regulate the issue trough soft law provisions have been provided by the UNCITRAL model Law on electronic signatures. At first, it seems that, despite some inevitable differences, in most cases, legislators have based such proposals on existing provisions on digital tools—e.g. digital signature, electronic document—adapting them as needed.

With regard to the system of dispute resolution, the development of new technologies and, consequently, of blockchain are affecting also the way through which individuals perceive justice and the way through which justice is delivered. It is therefore of outmost importance to explore how the cultural approach has been changed.

Firstly, it should be understood whether and how algorithms can be used before, or during a legal proceeding; Secondly, it should be questioned whether a judgment made by an individual—a Judge—can be substituted by one taken by a machine. In this regard, some software solutions are already being used in some national Courts in both EU and non-EU countries; pros and cons have to be carefully scrutinized.

From another perspective, Distributed Ledger Technology and blockchain are posing a threat to the traditional system of dispute resolution. Namely, there have been some projects developed on blockchain aimed at offering to their users' fora alternative to the domestic courts. It is therefore important to properly qualify these projects from a legal perspective. It is indeed to be seen whether they comply with international principles of procedural law.

As a matter of fact, it seems that most of them cannot be qualified as arbitral legal proceedings given that they are based on game theory or on the shelling focal point, without providing for any truly legal rules of procedure. As a consequence, their outcomes should not produce legal effects among parties. This result might be reached only if new rules of procedure are enacted according to, for instance, international commercial arbitration rules (UNCITRAL/New York Convention).

4 Part IV. The "Sustainable" Applications of Blockchain

This part scrutinizes in depth whether, and how, new technologies can be exploit in a sustainable way, abiding by the Sustainable development goals as enacted in the UN Agenda 2030. In this perspective, some considerations on blockchain and privacy issues along with the new role played by legal professionals must also be dealt with.

The broad development of distributed ledger technologies, and blockchain in particular, is modifying the dynamics of financial flows also in the field of humanitarian aid. In this context there are projects, already implemented in the field which use blockchain-based systems to undermine both the old system of transferring funds from a country to another, normally a less developed one, and techniques for doing micro finance.

There are many aspects that are all equally interesting. Amongst these, on concerns, in particular, the traceability of funds, from the donors down to the recipients, as well as the possible geo-location of disastrous events and the consequent definition of response times. The same tracking devices can also be guaranteed in the event of fundraising and their subsequent transfer.

Given the increasing popularity of these tools, to achieve a development that is truly sustainable, as required by the SDGs, the blockchain seems to represent an important medium as long as the most widespread access is guaranteed. The technical complexities of blockchain-based operating models is in fact a first great obstacle to be overcome, especially if such systems are meant to replace the centralized systems that have long been used in the field. This obstacle becomes even more significant when the interlocutors, recipients of a given project, are underdeveloped countries. In this sense, it is important to evaluate the role of licencing agreements as well as explore the possible use of other tools to promote universal access to the blockchain with all the benefits that can be derived from it (interesting to deal with a project that combines the use of blockchain and humanitarian aid/control of migration flows).

The potential of blockchain technology in relation to the pursuit of the SDGs can be particularly appreciated also in relation to the dynamics of foreign direct and indirect investments. The transition from centralized to decentralized technologies, including distributed ones, introduces a radically different logic in how direct and indirect foreign investments are made and carried out; among other things, these technologies are fostering a change in the direction of the monetary flows, which are increasingly being directed towards developing countries to implement sustainable projects based on the blockchain. This change concerns both the strictly infrastructural aspects (such as investment) and the involvement of institutional and private actors.

This scenario is well demonstrated by the many projects that are actually pursuing SDGs through blockchain. Amongst these, we can recall what is being done by the ESA, whose mission is to develop world-class Earth observation systems addressing scientific and societal challenges with European and global partners. One of the major lessons learned from the 2015 Millennium Development Goals (MDGs) has been the importance of data in the development agenda. Despite some significant improvement, critical data for informed policy making on development policies were still largely lacking especially in the developing world. A report requested by the UN Secretary General to analyse the data gaps and challenges, was published in November 2014 with the title "*A World That Counts: Mobilising the Data Revolution for Sustainable Development*". The report stressed the importance to have a UN-led effort that would mobilize the data revolution for all. The report also recognized that new technologies (including geospatial data and Earth Observations) are changing the way data are collected, analyzed and disseminated. In January 2017, the UN organized the first World Data Forum (WDF) on Sustainable Development Data. To be highlighted is the necessity to enhance capacity building in countries facing high data challenges, to modernize the national statistical systems, to encourage NSOs to embrace open data initiatives, to mainstream new technologies and new data sources in the activities of the NSOs, and to integrate geospatial data (and Earth Observation data) into statistical production programs at all levels.

On the other hand, however, DLT and blockchain could also impair the accomplishment of the SDGs. Reference is made to the goals n. 7 (affordable and clean energy) and the goal n. 13 (climate action).

Indeed, a blockchain such as Bitcoin consumes as much energy as that consumed annually by a small developed country. The consensus mechanism developed through, for instance, the proof-of-work is indeed energy consuming; as such, we either only favour blockchains based on energy-efficient consensus mechanisms, or each user shall bear the negative environmental externalities produced by the use of a non-efficient blockchain. This might mean that, for example, each user shall pay for the pollution produced by each transaction. In case of lack of legislative action in this filed, there is the concrete risk that blockchain' exploitation will soon become unsustainable.

The present volume also tackles the issue of blockchain and privacy. At present, these two fields seem indeed to be particularly connected to each other: the former might put at risk the latter; the concept of privacy now requires to be understood, and protected, in the light of the peculiarities of distributed ledger technologies.

As seen with regard to cryptocurrencies and crypto asset transaction, blockchain seems to allow individuals to act in manners not necessary falling in line with the GDPR. And the same conclusion may be reached if considering the U.S. regulations on privacy. Almost everywhere, data ownership issues along with the applicability of some rights, such as the right to be forgotten, raise the interest of both the general public and of practitioners and lawyers. In this regard, in some EU jurisdictions, the case law has for now endorsed a loose approach, thus guaranteeing only a partial and geographically limited right to privacy. In this regard, it is interesting to see whether and how these developments will impact daily relations, at least within the EU.

Lastly, the book considers if and how the use of DLT and blockchain may affect the way in which traditional legal professions are carried out. Namely, it should be assessed whether and how the development and the overwhelmingly widespread of blockchain technology has been putting at stake the way through which old legal professions have been traditionally carried out, in particular the one of "notaries". The question raises due to the fact that blockchain has the capability of guaranteeing transactions without a third-party certifying authority. Consequently, data registered on a block are certain, because certified through the system, and immutable. Accordingly, it has to be seen wither notaries should adapt and innovate their activities to consider the new solutions made possible by blockchain and, generally speaking, distributed ledger technologies.

The contributions are rounded off with a conclusion discussing the pros and the cons of blockchain technology. At this time it appears that there is a balance between the two. While trying to reduce its downsides, national and international legislation should aim to integrate as much as possible the new economic, financial and legal instruments made possible by DLTs. The desired outcome should be to make it possible to seamlessly use these new tools along with the more traditional ones.

The Co-Editors wish to warmly thank Professor N. Boschiero and D.-U. Galetta: they trusted the project since the very beginning.

A thank you goes also to the University of Milan, and in particular to the Department of National and Supranational Public Law for having co-sponsored both the Conference and the present Book.

Part I
Understanding Blockchain: the Legal Perspective

Blockchain Based Organizations and the Governance of On-Chain and Off-Chain Rules: Towards Autonomous (Legal) Orders?

Benedetta Cappiello

Contents

1 Introduction

G. Tomasi di Lampedusa was an Italian writer from Sicily who lived in the first half of the last century when Italian society was on the verge of change.[1] At that time, the need to blur the line between the rich and the poor, the noble and the bourgeoisie was strong and widespread. The latter were gaining their 'place' in high society: someone who was born the son of a farmer could indeed die as the owner of buildings and land. This was a deep shock for those noblemen who had always relied on the past glory and wealth of their ancestors; accepting that something was changing meant they had to welcome the 'newcomers' and blend in with them. With this picture of society in mind, G. Tomasi di Lampedusa, described the ability of a person to adapt to the status quo, writing: "Changing things so everything stays the same". Those

[1]di Lampedusa (2002).

B. Cappiello (✉)
Department of Italian and Supranational Public Law, University of Milan, Milan, Italy
e-mail: benedetta.cappiello@unimi.it

B. Cappiello, G. Carullo (eds.), *Blockchain, Law and Governance*,
https://doi.org/10.1007/978-3-030-52722-8_2

who were not capable of accepting change and acting accordingly, risked indeed failing and losing everything.

This glance at history leads us to scrutinize the challenges that states are now facing when tackling the issues—legal, economic and social—raised by the impressive growth in technological innovation.[2] In particular, this analysis will focus on blockchain protocols which are a type of Distributed Ledger Technology (DLT).[3] The intrinsic features of these technologies make it difficult to find a proper way to regulate them (they are transnational, distributed, without a center, and they are based on anonymous-pseudonymous transactions).

This analysis starts from the assumption that DLTs in general, and blockchains in particular, are not a space that cannot be regulated. The history of the internet has taught us that borders, governments and authorities will extend as much as they can whenever a legal intervention is possible. Accordingly, these new technologies too will soon (and somehow already have) proved not to be something existing in a vacuum; on the contrary, they are linked to all that was before and still is. The question is how to connect the two worlds: the old traditional one and the new one, which is bringing with it "a paradigm shift" to the way people think, pay, trade and connect with each other.

DLT and blockchain protocols could indeed affect the financial, legal, economic and social sectors: a number of applications in many fields could be developed thanks to blockchain technologies. Reference is made, for instance, to smart (legal) contracts, cryptocurrencies,[4] Initial Coins Offering (ICOs) and Security Token Offering (STOs).[5] Each of these applications allow the development of legal and/or paralegal tools, which in some way correspond to traditional ones. As a consequence, once the correspondence is found, proper regulation is needed that either follows the technological neutrality approach;[6] or through the enactment of *ad hoc* legal provisions, follows an approach at both the national and international level.

---

[2]DiMatteo et al. (2019), Schrepel (2019), Szostek (2019) and Kraus et al. (2019).

[3]Natarajan H et al., *Distributed Ledger Technology (DLT) and blockchain*, mber 2017. See http://documents.worldbank.org/curated/en/177911513714062215/Distributed-Ledger-Technology-DLT-and-blockchain

[4]Wang F. et al., *Financing Open Blockchain Ecosystems: Toward Compliance and Innovation in Initial Coin Offerings*, 2018. Bertoli (2018), pp. 395–428; Chaum (1983), pp. 199–203; (2014) The economics of digital currencies. http://www.bankofengland.co.uk/quarterly-bulletin/2014/q3/the-economics-of-digital-currencies. Ali R. et al. (2014) Innovations in payment technologies and the emergence of digital currencies.

[5](2019) Crypto-assets need common EU-wide approach to ensure investor protection. pp. 157–1391. Jabotinsky (2018) and Philipp and Chris (2018). European Parliament (2016) REP ORT on virtual currencies.

[6]The term was first used to describe the scope of the US Electronic Communications Privacy Act 1996. In synthesis the technological neutrality approach sees technological improvement as a tool that is different from those that were available before. Being just a question of form, they can be regulated according to the normative provisions already in force which simply have to be amended to include the new tools. As such, there should be the same online and off-line rules. To see an example of the technological neutrality approach see the UNCITRAL Model Law on Electronic

This analysis aims to scrutinize whether and how blockchain applications can also affect the traditional system of governance. The question arises because each blockchain protocol, while developing a certain application, also constitutes an autonomous blockchain based organization, pursuing its own aim and with its own rules of functioning.

Reference will be made to the so-called Diffuse Autonomous Organizations (DAOs), which are a *species* of the *genus* Diffuse Autonomous Applications (DApps). The aim is then to show that there is no legal standing to the claim that each blockchain constitutes an autonomous legal system detached from traditional ones.[7] Each blockchain constitutes, instead, just an organized network of relationships amongst people who do not know each other but who trust the technology. Moreover, given that these relationships might also produce some legal effect, each blockchain corresponds to an organization having the characteristics of a legal partnership, which is the oldest business entity.[8] Likewise, in the off-chain world, and also in the case of a blockchain based partnership, each participant exercises some power corresponding to the powers of the legislative, the executive, and the judiciary. This analysis will show that no blockchain can get rid of normative provisions issued at an international or national level, nor can they avoid national jurisprudential intervention.[9]

This analysis will question how on-chain rules, enacted within the blockchain, or other protocols linked to it, will apply along with the off-chain ones, which are the legal provisions enacted within legal systems—either national or international—to which the blockchain is linked.

To develop the analysis, Sect. 2 will focus on how blockchain technology works; then, Sect. 3 will scrutinize the role of each participant, highlighting the different level of power at his/her disposal. The subsequent Sect. 4 will analyze Decentralized Autonomous Organizations (DAOs), questioning their nature and the forms of governance they provide. Section 5 will then examine the DAO ("the Entity") case, scrutinizing in particular the application of on-chain rules; Sect. 6 then analyses the potentially applicable off-chain rules. Lastly, Sect. 7 will scrutinize whether it is possible to compare blockchains on-chain rules and the *lex mercatoria* in order to

Transferable Records. https://www.uncitral.org/pdf/english/texts/electcom/MLETR_ebook.pdf; Kresse (1987), Reed (2007) and Ali (2009).

[7]Zamfir (2019).

[8]Sjostrom Jr (2016) and Drake (2013).

[9]US: U.S. Court of Appeals for the first Circuit (2001). Sec v. SG Ltd, 265 F.3d 42, 46, 13 September, 2001; U.S. southern district Court of Florida (2018) United Corporation v. BITM AIN INC, et al., case 1:18-cv-25106-KMW; Italy: Brescia first degree Court (2018). decree 7556/2018, 18 July 2018; Florence, first degree Court (2019) Judgment n. 18/2019, 21 January 2019; Brescia Court of Appeal (2018) decree no. 207/2018 endorsing first degree judgment; France: Nanterre Commercial Court (2020), decision 26 February 2020; Paris court of Appeal (2013), case n. 12/00161 SAS Macaraja c/SA Credit industriel et commercial, 26 October 2013 (see here: https://www.lesechos.fr/finance-marches/banque-assurances/la-justice-francaise-assimile-le-bitcoin-a-de-la-monnaie-1182460).

understand whether the former share characteristics which render the latter a net of laws and principles which are accepted and applied by the whole community of merchants. Some conclusions will then be provided.

2 Blockchain: Understanding the ABC

Blockchain technology is a *species* of the *genus* DLTs; as such, it refers to a particular way of structuring and trading data in a distributed manner.[10] Also, the blockchain is the most well known and most often used DLT; the notorious first public blockchain ever released to the public was Bitcoin. Back in 2009, the not widely known Satoshi Nakamoto released the Bitcoin White Paper offering the public a new way to trade money.[11] The release had a disruptive effect: it was immediately clear that the technology developing and running Bitcoin represented a shift from internet protocols to other protocols. Indeed, currently, a transition from the internet to other protocols (e.g. blockchains) can be observed. The main difference between internet and blockchain protocols lies in what is the object of the transfer. Both allow the transfer of data, however, internet data is a series of bits corresponding to information, while blockchain data corresponds to an asset, both material and immaterial. Also, data on the internet is shared and used x number of times by y number of users, while tokens representing goods on a blockchain are either mine or yours. As such, blockchain technology has re-implemented the "artificial scarcity" of digital goods.[12] In actual fact, copyright laws represented the first attempt to craft the "artificial scarcity" of information: the reproduction of works was prohibited without the author's consent. However, due to the ease of reproducing identical copies, copyright infringement has become quite common and alternative technological measures of protection are used, such as digital rights management.[13] *Viceversa*, blockchain technology has the potential to effectively

[10]UK Cryptoassets Task Force (October 2018) final report, available here: https://assets.publishing.service.gov.uk/government/uploads/system/uploads/attachment_data/file/752070/cryptoassets_taskforce_final_report_final_web.pdf; see also UK Jurisdiction Task Force (2019) Report Legal statement on cryptoassets and smart contracts, available here https://www.lawsociety.org.uk/news/stories/cryptoassets-dlt-and-smart-contracts-ukjt-consultation/; FATF (2014) Virtual Currencies Key Definitions and Potential AML/CFT Risks. See Handerson and Raskin (2019). University of Chicago Coase-Sandro Institute for law & Economics Research Paper No. 858. Available here https://papers.ssrn.com/sol3/papers.cfm?abstract_id=3265295. Annunziata (2018).

[11]Nakamoto (1997).

[12]Morales A. (2018). Thinking Too Small: When Digital Scarcity Hurts The Future of Blockchain Games. Medium. De Filippi and Hassan (2018) and Ammous (2018).

[13]Ryadel (2019). DRM – when it's legit to remove it and how to do that. Medium.

implement ownership protection of digital data and this, in turn, might lead to a revival of the first sale doctrine (the so-called principle of exhaustion).[14]

Understanding what lies behind each and every blockchain protocol requires knowledge in, at least, computational law, computer science and computer engineering.[15] For the aims of the present analysis it will be enough to understand two technological aspects: how blockchains work (namely what does a distributed ledger on a blockchain mean) and how are blockchains managed. The latter aspect will be discussed in the next section.

With regards to how blockchains work, the technologies used to develop a blockchain are the result of already existing technologies. That is to say that blockchain protocols did not come out of the blue; instead, they are the unique combination of old technologies already developed to build decentralized networks. In a nutshell, each blockchain is a technology that is not guaranteed neither by a central bank nor by a public authority. Instead, it is a P2P network operating through a decentralized structure in which each participant (be it a node, a block or a peer) is contemporarily a supplier and a consumer of data and/or information. Actually, P2P networks were already available before the release of the first blockchain (see torrent or Napster);[16] however, blockchain protocols are something more. Indeed, blockchain protocols allow the trade of tokens representing values or goods, while P2P networks usually allow the transfer of already existing data.

In extreme synthesis, blockchains are a distributed database, joined by a network of computers, called nodes, located everywhere around the globe.[17] Each node retains identical copies of the whole ledger. As a result, the ledger is contemporarily shared by all. Using a figurative representation, each blockchain is made up of blocks storing any data or information that is used to perform the operation or transaction to which they are linked (it could be a certification, the transfer of property or any other contract).

A transaction occurs when interested party exchanges their corresponding public and private key:[18] the exchange is possible thanks to the cryptographic puzzle which allows the forwarding of encrypted messages—containing the transaction—between two parties.[19]

---

[14]Within the European Union, see the European Union Directive, 2001/29/EC of the European Parliament and of the Council of 22 May 2001 on the harmonization of certain aspects of copyright and related rights in the information society. O.J.L 167; within US, see: U.S. Copyright Act (2016) paras 17 et 109. See Rivaro (2014). Heath C. (1999). Parallel Imports and International Trade. Lehman (1995) and Ficsor (2002).

[15]Xu et al. (2019), Aaronson (2013), Goldwasser et al. (1989) and Goldreich and Oren (1994).

[16]Lambda (2018). P2P Network Systems- A Go-To Guide for Understanding How They Work. Medium.

[17]Low and Mik (2020).

[18]Goldreich et al. (1997).

[19]As clearly synthesized by the EBA: "a Bitcoin transaction occurs through a two-step phase: - Person A holds in a digital wallet 'public' and 'private' keys, generated via cryptography. Person B also holds 'public' and 'private' keys. The private keys are used to control the ownership of their

After the exchange occurs, miners work to approve the validity of the transactions that users have requested to be added to the blockchain. The miners have therefore to certify that the data encrypted in the transaction between two parties is correct. For instance, the miner checks that the object of the transfer, distinguished by a given code, has not already been transferred to a third party. Once a miner finds the solution it asks all the other miners to agree. This is the so-called "consensus mechanism". In this regard, the consensus mechanism was originally meant to frame a participative democracy, where all users could exploit the same power. However, the actual functioning of the consensus mechanism seems to be different. The one developed by Nakamoto is called Proof of Work (PoW): here a miner solves the cryptographic puzzle, then the transaction is approved if the majority of miners plus one reaches a consensus on the solution.[20] The miners who have more chances to solve a transaction are those who can exploit more computational energy: the more energy a miner uses, the higher its chance to be the first one to solve the cryptographic puzzle.[21] Aside from the unsustainability issue, this consensus mechanism also has another shortcoming, namely that the majority + 1 of miners forming the consensus risks not being a truly democratic solution.[22] The majority of the miners could indeed be part of the same miner's factory or they can be part of a parallel group acting to form a majority, in case of need, when deemed convenient.[23]

Aware of the above-mentioned shortcoming, developers have started to frame a different consensus mechanism, called Proof of Stake (PoS).[24] According to this mechanism each miner's vote has a different weight. The weight depends on the stake (which is equal to the sum of participation in the chain) at the miner's disposal: the more participation it has, the more its vote counts. Such a consensus proved to be plutocratic, to say the least: power depending on how much a miner has already earned.

To use a figurative representation: let's imagine that a sum of money, a property title of ownership, is transferred from A to B and subsequently to C. Irrespective of the type of contract (loan, purchase agreement etc.), all the information enabling

---

respective Bitcoins. Public keys are essential for identification and private keys (which are kept secret by the holders) are used for authentication and encryption.—Person A generates a transaction that includes A's address, B's address and A's private key (without disclosing what A's private key is). The transaction is broadcast to the entire DLT network, which can verify from A's private key that A has the authority to transfer the crypto-asset to the address it is sending from". See EBA (2019), Report, quoted, at. 9.

[20]Buterin (2018) On Public and Private Blockchains. Ethereum Blog, 2015. Duffield and Hagan (2014) and Bonneau and Miller (2015).

[21]de Vries A (2018) Bitcoin's Growing Energy Problem | Elsevier Enhanced Reader, pp. 801–805.

[22]Vukolic (2016).

[23]The attempt towards the democracy of the blockchain system was made clear, by the time it was discovered that the Bitcoin code contained a bug potentially allowing miners to maliciously inflate Bitcoin's supply. See BitcoinCore (2018). CVE-2018-17144 Full Disclosure at https://bitcoincore.org/en/2018/09/20/notice/. See Yermack (2017) and Wright and De Filippi (2015).

[24]Buterin (2018). The Ethereum so-called Casper will eventually convert Ethereum from a Proof of Work to a Proof of Stake; the decision is easy to grasp. See: https://github.com/ethereum/casper.

each step is stored in a dedicated block. The information stored in blocks A, B and C have the same base but: block B contains something more than block A; and block C something more than block A and B. This "something more" is the last transaction validated and appended to the block, after the consensus has been reached.

Therefore, the added value guaranteed by the blockchain is in its functioning: each block contains a hash of the prior block in the blockchain. Miners are in charge to ensure that all data in the overall blockchain has not been tampered with and remains unchanged. Therefore, the truthfulness of the information encrypted in the blocks is certified by third parties without the need to involve any central authority. Plus, each transaction is public (namely every user can see what, when and how a transaction has occurred) but no one can see who has made the transaction.[25] In this regard, it should be noted that the development and diffusion of distributed systems implies the passage from a context in which the identity of the parties is public, while the transactions remain private, to one in which the transactions are public, but the operators can remain anonymous. This requires a change in the legal protection logic of the parties involved, directly or indirectly.

To date, there exist different types of blockchain: a blockchain can be permissioned or permissionless.[26] A permissioned blockchain works pretty much as a private intranet: users can be part of the intranet only if they abide by the prerequisites required by the blockchain itself.[27] The use of permissioned blockchains seems to be preferred by big companies, such as IBM, which are now developing different types of private blockchain to better manage their activities. *Viceversa*, permissionless blockchains are the ones truly mirroring the idea of disruption to the nation state: public permissionless blockchain protocols are based on cryptography and guarantee immutability, decentralization and pseudo- anonymity.[28] All of this, without the need of a center of control. All these features should have led to a "virtual" society: open to all and making all equal. In fact, permissionless blockchains allow the entrance of *n'importe qui* who, using pseudonyms, can trade and update the chain.

What is of much interest, with this technology, concerns the object traded: each blockchain allows the exchange of so-called cryptoassets.[29] To date, there is not a single agreed definition of cryptoassets. In a broad sense, cryptoassets are a digital representation of actual goods, or of a value (a credit[30]) or they are a digital

---

[25]Low and Mik (2020).

[26]Lai and Lee (2018) and XXu et al. (2017).

[27]Antonopoulos (2017), p. 50.

[28]Bodó and Giannopoulou (2019), Tapscott and Tapscott (2016) and Swan (2015).

[29]OCSE (2010). The tokenisation of assets and potential implications for financial markets; EU (2019). Consultation document on an EU framework for markets in crypto-assets available at: https://ec.europa.eu/info/sites/info/files/business_economy_euro/banking_and_finance/documents/2019-crypto-assets-consultation-document_en.pdf; Chimienti et al. (2019), Spink et al. (2019), Vos (2019) and Robinson II (2019).

[30]Amongst others, WizKey, an Italian based company, has developed an Ethereum-based decentralized network that serves financial transactions and achieves other financial processes

representation of blockchain native goods, or of a native contractual right, such as Bitcoin or other cryptocurrencies. Native blockchain cryptoassets are usually issued through so-called Initial Coin Offerings (ICOs) and they are referred to as tokens. According to their characteristics, tokens can be distinguished as exchange, security and utility tokens.[31] Exchange tokens usually correspond to cryptocurrencies; security tokens amount to investment in a certain activity. These may correspond to transferable securities or financial instruments. Utility tokens might represent existing physical goods. Accordingly, each category is subject to the normative framework provided for the instruments to which the cryptoassets correspond.

3 Follow: Blockchain Participants' Power and Obligations

For each blockchain a number of participants take part acting behind the veil of pseudo-anonymity.[32] The combination of digital signatures and private and public cryptographic keys make it possible for a participant to store information and trade without being obliged to share their identity. The proper functioning of a blockchain disregards parties' identities.

Each participant therefore plays a different role in developing and running the blockchain. At this stage of technological development, it is safe to distinguish three categories of participants: core developers, miners, and users. Each category has its own functions and exploits a different level of power.[33]

Core developers are those who have developed the original blockchain protocol: they have written the original code which prescribes, for instance, the size of a block or the reward miners get for solving and adding a transaction to the blockchain. Also, developers can propose changes in the chain to the Community (see for instance the Blockchain improvement proposal to the Bitcoin blockchain[34] (BIP) or the

---

such as securitization, factoring and covered bond issuance. See: https://www.wizkey.io/en/platform/; see also the projects developed between Banks and financial institution: https://cryptonomist.ch/2020/03/18/banca-sella-bitcoin-hype/; https://www.coindesk.com/intesa-sanpaolo-trade-data-bitcoin-blockchain?amp=1.

[31]US: U.S. Court of Appeals for the first Circuit (2001). Sec v. SG Ltd, 265 F.3d 42, 46, 13 September, 2001; U.S. southern district Court of Florida (2018) United Corporation v. BITMAIN INC, et al., case 1:18-cv-25106-KMW; Italy: Brescia first degree Court (2018). decree 7556/2018, 18 July 2018; Florence, first degree Court (2019) Judgment n. 18/2019, 21 January 2019; Brescia Court of Appeal (2018) decree no. 207/2018 endorsing first degree judgment; France: Nanterre Commercial Court (2020), decision 26 February 2020; Paris court of Appeal (2013), case n. 12/00161 SAS Macaraja c/SA Credit industriel et commercial, 26 October 2013 (see here: https://www.lesechos.fr/finance-marches/banque-assurances/la-justice-francaise-assimile-le-bitcoin-a-de-la-monnaie-1182460).

[32]Wright and de Filippi (2018) and Narayanan et al. (2016).

[33]Schrepel (2020) and Shirky (2011).

[34]To understand how a Bitcoin improvement occurs see: https://github.com/bitcoin/bips.

Ethereum improvement proposal (EIP)[35]). In fact, just like any other technological tool, blockchains too need to be the object of minor or major updates which result in a change in the blockchain protocol.

Miners are those who allow the functioning of the blockchain, they create the chain. Accordingly, acting individually or as part of a so-called miner's factory,[36] miners exploit the computational power of their devices to solve the cryptographic puzzle covering all transactions occurring within a blockchain. Miners do not care about the content of the transaction: within the blockchain environment, the validation process does not have a legal value meaning it does not certify the legal validity of the transaction. On the contrary, the validation process refers to the automated, deterministic process of confirming that certain technical conditions have been met. The validation occurs when miners have certified that the new transaction contains all inputs and outputs of the previous ones, plus something more. Besides, miners also have the power to accept or to refuse all proposals raised by developers which significantly, or slightly, amend the blockchain. In both scenarios, when they validate a transaction or when they approve or reject a proposal, miners operate without any agreement; as such they can freely decide whether or not to mine. The decision depends on how much they can exploit from their mining activity.[37]

Lastly, users (also called nodes) are individuals who act in the blockchain by making transactions. Users can also exercise a limited power of choice: they can approve the way in which the chain is administered by staying and trading in the blockchain; or they can boycott the chain, using their exit power and selling the cryptoassets traded in the blockchain to which they were parties.[38] Plus, when they are requested, they can express their opinion regarding the updates proposed by developers. They cannot formally approve or refuse the change; however, they can express their view.

From the above scenario, it follows that each participant enjoys different powers, depending on its role.

To better grasp how core developers, miners and users get actively involved in a given blockchain development, reference will be made to the case where a change in the protocol occurs. In a blockchain based organization, changes are the result of either soft or hard forks: each leads to something similar to a "software update". A soft fork represents a minor change in the original blockchain protocol (it could perhaps correspond to a change in the layout). *Viceversa,* a hard fork implies a switch; for example one line of blockchain becomes two. Both kinds of fork result in a change to the way a given blockchain works.[39]

With regards to the former, the timeline for allowing a minor change in the blockchain protocol is the following: a blockchain core developer proposes changes

---

[35]To understand how an Ethereum improvement occurs see https://eips.ethereum.org.

[36]Wrigley (2020).

[37]Antonopoulos (2017), p. 26.

[38]Rodrigues (2019).

[39]Low and Ernie (2017).

to, for instance, boost the chain capacity or to ensure the blockchain's dominance. To be implemented, this soft fork is submitted to a first informal approval by the users' community. The change is proposed and explained in the blockchain forum where users can express their positive or negative judgment. Then, the change is subject to the miner's approval. It goes without saying that usually miners follow the majority decision expressed within the user's community. It is important to note that, in a case where the soft fork is approved, users are not obliged to abide by the changes. Instead, they can pursue the old version while still remaining part of the chain. In fact, after the fork, the resulting chain is still compatible with the previous version.

A hard fork is slightly different because it leads to the development of a new protocol that is incompatible with the previous one. Hard forks can be either planned, or controversial. The former is proposed when major changes are needed to guarantee the survival of the chain itself. The latter mostly occurs in response to an attack committed by an unknown source to the detriment of the original blockchain; the attack breaches the functioning of the original code, forcing a transaction favorable to the attacker, but not requested by users. This scenario can lead, as indeed it has led, to fraud and theft.[40] Some forks have been also been the object of judicial proceedings: a US district court of the southern district of Florida had to rule "*on a (alleged) knit network and organization to manipulate the market for Bitcoin Cash effectively hijacking the Bitcoin cash network, centralized the market, and violating all accepted standards, protocols and the course of conduct associated with Bitcoin since its inception*".[41]

When a breach in the protocol occurs, developers can propose a so-called "goes back": this will restore the situation as it was before the attack, deleting the fraudulent transaction. This decision might appear to be against the principle of the immutability of the protocol, no matter what. In other words, according to the ideas circulated when blockchain technologies started to emerge: one of the principles of crypto law was the sacrosanctity of the original code;[42] accordingly, no discussion might ever arise concerning its change. This approach might seem—as indeed it is—slightly repulsive towards the idea of democracy, participation and the exchange of political views. However, due to this reason, not all users might be in favor of the "goes back". In fact, the "goes back" is against the prerequisite of blockchain immutability; as a matter of principle the protocol cannot be broken. Accordingly, some miners might vote in favor and some against the fork. As a result, the very same blockchain will be divided into two autonomous branches, sharing the same origin, and users can decide autonomously where to stay.

[40]For some hard fork examples see: Ethereum blockchain forking permanently into Ethereum and Ethereum Classic (2016); Bitcoin forked into Bitcoin (BTC) and Bitcoin cash (BCH) in 2017. Also, the same year, it forked again into Bitcoin gold (BTG) forking and merging with ZClassic which in turn was a fork of ZCAsh: together they formed in 2018 BTCP.

[41]USSDC of Florida (2018) United Corporation v. BITMAIN INC, et al. case 1:18-cv-25106-KMW.

[42]Sklaroff (2017).

From the above it derives that each participant to the blockchain has its own prerogative and exploits different powers. In a blockchain "legal" system, developers act as the legislators, miners as those exploiting judiciary power, while users act as the executive power.[43] Each category has its own interests, sometimes conflicting with the other categories: developers are free to be, or not to be, interested in the development of a blockchain. They gain if the blockchain works properly and in an effective way but if this is not the case, they can just disregard it. Users have an interest in the increase in the value of the cryptoassets traded in the blockchain. The more they gain, the more they have an interest in not exercising their exit power. Miners have the most power: they know how to solve cryptographic puzzles, therefore they know how to certify and to add transactions. Plus, miners are those who approve or reject both minor and major changes. Contrary to users, miners receive a fee for each transaction solved so it is in the miners' interest to solve more puzzles, in less time. This, notwithstanding that the result will be a decrease in the blockchain's cryptoasset value. Miners' power to solve a transaction depends on the consensus mechanism applied to the blockchain and the consensus mechanisms so far provided pursue anything but democracy, equal participation and the equality of parties.

The proof of work is high energy consumption, which is possible only for miners running expensive and highly sophisticated devices capable of creating and validating blockchain transactions. Plus, a group of miners can easily agree to form the majority, so cancelling out any true democracy of the system. However, as it is, the proof of stake consensus mechanism also does not seem to pursue the ideal of democracy and equal participation in a free society. The vote of miners with a higher stake (meaning blockchain cryptoassets) counts more than others.

The analysis of how the blockchain protocol works and what is the role of each user, has led to a first conclusion: blockchain systems are truly decentralized but not as participative and equal as expected.

4 DAOs: Nature and Governance

Human beings have always felt the need to be part of a community regulated by legal provisions, which could be the expression of natural rights or of rights set by a God,[44] or enacted by a government, a tyranny or a monarch. As to the substance, rules have conferred rights, imposed obligations or defined relationships between private parties, operating within the same state or acting in different states. Rules have also regulated relationships between private parties and sovereign states. Lastly, rules have defined relationships between states in time of war and peace.

[43]Zamfir (2018) and Szabo (1997a, b).

[44]Gardner (2012).

Notwithstanding the multitude of rules, all have always shared the 'juridical ethos' of achieving justice, '*iustitium*', through the settlement of disputes between parties.

Blockchain technology was conceived to be disruptive to central authority and the traditional (allegedly) unequal organization of society. According to those defending the ideas lying behind distributed technologies, blockchain protocols should favour the constitution of a new form of social organization managed only by the rules enacted within the original blockchain code, written in the smart contract. This will also lead to a new system of governance: the governance of infrastructure, which is based on no party trust.[45]

To confirm the above assumption, it should be questioned how governance is enacted within blockchain based organizations: namely, it should be analyzed whether they run according to "internal" rules only, or whether they also abide by the principles of the legal system to which they are linked.

The blockchain technical name to qualify blockchain based organizations is Distributed Autonomous Organization (DAO), which are a kind of so-called Distributed Autonomous Application (DApp).[46] The latter are computer applications which run in a distributed way; the first DApps were released at the beginning of the new millennium (see BitTorrent, PopCorn) and ran on a P2P system on numerous PCs. Today, a P2P system can also run on blockchain protocol.[47]

A DApp becomes a DAO when the smart contract containing the rules of functioning also provides for rules of governance.[48] In other words, a DAO is a decentralized application that runs thanks to blockchain protocol and constitutes a new kind of organization among its participants. DAOs are developed to pursue a defined aim, or they pursue an interdisciplinary aim, combining legal, social, political and economic aspects. Also, DAOs can run either for profit or for no profit.[49] In both scenarios, they allegedly pursue their ultimate interest without any central authority. The communality of vision and of aim seems to render DAOs similar to the common law system's partnership.

---

[45]Finck (2018), De Filippi and McMullen (2018), Beck et al. (2018) and Merkle (2016).

[46]To better grasp the concept of DApp, see: https://ethereum.stackexchange.com/questions/383/what-is-a-dapp. As DApp examples see: Gnosis, Gnosis Ltd., last updated Jan. 2018. gnosis.pm; Civic, Civic Technologies, Inc., 2018. www.civic.com; and CryptoKitties, Axiom Zen, n.d. www.cryptokitties.co.

[47]The Swarm city: a blockchain based "city" grounded on a smart contract deployed on blockchain. The city functions as a marketplace; through blockchain technology it allows people—the participant—to communicate, to trade and to earn external reputation (see https://swarm.city).

[48]Schiller (2018), Savelyev (2017), Rühl (2019), Di Ciommo (2018), Woebbeking (2019), Schrepel (2019), Levi and Lipton (2018) and Mik (2017).

[49]See The LAO (2019a, b). A taxonomy for LAOs: making sense of the emerging LAO ecosystem (available here: https://medium.com/@thelaoofficial/a-taxonomy-for-laos-making-sense-of-the-emerging-lao-ecosystem-1122b035fe1a).

In a nutshell, DAOs correspond to a set of processes and rules enacted in a smart contract and operating autonomously on a blockchain.[50] With regards to the rules of governance, these lie at multiple levels, being both on-chain and off-chain.

The on-chain rules are provided on a two-level field, and the combination of the two levels forms the governance by the infrastructure.

At the first level there are the endogenous provisions, written in code and enacted within the White Paper; each DAO has one and it corresponds to its "founding chart". Per praxis, these provisions are based on economic incentives (so-called cryptoeconomics[51]) and game theory:[52] they provide for specific incentive structures to reward the good behavior of participants. In fact, cheating or committing fraud is economically not convenient and time and energy consuming.[53] In a case of cheating committed by a participant, blockchains have rules to punish them; for instance, miners could agree not to process a transaction requested by blacklist participants.

At the second level of on-chain provisions there are those provided for by the rules of the other platforms on which the DAO is linked. They form the on-chain exogenous rules because they are imposed outside the DAO reference community.

These exogenous on-chain rules are binding on the DAO. In fact, to function, the DAO itself requires multiple layers. The internet protocol is the first. It is a fact that blockchain protocol, as any other protocol, relies on the internet: therefore, it cannot ignore the internet level of governance. Internet governance can be exercised in multiple ways. The co-called internet service providers (ISPs) can control the transportation layer of the internet, they can target certain operations or they can adopt certain network management practices. These could affect the operation of a given blockchain system too. Reference is made to the internet governance capability to determine who can take an active part in a protocol; for instance, each user has a data cap which corresponds to the maximum amount of data that it can transfer monthly. Also, ISPs can prioritize services which have paid for priority (while downgrading the content that competes with their offerings). Mechanisms such as this are quite diffuse on ISPs even if they are against the alleged principle of net neutrality according to which (allegedly) all traffic on the internet should receive the same priority.[54] Plus, there is the so-called deep packet inspection (DPI) which can examine the content of data, transferred by users. Once tracked back, content of the given packet can be examined, even if encrypted. All these affect the blockchain's operation also.

The above-mentioned internet governance features can indeed unduly affect the operation of a blockchain based organization; it suffices here to recall that

---

[50]Smith and Barrett (2016).

[51]Mik (2017) and Zamfir (2015).

[52]Tadelis (2013).

[53]Szabo (1997a, b).

[54]Wu (2003). To a clear summary on where is the US Congress and Supreme Court with regard to the net neutrality bill, see: the WIRED Guide to Net Neutrality (2018) available here https://www.wired.com/story/guide-net-neutrality/.

blockchain protocols are meant to confer upon the participants unfettered access to the network and they are censorship resistant.

As well as the internet protocols, a blockchain must also abide by other on-chain exogenous rules; reference is made to the rules of blockchain networks on which the code is developed (see Bitcoin or Ethereum[55]), and the DApp framework (see Aragon, DAOstack).

All on-chain rules are conceived and written in code. On one side, they are strict and they cannot adapt to circumstances (unless the on-chain rule specifies how to amend itself).[56] On the other side, rules in code can be interpreted only in a single way and this should guarantee uniform application of the same rule.

With regards to the content, on-chain rules confer upon each DAO participant rights and duties of behavior; in case of non-compliance with the DAO on-chain rules, the (allegedly) guilty participant will get bad feedback, which puts them at risk of being forced out. Also, on-chain rules confer differing amounts of power upon participants. Namely, some participants decide the new projects to be run or developments to be endorsed; some express their view. It derives that DAOs, while pretending to get rid of central authority, assume the peculiarities of all market dynamics: absent a central institution, power is exercised by a small and concentrated group of powerful players.

Besides on-chain rules, there are off-chain provisions which provide for the so-called "governance of the infrastructure".[57] These rules are written in natural languages, they are less rigid but more ambiguous. As such they are subject to different interpretations. Besides, they are not automatically enacted: there should be a third party, a state authority, enforcing (or attempting to enforce) them on a case by case basis.

Off-chain rules can influence the development and the use of a given DAO, impacting on its social or institutional level. Accordingly, off-chain rules are endogenous when they consist of existing social norms and customs endorsed by the DAO community and enacted within the DAO White Paper, the aim being self-coordination and governance.[58] Conversely, off-chain rules are exogenous when they govern the blockchain from outside the community. They don't directly apply to a blockchain protocol but they can affect its functioning. These rules become applicable whenever the blockchain based organization's activity affects third parties; or, when blockchain participants are damaged by on-chain activity but there are no available (and effective) dispute resolution mechanisms offered within the chain. Also, off-chain rules might be imposed by a third-party authority to

[55]Decentralized Autonomous Organization, ETHEREUM, https://www.ethereum.org/dao [https://perma.cc/2KXE-3MYU].

[56]Tezos, one of the first blockchains allowing token holders to modify the rules of the underlying blockchain protocol in a fully automated way (https://tezos.com).

[57]Wang et al. (2017).

[58]These rules might correspond to the social norms and principles taken from living society that a given blockchain community decides to abide by. Per praxis, they are named in the blockchain White Paper.

ensure, amongst other things, that the on-chain activities abide by the principle of national and international public order. Undoubtedly, each blockchain based organization refers to the normative framework provided by the national legal system. For example, if a blockchain is operating as a DAO crowdfunder, it must respect the relevant national provision of the state from where the money is collected. Also, international law provisions and principles could play a role, particularly with regards to the relationship between international public law and the governance of the blockchain.[59] According to some, international law is already governing blockchains.[60] This relies on the assumption that all blockchain based organizations are transnational in nature. As such, they lie within the international community and should at least abide by the principles of international law.[61] Reference is made, for instance, to the principle of international procedural law, whenever the blockchain based organization provides for a mechanism of dispute resolution.[62] The principles of international law protecting fundamental values should also be taken into consideration when developing a blockchain based organization. The latter could be exploited for illicit aims, breaching the founding principles of the international community. Indeed, there have been blockchains, or other DLTs, developed to pursue illegal activities (such as narcotraffic or the trafficking of human organs).[63] These illicit applications, referred to as "dark boxes", require regulators to urgently develop truly global regimes for detecting and prosecuting them. A truly global framework of provisions will, in turn, guarantee uniform application and enforcement, notwithstanding where the breach is committed or the damage that occurs. In addition, states will remain engaged in controlling unwanted activities and pursuing them within their own jurisdictions.

From the above it derives that each blockchain organization in general, and the DAOs in particular, do rely on multiple levels of governance. This leads to the assumption that neither of them corresponds to either an autonomous legal order or a blockchain based organization. However, they do heavily rely on other systems of rules, both on-chain and off-chain, the main difficulty being to combine the two levels.

---

[59]Koh (1997).

[60]Clean App (n.d.). Blockchain Governance 105: International Law. Global blockchains = global blockchain governance. CryptoLaw Review. Available here: https://medium.com/cryptolawreview/blockchain-governance-105-international-law-3c7ebd025a43; see also Maupin (2017).

[61]Crawford (2019), Salerno (1996), Bobbio (1994), Simma and Alston (1992), Bassiouni (1990), Abi-Saab (1987), Verdross (1968), Fitzmaurice (1958), Sørensen (1960), McNair (1957) and Schwarzenberger (1955).

[62]Cappiello (2019), Givari (2018), Kotuby (2013) and Kolb (2006).

[63]Segall (2015).

5 The DAO Case: On-Chain Provisions to Develop an Autonomous Legal Order

The section above has attempted to clarify how the rules of governance manage blockchain based organizations. Given the above framework, one might wonder if and how on-chain and off-chain levels of rules combine with each other; the question is then how a DAO is connected with a given national legal order and if it has to abide by the principles of international law.

To better grasp the concept, it is worthwhile to refer to the DAO (the "Entity") case; in this regard, we will scrutinize how the DAO was meant to work, paying attention to the role conferred upon each participant. The aim is to understand whether and how the DAO was meant to connect with national legal systems.

The DAO was a smart contract deployed on the Ethereum blockchain network; the smart contract enacted the rules to build a platform collecting money to fund a sponsored project. The DAO White Paper was published in 2016 and its author, C. Jentzsch, was the Chief Technology Officer of Slock.it (a blockchain and IoT solution company incorporated in Germany) and was co-founded by C. Jentzsch, S. Jentzsch and S. Tual.[64] The White Paper explained the basic rules of procedure of the DAO which purported to be an example of an autonomous and democratic organization. Interestingly to note, the DAO was presented as an Entity that *"can be used by individuals working together collaboratively outside of a traditional corporate form. It can also be used by a registered corporate entity to automate formal governance rules contained in corporate bylaws or imposed by law"*.[65] According to the White Paper the smart contract deployed on the DAO would have solved all governance issues typical of any legal corporation. The Entity would then supplant the mechanism of traditional governance and management through formalizing and automating the enforcing of traditional contractual terms.[66] With regards to the scope, the Entity was meant to create a crowdfunding contract to raise funds for companies active in "crypto space".[67] Each interested participant was to act using a pseudonym.

All funds were raised and collected in the Ethereum DAO's address and then distributed to the project to which they were originally intended for. Funding could be done by anyone sending the DAO tokens to the DAO wallet address. Hence, each interested participant was first required to invest in the DAO token, paying for them

---

[64]https://slock.it.

[65]The DAO White Paper available here: https://github.com/the-dao/whitepaper.

[66]In: *If Rockfeller was a Coder,* Reyes has argued that: "The DAO would "hold the trust property in the form of digital assets," and there would be trustee token holders as well as certificate token holders. Only a trustee token, and not a certificate token, would be endowed with the right to transfer or otherwise dispose of the DAO's property", in Reyes (2019).

[67]See Slockit, Slock.it DAO demo at Devcon1: IoT + Blockchain, YOUTUBE (Nov. 13, 2015), https://www.youtube.com/watch?v=49wHQoJxYPo.

in Ethereum (ETH[68]); and secondly, to invest them (in whole or in part) in the project (s) sponsored by the DAO platform. Each DAO token conferred, upon its owner, voting and ownership rights. The DAO earned a profit by funding the project and provided DAO token holders with a return on their investment.[69] Interestingly, each DAO token holder could also decide to re-sell the token in the secondary market, thus monetizing his/her investment. In fact, after the first offering period, Slock.it solicited some web-based exchange platforms (one was located in the US[70]) to trade the DAO tokens.

The functioning of the DAO was clearly explained on the DAO website which also contained a link via which the DAO token could be purchased. As such, the website was used to promote DAO communication with the public enabling the latter to understand the project and its functioning.[71]

At a first scrutiny the functioning of the DAO seems easy to understand: on its face it did not seem to frame anything unseen before as the DAO was meant to (and in fact did) operate as a crowdfunding platform.

Much interest therefore arises out of the governance issue. The DAO presented itself as a truly autonomous corporation, managed in an innovative and never before seen way. This was the claim, however, on closer scrutiny, it seems that the DAO operated as any other corporation, conferring upon each category of participant different powers and roles. These could be project developers; investors; or those choosing which project to include within the DAO; or the core developers of the DAO itself. Each category of participant contributed to the functioning of the DAO, exercising different powers.

So-called contractors, submitted proposals for projects that could potentially provide a return. To be a contractor, the individual had to abide by two conditions: they had to own at least one DAO token and they had to pay a deposit in ETH that would then be forfeited to the DAO if the proposal failed to reach quorum. To submit a proposal, the contractor had to write a smart contract (on the Ethereum blockchain) and post all project details on the DAO website.

Before being handed over to the Community voting process, a proposal had to firstly be approved by the so-called curators. These were individuals chosen autonomously by the DAO developers on the basis of expertise and credentials. According to the White Paper, these curators exercised "considerable power" given that they maintained ultimate control over which proposal could be submitted to a vote. As

---

[68]https://ethereum.org/developers/.

[69]According to the DAO White Paper, the DAO token holder would receive rewards defined as any ETH received by the DAO generated from the projects to fund new projects or to distribute the ETH to DAO token holders.

[70]Within the US the platforms trading fiat and crypto currencies must be registered at the Financial Crime enforcement Network (FINCEN) as a monetary services business and provide customers the possibility to exchange virtual currencies for other virtual or fiat currencies.

[71]Securities and Exchange Commission (SEC). Securities exchange act of 1934. Release No. 81207 / July 25 2017: Report of investigation pursuant to Section 21(a) of the Securities Exchange Act of 1934 Report, at 7–8.

publicly stated, "*the Curator had complete control over the whitelist* . . . *the order in which things get whitelisted, the duration for which proposal get whitelisted, when things get whitelisted and clear ability to control the order and frequency of proposal*".[72]

Once the curators had approved the project, it could become publicly available on the DAO website and on other exchange platform websites. Then the DAO's token holders were required to cast their vote with each vote weighted differently according to the total number of tokens owned by the voter. This voting process can be easily criticized: as the vote was weighted according to the sum of tokens owned by the participant, then the more participants spent on buying the DAO tokens the more power he/she obtained; the principle is anything but democratic. Plus, the voting process itself could be distorted and did not necessarily mirror the consensus of the DAO holders.[73]

From the above, it is clear that the DAO was built to be managed by the core developers along with the curators. The DAO token holders were only meant to act as traditional shareholders in any company: investing in a project in order to receive a return. And in fact, throughout 2016, DAO Token holders were buying and selling the DAO tokens in the secondary markets.

Contrary to all expectations, while the DAO token offering period was still pending, the DAO project raised concerns regarding its safety and security. Due to this, the developers, in early May 2016, issued a proposal to develop certain updates. However, on 17 June 2016, an individual, or a group of individuals, who were already part of the DAO community began to divert from the DAO wallet and the ETH already invested in it and the attack stole 3.6 million ETH.[74] According to the rules provided in the DAO code, any sum diverted from the DAO wallet was to be held for 27 days before a withdrawal was possible. During this period, the DAO developers proposed and endorsed a hard fork, aimed at securing the diverted ETH and returning it to the DAO token holders. The hard fork would have returned the money as if the attack had never occurred. The fork was implemented on 20 July 2016 thanks to a majority of participants' approval. However, some decided not to endorse the fork as, according to this minority, blockchain systems were *per se* immutable, hence, no "goes back" should be allowed. Plus, nothing in the original smart contract qualified the diversion of money from one wallet to another as a breach of contract. Accordingly, a literal interpretation of the smart contract would have not impeded the attack: the DAO contractual terms were enclosed in this code *0xbb9bc244d7983fde783fcc1c72d3bb8c189413*. Accordingly, absent any further details, the code could have been meant to allow third parties to move the token from one wallet to another.

---

[72]EB134- Emin Gün Sirer and Vlad Zamfir: on a Rocky DAO. (June 6, 2016), https://www.youtube.com/watch?v=ON5GhIQdFU8.

[73]According to the SEC, "voting rights were limited. DAO token holders were substantially reliant on the managerial efforts of Slock.it, its co-Founders and the Curators. Even if an investor's effort helps to make an enterprise profitable, those efforts do not necessarily equate with a promoter's significant managerial efforts or control over the enterprise". See, SEC Report quoted at 13.

[74]Thompson (2016).

6 Follow: The Off-Chain Rules Applicable to the DAO

As seen above, on-chain rules were developed to regulate the DAO's functioning; however, nothing was provided for in the case of a breach of code (as indeed happened).

It is now worth changing perspective, questioning whether, at least in theory, the DAO could have been regulated by off-chain rules as well. The answer is positive: in fact, the DAO operation, along with its attack, did not stay in the vacuum of its own code of functioning; instead, both raised the attention of the government and of the national market authority. Namely, 1 year after the DAO hard fork the US Securities and Exchange Commission (the SEC/the Commission) opened an inquiry aimed at qualifying the nature of the operation that had occurred on both the DAO platform and the other web-based exchange platform involved. The SEC scrutiny was legitimate given that DAO tokens were also traded within US borders, through the means of a US web-based exchange platform. Thus, the Commission deemed it appropriate, and in the public interest, to scrutinize the activity pursued by the DAO so as to understand which US federal law would apply.

The Commission concluded by acknowledging that the DAO tokens were securities and they should have been regulated accordingly. Firstly, the DAO token holders were indeed entering into an investment contract (according to US case law, the investment of money need not necessarily take the form of money[75]). Secondly, the DAO token holders were investing with the expectation to earn money. Thirdly, the profit depended on the managerial effort pursued by others: the Entity's developers along with the DAO curators. With all these characteristics, the DAO should have been registered as an issuer, which is broadly defined as *"every person who issues or proposes to issue any security and person include any unincorporated organization* (U.S.C. §77b(a)(4))".[76]

The SEC report also proved that (allegedly) pure blockchain based organizations are subject to the normative framework provided for in the national territory in which the blockchain or the operation developed is linked. In this case, it was in the US; however, it could have also been in Germany, as this was the state in which the company which developed the DAO was incorporated. Potentially, it could have also been all the other national states where the exchange platform trading the DAO tokens was active. The SEC assumption was useful not in that it held some individuals accountable but to prove that, in the future, (blockchain) platforms under its scrutiny would be required to abide by US federal law. As a result, after the report was made public, all web-based exchange platforms stopped trading the DAO tokens.

[75]Uselton v. Comm. Lovelace Motor Freight, Inc. 940, F.2d, 564, 574 (10th Cir. 1991); See SEC Report, quoted, at 11.

[76]Uselton v. Comm. Lovelace Motor Freight, Inc. 940, F.2d, 564, 574 (10th Cir. 1991); See SEC Report, quoted, at 15.

In the light of the above, it must be stressed that the on-chain and off-chain can only concur in regulating the blockchain based organization if the latter has an interface with the off-chain real world. Off-chain rules can be truly effective in certifying a breach, and holding the person responsible accountable, only when there is someone real to refer to whose identity is known (whether a legal person or an individual). As in the case of the DAO, the SEC opened the procedure because the DAO was also operating through a US web-based exchange platform. Besides, there are indeed some national jurisdictions which already have rules on alleged wrongdoing committed within some blockchain chains:[77] the breach and the harm caused was geographically located and linked to the blockchain's off-chain interface. However, national jurisdictions, might not have the power to remedy the situation.

In fact, national jurisdictions cannot force a change in the protocol. Another shortcoming is that a national court rules only over a given situation that occurred within its borders, without its judgment having effect on the blockchain itself. In fact, blockchains are transnational thus a national ruling affecting the whole chain would imply the extraterritorial application of a national provision. Or, it would imply the arisal of a customary international law provision allowing for the emergence of extraterritorial application of national interventions at least in public hyper utility blockchains (which are processes and data that create global-scale social utility).

Besides, absent any connection with the off-chain world, wrongdoing committed within a blockchain based organization has to be solved at the blockchain organization level.

7 The (Implausible) Comparison Between Blockchain On-Chain Rules and the *lex mercatoria*

The above analysis leads to a conclusion: blockchain based organizations do not lie in a vacuum. To the contrary, they are strictly linked with national states, along with the whole international Community. From this, there is a last point worth considering; one might question whether the on-chain rules, enacted as the code running the blockchain, form an autonomous legal order. According to some *"Nick Szabo forged*

[77]US: U.S. Court of Appeals for the first Circuit (2001). Sec v. SG Ltd, 265 F.3d 42, 46, 13 September, 2001; U.S. southern district Court of Florida (2018) United Corporation v. BITM AIN INC, et al., case 1:18-cv-25106-KMW; Italy: Brescia first degree Court (2018). decree 7556/2018, 18 July 2018; Florence, first degree Court (2019) Judgment n. 18/2019, 21 January 2019; Brescia Court of Appeal (2018) decree no. 207/2018 endorsing first degree judgment; France: Nanterre Commercial Court (2020), decision 26 February 2020; Paris court of Appeal (2013), case n. 12/00161 SAS Macaraja c/SA Credit industriel et commercial, 26 October 2013 (see here: https://www.lesechos.fr/finance-marches/banque-assurances/la-justice-francaise-assimile-le-bitcoin-a-de-la-monnaie-1182460).

a crypto law and popularized a legal theory that created software that is way more autonomous than society is capable of creating without the use of law".[78] If this assumption were correct, then blockchain based rules should share the same features as the rules and principles forming the lex mercatoria.[79] Interestingly to note, this very same conclusion was first proposed when internet protocols[80] (then open source software) started to be widespread.[81] In both cases, the claim has been wisely rejected. The same conclusion can now be reached also with regards to the blockchain based rules which form the so-called *lex cryptographia* or rules of code.[82]

To prove this, a closer comparison of the features of *lex mercatoria*, *lex informatica*, open source software and *lex cryptographia* is necessary.

With regards to the first, the history of the lex mercatoria goes back to the Medieval era when communities of merchants started to agree on a set of uniform legal principles developed independently from the medieval central authorities and the rules enacted by them. The provisions and the principles forming the lex mercatoria are thus the result of a bottom up approach, legitimizing customs and practices.[83] Given this, the process leading to the conferring of legal legitimization upon the lex mercatoria rules and principles took centuries: states have always been indifferent to normative provisions not enacted by state authorities.

To date, while a uniform definition of lex mercatoria is still missing, that *corpus* of laws has received legitimization at all levels, national and international.[84] This means that economic operators can freely decide to regulate their relationships according to rules or principles that form part of the lex mercatoria.[85] Given this legitimization, the question has then become how broad and deep the implications of the lex mercatoria are with respect to the nature and the functioning of that *corpus* of laws in the context of globalization. Nowadays, lex mercatoria is indeed in a position to play a significant role within the international community and its functionality is grounded on three specific characteristics.

---

[78]Zamfir (2019).

[79]For an overview on such a broad issue see, among others: Boschiero (2005), Konradu and Fix-Fierro (2005), Goldman (1964, 1993) and Schmitthoff (1964).

[80]Barlow (1996), Lessig (1999), Goldsmith (1998), Fischer-Lescano and Teubner (2004), Appelbaum et al. (2001), Goldsmith and Wu (2006), Loader (1997), Trotter (1994) and Mefford (1997).

[81]Marrella and Yoo (2007) and Mann (2006).

[82]Wright and de Filippi (2018).

[83]Johnson and Post (1996).

[84]*Contra:* S. Bond, while Secretary General of the ICC International Court of Arbitration in Paris, found that arbitration clauses were determining, as applicable, the national provision. From this, he derived that parties prefer domestic law to international law (see Bond 1990). However, this conclusion seems not to be the correct one: a closer scrutiny of the case law leads to the opposite conclusion. Fouchard et al. (sous la direction) (1997).

[85]Berman and Felix (1998).

Lex mercatoria rules and principles form the so-called third legal order, autonomous from both the national and the international ones. In this regard, it is worthwhile to highlight that autonomy means that its existence and development do not depend on other legal systems.[86] Accordingly, private economic operators can freely produce laws, without previous authorization by nation states which return to the scene in case enforcement is needed. This "return" to the national states also proves that the lex mercatoria legal order is autonomous but not detached from other legal orders. Thinking the other way around, it is a dogma. Secondly, lex mercatoria provisions are universally accepted and applied all around the globe.[87] Thirdly, lex mercatoria provisions and principles are the result of spontaneous activity coming from its community. This means that lex mercatoria is not the result of the exercise of governmental power or intergovernmental process. To the contrary, it is the result of a bottom up approach which reflects "*the collective freedom of entire trading community*".[88]

Given the above, neither internet protocols nor open source software have the features to be considered independent legal orders.

Internet protocols were claimed to be ruled by a set of autonomous provisions forming the so-called *lex informatica*. Namely, the provisions forming the *lex informatica* were made up of informatic protocols, software, hardware, algorithm and binary codes developed and built by software engineers.[89] However, *lex informatica* has never reached the status of an autonomous legal order; internet protocols and programs soon started to be regulated by either national or international law provisions. For governments, at all levels, it was just a matter of understanding how to deal with new technology. In the end, governments understood that they could either follow a neutrality approach towards technology[90] or, where needed, they enacted new provisions.

With regards to open source software, these are distributed along with their original code: any software amendment is therefore available to all users. According to Lessig, the more widespread use of open source software may have increased the

[86]*Contra* there are some academics who confer upon lex mercatoria a more restricted role. According to them, lex mercatoria could only be used to solve disputes among merchants (Jones 2003). The settlement of mercantile disputes by merchants: an approach to the history of commercial law. Lecture addressed at the University of Chicago Law School Symposium: The Empirical and Theoretical Underpinnings of the Law Merchant Oct. 16–17, 2003). Or, lex mercatoria could be used only to fit the gap left by existing national law (see Berger K.P. (1999), The creeping codification of the lex mercatoria, at 40).

[87]See Berman H. J. (1982). *Contra*, according to some academics there should be a distinction between "macro" lex mercatoria, containing principles and rules shared by all, or the majority, of states; and micro lex mercatoria which should correspond to the legal principles contained in a given contract. Maniruzzaman (1999).

[88]Hayek (1973) (cited by Marrella F., Yoo C. at 7).

[89]Maestri (2017).

[90]ESMA (2019). Advice on Initial Coin Offerings and Cryptoassets, ESMA 50-157-1391; Jabotinsky (2018) and Hacker and Thomale (2017). European Parliament (2016) Report on Digital Currencies (2016/2007(INI)) at 22.

ability to resist governmental control. However, this conclusion was soon proved to not have taken into proper consideration the real features of open source software. Each open source is grounded on the principle of lack of central authority. It is true that, once accepted, under the open source licence's terms each user can amend the software code. However, it is not possible for open source software to concur, as necessary, to form autonomous legal systems. This conclusion can easily be reached for three reasons: firstly, open sources are not universally accepted; indeed, a universal open source software, governed by the same rules, does not exist. To the contrary, each open source software, for example GNU/Linux or LibreOffice—has its own regulations. In fact, as of today, there is a proliferation of open source licenses (more than 50).[91]

Secondly, open source codes are developed by individuals who want to achieve a particular aim. What is included in the open source's license reflects the will of its developers to shape the values of the given open source community.[92] As such, the code is not the result of a spontaneous emergence of practices.[93] Lastly, like the internet, open source systems are more dependent on national law than lex mercatoria is. Open source does not have provisions for dispute resolution and so protection for any breach of copyright must be sought from a legal system. For all the above reasons, neither internet protocol nor open source software has reached the standing of an independent legal order.

By the time distributed ledger technologies in general, and blockchain technologies in particular, started to become widespread, some academics perceived the rise of a new legal system regulated by its own rules. According to some, these new technologies, along with the projects they could develop, would be regulated by an autonomous corpus juridicium, called lex cryptographia, consisting of rules written in code.[94] Code is in fact presumed to be the only language available to govern these new technologies. According to these academics, each blockchain then constitutes a new legal system, detached from all others and governed by its own rules. In fact, contrary to the older technologies, blockchains should allow for enforcement provisions also, therefore cutting off the necessity to return to the state's legal system.[95]

However, claims of the independence of the internet and open source software should be rejected. Each blockchain is created and operates to achieve an autonomous aim. This is to say that on-chain rules are not uniquely framed for the whole community. Besides, they neither have, nor would potentially have, legal legitimization. On-chain rules both exogenous and endogenous, are more a code of conduct. They consist of a series of software protocols regulating the functioning of the chain and the handling and prevention of disputes that might arise in blockchain

---

[91]For a complete list see: Open Source Initiative, The Approved Licenses, http://www.opensource.org/licenses.

[92]Stallman (1999) and Raymond (2000).

[93]Padoa Schioppa (2005).

[94]Schrepel (2020) and Wright and De Filippi (2015).

[95]Ortolani (2019) and Cappiello (2019).

governance. Also, if breached, on-chain rules have limited—and only soft—instruments to hold the responsible party accountable: the worst scenario being to gain a bad reputation or being obliged to exit the chain.

Also, on-chain rules might eventually produce legal effects recognized by a national legal order when the blockchain has an off-chain interface connecting it to the off-chain world. For instance, a smart contract becomes a smart legal contract if, in case of a breach, the damaged party pursues damages or enforcement before a national court which finds that the smart contract has the form and content of a traditional contract.[96] The same holds true when a web-based organization is required to abide by national rules even when it trades cryptoassets or any other native blockchain goods.

Given the above, by the time a blockchain based organization "exits" the on-chain world, it loses its alleged autonomy and must abide by the off-chain rules. This is to say that, as seen in the DAO case, the nation state will always have ultimate control over a given blockchain's functioning and legitimization. Accordingly, instead of presenting blockchains as new legal orders based on new governance (that of the governance of the chain), it would be preferable to view blockchain technology as a new tool to achieve aims or to create and manage entities.

8 Conclusion

Law and technology can influence each other; indeed, they interact through a complex system of dependencies and interdependencies.

History has shown that new technologies can profoundly impact the way human society trades, connects and communicates. New technologies do indeed represent a new environment for human expression and living within society. As Schwab suggested, we are leaving a fourth technological revolution which has brought together digital, physical and biological systems. In does not change what we are doing, but it changes us.[97]

DLT technologies in general, and blockchains in particular, are about to lead—and in part already have led—our society to a paradigm shift. Thanks to blockchain technologies, individuals are experiencing a new form of trust: the no party trust, where parties do not trust each other—they do not even know each other—but they trust the technology. Blockchain technologies are also crafting the scarcity of digital goods. Differently from before, goods traded on a blockchain protocol can have only one owner, regardless of the nature of the token itself which can correspond to the digital representation of the value of a good, a security or a right. Also, blockchain technologies are making new forms of governance available; reference has been

[96] Cappiello (2020).

[97] Schwab (2016).

made to the combined governance of both on-chain and off-chain rules. As such, the governance of the blockchain runs in parallel with the governance of the blockchain.

Besides, blockchain technology, as those before it, does not entail the fall of sovereign nation states. to the contrary, the latter are only required to amend their functioning and, (where necessary) their normative provisions, to accommodate new technologies. A prompt and serious legitimization of new technologies is much needed: entailing a clear distinction between what is legitimate and what is an illegitimate technology exploitation.

Distribution and decentralization do not mean anarchy. Instead, these will be used to solve the failure and the shortcomings of nation states. Where states are lacking, technology responds in a continuous dialogue. This analysis has also shown that behind the blockchain developers' claims of openness, autonomy, participation and equality, at closer scrutiny blockchain based organizations seem to function *verbatim* as a partnership. In fact, participants do not have the same role and the power is distributed depending on the economic share of each participant. Accordingly, instead of a participative democracy, blockchain systems seem more alike to plutocratic government. Given this, the positive effects deriving from a legitimate and proper exploitation of these new technologies should not be dismissed. To the contrary, it is now time for the "two worlds" to open a dialogue. Not disruptive, but constructive.

References

Aaronson S (2013) Quantum computing since democritus. Cambridge University Press, Cambridge

Abi-Saab (1987) Cours general de droit international public. Recueil des cours de l'Académie de droit international de La Haye, t. 207, Dodrecht/Boston/Leiden

Ali R (2009) Technological neutrality. Lex Electronica

Ammous S (2018) The Bitcoin standard: the decentralized alternative to central banking. John Wiley & Sons Inc, Hoboken

Annunziata F (2018) La disciplina delle trading venues nell'era delle rivoluzioni tecnologiche: dalle criptovalute alla distributed ledger technology. Orizzonti del diritto commerciale

Antonopoulos AM (2017) Mastering Bitcoin: unlocking digital cryptocurrencies, 2nd edn. O'Reilly media, Sebastopol

Appelbaum R, Felstiner W, Gessner L, Volkmar G (2001) Rules and networks. The legal culture of global business transactions. Oxford University Press, Oxford

Barlow JP (1996) A declaration of the Independence of cyberspace. http://homes.eff.org/~barlow/Declaration-Final.html

Bassiouni MC (1990) A functional approach to general principles of international law. Mich J Int Law 11:768–818

Beck R, Müller-Bloch C, King J (2018) Governance in the somy: a framework and research agenda. J Assoc Inf Syst 19:1–36

Berman HJ, Felix JD (1998) The 'new' law merchant and the 'old': sources, content, and legitimacy. In: Carbonneau TE (ed) Lex Mercatoria and arbitration. A discussion of the new law merchant. Revised edition. Juris Publishing/Kluwer Law International, The Hague, pp 53–69

Bertoli P (2018) Virtual currencies and private international law. Rivista di diritto internazionale privato e processuale 54:2

Bobbio N (1994) Principi generali di diritto. In: Bobbio N (ed) Contributi ad un dizionario giuridico. Giappichelli, Turin, pp 257–279

Bodó B, Giannopoulou A (2019) The logics of technology decentralization – the case of distributed ledger technologies. In: Ragnedda M, Destefanis G (eds) Blockchain and web 3.0: social, economic, and technological challenges. Routledge, Abingdon

Bond S (1990) How to draft an arbitration clause (revisited). ICC Bull 1.2:14–27

Bonneau J, Miller A (2015) Sok: research perspectives and challenges for bitcoin and cryptocurrencies. In: 2015 IEEE symposium on security and privacy. IEEE, pp 104–121

Boschiero N (2005) La lex mercatoria nell'era della globalizzazione: considerazioni di diritto internazionale pubblico e privato. Sociologia del diritto 2:83–155

Buterin V (2018) Governance, Part 2: plutocracy is still bad' blog post at https://vitalik.ca/general/2018/03/28/plutocracy.html

Cappiello B (2019) Where is justice taking place? Blockchain technology as a tool to fill a gap. Rivista di diritto internazionale privato e processuale 3:652–680

Cappiello B (2020) Dallo "smart contract" computer code allo smart (legal) contract. I nuovi strumenti (para) giuridici, alla luce della normativa nazionale e del diritto internazionale privato europeo; prospettive de jure condendo. Rivista del commercio internazionale 2:325–388

Chaum D (1983) Blind signatures for untraceable payments. In: Chaum D, Rivest RL, Sherman AT (eds) Advances in cryptology. Springer US, Boston, pp 199–203

Chimienti MT, Kochanska U, Pinna A (2019) Understanding the crypto-asset phenomenon, its risks and measurement issues. ECB Economic Bulletin

Clean App (n.d.) Blockchain Governance 105: International Law. Global blockchains = global blockchain governance. Crypto Law Review. Available here: https://medium.com/cryptolawreview/blockchain-governance-105-international-law-3c7ebd025a43

Crawford J (2019) Brownlie's principle of public international law. Oxford University Press, Oxford

De Filippi P, Hassan S (2018) Blockchain technology as a regulatory technology: from code is law to law is code. arXiv preprint arXiv:180102507

De Filippi P, McMullen G (2018) Governance of blockchain systems, governance of and by distributed infrastructure. A COALA + blockchain research Institute big IDEA White Paper

Di Ciommo E (2018) Smart contracts and (non-)law. The case of the financial markets. Law Econ Yearly Rev 7:291–325

di Lampedusa GT (2002) Il gattopardo. Feltrinelli Editore, Milano

DiMatteo LA, Cannarsa M, Poncibò C (2019) The Cambridge handbook of smart contracts, blockchain technology and digital platforms. Cambridge University Press, Cambridge

Drake DJ (2013) Business organizations in a planning context, cases, materials and study problems. West Academic, Saint Paul

Duffield E, Hagan K (2014) Darkcoin: peer to peer cryptocurrency with anonymous blockchain transactions and an improved proof of work system. bitpaper info

Ficsor M (2002) The law of copyright and the internet: the 1996 WIPO treaties, their interpretation and implementation. Oxford University Press, Oxford

Finck M (2018) Blockchain regulation and governance in Europe. Cambridge University Press, Cambridge

Fischer-Lescano A, Teubner G (2004) Regime collisions: the vain search for legal unity in the fragmentation of global law. Mich J Int Law 25:999–1046

Fitzmaurice G (1958) Some problems regarding the formal sources of international law. In: van Asbeck FM et al (eds) Symbolae Verzijl. Nijhoff, La Haye, pp 153–176

Fouchard P, Gaillard E, Goldman E (1997) Traité de l'arbitrage commercial international. Revue de droit comparé, pp 269–271

Gardner J (2012) Law as a leap of faith: essays on law in general. Oxford University Press, Oxford

Givari D (2018) Can the application of blockchain technology broaden the horizon for arbitration?. Kluwer Arbitration Blog

Goldman B (1964) Frontières du droit et lex mercatoria. Archives de philosophie du droit IX:177–192

Goldman B (1993) Nouvelles réflexions sur la lex mercatoria. In: Etudes de droit international en l'honneur de Pierre Lalive, Bâle et Frankfurt s/Main, pp 241–255

Goldreich O, Oren Y (1994) Definitions and properties of zero-knowledge proof systems. J Cryptol 7:1–32

Goldreich O, Goldwasser S, Halevi S (1997) Public-key cryptosystems from lattice reduction problems. In: Annual international cryptology conference. Springer, Berlin, pp 112–131

Goldsmith J (1998) Against cyberanarchy. Univ Chicago Law Rev 65:1199–1250

Goldsmith J, Wu T (2006) Who controls the Internet? Oxford University Press, Oxford

Goldwasser S, Micali S, Rackoff C (1989) The knowledge complexity of interactive proof systems. SIAM J Comput 18:186–208. https://doi.org/10.1137/0218012

Hacker P, Thomale C (2017) Crypto-securities regulation: ICOs, token sales and cryptocurrencies under EU financial law. http://ssrn.com/abstract=3075820

Handerson M, Raskin M (2019) A regulatory classification of digital assets: toward an operational Howey test for cryptocurrencies, ICOs, and other digital assets. Colum Bus Law Rev 2019:443

Hayek FA (1973) Law, legislation and liberty. Vol. 1: rules and order, pp 8–34 (cited by Marrella F., Yoo C. at 7)

Jabotinsky H (2018) The regulation of cryptocurrencies – between a currency and a financial product. Legal research paper no. 18-10. Hebrew University of Jerusalem

Johnson DR, Post D (1996) Law and borders – The rise of Law in cyberspace. First Monday 1(1) Available from https://journals.uic.edu/ojs/index.php/fm/article/view/468

Jones W (2003) The settlement of mercantile disputes by merchants: an approach to the history of commercial law. Lecture addressed at the University of Chicago Law School Symposium: The Empirical and Theoretical Underpinnings of the Law Merchant Oct. 16–17, 2003

Koh HH (1997) Why do nations obey international law? Yale Law J 3:2599–2659

Kolb R (2006) General principles of procedural Law. In: Zimmermann A, Tomuschat C et al (eds) The statute of the international court of justice: a commentary. Oxford University Press, Oxford, pp 871–908

Konradu W, Fix-Fierro H (2005) Lex mercatoria in the mirror of empirical research. Sociologia del diritto 2:205–226

Kotuby C (2013) General principles of law, international due process and the modern role of private international law. Duke J Comp Int Law 23:411–443

Kraus D, Obrist T, Hari O (2019) Blockchains, smart contracts, decentralised autonomous organisations and the law. Edward Elgar Publishing, Cheltenham

Kresse KJ (1987) Privacy of conversations over cordless and Cellular telephones: federal protection under the electronic communications privacy act 1996. George Mason Univ Law Rev 9:335

Lai R, Lee DKC (2018) Handbook of blockchain, digital finance, and inclusion, vol 2. Academic Press, Cambridge

Lehman BA (1995) Intellectual property and the National information infrastructure: the report of the working group on intellectual property rights. Information Infrastructure Task Force, Washington, D.C.

Lessig L (1999) Code and other laws of cyberspace. Basic Books 6–8:20–21

Levi S, Lipton A (2018) An introduction to smart contracts and their potential and inherent limitations. Available at: https://corpgov.law.harvard.edu/2018/05/26/an-introduction-to-smart-contracts-and-their-potential-and-inherent-limitations/

Loader B (ed) (1997) The governance of cyberspace. Routledge, Abingdon

Low KFK, Ernie T (2017) Bitcoins and other cryptocurrencies as property? Law Innov Technol 2:235–268

Low KFK, Mik E (2020) Pause the blockchain legal revolution. Int Comp Law Q 69:135–175

Maestri E (2017) Lex informatica and soft law. Le architetture normative del cyberspazio. In: Maestri E, Moro P, Sarra C (eds) Tecnodiritto. Temi e problemi di informatica e robotica giuridica. Franco Angeli, Milano, pp 157–177

Maniruzzaman FM (1999) The lex mercatoria and international contracts: a challenge for international commercial arbitration? Am Univ Int Law Rev 3:657–733
Mann RJ (2006) Commercializing open source software: do property rights still matter? Harv J Law Technol 20:10–21
Marrella F, Yoo CS (2007) Is open source software the new lex mercatoria?. Faculty Scholarship. Univ Pa Law School 165:808–837
Maupin J (2017) Mapping the global legal landscape of blockchain and other distributed Ledger Technologies. CIGI Papers No. 149
McNair AD (1957) The general principles of law recognized by civilized nations. Br Yearb Int Law 33:1–19
Mefford A (1997) Lex Informatica: foundations of law on the Internet. Indiana J Global Legal Stud 5:211–237
Merkle R (2016) DAOs, democracy and governance. Cryonics Mag 4:28–40
Mik E (2017) Contracts: terminology, technical limitations and real-world complexity. Law Innov Technol 9:269–300
Nakamoto S (1997) Formalizing and securing relationships on public networks. First Monday 2
Narayanan A et al (2016) Bitcoin and cryptocurrencies technologies. Princeton University Press, Princeton
Ortolani P (2019) The impact of blockchain technologies and smart contracts on disputes resolution: arbitration and court litigation at a crossroads. Uniform Law Rev 2:430–448
Padoa Schioppa A (2005) Brevi note storiche sulla lex mercatoria. Sociologia del diritto 2:75–83
Philipp H, Chris T (2018) Crypto-securities regulation: ICOs, token sales and cryptocurrencies under EU financial law. Eur Company Financ Law Rev 15:645–696
Raymond R (2000) The revenge of the hackers, Available here: http://catb.org/~esr/faqs/hacker-revenge.html
Reed C (2007) Taking sides on technology neutrality. SCRIPTed 4:263
Reyes C (2019) If Rockfeller were a coder. George Wash Law Rev 87:373–429. at 413
Rivaro R (2014) L'applicazione del principio di esaurimento alla distribuzione digitale di contenuti protetti. Giurisprudenza Commerciale:1149–1164
Robinson RA II (2019) The new digital wild west: regulating the explosion of initial coin offerings. Tenn Law Rev 86:898–960
Rodrigues UR (2019) Law and the blockchain. Iowa Law Rev 2:679–729
Rühl G (2019) The law applicable to smart contracts, or: much ado about nothing?, Oxford Business Law Blog
Salerno F (1996) Principi generali di diritto (Diritto internazionale). Digesto delle discipline pubblicistiche XI:524–557
Savelyev A (2017) Contract Law 2.0: smart contracts as the beginning of the end of classic contract law. Inf Commun Technol Law 2:116–134
Schiller K (2018) Smart contracts – Übersicht und Erklärung, Blockchainwelt. Available at: https://blockchainwelt.de/smart-contracts-vertrag-blockchain/
Schmitthoff C (1964) The law of international trade. its growth, formulation and operation. In: Schmitthoff C (ed) The sources of the law of international trade. Butterworth, London, pp 137–169
Schrepel T (2019) Collusion by blockchain and smart contracts. Harv J Law Technol 33:118–168
Schrepel T (2020) The theory of granularity: a path for antitrust in blockchain system, pp 3–49. Available here https://papers.ssrn.com/sol3/papers.cfm?abstract_id=3519032
Schwab K (2016) The fourth industrial revolution: what it means, how to respond available here: https://www.weforum.org/agenda/2016/01/the-fourth-industrial-revolution-what-it-means-and-how-to-respond
Schwarzenberger G (1955) The fundamental principles of international law. Recueil de cours de l'Aie T. 87, Dodrecht/Boston/Leiden, pp 195–383
Segall L (2015) Silk Road's Ross Ulbricht sentenced to life", CNN available here: money.cnn.com/2015/05/29/technology/silk-roadross-ulbricht-prison-sentence/

Shirky C (2011) Here comes everybody: the power of organizing without organizations. Penguin, London
Simma B, Alston P (1992) The sources of human rights law: custom, jus cogens and general principles. Am J Int Law 12:82–108
Sjostrom WK Jr (2016) Business organizations: a transnational approach. Wolters Kluwer, New York
Sklaroff J (2017) Smart contracts and the cost of inflexibility. Univ Pa Law Rev 166:263–303
Smith R, Barrett DE (2016) The DAO's wild ride: where does blockchain go from here?, FORBES. https://www.forbes.com/sites/realspin/2016/07/01/the-daos-wild-ride-where-does-blockchain-gofromhere/#4f1e637e3e5c
Sørensen M (1960) Les principes de droit international public. Cours général de droit international. Recueil de cours de l'Aie 101:1–254
Spink A, Butler S, Bell C (2019) Cryptoassets and smart contracts: the UKJT legal statements
Stallman R (1999) The gnu operating system and the free software movement. In: DiBona C (ed) Open sources: voices from the open source revolution. O'Really Media, Sebastopol, pp 67–70. Available at http://www.gnu.org/gnu/thegnuproject.html
Swan M (2015) Blockchain: blueprint for a new economy. O'Reilly media, Sebastopol
Szabo N (1997a) The idea of smart contracts. Available here: https://nakamotoinstitute.org/the-idea-of-smart-contracts/
Szabo N (1997b) Smart contracts: formalizing and securing relationships on public networks. First Monday 2. Available at: https://doi.org/10.5210/fm.v2i9.548
Szostek D (2019) Blockchain and the Law. Nomos Verlag, Baden-Baden
Tadelis S (2013) Game theory. An introduction. Princeton University Press, Princeton
Tapscott D, Tapscott A (2016) Blockchain revolution: how the technology behind bitcoin is changing money, business, and the world. Portfolio, New York
The LAO (2019a) The LAO: A for-profit, limited liability autonomous organization. Medium. Available here: https://medium.com/openlawofficial/the-lao-a-for-profit-limited-liability-autonomous-organization-9eae89c9669c
The LAO (2019b) A taxonomy for LAOs: making sense of the emerging LAO ecosystem available here: https://medium.com/@thelaoofficial/a-taxonomy-for-laos-making-sense-of-the-emerging-lao-ecosystem-1122b035fe1a
Thompson C (2016) The DAO of Ethereum. Analyzing the DAO hack, the blockchain, Smart contracts, and the law available here: https://medium.com/blockchain-review/the-dao-of-ethereum-e228b93afc79
Trotter HI (1994) The proper legal regime for "Cyberspace". Univ Pittsbg Law Rev 993:1019–1021
Verdross A (1968) Les principes généraux de droit dans le système des sources du droit international public. In: Guggeheim P (ed) Receuil d'études de droit international en hommage à P. Guggenheim. La Librairie de l'Université, Georg, Geneva, pp 521–530
Vos G (2019) Cryptoassets as property: how can English law boost the confidence of would-be parties to smart legal contracts?. Joint Northern Chancery Bar Association and University of Liverpool Lecture
Vukolic M (2016) The quest for scalable blockchain fabric: proof-of work vs. BFT replication. In: Camenisch J, Kesdoğan D (eds) Open problems in network security, lecture notes in computer science, vol 9591. Springer, Berlin, pp 112–125
Wang S, Vergne JP, Hsieh Y-Y (2017) The internal and external governance of blockchain-based organizations: evidence from cryptocurrencies. In: Campbell-Verduyn M (ed) Bitcoin and beyond: blockchains and global governance. RIPE/Routledge Series in Global Political Economy, New York
Woebbeking M (2019) The impact of smart contracts on traditional concepts of contract law. J Intellect Prop Inf Technol E-commerce Law 10:105–112
Wright A, De Filippi P (2015) Decentralized blockchain technology and the rise of the Lex Cryptographia

Wright A, de Filippi P (2018) Blockchain and the law: the rule of code. Harvard University Press, Cambridge

Wrigley S (2020) When people just click: addressing the difficulties of controller/processor agreement online. In: Corrales C, Fenwick M, Happio H (eds) Legal tech, smart contracts and blockchain. Springer, Berlin, pp 221–252

Wu T (2003) Network neutrality, broadband discrimination. J Telecommun High-Tech Law 2:141–176

Xu X, Weber I, Staples M (2019) Architecture for blockchain applications. Springer, Berlin

XXu et al (2017) A taxonomy of blockchain-based systems for architecture design. In: IEEE International Conference on Software Architecture (ICSA), Gothenburg, pp 243–52

Yermack D (2017) Corporate governance and blockchains. Rev Finance 1:7–31

Zamfir V (2015) What is cryptoeconomics? Mountain View, CA: Cryptoeconomicon. Available here: https://www.youtube.com/watch?v=9lw3s7iGUXQ

Zamfir V (2018) Blockchain Governance 101. Medium. Available here: https://blog.goodaudience.com/blockchain-governance-101-eea5201d7992

Zamfir ZV (2019) Against Szabo's law, for a new Crypto legal system. Crypto Law Review

The Role of Blockchain in the Public Sector: An Overview

Gherardo Carullo

Contents

1 Introduction: Centralization and Decentralization of Data

With the transition to the digital era we have witnessed a profound change in the methods of data management, including in the public sector. For some time now, information is kept in digital archives that allow—in various ways and according to different logics—the cataloguing, structuring and indexing of the data contained therein.

This innovation, among the numerous effects it entails, has the important consequence of giving a new dimension to information, if considered as a whole. From catalogues kept statically in paper archives, the materials in public hands, organized and structured with the tools offered by information and communication technologies (ICT), become a dynamic asset stored in digital databases.

G. Carullo (✉)
Department of Italian and Supranational Public Law, University of Milan, Milan, Italy
e-mail: gherardo.carullo@unimi.it

B. Cappiello, G. Carullo (eds.), *Blockchain, Law and Governance*,
https://doi.org/10.1007/978-3-030-52722-8_3

In recent years we have witnessed a growing push towards the centralization of such databases.[1] Due to technical, economic or commercial reasons, as well as for organizational efficiency, both in the public sector and private sector databases have often been physically located in data centers acting as a central place of collection and management of data.[2] This organizational model, for various reasons that go beyond the scope of this chapter,[3] has been largely adopted in the public sector, where there has been a general trend towards the centralization of ICT systems[4] within each level of governance.[5]

At the other end of the spectrum, there are peer-to-peer (P2P) communications. In a P2P system each user participating in the network—commonly known as a node—, can, and normally does, retain a (full) copy of the data being shared. This model was rapidly adopted for the illegal exchange of copyrighted files.[6] As there is no central data collection point—that is, a single data center—, it can be particularly difficult for authorities to block the activities of the distributed network.

The lack of a single data collection point, however, presents the arduous problem of identifying a single source of truth. As the nodes on which the data are stored multiply, it becomes essential to identify which version is the most up-to-date and correct, in order to avoid collisions, tampering or frauds. As explained in Chap. 4,[7] blockchain addresses such problem with mathematical algorithms that can prevent collisions in the data, while guaranteeing its integrity and resilience with respect to tampering attempts.[8]

Blockchain technology therefore enables the creation of decentralized and secure systems that can profoundly innovate some of the inner concepts upon which centralized systems work. Even where the participants of a given network have no particular mutual trust.

These unique features of blockchain have stimulated numerous initiatives aimed at developing decentralized systems,[9] also with the aim to overcome the data monopoly of some of the current players in the digital market.[10] In the public context, however, despite some interesting attempts to implement

[1]It has been noted that centralization and decentralization are cyclical in computing, Peak and Azadmanesh (1997).

[2]For an early analysis of such trend, see Warren Axelrod (1999).

[3]For a brief overview of the advantages of centralized systems, in particular in comparison to decentralized ones, see Wüst and Gervais (2018), p. 46.

[4]For example, for the US federal government see Brown and Garson (2013), p. 78.

[5]It should be noted that, as per the organization of public powers, "*decentralisation is a major trend everywhere*", as noted by Benamou et al. (2004), p. 84. For this reason, when we refer to centralization of ICT systems, we mean within each center of power.

[6]Steinmetz (2005), pp. 18–24.

[7]See the chapter by C. Biondi Santi and V. Vespri.

[8]This system of course does not prevent, however, other kinds of malicious behaviors as for example explained by Bartoletti et al. (2018).

[9]Wessling et al. (2018).

[10]Yano et al. (2019).

blockchain-based solutions,[11] the widespread use of this technology faces additional multiple challenges.

Among these, it must be considered that most public administration ICT systems have usually been implemented according to a centralized logic. This could therefore slow down, if not even prevent, the transition to a decentralized paradigm. Switching costs could indeed constitute a major obstacle to the widespread use of decentralized systems. It has to be considered that the remodulation of an ICT system entails costs and can lead to failures.[12] As a result, decision makers in public institutions might prefer to avoid the risk of wasting public money, especially if there are no or little incentives for innovating.[13]

It must also be considered that blockchain was initially conceived with the aim of removing the need to have a central governing authority.[14] As a matter of fact, such self-regulation capacity has allowed blockchain to become quite popular in the cryptocurrency sector, starting from Bitcoin. As confirmed also by the case law of the Court of Justice, Bitcoin "*does not have a single issuer and instead is created directly in a network by a special algorithm*".[15] This stands in stark contrast to modern systems of public law, where a body of some kind is normally entrusted with authoritative powers to purse a public interest.[16] This alone could therefore cast doubts on the very usefulness of blockchain in the public sector.

It is therefore necessary to investigate if any, and what, utility the blockchain could have in the public sector.[17] To answer this question, it is necessary to clarify some fundamental concepts, starting with the one of "database", which is a critical element of this topic.

2 Essential Notions on the Concept of Database

To understand the meaning of the term database, from a legal point of view we can refer to the definition contained in article 1, paragraph 2, of Directive 96/9/EC on the legal protection of databases. According to this provision, "*database*" means "*a*

[11]See for example the blockchain-based app developed by *Regione Lombardia* in Italy for enrolments in nursery schools, www.lombardiaspeciale.regione.lombardia.it/wps/portal/LS/Home/News/Dettaglio-News/patto-per-lo-sviluppo/2019/09-settembre/regione-lombardia-sperimenta-blockchain-per-accesso-a-suoi-servizi/regione-lombardia-sperimenta-blockchain-per-accesso-a-suoi-servizi.

[12]Roman (2013), p. 112.

[13]While in the private sector it has been observed that competition can in itself stimulate innovation, Tang (2006).

[14]Xu et al. (2019), p. 46.

[15]See judgment of 22 October 2015 in case C-*264/14 Hedqvist*, paragraph 11.

[16]Amongst the many studies that have analyzed this aspect of public law, see for example Goodnow (1983), p. 48.

[17]From a technical point of view, in comparison with centralized systems, this question has been addressed by Wüst and Gervais (2018), p. 45 et seq.

collection of independent works, data or other materials arranged in a systematic or methodical way and individually accessible by electronic or other means".[18] We can also refer to the vocabulary of the *International Organization for Standardisation* (ISO) n. IEC 2382: 2015, according to which a database is a "*collection of data organised according to a conceptual structure describing the characteristics of these data and the relationships among their corresponding entities, supporting one or more application areas*".[19]

These definitions provide us with some useful directions regarding the elements that constitute a database. First, we can note that neither the support on which it is stored (hardware), nor any computer program necessary for its operation (software) are mentioned. The only elements that are relevant are the records contained in the database, the structure according to which they are stored, their characteristics and their relationships. Therefore, these elements have their own (digital) consistency, which is independent from the physical infrastructure (hardware) and the computer programs (software) necessary for their operation.

The twenty-third recital of Directive 96/9/EC also confirms that "*the term 'database' should not be taken to extend to computer programs used in the making or operation of a database*". This is because the database can exist and have its own (digital) consistency regardless of the computer programs needed to access its contents. As a matter of fact, there can be multiple computer programs capable of accessing a database.

Another important feature of databases is that they, as digital resources, can be replicated an indefinite number of times, on any system capable of hosting them. Such replicas can be identical to the source, so that each copy cannot be distinguished from the original data source. Moreover, replicating a given data set does not normally compromise the integrity of the source from which it is extracted. This is particularly relevant in the perspective of decentralized systems as it allows to have multiple copies of a database shared among multiple nodes of a distributed network.

Under this perspective, as per the infrastructural aspect, the fact that a database can be independent from the *hardware* on which it is hosted is also important for distributed systems. The fact that the database can be hosted on a variety of hardware settings means that each node can choose, to a certain degree, whichever system it deems more convenient or appropriate, without compromising its ability to be part of the distributed network.

[18]It should be noted that this article expressly states that the collections in question can be "*accessible by electronic or other means*", so that it is also possible to have databases stored on analogical supports. In the context of this chapter, however, we only deal with profiles related to digital ones.

[19]See definition n. 2121413, at https://www.iso.org/obp/ui/#iso:std:iso-iec:2382:ed-1:v1:en.

3 Data Centers in Centralized Systems

In order to be digitally stored, data must be saved on physical devices. As the volume of data grows, the complexity of the infrastructure required to store it increases. For masses of data such as those owned by public administrations it is usually necessary to set up infrastructures specifically designed to store data. These are the so-called data centers, also commonly known as a *cloud*.[20]

It is worth underlining that the term *cloud* can be misleading: these structures are usually deep-rooted in the ground, inside buildings equipped with complex systems designed to optimize performances and are normally well protected, both from cyber threats and real world dangers, such as natural disasters.

These data centers have the function of hosting all the hardware, and thus software, needed for data storing and managing in one place. Normally, backup copies are routinely made to prevent any loss of data. This can be done at the same site, or in a different infrastructure, sometimes even geographically distant, in order to minimize risks.[21]

To ensure business continuity, therefore, normally the original data source is supported by one or more secondary copies for disaster recovery. However, it should be emphasized that in a centralized model, even if there are multiple secondary centers, the source of truth is identified in a primary data center, while the others—under normal service conditions—have the only function of passively replicating the information contained in the original data source. In other words, even if there are multiple copies of the same database, only one acts as the origin of information, while the others are secondary copies.

4 Blockchain As a Decentralization Tool

Blockchain is usually classified as a Distributed Ledger Technology (DLT). It is composed of a series of technologies and protocols that use a shared, distributed, replicable, simultaneously accessible, architecturally decentralized ledger based on cryptography. It allows the recording, validation, updating and storage of data, both in clear text and encrypted. The integrity of the ledger is verifiable by each participant, and it normally cannot be altered or modified.[22]

Among its most important features, the concept of distributed ledger is fundamental. By the term ledger, in this case we mean in essence, a digital document in which information is stored according to a predefined structure. In other words,

---

[20]The US federal government has for example created the service cloud.gov, which "*helps teams build, run and authorize government cloud systems quickly and cheaply*" (https://cloud.gov).

[21]On the various strategies to optimize backup and recovery procedures, see Hiatt (2000), p. 39 et seq.

[22]For a thoughtful analysis of how blockchain works, see Xu et al. (2019).

ledger refers here to the notion of database as described above. The substantial difference, however, is that, in this case, such database is decentralized.

The distributed nature of the database used by DLT implies that it is shared on a network in which each participant—i.e. each node—normally holds a copy of the ledger. The notable difference with respect to centralized systems is that in this case such copies are not mere backups. Each node on which the database is stored can have—and normally has—the same authority as the others in the distributed network. As a general rule, there are no passive or secondary nodes. This has the double advantage of allowing perfect transparency of the contents of the ledger, and of avoiding a single point of failure.

An important feature for public administrations of DLTs is that the network can be public or private. In public blockchains, anyone can store the entire distributed ledger on their device and can thus become a full node on the network. In private ones, on the contrary, only those authorized to do so have access to the ledger.

Another important difference is between permissioned and permissionless DLT systems. The former is based on an authentication system whereby not all users have the same power over the data stored in the distributed ledger. The latter is instead devoid of any authentication measure, so that anyone can perform operations on the data stored in the registry if they comply with the rules set by the network itself for doing so.[23]

As previously outlined, the distributed nature of the ledger on which blockchain technologies are based is at the basis of the need to manage the recording, validation, updating and storage of data on a cryptographic basis. The distributed nature of the database imposes the use of complex mathematical algorithms to validate the contents and operations carried out on the DLT.

Unlike traditional databases, DLTs implement a cryptographic information concatenation system that allows anyone to verify every change recorded in the database. Through complex mathematical algorithms this concatenation guarantees over time that the information contained in each block cannot be altered. Even if the database is distributed on a very large number of nodes, it can always be verified that each copy of the ledger is intact and that therefore all the information distributed on all the nodes are concordant with each other.

Distributed consensus mechanisms are normally also implemented to add new blocks. Such consensus mechanisms are complex mathematical models capable of validating the information of each block with the other participants in the network.[24]

These features of DLTs guarantee the integrity and functioning of the system without a central authority. The mathematical models that manage the network themselves guarantee the correct functioning of the system and its full integrity and immutability. Therefore, in light of these characteristics, we can now evaluate in what terms blockchain, especially public and permissionless ones, can play a role in ensuring the transparency of public administrations.

[23] See also Wüst and Gervais (2018), pp. 45–46.

[24] See chapter by C. Biondi Santi and V. Vespri

5 Blockchain As a Transparency Tool in the Public Sector. Potentialities and Limits

Transparency of public administrations is an issue that has recently become increasingly important in the public debate. Access to information held by public subjects is considered more and more relevant from multiple points of view. It can favor the democratic process, the participation of citizens in public decision-making processes or as a tool for fighting and preventing corruption.[25]

In a context in which information is stored in digital databases, it is therefore certainly interesting to evaluate in what terms blockchain could facilitate access to data. As outlined above, this technology can be used to create decentralized public networks, in which every participant has access to the distributed database. This tool could thus favor the transparency of the administration by implementing a new radical system to disseminate open data.

At this regard it is worth recalling that the expression open data usually identifies information that is made accessible for free, to anyone, even for commercial purposes, through the tools offered by ICT, in open formats that are likely to be processed even without human intervention, i.e. automatically by computer programs.

Legal barriers are removed, through the adoption of licenses that allow the reuse of data without particular limits. From a technical point of view, the distribution through digital channels (e.g. internet) and in machine readable formats, ensure that data is the most accessible possible. Such formats are:

The notion of "*machine readable format*" is provided by art. 2, paragraph 1, lett. 13) of Directive 2019/1024/EU, which replicates the same definition already dictated by the previous Directive 2003/98/EC. According to both Directives, it is a "*'machine-readable format' means a file format structured so that software applications can easily identify, recognise and extract specific data, including individual statements of fact, and their internal structure*".

This characteristic of the data is of particular importance since, in the absence of it—where therefore the data is not distributed in machine-readable formats—it would be much less convenient to process it.

In this regard, it has to be outlined the relationship between the notion of open data and that of big data. While open data refers to the accessibility of data, both from a technical and legal perspective, "*big data is the information asset characterised by such a high volume, velocity and variety to require specific technology and analytical methods for its transformation into value*".[26]

---

[25]Blanke and Perlingeiro (2017). As a tool aimed toward "*the transparency of the performance of the administration and of public services, and prevention of corruption*", see for example Galetta (2018), p. 355.

[26]According to the definition proposed by De Mauro et al. (2016).

On the basis of this last definition, it can therefore be noted that open data and big data are distinct and autonomous concepts. An open data set might not be qualified as big data, just as big data might not be open data, and *vice versa*.

On the other hand, it should be borne in mind that "*the public sector of the Member States collects, produces, reproduces and disseminates a wide range of information in many sectors of activity, for example social, political, economic, legal, geographical information, environmental, meteorological, seismic, tourism, information on business, patents and education*".[27] Therefore, it can normally be assumed that the amount of data processed in the public sector is such as to qualify a large part of the data sets held by administrations as *big data*.

Making open data available in machine readable formats, especially if it also qualifies as big data, is very important because in this way it is easier to use and analyses it.

In this sense, permissionless and public blockchains can be useful. As seen in this type of system, data is available to any participant as provided by the protocol implemented by the DLT. Furthermore, the fact that data is registered on the blockchain ensures that it is structured according to a predefined schema. This can generally guarantee that such data is in a "*machine-readable format*".

The problem, however, is that blockchain technology is not usually used to storing large amounts of data sets. Since all the information is stored into linked blocks, and because all such blocks are required to be checked in order to ensure integrity of the chain,[28] it can be particularly expensive and inefficient to save large amounts of data. As an example, the Bitcoin blockchain, which saves small pieces of information on transactions[29]—each of which "*are typically ~250 bytes of data*"[30]—, in a few years has already passed over 270 GB.[31]

Blockchain therefore does not seem suitable for saving the kind of documents and data that are generally made public by administrations to ensure a high level of transparency of the public sector. On the contrary, this technology seems more suitable to store small fragments of data. As a consequence, given the current implementations of blockchain technology, it seems that it would not be optimal to save documents and data to be made public directly on the blockchain.

---

[27]Directive 2019/1024/EU, eighth recital.

[28]The problem is described, amongst others, by Bragagnolo et al. (2019). It should be added, however, that there are some proposals to overcome such problem, Palm et al. (2018). See also Ren et al. (2018).

[29]Although in some minor cases users have been able to store other pieces of information, the Bitcoin blockchain currently only allows specific small sets of data as the "transaction" value, as explained by Bistarelli et al. (2018). On the other hand, the "OP RETURN <DATA>" field, which supports any arbitrary value, is limited to 40 bytes, Talk Crypto Blog » OP_RETURN 40 to 80 bytes. http://www.talkcrypto.org/blog/2016/12/30/op_return-40-to-80-bytes/.

[30]Analysis of Bitcoin Transaction Size Trends. In: TradeBlock. https://tradeblock.com/blog/analysis-of-bitcoin-transaction-size-trends.

[31]As of March 20, 2020. The problem is widely discussed, see for example Zima (2018).

On the other hand, small pieces of information that can guarantee the integrity and authenticity of such data could very well be saved on the blockchain. For example, a hash representing the data to be certified,[32] along with a timestamp, could be stored on a blockchain to guarantee that a given document had a certain content at a given moment.[33] In this case the document could be stored on any device, without the need to save its contents on the blockchain. Then, at any later time, the integrity of this document could be verified by checking the fingerprint stored on the blockchain.

Considering the growing importance that legislation on the protection of personal data has, it is however necessary to consider if and what limits this discipline may curb the possibility of using blockchain in the public sector.

6 Blockchain in the Public Sector and Personal Data: The Problem of Cross-Analysis for Identification of a Natural Person

Regulation of 27 April 2016 relating to the protection of individuals with regard to the processing of personal data, as well as the free circulation of such data (the so-called General Data Protection Regulation, GDPR) provides a comprehensive set of rules on how personal data can be processed, including by public authorities.[34] It is therefore necessary to assess if, and to what extent, the GDPR might have an impact on the possibility of using blockchain in the public sector.

As many authors have already thoughtfully analyzed the provisions of the GDPR, and how such rules require specific actions to comply with, we can focus here on two main aspects related to the use of blockchain in the public sphere.

First, the notion of "controller" does not seem to pose particular problems in light of the peculiarities of blockchain technology. Article 4(1)(7) identifies the data controller as "*the natural or legal person, public authority, agency or other body which, alone or jointly with others, determines the purposes and means of the processing of personal data*". It is therefore not important whether the data is saved on a centralized or distributed system. For the purposes of identifying the data controller, and therefore whoever will be responsible for such data, this characteristic of the computer system appears to be irrelevant.

---

[32]"*Hashing means creating a fingerprint (a formula made of numbers and letters) of the data elements in the transaction message*", Zwitter A, Herman J, *Blockchain, development and humanitarism*, 2018, p. 9.

[33]See for example the project *OpenTimestamps* at https://opentimestamps.org/, which "*defines a set of operations for creating provable timestamps and later independently verifying them*".

[34]Article 4(1)(7) of the GDPR provides that the definition of "*controller*" includes any "*public authority*", and Article 6(1)(e) confirms that processing personal data "*for the performance of a task carried out in the public interest or in the exercise of official authority vested in the controller*" is lawful, provided that all conditions set by the GDPR itself are met.

The second aspect that requires attention is related to the right to be forgotten. Article 17 of the GDPR provides that "*the data subject shall have the right to obtain from the controller the erasure of personal data concerning him or her without undue delay and the controller shall have the obligation to erase personal data without undue delay*" where certain conditions are met.

This can pose a problem since, normally, blockchain does not allow the deletion of blocks and of the data stored therein. Consequently, this could mean that such technology might not be used whenever some data might be considered as personal data. Before assessing what kind of data falls into such category, however, it is worth underlining that the term blockchain does not refer to a single type of technology. On the contrary, there are potentially infinite variations of such systems. So, it cannot be *a priori* excluded that a blockchain that supports data deletion might be introduced.[35]

If that were the case, blockchain could even be more suitable to ensure data deletion than a centralized system. Pursuant to Article 17, paragraph 2, GDPR the controller "*shall take reasonable steps, including technical measures, to inform controllers which are processing the personal data that the data subject has requested the erasure by such controllers of any links to, or copy or replication of, those personal data*". A blockchain-based system supporting data deletion could help in this process as it could be configured to automate the deletion of data on all the devices on which the distributed database is replicated.

In any case, it must be recalled that normally blockchain is not designed to store personal data. As seen in the previous paragraph, on blockchain it is usually preferable to save data identification codes (hashes), rather than the actual data.[36] It follows that administrations should not store personal data on the blockchain, but only metadata (e.g. hashes) of such information.

In this regard, however, it must be considered that the concept of personal data is very broad. As a consequence, even hashes stored on the blockchain might, in certain conditions, be considered as personal data. To better clarify this concept, it is necessary to briefly analyses the notion of personal data provided by the GDPR.

Pursuant to article 4(1)(1) of the GDPR, "*'personal data' means any information relating to an identified or identifiable natural person ('data subject'); an identifiable natural person is one who can be identified, directly or indirectly, in particular by reference to an identifier such as a name, an identification number, location data, an online identifier or to one or more factors specific to the physical, physiological, genetic, mental, economic, cultural or social identity of that natural person*".

First of all, it should be noted that only data relating to natural persons is contemplated. It must therefore be deduced that the data of legal entities is not

[35]For example, it has already been proposed a "*a method for achieving revocation with a practical approach, while not diverging from the open and decentralized nature of Bitcoin*", see Karasavvas (2018).

[36]In line with this idea has been proposed a "*digital identity management platform on the touchstone of the GDPR*", Kulhari (2018), p. 33.

protected by Regulation 2016/679/EU. As for the data of natural persons linked to legal persons, the Court of Justice has clarified several times that in order to guarantee legal certainty in relations between companies and third parties within the common market it is essential that anyone wishing to enter into business relationships with companies based in other Member States can easily know the essential constituent data of commercial companies and essential data relating to the powers of their representatives.[37] This therefore imposes a balance between the right to the protection of personal data and need for the names of such natural persons to be made public in the business registers of member states.

As for the types of data that can be considered suitable to make a natural person identifiable, it must first be noted that the list provided by article 4 is an open one. The European legislator has in fact expressly used the expression "*such as*" in providing the aforementioned list, thereby indicating that even further categories of data can be considered personal. Therefore, it is necessary to verify, on a case-by-case basis, with respect to all the circumstances of the specific case, whether or not certain data can identify a natural person and, therefore, qualify as personal data.

It must also be considered that the ability of data to make a natural person identifiable must be assessed in relation to all available information. This means that even where data, considered in itself, is not suitable for identifying a natural person, if combined with other data can achieve this result, it must be considered together with all the other data, as personal data. In this regard, recital 30 of the GDPR states that the "*online identifiers produced by the devices, applications, tools and protocols used, such as IP addresses, to temporary markers (cookies) or to other identifiers, such as identification tags radio frequency* [...] *can leave traces which, in particular if combined with unique identifiers and other information received from the servers, can be used to create profiles of natural persons and identify them*".

As for "*the image of a person recorded by a camera*", the jurisprudence of the Court of Justice has for example already clarified that it "*constitutes 'personal data' [. . .] inasmuch as it makes it possible to identify the person concerned*".[38] According to this case-law, a mere image, without any reference to the identity of the subject, or of the subjects, represented therein is not in itself capable of identifying the person, or persons, to whom the images relate. Vice versa, where the image is associated with data capable of linking it to a natural person, for example because in the image there is the person's name and surname, then it must be concluded that said image constitutes personal data.

A similar discussion can be conducted in relation to an IP address, that is, a numeric or alphanumeric string that identifies the points of origin and destination of the information on the internet. Indeed, it may not always be clear whether such data

---

[37]See most recently in the judgment of 9 March 2017, in case C-398/15, *Manni*, ECLI:EU:C:2017:197, paragraph 50.

[38]Court of Justice, judgment of 14 February 2019, C-345/17, *Buivids*, ECLI:EU:C:2019:122, paragraph 31.

should be considered as information capable of identifying a natural person. The answer to such a question will necessarily depend on the context in which this IP address is generated and collected, and on the ability of this data, possibly together with other data, to identify a natural person. If, for example, a user surfed the internet through a public network, such as a university's WI-FI, it is reasonable to exclude that the IP in itself could uniquely identify one natural person, since the same IP would refer to multiple users connected to that WIFI. Vice versa, if a unique identification code were associated with such IP address, connecting a specific user to a given identity, then it should be concluded that the IP address would be personal data.

In line with this reasoning, the Court of Justice has stated that "*a dynamic IP address registered by an online media service provider when a person consults a website that such provider makes accessible to the public constitutes, towards this supplier, a personal data within the meaning of this provision, if that supplier has legal means that allow him to identify the person concerned thanks to the additional information available to the internet access provider of that person*".[39]

Therefore, given the wide range of data that can qualify as personal data, it can be assumed that most of the time the data managed and exchanged by public administrations will probably have to fall into this category. This can happen first of all because the data is in itself directly capable of identifying a natural person. This could be the case, for example, of the tax code which, as a "*tax identification number*", "*is by its very nature a tax data that refers to an identified or identifiable natural person and, therefore, is a personal data*".[40] In other cases, data held by a public authority might be considered as personal due to the wide range of information in possession of public administrations on natural persons.

On this latter point, it should also be borne in mind that the Court of Justice has already had the opportunity to clarify that "*for information to be treated as 'personal data' [...] there is no requirement that all the information enabling the identification of the data subject must be in the hands of one person*".[41] Which means that to assess the suitability of data in possession of an administration to identify a natural person, it is not enough to consider the additional data available to that single administration, but it must instead be evaluated how that data can interact with all the data held by other entities to which said administration has access. As a consequence, the combination of all this data can indeed many times allow tracing back to a specific subject information that, individually considered, would not necessarily be relevant pursuant to the GDPR. It follows that the possibility of

[39]Court of Justice, judgment of 19 October 2016, C-582/14, *Breyer*, ECLI:EU:C:2016:779, paragraph 49.

[40]Court of Justice, judgment of 16 January 2019, C-496/17, *Deutsche Post*, ECLI:EU:C:2019:26, paragraph 56.

[41]Court of Justice, judgment of 20 December 2017, C-434/16, *Nowak*, ECLI:EU:C:2017:994, paragraph 31.

interconnecting all information made available by public bodies can significantly extend the scope of the notion of personal data.

For this reason, even when publishing anonymized data (e.g. hashes) on a public blockchain, it is necessary to consider which interconnections between data can be made in order to reveal the identity of the natural person behind such data. In other words, it is necessary to ensure that the cross-analysis of datasets published by administrations does not allow identification of a natural person where the personal data of the latter should not or cannot be made public.

7 Conclusions: Which Concrete Applications Are Suitable for Blockchain in the Public Sector

Considering the main characteristics of blockchain technology, to conclude we can make some proposals on how tools and ICT systems based on such technology might contribute to the improvement of administrative functions.

First of all, DLTs could have some utility in complex procedures, that is, where multiple administrations have to interact to exercise a certain public power, especially in cases where this occurs supra-state level, for example in cases of European co-administration.[42] In these instances, the exchange of information between administrations could take place thanks to private blockchains on which each body has the right to store data of its competence, as well as access the datasets stored by other public bodies that are functional to the performance of its tasks. The advantage over a centralized system would be the equality of all the nodes, that is, of all the administrations involved, by removing the need to provide a central collection point.

Alternatively, if an administration must check a person's data from multiple other public bodies, instead of copying the data to its database, thus multiplying the user's personal data and related risks, it could instead save only the hashes that identify such data. In this way the administration, once done, could certify its activities without needing to save the data in its databases. In order to later verify the results, it would be enough to cross the hashes saved on the blockchain with the original data contained in the databases of the other entities. In this way, anyone having access to the blockchain and the third parties' databases could at any time check the accuracy of the data, without having to duplicate it in multiple places.

It can also be envisaged that the DLTs may allow for greater transparency in the sharing of publicly accessible data with private individuals. This could happen thanks to a horizontal data distribution through public permissioned blockchains in which the public authority maintains control over the updating of the data, while allowing private individuals to have access to them immediately and directly. In this case, the advantage over centralized systems could be represented by the fact that a

[42]This could be the case, for example, for immigration controls in the EU area, as proposed by Patel et al. (2018).

DLT-based system would allow citizens to be themselves co-custodians of the information of their interest, thus being able to access it directly without the intermediation of services aimed at allowing access to data.

It should be emphasized once again, however, that, as explained in the previous paragraphs, the data that would be saved on the blockchain would consist, most likely, in small pieces of information. Therefore, as in the previous examples, the most likely scenario would be that the blockchain would store only the hashes of the data to be made public. The actual information would then be exchanged with other more efficient means than blockchain.[43]

Finally, it is also possible to envisage the possibility that private individuals participate in the co-creation of the distributed database, by entering certain information themselves. This could be of some use whenever the administration needs to acquire data from private individuals. This could be done through public or private blockchains, ensuring adequate levels of authentication and validation of the information entered with respect to the various cases considered. This could allow administrations to acquire the information they need with the guarantee of immutability that the blockchain system assures, including complete traceability of all operations carried out on the distributed ledger.

References

Bartoletti M, Pes B, Serusi S (2018) Data mining for detecting Bitcoin Ponzi schemes. In: 2018 Crypto Valley Conference on Blockchain Technology (CVCBT). CPS. IEEE, Piscataway, pp 75–84

Benamou N, Busson A, Keravel A (2004) Impact of e-Government interoperability in local governments. In: Traunmueller R (ed) Electronic government: third international conference, EGOV 2004, Zaragoza, Spain, August 30–September 3, 2004, Proceedings. Springer-Verlag, Berlin

Bistarelli S, Mercanti I, Santini F (2018) An analysis of non-standard Bitcoin transactions. In: 2018 Crypto Valley Conference on Blockchain Technology (CVCBT). CPS. IEEE, Piscataway, pp 93–96

Blanke H-J, Perlingeiro R (eds) (2017) The right of access to public information: an international comparative legal survey. Springer, Berlin

Bragagnolo S, Marra M, Polito G, Gonzalez Boix E (2019) Towards scalable blockchain analysis. In: 2019 IEEE/ACM 2nd International Workshop on Emerging Trends in Software Engineering for Blockchain (WETSEB). IEEE, Piscataway, pp 1–7

Brown MM, Garson GD (2013) Public information management and E-Government: policy and issues. Idea Group Inc (IGI), Hershey

De Mauro A, Greco M, Grimaldi M (2016) A formal definition of Big Data based on its essential features. Library Rev:122–135. https://doi.org/10.1108/LR-06-2015-0061

Galetta D-U (2018) Access to administrative documents and to public sector information in Italy. In: Blanke H-J, Perlingeiro R (eds) The right of access to public information: an international comparative legal survey. Springer, Berlin, pp 343–367

[43] Thanks to the data certification performed with blockchain, for example, we could hypothesize the dissemination of data by the torrent data sharing system.

Goodnow FJ (1983) Comparative administrative law: an analysis of the administrative systems, National and Local, of the United States, England, France, and Germany. G. P. Putnam's Sons, New York

Hiatt CJ (2000) A primer for disaster recovery planning in an IT environment. Idea Group Inc (IGI), Hershey

Karasavvas K (2018) Revoking records in an immutable ledger: a platform for issuing and revoking official documents on public blockchains. In: 2018 Crypto Valley Conference on Blockchain Technology (CVCBT). CPS. IEEE, Piscataway, pp 105–111

Kulhari S (2018) Building-blocks of a data protection revolution: the uneasy case for blockchain technology to secure privacy and identity. Nomos Verlagsgesellschaft, Baden-Baden

Palm E, Schelén O, Bodin U (2018) Selective blockchain transaction pruning and state derivability. In: 2018 Crypto Valley Conference on Blockchain Technology (CVCBT). CPS. IEEE, Piscataway, pp 31–40

Patel D, Balakarthikeyan, Mistry V (2018) Border control and immigration on blockchain. In: Chen S, Wang H, Zhang L-J (eds) Blockchain – ICBC 2018. Springer International Publishing, Cham, pp 166–179

Peak DA, Azadmanesh MH (1997) Centralization/decentralization cycles in computing: market evidence. Inf Manag 31:303–317. https://doi.org/10.1016/S0378-7206(97)00002-5

Ren Z, Cong K, Aerts T et al (2018) A scale-out blockchain for value transfer with spontaneous sharding. In: 2018 Crypto Valley Conference on Blockchain Technology (CVCBT). CPS. IEEE, Piscataway, pp 1–10

Roman AV (2013) Realizing E-government: delineating implementation challenges and defining success. In: Halpin EF, Griffin D, Rankin C et al (eds) Digital public administration and E-government in developing nations: policy and practice. IGI Global, Pennsylvania, p 112

Steinmetz R (2005) Peer-to-peer systems and applications. Springer Science & Business Media, Berlin

Tang J (2006) Competition and innovation behaviour. Res Policy 35:68–82. https://doi.org/10.1016/j.respol.2005.08.004

Warren Axelrod C (1999) Reverting to centralized data center management. In: Blanding SF (ed) Handbook of data center management, 1998 edition, II. CRC Press, Boca Raton, pp 75–83

Wessling F, Ehmke C, Hesenius M, Gruhn V (2018) How much blockchain do you need? Towards a concept for building hybrid DApp architectures. In: Proceedings of the 1st international workshop on emerging trends in software engineering for blockchain. Association for Computing Machinery, Gothenburg, pp 44–47

Wüst K, Gervais A (2018) Do you need a blockchain? In: 2018 Crypto Valley Conference on Blockchain Technology (CVCBT). CPS. IEEE, Piscataway, pp 45–54

Xu X, Weber I, Staples M (2019) Architecture for blockchain applications. Springer International Publishing, Cham

Yano M, Dai C, Masuda K, Kishimoto Y (2019) Creation of a blockchain and a new ecosystem. RIETI policy discussion papers

Zima M (2018) (Short Paper) Inputs reduction for more space in Bitcoin blocks. In: 2018 Crypto Valley Conference on Blockchain Technology (CVCBT). CPS. IEEE, Piscataway, pp 112–115

Some Historical and Philosophical Remarks on the Rule of Law in the Time of Automation

Jean Lassègue

Contents

1 Introduction

The viewpoint that is defended in the following pages claims that the history of writing and computing systems can help clarify today's digital turn in the rule of law. As a philosopher of science and not a jurist, the basic point I would like to make is that there is a rather hidden connection relating current conflicts of legality with computation and the history of writing.

Indeed, there is something very new and very old at the same time in the transformations of the rule of law we experience today. Something very old: the rise of digital norms does not come out of the blue and my hunch is that it can be better understood and clarified if we put it in a broader historical perspective. Instrumental

J. Lassègue (✉)
Centre Georg Simmel - Recherches Franco-Allemandes en Sciences Sociales (CNRS-UMR 8131), École des Hautes Études en Sciences Sociales, Paris, France
e-mail: jean.lassegue@ehess.fr

B. Cappiello, G. Carullo (eds.), *Blockchain, Law and Governance*,
https://doi.org/10.1007/978-3-030-52722-8_4

in this attempt is the notion of literacy,[1] i.e. individual and social processes related to reading, writing and computing that are all intertwined since Antiquity. The first claim I would like to make is therefore the following: if computer science is considered as the latest step in the long history of writing in the West,[2] its use in legal matters should be referred to this long history if we want to make sense of it. But, from another perspective, the present state of affairs is unprecedented: original forms of social transactions like those performed by blockchains operate within social frameworks that tend to restrict social interaction to completely computable microworlds, that is to say worlds that are limited to a finite number of elements the mutual connection of which can be exhaustively determined. This is all the truer today since the total number of cell phones reached the number of the entire world population in 2014, virtually making every one of us an atomic node on a global network.[3] In this interconnected world, blockchain technology is exemplary: it is supposed to percolate from local microworlds through society as a whole by transforming social interactions warranted by law into computable transactions, the ultimate goal being the replacement of legal institutions by purely technological solutions. This is certainly something new as it disrupts the role played by institutions in the very idea of body politic. But it presupposes an all-encompassing applicability of decidable computable processes to the social world that should be questioned for it was demonstrated as early as the 1930s that the concept of computation had inner limitations in terms of decidability[4] and even before, that chaotic behaviors in physical processes would resist any form of computational prediction.[5] My second claim is therefore that these theoretical limitations are not restricted to the domain of science but have social consequences bearing on the conception of law and legality: if this is true, these limitations affect the very idea of an expansion of computable processes to society as a whole. It is therefore doubtful that microworlds, especially those designed by blockchains, can expand to society as a whole without deeply modifying the way legal norms should be conceived.[6] In this respect, the always re-emerging debates on whether "artificial intelligence" can "overcome" human intelligence should be interpreted in sociological terms as

[1]Havelock (1976), p. 19: "Literacy, though dependent on the technology employed in inscription, is not to be defined by the simple existence of that technology. It is a social condition which can be defined only in terms of readership."

[2]Herrenschmidt (2007).

[3]"Measuring the Information", International Communication Union, United Nations special Agency, Geneva, Switzerland, Society Report, 2014, p. 21 (https://www.itu.int/en/ITU-D/Statistics/Pages/publications/mis2014.aspx). It doesn't mean of course that the penetration rate of cell phones is uniformly spread over all the continents.

[4]Longo (2010), pp. 219–262.

[5]Poincaré (1893).

[6]This was already the case with the relationship between society and economy as described by Polanyi (2001) in which he showed how economy would tend not only to claim independence from society but also to rule it.

debates on what level of mechanization should be considered as the norm in social interactions[7] and this is of course a normative question jurists have to tackle.

There is, therefore, a conflict between two forms of legality in today's rule of law: the first one is based on legal texts written in technical but natural languages that are the expression of political sovereignty; the second one is based on unreadable pieces of software the authority of which derives from a collective trust given to machines, a trust that has not yet reached the level of legal expression. Whether this trust can become the base of a legal system is an open question I shall raise in due course. Let me start first with a few remarks on writing and computing systems both in Antiquity and in recent times. Strangely enough, we have to start with the way linguistic and computational signs were written in order to understand what computation is about in today's rule of law for there has always been a strong connection between computing writing languages and writing the law since Antiquity.[8]

2 Automation in the History of Literacy

Of course, it would be preposterous to try and describe the fifty-four centuries of western literacy in just a few paragraphs—starting from Mesopotamia in -3300 BC up to today's global networks—and I shall certainly not take this road. I will instead take the risk of leaving aside points that would be worth mentioning and rather dwell on two directions taken by the automation of literacy processes that seem to me particularly important for our present purpose which is the description and evaluation of today's rule of law.

[7]This was already Turing's point in 1947 just before the first computer became operational (June 1948): "Roughly speaking those who work in connection with the ACE [an experimental computer called either a "calculator" or a "computer" in the rest of the text] will be divided into its masters and its servants. Its masters will plan out instruction tables for it, thinking up deeper and deeper ways of using it. Its servants will feed it with cards as it calls for them. [. . .] As time goes on the calculator itself will take over the functions both of masters and of servants. [. . .]. The masters are liable to get replaced because as soon as any technique becomes at all stereotyped it becomes possible to devise a system of instruction tables which will enable the electronic computer to do it for itself. It may happen however that the masters will refuse to do this. They may be unwilling to let their jobs be stolen from them in this way. In that case they would surround the whole of their work with mystery and make excuses, couched in well-chosen gibberish, whenever any dangerous suggestions were made. I think that a reaction of this kind is a very real danger. This topic naturally leads to the question as to how far it is possible in principle for a computing machine to simulate human activities." Turing (2004), p. 392.

[8]Lassègue and Longo (2012), pp. 450–461.

2.1 *Reading in Antiquity*

Western writing systems from -3300 BC (Mesopotamian origin of writing) to -800 BC (emergence of Greek alphabet) evolved towards a representation of the phonetic reality of language, gradually leaving aside ideograms (marks standing for a meaning) and logograms (marks independent of their acoustic counterpart) except in the particular case of the representation of numbers. Logogrammatic representation of numbers and mathematical signs as we know them ("2", "45", "π", "∫", etc.) played a crucial part in the origin of writing in Mesopotamia[9] and since then lived a life of their own in the middle of phonetic signs[10] until the twentieth century and the "Hilbert program" to which I will come later. But basically, what was represented by written marks was the sounds of languages first conceived as syllables (in the Mesopotamian, Egyptian and Semitic writing systems), then as phonemes (in the Greek alphabet). The Greek alphabet, although strongly connected to previous writing systems, was innovative on at least three major points.

First, by writing down phonemes, the Greek writing system became a full-fledged alphabet: all the sounds of Greek were represented, contrary to former alphabets first designed for Semitic languages (like Phoenician) where only consonants were written down because the written representation of vowels in these languages, only three in number, was not deemed necessary.[11] The phonematic representation of the Greek alphabet introduced a clear cut distinction between the marks themselves and their meanings: the alphabet dealt with the objective sounds of Greek, i.e. phonemes, and not with its meanings that are already apparent in syllables.[12] The second consequence is that the reader of a text written with the Greek alphabet (or its Latin or Cyrillic derivatives) is not supposed to know in advance the language he or she is reading because the phonematic decomposition made possible by the alphabet is independent of the meaning of the text. Said differently, the Greek alphabet is potentially mechanizable for it reduces the process of reading to an automatic scanning which is independent of any previous knowledge of the language that is scanned: reading became *automatic* through the Greek alphabet.[13] Thirdly, the use of the alphabet does not require the intervention of scribes as specialists of

[9]Schmandt-Besserat (2010).

[10]Cajori (1994).

[11]Havelock (1976), pp. 80–81: "The pre-Greek systems set out to imitate language as it is spoken in these syllabic units. The Greek system took a leap beyond language and beyond empiricism. It conceived the notion of analyzing the linguistic unit into its two theoretic components, the vibrating column of air and the mouth action imposed upon this vibration."

[12]For example, "ball", "bubble", "bowl" and "balloon" certainly means that the "ba" "bu", "bo" syllables have to do with something round in shape; this is not the case anymore with the phonematic decomposition of linguistic sounds. One can see that the two sides of signs were slowly distinguished from one another and became the "material side" and the "meaningful one": this is not a given "fact", it's a historical and social process that took many centuries to happen.

[13]We all know too well that when we are tired, we can read a page and realise in the end that we haven't caught anything from it although the automatic reading was successfully made.

interpretation to be read because all the alphabetical marks necessary for reading are publicly on display. Reading as a social practice took many centuries and tremendous collective efforts to become public knowledge but being able to read the law then became very much part of modern democratic citizenship. Of course, even though it is written in natural language, reading the law today most of the time requires the intervention of jurists as "law scribes" but the technical jargon is still at walking distance, so to speak, from the natural tongue of lay individuals.

To wrap up, one can say that with the Greek alphabet (and its derivatives), every language can be written alphabetically and everyone can learn to read (even machines can!). The political representation attached to reading is what the Greek called *isonomia*, "equality before the law" by the recognition that written laws impose the same obligations to all. Law is discussed collectively and public discussion is based on a medium that is not the exclusive property of scribes and those who employ them: alphabetic reading goes hand in hand with citizenship.

2.2 Writing in Present Times

I will briefly show that in the course of the twentieth century, a new step in the history of literacy was reached when the *writing* process became partly automatized under the name of "computer programming". The control over the writing process was henceforth completely lost by individuals and became a collective enterprise nobody alone could have a full grip on. This lead to the situation we know of today in which most of us are illiterate as far as writing code, i.e. "programming", is concerned. Even computer scientists, as knowledgeable as they are in the writing of codes, do not master the whole process of writing programs which can sometimes be made up of millions of lines of code: writing codes has become a very collective and industrial kind of work. The social consequence is that it is indeed paradoxical that literacy which had been such an instrument of political emancipation for many centuries unknowingly became quite the opposite and required once again today the intervention of a class of modern scribes: the computer scientists. This has far-reaching consequences on the rule of law that I will touch upon later. But for now, I will briefly sketch the three steps that led to the possibility of the digitalization of law by making the new form of writing automatic.

At the end of the nineteenth century, the emergence of various "non-Euclidean" geometries contradictory to one another as well as of paradoxes in set theory which was supposed to be instrumental in finding a foundation for all mathematics triggered a crisis known as the "foundational crisis". The German mathematician David Hilbert (1862–1943) tried to circumscribe a "safe zone" in mathematics where the various geometries could be dealt with and no paradox would appear. Arithmetic was this safe zone and Hilbert showed how all axiomatic systems could be reduced to a unique, arithmetic one. The goal was then to generate theorems from this axiomatic system in the most secure way so as to avoid generating contradictions. But there was no way the problem could be dealt with by reducing this axiomatic system to a more fundamental one: the generation of theorems had to be justified from within. To solve the problem, Hilbert used the same alphabetic strategy that was used with Greek language: by making a clear-cut distinction between the level of marks and the level of meaning and by focusing on the level of marks only, he could determine which were the lawful (i.e. logical) connections between these marks without taking into account their meanings the interpretation of which remained questionable. According to Hilbert, introducing the alphabetical stance would therefore avoid the dangerous situation that prevailed in mathematics at the beginning of the twentieth century and allow for a general method capable of checking the validity of propositions. To make sure that the logical connections leading from axioms to theorems were secured, the "mechanical" way was the most promising one because it was independent from any uncontrolled and possibly paradoxical meaning. This "mechanical" way was still to be defined. Three steps would be necessary.

The first step towards a mechanical checking of theorems was therefore to make sure that mathematical propositions were transcribed in a canonical form from an alphabet of written marks. Mathematical texts which were up to then a mixture of propositions written in formal and natural language as well as diagrams were now composed of alphabetical marks combined by logical laws.[14] These logical laws were considered by Hilbert as entrenched in the human mind which had no other choice but to follow them.[15]

The alphabetization of mathematics was followed by a second step that would reinforce the arithmetic stance developed by Hilbert, the so-called "arithmetization" of the alphabetical marks. Kurt Gödel (1906–1978) showed that it was possible to connect specific numbers to the marks of the alphabet: checking the validity of the logical connection between marks was therefore reduced to computing numbers.[16] Contrary to Hilbert's viewpoint who had to presuppose a "mind" external to the writing process which was capable of following the rules of logic, Gödel's depended only on the writing procedure consisting in connecting marks for signs with marks for numbers and to compute on the latter ones: only the computational "mind" was presupposed in Gödel's analysis.[17]

[14]Hilbert (1926), pp. 161–190.

[15]Hilbert (1923), pp. 151–165: "[. . .] our thinking is finitist, when we think, a finitist process takes place."

[16]This would be of fundamental interest when programming languages would appear after the Second World War.

[17]Gödel (1931), pp. 173–198: "The formulas of a formal system in outward appearance are finite sequences of primitive signs (variables, logical constants and parentheses or punctuation dots), and it is easy to state with complete precision which sequences of primitive signs are meaningful formulas and which are not. Similarly, proofs, for a formal point of view, are nothing but finite sequences of formulas (with certain specifiable properties). Of course, for metamathematical considerations it does not matter what objects are chosen as primitive signs, and we shall assign natural numbers to this use. Consequently, a formula will be a finite sequence of natural numbers, and a proof array a finite sequence of finite sequences of natural numbers."

In a third step, the "computational mind" would be reintegrated by Turing (1912–1954) in the writing process itself. The "computational mind" was no "mind" after all but just a writing procedure that could be made entirely at hand in the open: there was no need of folk psychology to address the issue. Before Turing, it was still unclear what "computation" and "mechanical" exactly meant[18] but he clarified the matter by showing that the notion of computation could be performed by an abstract machine which would be limited to a writing and reading process performed by what would be called after his article of 1936,[19] a "Turing machine". A Turing machine is not a material machine: it is the diagram of an abstract machine capable of reading, writing and moving its reading-writing head on the boxes of a tape of indefinite length, each box containing only one mark or none. A Turing machine is therefore a reading and writing device that transforms numbers given as inputs into numbers generated as outputs through a "program", i.e. a list of transforming rules (written also as a sequence of numbers) the machine uses to perform the computation. The Turing machine is the logical structure of all computers in the world today which are only finite and material replica of this abstract device. The important point is that computer programming *automatically* transforms a set of written marks into another set of other written marks: the writing process is automatized without human intervention once the program had been written. From a social point of view, this is precisely what completely modifies today's literacy: when programs are efficient (a point which cannot be proved in advance), computers write and re-write numbers representing data without human control. This fact fuels the social imaginary of science-fiction novels and films where humans become enslaved to "superior" machines. But this is imaginary only, the reality is very different because computers as descendants of Turing machines have nonetheless inner limitations.

One would first think that because the concept of a Turing machine is capable of computing any computable processes, every problem that can be defined logically can be represented as a computable problem and receive a computable solution that the right program (if it exists) can perform on the material counterpart of a Turing machine, viz. a computer. One could therefore think that the Turing machine was the last piece of a jigsaw puzzle that would make the Hilbert program work for good. In fact, just as it was already the case with the important limitation results made clear by Gödel, it utterly destroys it: Turing shows in his article of 1936 that his very simple device is certainly able to compute any type of computation but that there are nonetheless problems which cannot be computed and never will. The proof of such a limitation is a real tour de force: within the strictly computable framework of Turing machines, one can imagine computable procedures[20] that are able to generate uncomputable numbers no machine can ever compute. This has important consequences regarding Hilbert program: if computation is a way of checking the

[18]Gandy (1988), pp. 55–111, § 5.

[19]Turing (1938), pp. 230–265.

[20]Such as the Cantorian "diagonal procedure" quoted by Turing in his 1936 article.

validity of mathematical expressions, there must be mathematical expressions the validity of which cannot be checked by computation. It is therefore possible to prove that certain mathematical propositions escape all formalized axiomatic systems. I can then go back to the claim I made in the beginning, namely that limitations of axiomatic systems also have social consequences. Digitalization is certainly possible on some issues in the social world as the incredible multiplication of pieces of software amply shows today but there is no reason to believe it should be considered a universal solution to all social issues since computing limitations are already present in the mathematical domain: why should social problems be more computable than mathematical ones? We have now to explore the consequences of this epistemological situation on the particular case of the rule of law.

3 Consequences on the Rule of Law

The gradual digitalization of society certainly modifies the types of breach of the law that are committed. Today's digitalization has therefore an impact on the content of various laws as well as on new laws covering new domains, especially regulations of electronic exchange on the internet. But this is only the tip of the iceberg for it does not modify legality as such. More than the legal content (in various domains such as competition law, law of intellectual property, etc.), it is rather the legal form, i.e. legality, which is being transformed through digitalization.

The transformation of legality has two aspects that seem unconnected at first. The first one has to do with the relationship between legality and mathematics: is there a common ground between the formalist take in mathematics that gave birth to computer science as briefly sketched earlier and the formal aspects of law? The legal domain, precisely because of its formal aspects, seems to be an adequate candidate for digitalization: more than many other types of institution, law has a long tradition of formalism that goes far beyond the usual reference to Aristotelian syllogism.[21] The question is therefore how relevant the transfer from computer science to the legal domain is. To answer this question, one could stick to the analysis of formalism in the two domains and see how far they can be made compatible. Computer science would then appear as the modeling source applied to law, a rather late-comer in the digital transformation of society. The drawback of this approach is twofold. First, the specificity of the legal domain disappears and law is made part of an homogeneous and passive field that is liable to digitalization. Secondly, it completely puts aside the second aspect of legality which is the relationship between legality and anthropology: laws become legal through instituted procedures of collective agreement, something which is completely foreign to

[21]Leibniz who was both a jurist and a mathematician is a key figure in that respect since he tried, with a rather elusive success, to develop a formalist and mechanistic approach to law from the Leibniz (1666). Reprint Leibniz (2018), pp. 30–105.

the mathematical approach. For example, why is the partial delegation of judgement to specific pieces of software and database being now collectively agreed upon in various court cases? Where does this consensus come from? And how does it become constraining? These are questions only an anthropological viewpoint on legality can answer. The problem we are confronted with is therefore: how is it possible to keep together the two aspects, the mathematical and the anthropological one, of legality? What is claimed here is that only the analysis of signs both in their formal and collective aspects makes it possible to take into account the two aspects, mathematical and anthropological, of legality. It is therefore necessary to go back to the way law has been written in the past and is being written today in the context of digital society to have a better view on the transformation of legality. Three steps in the recent history of the relationship between computing and law can be distinguished: translation, competition and replacement. I will particularly insist on the third step that deals with blockchain.

3.1 Translating Legal Texts into Computable Code

The historical relationship between computer science and law seems at first to be governed by convenience only. As soon as it became cheap enough to store large amounts of legislative, administrative or jurisprudential texts in an electronic format, it became also clear that reading laws and regulations from thick and heavy books stacked in specialized libraries could be replaced by immediate online access for both professionals and citizens. But it was less clear that what at first was just a convenient mode of access would also modify the legibility of law itself. Like any other type of knowledge transformed into data, looking for the relevant legal information could not be performed by reading only: keywords had to be designed, i.e. *a priori* categories that would assist with data navigation. This had of course an impact on the way cases were cognitively represented by readers because the various narratological strategies used to make sense of a case when presented as a continuous narrative would have to be modified: the way a case is made sense of through keywords automatically leads up to a more fragmented representation of it. It also leads up to another level of generalization than the case itself by bringing it closer to other cases, a generalization which modifies the representation of the case under scrutiny. Thus the digitalization of legal corpora modified the relationship between the levels of generality between case and law. In the same way, the systematic use of statistics made it gradually clear that a new type of information was henceforth available both in finding similarities between cases as well as in revealing tendencies in behaviors of plaintiffs as well as biases in the way justice was done. The relevance of keywords for data navigation and the use of statistics became therefore a major issue law professionals could not leave to computer scientists only: joint work had to be done to make sure that the relevance of keywords in specific database was monitored according to what was under scrutiny (establishment of facts, type of law involved, etc.) and that the statistical knowledge which was gained was an additional asset to the rule of law and not a way to devaluate its authority by underlining its practical shortcomings. From a sociological point of view, it meant that reading the law had to become a combined effort performed by several communities that were not used to work together. In any case, reading the law was not the preserve of "law scribes" anymore. This is also the case as far as writing the law is concerned.

3.2 The Competition Between Textual and Digital Law

Before the emergence of digital law, Western democracies would strive to draw a virtuous circle in the way they would set up a legal order: the process of making law effective would start with a discussion held in natural language (as opposed to a formal one which has a written form only) among members of various parliamentary instances, assisted in this task by jurists whose role was to help switching the future law from an oral to a written form. The process would end up by the written enactment of the law which relied on the capacity to read from citizens who, after a tremendous collective effort over several centuries, had become literate. This general literacy would hopefully contribute to the obedience to the law and the political participation to common affairs. But the emergence of digital law disrupts this legal flux between various institutions by departing from natural language and the community of speakers it makes possible: by delegating the very content of the law to a form exclusively written in a logical language operated on computers, the very notion of a community that natural language and symbolic institutions made possible was left behind. All of a sudden, citizens but also the most trained jurists became illiterate as they were confronted to the actual computer coding of legal texts. And in a way, it was the case with computer scientists themselves: no one can follow the millions of operations that are needed to run a program on a computer as no one can write the millions of lines that are need to complete a large program either. But more than the actual limitations of human cognitive capacities, it was the seemingly autonomy of writing performed by computers that was entirely new: according to data processed, the logical connector 'if…then' in programs would introduce possible choices that were made neither by the programmers nor by the users but were left for the computer to decide. For example, software programs such as Compass used since 2010 in many penal courts in the United-States which is described as a "risk assessment tool for criminal justice practitioners" would dramatically change the way liberation on parole before the trial would be assessed… and would give rise to much scandal when it was statistically discovered that African-Americans were massively discriminated in this process. In less dramatic examples, one can imagine that courts of justice (just like private companies like Ebay already do) would develop applications that could be implemented on mobile device in order to resolve small-scale conflicts (missing or unsuitable delivery, neighbourhood disputes) without the judge's intervention.

The point that is underlined as far as software use is concerned is that writing does not entirely depend on human intervention—a deep change the consequences of which are still waiting to be fathomed. If we leave aside the purely imaginary reactions spanning from thinking robots to transhumanism, it is the immaterial and computable aspects of writing which deprive human beings of their capacity to be held responsible for what they write legally by breaking the reading-writing circulation between well-defined institutions that up to now had made legality possible. Legality becomes problematic since it is partially located out of the sphere of individual judgement and the collective institutions founded on a political order rooted in a shared history that make the production of this judgement possible.[22]

The conflict between legal texts and legal codes has a graphic origin and shows how difficult it is to hang together a mute mode of writing which is socially hermetical and a collective space where human beings can recognize but also clash with one another according to socially admitted modes of justice. It generates a symbolic mutation[23] between two forms of legality that can be coined as "rule of text" and "rule of code". The challenge is the following: how is it possible to reintegrate the out of space, purely written code in a spatial environment which is meaningful for humans, i.e. where humans can feel recognized as subjects? Put simply: how do we make code socially readable? The question becomes all the more important when confronted to a third step in the relationship between computer science and law, which has to do with the rise of blockchain technology.

3.3 Replacement of Textual and Code Law: The Case of Blockchain Technology

Blockchain is what was called in the beginning a "microworld". It is a software technology which became famous with the emergence of cryptocurrencies like bitcoin in 2009 or Etherum in 2015 and which is supposed to be the ultimate solution for preventing monopolistic mediations to appear or reappear. Its avowed purpose is to get rid of symbolic mediations depending on "rule of texts" (from notaries to central banks) as well as digital ones depending on "rules of code" which almost naturally tend to re-establish a monopolistic mediation by way of universally used platforms (for example Uber, Amazon or Facebook). Blockchain technology is based on the traceability of sets of objects (diamonds, vintage cars, etc.) which creates a restricted world in which exchange through peer-to-peer protocols can take place without a central authority, be it symbolic or digital. It presupposes an ontology reduced to atomic components governed by purely deterministic processes (essentially, tagging, authenticating, buying and selling) within a network. From this

[22]Lassègue (2019), pp. 255–274.

[23]By "symbolic mutation", I mean a process in which the authority of norms is elaborated differently through a collective work on institutions, from linguistic signs to political assemblies.

point of view, blockchain technology entirely pertains to the world of writing and claims full independence from an outer counterpart: the difference between objects and their tags is supposed to be non-existent.

Sticking to a microworld is supposed to solve the problem of mediation by making it mechanically decidable: in a finite world of tagged objects and of participants, it is possible to compute one-to-one mappings between the participants willing to exchange as well as one-to-one mappings between the written tags and the physical objects the tags stand for. It is therefore possible to operate within a completely decidable structure where the exchange of goods is a simple consequence of written, traceable exchange of tags. From a purely logical point of view, because of its decidability, any blockchain structure operates within a digital world which is not "Turing-complete", i.e. which does not allow for undecidable results.[24] Said differently, blockchain technology creates microworlds that are too "small", i.e. too arithmetically poor, to accommodate even all computational processes. This would be of no consequence if it was possible for the participants to stick to the decidable relationships that are effective in blockchain networks but this is not the case: as they are implemented through pieces of software, they are subject to computational limitations. In particular, because of the proof in the 1936 paper by Turing that there is no program that can predict if another piece of program will or will not terminate, the possibility always remains that a piece of software used to run a blockchain will sooner or later have an unpredictable bug. In this case, the blockchain in question will not be restricted to its own microworld and will need external fixing. But if no instance of government is anticipated as should be the case in a structure devoid of centralized and institutionalized mediation, who will take the responsibility to modify the program? It will be fixed by an occult form of government all the participants of the blockchain are not aware of and do not participate in electing those in charge. It is therefore for computational reasons that mediations of the classical type like the institution of a government are bound to be necessary—even in decidable microworlds like blockchain structures.

From a more general point of view, it is therefore very hard to imagine how blockchain technology could be extended to forms of social transaction that we have every reason to believe to be not computably decidable. Moreover, non-computable processes are everywhere in the natural world where chaotic systems are the rule and not the exception[25] just as cultural phenomena, from natural languages to institutions of government, cannot be even approached by computable models only even when they are limited to very simple structures.[26] In the case of law, it seems therefore

[24]In this sense, a blockchain operate in the same kind of environment as first order predicate logic which Gödel proved to be complete. Cf. Gödel (1930), pp. 349–360.

[25]Pisanti and Longo (2012), pp. 28–31.

[26]In the case of natural languages for example, the very idea of a completely stabilized linguistic meaning which would be fixed in advance like in logical languages does not do justice to the constant shift of meaning through usage. Just as in physics where the problem of perturbation under the threshold of measure can trigger unpredictable evolutions, so is the case with linguistic meanings the evolution of which is also unpredictable.

clear that blockchain technology can be used (for certification and contracts for example) but have to be merged in richer worlds in order to make real sense. Decidable structures can be of great help to partially secure transactions but cannot replace social relationships which are of a different order of complexity which is not possible to determine in advance.

4 Conclusion

The relationship human beings have to external reality, natural or social, is not limited to decidable structures like blockchain. It would therefore be illusory to think that legal institutions could be replaced one day by decidable processes that can be written in advance. Law is not limited to a set of written rules that can be mechanically applied even in the simplest case of decidable structures. Law is a process which opens up a future that remains to be written collectively.

References

Cajori F (1994) A History of Mathematical Notations [1929]. Courier Corporation, Mineola
Gandy R (1988) The confluence of ideas in 1936. In: Herken R (ed) The universal turing machine: a half-century survey. Oxford University Press, Oxford, pp 55–111
Gödel K (1930) Die Vollständigkeit der Axiome des logischen Funktionenkalküls. Monatshefte für Mathematik und Physik 37:349–360. Reprint with English translation in K. Gödel, Collected Works, vol. 1, Oxford University Press, Oxford, 1986, pp 60–101
Gödel K (1931) Über formal unentscheidbare Sätze der Principia Mathematica und verwandter Systeme I. Monatshefte für Mathematik und Physik 38:173–198. Reprint with English translation in K. Gödel, Collected Works, vol. 1, Oxford University Press, Oxford, 1986, pp 144–195
Havelock EA (1976) Origins of western literacy. Four lectures delivered at the Ontario Institute for Studies in Education, Toronto, March 25-28, 1974. Monograph Series No. 14. The Ontario Institute for Studies in Education. The Ontario Institute for Studies in Education, Toronto
Herrenschmidt C (2007) Les trois écritures: langue, nombre, code. Gallimard, Paris
Hilbert D (1923) Die logischen Grundlagen der Mathematik. Mathematische Annalen 88:151–165
Hilbert D (1925) Über das Unendliche. Mathematische Annalen 95(1926):161–190
Lassègue J (2019) Ambivalence du calculable et crise du jugement. Archives de Philosophie 82:255–274
Lassègue J, Longo G (2012) What is Turing's comparison between mechanism and writing worth? In: Cooper SB, Dawar A, Löwe B (eds) How the world computes, turing centenary conference, Lecture notes in computer science 7318. Springer, Berlin, pp 450–461
Leibniz GW (1666) Dissertatio de Arte Combinatoria. Reprint in Die philosophischen Schriften, Gerhardt (ed.) band IV, pp 30–105
Leibniz GW (2018) De Justitia et Novo Codice Legum Condendo [1679]. Reprint Textes inédits d'après les manuscrits de la Bibliothèque provinciale de Hanovre, G. Grua (ed.) Paris, Presses Universitaires de France, 1998, t. II, pp 621–623
Longo G (2010) Incompletezza. In: La matematica, vol 4. Einaudi, Turin, pp 219–262
Pisanti N, Longo G (2012) Le equazioni della natura. Sapere, London, pp 28–31. Agosto 2012
Poincaré H (1893) Les méthodes nouvelles de la mécanique céleste. Gauthier-Villars, Paris

Polanyi K (2001) The great transformation: the political and economic origins of our time. Beacon Press, Boston
Schmandt-Besserat D (2010) How writing came about. University of Texas Press, Austin
Turing A (1936) On computable numbers, with an application to the Entscheidungsproblem. Proc London Math Soc 2(42):230–265. Reprint in The Essential Turing, Jack Copeland (ed.) Oxford University Press, Oxford, 2004, pp 58–93
Turing A (2004) Lecture on the automatic computing engine, [1947]. Reprint in The Essential Turing, Jack Copeland (ed.) Oxford University Press, Oxford, pp 378–394

Solving Cryptographic Puzzles: How to Mine?

Clemente Biondi Santi and Vincenzo Vespri

Contents

1 Introduction

In this chapter we will examine the activity of *mining* in the peer-to-peer electronic payment system Bitcoin, empathizing its importance for the maintenance and security of the blockchain.

A blockchain is a growing chain of blocks containing records of data, linked together using techniques of cryptography. It is an "open, distributed ledger that can record transactions between two parties efficiently and in a verifiable and permanent way",[1] so it is resistant to data modification.

Although its dimension is able to grow in time, its content will not be modifiable nor deletable without invalidating the whole structure, this gives the blockchain the propriety of being immutable. Apart from its security, another property is the transparency of the records held in a public blockchain. Since the system is distributed, there is no presence of a central authority and participants need to cooperate with each other to maintain the order.

[1]Narayanan et al. (2016).

C. Biondi Santi (✉) · V. Vespri
University of Florence, Department of Math and Computer Technology, Florence, Italy
e-mail: vincenzo.vespri@unifi.it

B. Cappiello, G. Carullo (eds.), *Blockchain, Law and Governance*,
https://doi.org/10.1007/978-3-030-52722-8_5

The white paper proposed by Satoshi Nakamoto[2] describes Bitcoin's system as "a purely peer-to-peer version of electronic cash" that "would allow online payments to be sent directly from one party to another without going through a financial institution". The transactions made within the network are "saved" into an ongoing chain of hash-based proof-of-work, forming a record that cannot be changed without redoing the proof-of-work. The proof-of-work consists in an electric consumption due to the high usage of the CPU that is needed to solve a cryptographic puzzle. As long as the majority of CPU power is controlled by participants that are cooperating, a longer chain will be generated by these nodes, outpacing malicious attackers. The process of adding a new block by solving a cryptographic puzzle is called "mining".

Mining through the solution of cryptographic puzzles, is the process by which transaction are verified and added to Bitcoin's public blockchain. Bitcoin is a digital currency based on a peer-to-peer decentralized network presented in 2009 by Satoshi Nakamoto, a pseudonym for an unknown person or collective.

In Bitcoin's network, every machine participating is called a "node". Every node is able to store, create, receive and send data to others. Special nodes called "miners", have the ability to aggregate pending transactions into blocks and add them to the main blockchain. The miner is required to provide various information about the transactions and a valid Proof-of-Work to successfully add a new block.

The Proof-of-Work is a verification process in which a cryptographic puzzle has to be solved through the expense of computational power. This method was proposed as a solution to the Byzantine Generals Problem.

2 Byzantine Generals Problem

The Byzantine Fault (or Byzantine failure[3]) is a condition of a computer system, which mainly appears in distributed computing systems, where components may fail and there is imperfect information on whether a component has failed.

The name Byzantine Generals Problem comes from an allegory that pictures a condition of stall for members of a system, some of which are unreliable, where a coordination or agreement is needed.

This condition consists of two or more generals, with their respective army, that need to coordinate an attack by being far away from each other. An obvious answer would be sending messengers to deliver an order of attack to the other armies and probably sending other messengers to confirm that orders have been received. The issue is that a messenger could be killed or captured by the enemy resulting in a missing or tampered message respectively, hence a failed coordination. The generals need an algorithm to perform a coordinated attack, they need to find consensus.

[2]Nakamoto (2008).

[3]Kirrmann (2005), p. 94.

Every general can be seen as a node in a peer-to-peer decentralized network: in order to be able to function properly, a mechanism is needed to coordinate all the nodes.

3 Proof-of-Work

Proof-of-Work (PoW)[4] is a mechanism that secures the network's consensus, even in the presence of non-compliant nodes. Every node is made of software and hardware and can perform various operations, including the following:

- make transactions;
- receive transactions;
- verify transactions;
- broadcast transactions to other nodes.

Due to the lack of a central authority in a peer-to-peer system like Bitcoin's network, every node is able to observe the others. In a scenario where a node wants to send Bitcoins to another node, it needs to declare it publicly in order to communicate to the miners that the transaction needs to be processed and verified.

A miner is constantly listening to broadcasted transactions and, after a collection and verification process, adds them to the blockchain through the solution of a 'hash puzzle'.

The hash puzzle is a piece of data which is difficult to produce but easy for others to verify and which satisfies certain requirements. Since the puzzle can be a random process with low probability, it is solved by trial and error and the whole process has a heavy cost in terms of electricity and time. As a Proof-of-Work scheme, Bitcoin uses Hashcash[5] based on SHA-256.

The Proof-of-Work is required by a miner to successfully add a new block to the blockchain and it "fixes" its difficulty to limit the rate at which new blocks can be generated by the network to one every 10 min.

4 Mining: The Validation Process

When new transactions are broadcasted, mining nodes collect and aggregate all the data found and automatically apply, through Bitcoin's software installed on the machine, a series of controls, such as:

[4]Gervais et al. (2016), pp. 3–16.

[5]Back (2002).

- track the source of the transaction;
- check if the sender has enough Bitcoin in his wallet;
- check if the sender has already spent his Bitcoins (prevents double spending);
- check if the amount of Bitcoins in the transaction is within the range of 0 and 21 million.

If all requirements are satisfied, the transaction is placed in a Memory Pool where it will wait until a miner takes it for confirmation. A Memory pool (or Mempool) is a simple 'list' of pending transactions that are waiting for the approval of a miner. The order in which transactions are chosen is proportional to the fee paid by the sender of the transaction.

All the miners in the network are competing with each other to create a new block, since only the first successful creation will be awarded with the reward by the system. Once a miner has gathered enough transactions from the Mempool, it needs to control that none of them is already in the blockchain. After this last control, the miner creates a 'candidate block' with the transactions gathered and a 'block header' which consists of:

- timestamp of the block;
- the list of the transactions in the candidate block;
- a link to the previous block in the blockchain;
- a valid Proof-of-Work.
- other data such as the reward for the miner and the size of the block.

The first miner that successfully builds a valid block and adds it to the blockchain receives a reward for his work. An example of the information contained in the 'block header' is presented in Table 1. Since Proof-of-Work requires a considerable computational power expense (which means a lot of electricity consumed), the first miner to successfully present a valid PoW is rewarded with newly generated Bitcoins.

5 Cryptographic Puzzles: One-Way Hash Functions

A *hash function* is any function that can be used to map data of arbitrary size to fixed-size values, called *hash values* or *digest*. Furthermore, a *one-way hash function* is designed in such a way that is hardly reversible, that is, to find a string that hashes to a given value. The slightest change in an input string may cause the hash value to change drastically, this phenomenon is called *avalanche effect*.

Before going through the properties required to all good cryptographic hash functions, let's consider the following example of use: suppose C needs to patent a new invention. Then C will need to present the project P to the patent office where, once delivered, no modifications will be allowed, and it will be added to the queue. It is possible that in this time, a malicious attacker could breach in the office and steal the ideas in C's project. To solve this issue, C could arrange with the patent office to

Table 1 Example of the information stored in a block of the Bitcoin Blockchain[a]

Block #599857	
BlockHash 0000000000000000014508924dcb8c3d219e48303154276b4023c6c31bc330f	
Number of transactions 3144	**Difficulty** 13008091666971.898
Height 599857(mainchain)	**Bits** 1715a35c
Block reward 12.5 BTC	**Size** (bytes) 890974
Timestamp Oct 18, 2019 4.56.20 AM	**Version** 549453824
Mined by *omissis*	**Nonce** 3929938969
MerkleRoot 74298f9df6354577be2eb88516b359	**Next Block** 599858
Previous block 599856	
Transactions:[b]	
Transaction ID	**Mined on**
ff38b246c3c8ea9f49aebe47a5daa5b3308ae200410ef587cd930c8a3c14f182	18/10/2019 4:56:20
Transferred from	**Amount**
17A16QmavnUfCW11DAApiJxp7ARnxN5pGX	2.10531439 BTC
Transferred to	**Amount**
1MNADL2qAj8esSw2bYtUBA6e4KbrJ2t1g6	0.0065 BTC
3DhzqB6VLAXq6pLfbA7B2RhgbHntUwXVu5	0.01978164 BTC
17A16QmavnUfCW11DAApiJxp7ARnxN5pGX	2.07803275 BTC

[a]The information presented in Table 1 is an extract of the data actually stored on the Bitcoin blockchain. This data can be verified for example through one of the many blockchain explorers available online, such as https://www.bitcoinblockexplorers.com

[b]For example, only one transaction data is shown, the block in question contains 10 transactions

present, instead of the project P, its unique hash value H(P). Doing so the attacker stealing H(P) would have no useful information to find the project P. Moreover, at the time of registration of the project, at the end of the waiting queue, C would have to provide the project P to the patent office to confirm that its hash value coincides with H(P).

Good cryptographic hash functions are requested to possess the following properties to withstand all known types of cryptanalytic attacks:

- a hash function H can be applied to inputs of any size;
- the hash value H(M) (or digest) has a fixed size;
- given an input M, the hash function H(M) is feasible to compute;
- given the hash value it should be difficult to find any input M such that h = H(M). This property is also known as *pre-image resistance* or the property of being one-way;
- given an input M, it should be difficult to find a different input M’ such that H (M)=H(M’). This property is also known as *weak collision resistance* or *second pre-image resistance*;
- it should be difficult to find a pair of two different inputs <M, M’> such that H (M)=H(M’). Such pair is called a *cryptographic hash collision* and the property takes the name of *strong collision resistance.*

The need of the first three properties is obvious. However, the necessity of the last three properties could be explained by examining a violation from an attacker. If property (5) would be violated, an attacker could switch the real message M with a tampered message M’ such that H(M) = H(M’), and the receiver would accept the result as if it was authentic. If property (4) would be violated, the attacker could make a similar attack even in the case that only H(M) is known. Lastly, property (6) is referring to the resistance of H to a class of attacks known as *birthday attacks*,[6] that presuppose that the attacker has a temporary access to the hashing mechanism.

Bitcoin uses SHA-256 (Secure Hash Algorithm, 256 bits) as a hashing function, which yields a unique output with a fixed size of 256 bits. This function is one-way since knowing its output gives no information about the input, making it secure and reliable.

SHA-256 belongs to the SHA-2 cryptographic hash functions set, designed by the NSA. They compare the computed digest to a known and expected hash value to verify data’s integrity.[7] In Bitcoin’s network, SHA-256 is used in the Proof-of-Work algorithm and in the creation of the Bitcoin addresses.

The only known way to find the input of the SHA-256 given the output is by trial and error. The attacker would have to guess an input, encrypt it through the SHA-256 and check if it matches the desired output, otherwise the aggressor will need to guess again (this attack is also known as a ‘Brute Force Attack’).

---

[6] Katz and Lindell (2014).

[7] Penard and van Werkhoven (2008).

The SHA-256 is used to determine the 'BlockHash' which is a unique fingerprint (or ID) of each block. A BlockHash is made of concatenated information about the block, such as timestamp, nonce, hash of previous block... passed through the hash function SHA-256.

A 'nonce' is an arbitrary number guessed by the miner in order to create a blockhash that starts with *n* zeros, after the application of SHA-256. In this hashing function, a minor change in the input completely changes the output. The creation of such blockhash is achieved through brute forcing the value of nonce, trying all its different values. Once a miner finds a nonce that, passed through the SHA-256 along with other information, yields a blockhash starting with *n* zeros, the Proof-of-Work is complete, and that miner adds the block to the blockchain. The number of zeros *n* depends on the 'difficulty' field, which increases proportionally to the number of people trying to mine the next block.

6 Elliptic-Curve Cryptography (ECC)

Elliptic-curve cryptography (ECC) is an approach to public-key cryptography based on the algebraic structure of elliptic curves over finite fields. It is the approach used to secure the blocks in bitcoin blockchains. ECC requires smaller keys compared to non-ECC cryptography to provide equivalent security. Elliptic curves are applicable for key agreement, digital signatures, pseudo-random generators and other tasks. Indirectly, they can be used for encryption by combining the key agreement with a symmetric encryption scheme. Public-key cryptography is based on the intractability of certain mathematical problems. Early public-key systems are secure assuming that it is difficult to factor a large integer composed of two or more large prime factors. For elliptic-curve-based protocols, it is assumed that finding the discrete logarithm of a random elliptic curve element with respect to a publicly known base point is infeasible: this is the "elliptic curve discrete logarithm problem" (ECDLP). The security of elliptic curve cryptography depends on the ability to compute a point multiplication and the inability to compute the multiplicand given the original and product points. The size of the elliptic curve determines the difficulty of the problem.

For current cryptographic purposes, an elliptic curve is a plane curve over a finite field (rather than the real numbers) which consists of the points satisfying the equation

$$y^2 = x^3 + ax + b$$

along with a distinguished point at infinity. In the mathematics of the real numbers, the logarithm $\log_b a$ is a number x such that $b^x = a$, for given numbers a and b. Analogously, in any group G, powers b^k can be defined for all integers k, and the discrete logarithm $\log_b a$ is an integer k such that $b^k = a$. The use of elliptic curves in cryptography was suggested independently by Neal Koblitz[8] and Victor S. Miller[9] in 1985. Elliptic curve cryptography algorithms entered in wide use in 2005.

The curve used by Bitcoin, secp256k1, in the normal Weierstrass form has equation $y^2 = x^3 + 7$. The elliptic curve can take characteristic shapes in the plane according to its coefficients, but each one is symmetrical with respect to the abscissa axis, since for each value of x there will be a positive and a negative value for y, that is: $y = \pm(x^3 + ax + b)^{(1/2)}$. In cryptography, curves are used on which some algebraic properties can be defined with respect to an internal composition operation, therefore only non-singular curves will be taken into consideration, discarding all those curves with cusps or with self-intersections.

To verify the non-singularity of the curve, it is necessary to impose that its determinant is different from 0, i.e. that the inequality exists: $4a^3 + 27b^2$ different from 0 The points of a non-singular curve, combined with a special element 0 called point to infinity or zero point, represent a set G, defined in this way:

$$G = \{(x, y) \in R^2 | y^2 = x^3 + ax + b, 4a^3 + 27b^2 \text{ different from } 0\} \cup \{0\}$$

A commutative, or abelian, group[10] is a non-empty set on which a binary operation "x" is defined to satisfy certain properties:

- the set is closed with respect to the operation, i.e. if a and b belong to the set G then also $c = a \times b$ belongs to G;
- the operation respects the associative property, or $(a \times b) \times c = a \times (b \times c)$;
- there is a 0 element, called identity element, such that $a \times 0 = a$ and $0 \times a = a$ for every a;
- each element has its inverse, that is, for every a, there exists b such that $a \times b = 0$;
- the operation respects the commutative property, or $a \times b = b \times a$ for each a and b belonging to the set.

A group that contains a finite number of elements is called a finite group and the number of elements in the group is the group order, otherwise the group is called an infinite group. On a G group you can define the operation of elevation to power as the repeated application of the group operator, so $a^3 = a \times a \times a$. A G group is called cyclic if each element of G is a power a^k of a fixed element $a \in G$, with $k \in N$, in this case it is he says that the element a generates the group G or that is a generator of G, moreover a cyclic group is always abelian and can be finite or infinite. In the case of elliptic curves,[11] the composition operation is the sum, indicated with the symbol +.

[8]See for instance, Koblitz (2012a, b, 1998).
[9]Miller (1985).
[10]For elementary properties of Abelian groups, see Fuchs and Gobel (1993).
[11]See for instance Miller (1985).

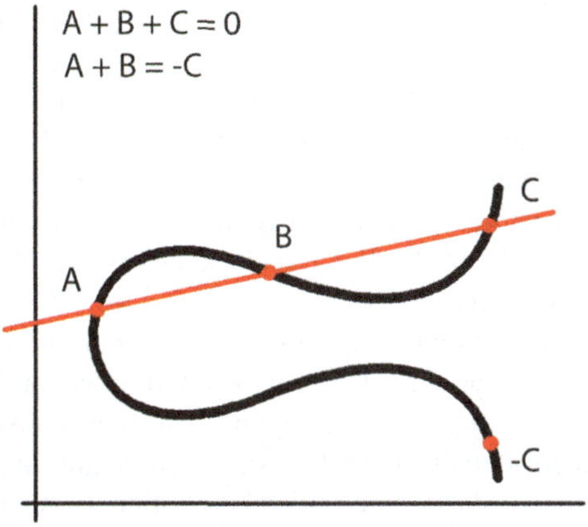

Fig. 1 Elliptic curve cryptography

Moreover:

- the inverse of a point $P(x_P,y_P)$ is defined as the point $-P(x_P,-y_P)$ symmetric of P with respect to the axis x;
- the identity element is represented by the point to infinity, or zero-point O for which is worth $0 = -0$ and for every point P belonging to G we have $P + O = O + P = P$;
- the sum operation, indicated with + is defined by the rule $A + B + C = O$, with A, B and C belonging to the set G and are aligned.

Let us explain in the geometric setting what is the sum operation for elliptic curves. The elements of the group can be represented as points on the Cartesian plane and also the law of internal composition can be interpreted in a geometric way, establishing that if three points of the curve lie on the same line, or are aligned, their sum is zero. As we have to do with abelian group, it is guaranteed that each element has an inverse element with respect to the sum and that the operation of sum has the commutative property, so that the rule for the sum can be rewritten as $A + B = -C$ where A, B and C are aligned points, as see on Fig. 1. To calculate the sum between two points A and B belonging to the curve we must draw a straight line between them until you find a third intersection point C,. Note that this point always exists. For a third degree equation, two real roots implies that also the third is real.[12] The result of the sum will be the inverse of the point of intersection—C, symmetric of C with respect to the x axis.

In the particular case where we want to define the sum P + P we have to use the tangent to the curve in point P and it is necessary to use the formula of the first derivative with respect to x of the curve equation:

[12]By Gauss Theorem an equation of degree n has exactly n solutions in the complex number (the complex plane contains also the Real Numbers Line). The strictly complex roots are at couple, so they are even. So, for an equation of third degree can be two or zero. Therefore, if there are two real solutions, also the third is real.

$$m = (3x^2{}_P + a)/(2y_P)$$

This allows us to define a scalar multiplication operation of a point P belonging to the curve, for a natural number: nP = P + P + ... + P for n times. The multiplication of an element of the group for a scalar, that is the repeated application of the sum operator, by definition represents the elevation to power within the group G, or $P^3 = 3P = P + P + P$ and the inverse of this operation will be called logarithm on elliptic curves.

Based on the algebraic formulas introduced previously for the sum of two points, we can perform the previous multiplication by making n−1 sum operations, actually, with the use of appropriate algorithms we can do much better. One of the algorithms that can be used to efficiently implement the scalar multiplication operation is the double and add algorithm. Given the product n*P, with $n \in N$ and $P \in G$, a generic scalar n can be written as the sum $n_0 + 2n_1 + 2^2n_2 + \ldots + 2^m n_m$, where the numbers $n_0, \ldots, n_m \in \{0,1\}$ and m + 1 is the number of digits of the binary representation of n. Suppose we want to multiply the generic point P for 151, whose binary representation is 100101112, then we can write:

$$151P = 2^7P + 2^4P + 2^2P + 2^1P + 2^0P$$

The double and add algorithm[13] tells us:

- initialize the result Q to 0;
- with i = 0, since $d_0 = 1$ we add P to Q and store the result in Q and double P;
- with i = 1, since $d_1 = 1$ we add P to Q and store the result in Q and double P;
- with i = 2, since $d_2 = 1$ we add P to Q and store the result in Q and double P;
- with i = 3, since $d_3 = 0$ we do not execute any sum, but we double P;
- with i = 4, since $d_4 = 1$ we add P to Q and store the result in Q and double P;
- with i = 5, since $d_5 = 0$ we do not execute any sum, but we double P;
- with i = 6, since $d_6 = 0$ we do not execute any sum, but we double P;
- with i = 7, since $d_7 = 1$ we add P to Q and store the result in Q and double P;
- no binary digits of n are left to be taken into account, then returns Q.

The algorithm gives the result of multiplication by executing 5 sums and 7 multiplications. For each iteration of the loop this algorithm performs a summing operation, or alternatively a summing operation followed by another summing operation (doubling P), the loop is executed as many times as the binary digits of n, this leads us to estimate a cost of O(logn). So far, we have talked about elliptic curves in which the variables and the coefficients belong to the real numbers, but in their cryptographic application both the variables and the coefficients are restricted to the elements of a finite field. In mathematics, a finite field, or Galois field,[14] is a

[13]See for instance Hankerson et al. (2004).

[14]See for instance Applications (2008).

field with a finite number p^n of elements, with p prime number and is often denoted as $Z(p^n)$ or GF (p^n).

The security of elliptic curve cryptography depends on the difficulty with which it is possible to perform the inverse operation, i.e. to determine n when nP and P are given. This problem is called the discrete logarithm[15] of the elliptic curve and it is a problem that is considered hard.[16] Currently the fastest known technique for calculating the logarithm is called the Pollard rho method.[17] Designed by John Pollard[18] in 1975, it was used in 1981 to factor Fermat's eighth number issue (a Fermat number,[19] named after Pierre de Fermat[20] who first studied them, is a positive integer of the form $F_n = (2^2)^n + 1$. It was conjectured that all the Fermat number were prime number, conjecture that was proved to be false) It is a probabilistic algorithm, in the sense that it does not guarantee to produce a result.

In reality there are some elliptic curves for which it is possible to find specific algorithms that solve the discrete logarithm in polynomial time, such curves are not suitable for cryptographic uses and are therefore called weak. The possibility that some curves are intrinsically weak to a cryptographic analysis imposes several questions related to the trust that it is legitimate to place in objects of this type. Suppose, in fact, that someone proposes the use of a curve, how can we be sure that it does not have some kind of mathematical vulnerability not yet discovered that makes the problem of the logarithm solvable in polynomial times? To avoid the eventuality that some attacker can forge a curve so as to include in it some mathematical backdoors[21] it is used the principle called nothing up my sleeve,[22] that is it is introduced a random number, called seed, which is used to generate curve parameters and the generator point, using hash functions. A curve generated by the use of a seed is called verifiably random, or randomly verifiable.[23] The elliptic-curve cryptography is resistant to nowadays computers. Only the introduction of quantum computing[24] can make breakable ECC.

[15]See for instance Weisstein EW Discrete Logarithm. https://mathworld.wolfram.com/DiscreteLogarithm.html.

[16]See for instance Bovet and Crescenzi (1994).

[17]See for instance Montgomery (1987).

[18]Brent and Pollard (1981), pp. 627–631.

[19]See for instance Krizek et al. (2001).

[20]See for instance Pierre de Fermat—Biography, Facts and Pictures. https://www.famousscientists.org/pierre-de-fermat/.

[21]Diffie and Hellman (1976), pp. 644–654.

[22]"Nothing up my sleeve" is a phrase associated with magicians, who sometimes preface a magic trick by holding open their sleeves to show they have no objects hidden inside.

[23]In cryptography, the concept of a verifiable random function was introduced by Micali et al. (1999), pp. 120–130.

[24]See for instance Shor (1999).

References

Applications IC on FF (2008) Finite fields and applications: eighth international conference on finite fields and applications, July 9–13, 2007, Melbourne, Australia. American Mathematical Soc., Providence

Back A (2002) Hashcash-a denial of service counter-measure

Bovet D, Crescenzi P (1994) Introduction to the theory of complexity. Prentice Hall, New Jersey

Brent RP, Pollard JM (1981) Factorization of the eighth Fermat number. Math Comput 36:627–630

Diffie W, Hellman M (1976) New directions in cryptography. IEEE Trans Inf Theory 22:644–654

Fuchs L, Gobel R (eds) (1993) Abelian groups. CRC Press, New York

Gervais A, Karame GO, Wüst K, et al (2016) On the security and performance of proof of work blockchains. In: Proceedings of the 2016 ACM SIGSAC conference on computer and communications security, pp 3–16

Hankerson D, Menezes AJ, Vanstone S (2004) Guide to elliptic curve cryptography. Springer Science & Business Media, New York

Katz J, Lindell Y (2014) Introduction to modern cryptography, II. CRC Press, London

Kirrmann H (2005) Fault tolerant computing in industrial automation. ABB Research Center, Baden

Koblitz N (1998) Algebraic aspects of cryptography. Springer Science & Business Media, New York

Koblitz N (2012a) A course in number theory and cryptography, II. Springer Science & Business Media, New York

Koblitz NI (2012b) Introduction to elliptic curves and modular forms, II. Springer Science & Business Media, New York

Krizek M, Luca F, Somer L (2001) 17 Lectures on Fermat numbers: from number theory to geometry. Springer Science & Business Media, Burnaby

Micali S, Rabin M, Vadhan S (1999) Verifiable random functions. In: 40th annual symposium on foundations of computer science (cat. No. 99CB37039). IEEE, Piscataway, pp 120–130

Miller VS (1985) Use of elliptic curves in cryptography. In: Conference on the theory and application of cryptographic techniques. Springer, Berlin, pp 417–426

Montgomery PL (1987) Speeding the Pollard and elliptic curve methods of factorization. Math Comput 48:243–264

Nakamoto S (2008) Bitcoin: a peer-to-peer electronic cash system. 11

Narayanan A, Bonneau J, Felten E et al (2016) Bitcoin and cryptocurrency technologies: a comprehensive introduction. Princeton University Press, Princeton

Penard W, van Werkhoven T (2008) On the secure hash algorithm family. In: Tel G (ed) Cryptography in context

Shor PW (1999) Polynomial-time algorithms for prime factorization and discrete logarithms on a quantum computer. SIAM Rev 41:303–332

Part II
Governance and Regulatory Issues

Cyberspace, Blockchain, Governance: How Technology Implies Normative Power and Regulation

Andrej Zwitter and Jilles Hazenberg

Contents

1 Introduction

The modern world has brought many technological changes to the daily lives of citizens. The plethora of data that is being collected by companies such as Google and Facebook exceed petabytes of data daily. This data is also the driver of new technologies such as machine learning and artificial intelligence. It fuels economies as much as intergovernmental services such as development aid and humanitarian action.[1] In addition to data collection and usage, information infrastructures such as digital ledger technology, specifically blockchain technology, are also adding to the complexity of data and information management. Specifically, since the rise of Bitcoin, blockchain technology is almost being seen a panacea for the management of logistic, governance and information management problems. It has become a *sine qua non* technology of aspiring companies, start-ups, and government agencies as

[1] Qadir et al. (2016) and Ali et al. (2016).

A. Zwitter (✉)
University of Groningen, Campus Fryslan, Groningen, The Netherlands
e-mail: a.zwitter@rug.nl

J. Hazenberg
University of Groningen, Faculty of Science and Engineering, Groningen, The Netherlands

B. Cappiello, G. Carullo (eds.), *Blockchain, Law and Governance*,
https://doi.org/10.1007/978-3-030-52722-8_6

well as international organizations alike.[2] Its application spans from crypto currency, supply chain management, smart contracts, digital identity management and many more.

However, technologies are not neutral in the sense of normative implications that they impose on its users. For example, user interfaces that have become the access to all features of databases, such as social media platforms in the form of Facebook or Instagram. These in part determine whether certain actions are even possible. Until the introduction of different emojis for Facebook likes, there was only the like button with a thumbs-up. By the mere limitation of the user interface, a dislike, such as in YouTube, was not even possible. The lack of a dislike button on Facebook served the purpose of creating a positive atmosphere on the social Media platform. The code behind the user interface of Instagram, for example, does not allow the use of hyperlinks in picture descriptions. These are in fact design choices with certain purposes in mind. All these design choices determine user behavior and can assume regulatory function.

Technology implies norms and governance embedded in its code and infrastructure. The above examples already illustrate that even without explicit normative framing, technological design choices impose limitations to the actions of users. In his book "Code and Other Laws of Cyberspace", Lawrence Lessig explains how Indeed digital code has become equal to law in that it imposes certain actions, allows for certain freedoms, and limits other actions. The structure of blockchain technology and digital ledger technology brings Lessig's argument to a higher level of governance. Extending beyond his line of reasoning, we suggest in this chapter that design choices around blockchain technology are at the same time design choices for norms of governance. We argue that if this is the case, then state regulators need to treat the implementation of new technologies with governance implications as laws and contracts that need to be assessed vis-à-vis the existing legal framework.

This chapter will first introduce traditional notions of governance as old (Mode I) and new (Mode II) governance. In the next section, we will argue that technology imposes governance principles through design choices. Some of these design choices are made with governance in mind, others are guided by more general norms of human interaction, and again others are even implemented without any consideration of their normative power. The section will illustrate how Cyberspace imposes meta-principles of governance that allow for a whole new conception of regulation, which we call "Cyber-Governance". We will show that these meta principles often remain implicit while still having a big impact on our daily interactions. Thereafter, we will turn our attention to software architecture design choices of blockchain technology in particular and argue that these impose specific governance principles. For that purpose, we will analyze design choices such as decentrality, immutability, and trustlessness. The arguments in this chapter will be predominantly legal theoretical and philosophical rather than technical. The purpose is to explain the normative power of technological design specifically in the realm of governance.

[2] Zwitter and Boisse-Despiaux (2018) and Zwitter (2015).

2 Traditional Governance: Old and New

Governance is a highly contested concept and definitions are as elusive as for example definitions of "sustainability" and "cyber".[3] Governance as a policy concept is defined by David Levi-Faur as a "signifier of change" in policy-making which concern shifts of processes of policy making and policy making authority.[4] Such shifts can for example be vertically to regional, international, transnational, and to the local, and horizontally to private spheres of society.[5]

Besides that, governance is often depicted as modes, referring to 'old' and 'new' forms of governance or Mode I and II governance.[6] 'Old' governance (Mode I) in this context mostly refers to hierarchical command and control structures traditionally embedded in the state, whereas "new governance" (Mode II) commonly refers to horizontal modes of policy making. Lately, the term network governance has emerged with the emergence of social networks and governance processes of regulatory nature sometimes embedded entirely in the private sphere.[7]

Firstly, *public-private governance* is a form of Mode II governance in which non-state actors are integrated into public policymaking. Increasingly the expertise of private actors is sought in developing regulation. Public-private governance relies on networks and market-mechanisms of competition to achieve policy-goals.[8] Policy goals are often set by either within public private partnerships or in public institutions. Public-private governance consequently delegates the performance to achieve these goals to non-state actors for more efficient, effective, or expert based performance.[9] Oversight of this process is often assigned to non-majoritarian institutions who keep a check on private-actors performance's in correspondence with the public interest. Text-book examples of such public private governance are the large-scale privatizations of public institutions in the 1990s where the deliverance of public goods was brought to the market while semi-public regulators performed oversight. Between state actors, intermediary institutions, and private actors, policy networks are established that through partnerships govern practices from telecom to the provision of basic goods such as housing.

Secondly, *non-autonomous self-governance* is a form of governance without the direct involvement of a public actor in the policy-making process. Rather it refers to governance by non-state actors to keep hierarchical commands by public actors at bay. These non-state actors can be for-profit corporations and private individuals but also semi-public intermediary institutions and state-owned corporations.

[3]Levi-Faur (2012), Van Kersbergen and Van Waarden (2004), Kooiman (2003) and Colombi-Ciacchi (2014).

[4]Levi-Faur (2012), pp. 7–8.

[5]Hazenberg and Zwitter (2017).

[6]Lobel (2012), Mayntz (2003), Bevir (2010) and Rhodes (1996, 1997).

[7]Hazenberg and Zwitter (2017).

[8]Bevir (2010, 2013).

[9]Majone (2001).

Non-autonomous self-governance is governance under the shadow of hierarchy, i.e. the threat of hard-law commands.[10] Privacy standard setting by private corporations can be an example of this. Moreover, soft-law and international agreements play an important role in this form of governance. Often soft-law norms indicate what is expected of non-state actors but leaves open the manner in which to meet these expectations. Other examples include sectorial agreements on labor standards above and beyond what is legally required.

Thirdly, *autonomous self-governance* resembles the previous form with the exception that there is no shadow of hierarchy pressuring private governance initiative. Autonomous self-governance is regulation and policymaking originating out of free, often market, interactions between private actors. Codes of conduct, best practices, and standard setting can be instances of such autonomous self-governance. Moreover, pressures from private market actors, such as consumers, often trigger self-regulation. In other words, autonomous self-governance is governance arising from the private sector without involvement of public bodies. The commonalities between these three sub-forms of Mode II governance is that different actors, both public and private, perform different roles based on what they can deliver or are best at delivering in the policy-process from policymaking to its enforcement.[11]

Opposed to the relatively rigid structure of identity-based Mode I governance, role-based governance is more fluid. Multiple actors perform different governance roles in different spheres, often simultaneously: a corporation can be regulator as part of a policy-network developing regulatory policies; at the same time, it can be the regulated subject by external actors in other areas. Generally, roles are variable within policy spheres and consequently multiple actors perform different governance roles. One of the important consequences of such role-based governance is that the role an actor performs or its ability to perform it becomes the relevant aspect of power rather than the identity of the actor as per Mode I governance. Within Mode II governance power relationships are thus governed through a multitude of practices of soft law to optimize the ability of all actors to perform their governance roles effectively and efficiently. Power is perceived as static when roles are assumed to be fixed. This is predominantly the case in public-private governance where specific governance tasks are performed by actors based on their capability to perform certain tasks, i.e. under a clear division of labor. Within non-autonomous and autonomous self-governance, however, power is variable because roles are no longer fixed but are, often simultaneously, performed by multiple and changing actors. Within these forms of Mode II governance actors govern on a more ad-hoc basis and not necessarily in a structured manner. Power relationships thereby become more diffuse and networked with multiple actors having power over others corresponding to different roles they perform at a given time within a governance network.

[10] Börzel and Risse (2010).

[11] Majone (2001).

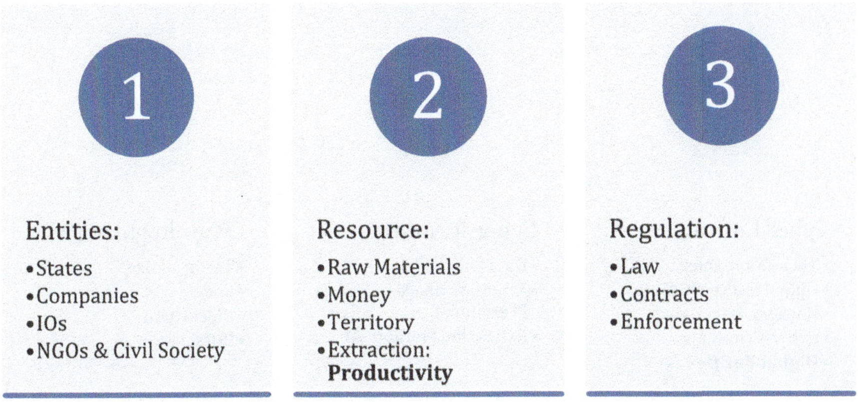

Fig. 1 Traditional Governance (old and new)

3 Cyber-Governance: How Technology Imposes Governance Principles

Lawrence Lessig's book "Code and Other Laws of Cyberspace" and his landmark article "Code is Law" drove home a very fundamental insight into the nature of law and Cyberspace.[12] It explained that code regulates actions in Cyberspace just as laws do in the real world. However, the extent to which our world and Cyberspace are interconnected has dramatically changed over the past two decades. The domain of the Cyberspace determines by and large our physical reality and the interactions between both are very fluid. Many of our payments today are being done digitally and the use of paper money becomes increasingly an exception. Online shopping has become the norm rather than the exception and digital commodities are ubiquitous. This development has gone so far that even the military has recognized Cyberspace as a discrete domain of warfare next to land, sea, air and space.[13]

From a perspective of governance, Cyberspace imposes fundamentally different rules than we are used to from the principles that lay the foundation of our current legal system. We can look at the different forms of governance, traditional governance and Cyber-governance, from the perspective of legal entities, resources, and regulation. Traditional governance (see Fig. 1) in general recognizes the following entities: States, companies, international organizations, non-governmental organizations, civil society organizations, individuals, and other legal entities sui generis. As resources traditional governance would consider physical commodities, to some extent digital commodities and intellectual property. Furthermore, it includes raw

[12]Lessig (1999, 2000).

[13]McGuffin and Mitchell (2014).

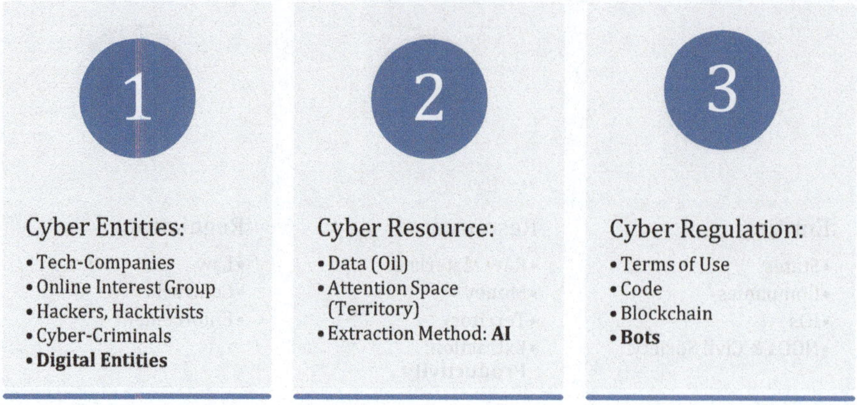

Fig. 2 Cyber-Governance

materials, money, and territory. The underlying assumption behind these resources is that any sort of value is being extracted through the method of productivity. In terms of regulation, traditional governance considers laws, regulations, contracts and traditional means of legal enforcement, such as courts and the executive functions of the State. All these aspects taken together, traditional governance is built on the underlying assumptions that individual agency and legal norms are bound to the principle of territoriality and its national and regional enforcement through the judiciary and executive branches.

Cyber-governance (see Fig. 2) could be defined as traditional governance augmented by the fact that Cyberspace increasingly determines physical reality, social and legal interaction, forms of possible legal and contractual interaction and the entities with which can be interacted. It puts a big question mark behind the underlying assumptions that the original principle of territoriality and its enforcement are still equally valid. New entities are starting to become increasingly relevant for governance, such as, technological companies in particular, online interest groups, hackers and hacktivists, cybercriminals, and a completely new domain of entities, which we would summarize as digital entities. These digital entities are comprised of bots and botnets, viruses and worms, artificial intelligence, and other forms of code that can act to some extent autonomously of its creator. These digital entities, indeed, are becoming a legally tangible phenomenon as can be seen in the European discussions on Robot-rights and the rights and duties of artificial intelligence.[14]

In Cyber-governance data is the new oil, and human users' attention space is the new territory that is open for conquest. The new method of extraction of value from data and attention space is machine learning and artificial intelligence. In terms of regulation, the Cyber-domain also opens up new opportunities for private entities to

[14]Zwitter (2016).

become lawmakers and regulators. We have already mentioned code-as-law. In addition, "terms of use" have become new means of regulation of the user bases of any service. Terms of use determine the rights of clients of social media platforms and other digital services. These rights do not only concern the service in and of itself but also modes of social interaction (e.g. which kinds of messages are allowed on Twitter) and its side products, namely data. Given the lack of legal regulations of data ownership outside of the realm of privacy regulation and intellectual property rights, contracts are the only way to enforce data ownership. Such contracts in many cases take the form of terms of use. However, given the power imbalance between users and service providers in the cyber-domain (compare for example terms of use for services of Google, Facebook, Microsoft, Instagram, WhatsApp, etc.) new digital service providers act as de facto regulators rather than as equal contract partners. In other words, if Facebook was a country, it's constitution (formed by its terms of use, its limitations imposed by the user interface and other forms of codes) would be applicable to 2.5 billion active users.[15] Blockchain, in this regard, can be seen as a specific form of regulating code, implying specific design principles and thereby normative principles of governance. What kind of executive, regulative and law enforcement functions digital identities such as bots will be able to play in the future, remains to be seen.

4 Blockchain Design Choices As Normative Choices

As mentioned in the previous section, all software design choices have inadvertently also normative effect. This is particularly true in blockchain technology. This section will take a closer look at the effects of blockchain technology features such as decentrality, immutability, and trustlessness. Before that it is worthwhile to have a brief look at blockchain applications, e.g. Bitcoin, in the history of thought.

In 2008, Satoshi Nakamoto wrote a white paper on blockchain technology and Bitcoin.[16] The governance model embodied by this new technology was one that aimed to decentralize otherwise centralized services such as the financial system. Bitcoin as a peer-to-peer money system was potentially foreshadowing a peer-to-peer society.[17] The nature of this decentralized, almost anarchic system becomes particularly visible when looking at decentralized autonomous organizations (DAOs), a specific form of governance system within blockchain based services. So-called DAOs can be defined as non-hierarchical organizations performing and recording tasks that are routinely conducted on a peer-to-peer, cryptographically

[15] Akinpelu O (2020) Facebook is Still King as the Social Media Giant Hits 2.5bn Monthly Active Users. In: Technext. https://technext.ng/2020/01/31/facebook-is-still-king-as-the-social-media-giant-hits-2-5bn-monthly-active-users/.

[16] Nakamoto (2008).

[17] Swartz (2018).

secured network. The DAO relies entirely on its stakeholders to voluntarily operate, manage and evolve the governance model through democratic consultations.[18] And the political visions of a group of market-anarchist cryptographers determined the design choices that were embedded in the blockchain technology underlying Bitcoin:[19] decentrality, transparency, trustlessness, immutability. Let us have a closer look at these design choices with a view to the normative effects on governance structures.

Decentrality is expressed by the feature that the ledger on which transactions are recorded is shared across all nodes in the network. As a design choice, it ensures that every node (or actor) is always having access to the whole ledger and all its encompassing transaction data. This ensures the transparency of all transactions. This feature also comes at a price. Decentrality puts a limit on the scalability of digital governance solution. For example, Bitcoin technology is said to require with 61,76 terawatt-hours per year, approximately 0.28% of total global electricity consumption. This is as much electricity as if Bitcoin were the 41st most-energy-demanding nation on the planet.[20] If a governance solution is indeed to be implemented on a larger scale, it requires that the norms can be broadly disseminated through the means of their execution. By extension, power consumption as in the case of Bitcoin technology inherently limits the possibilities of its deployment. Scalability becomes a factor in blockchain's utility as a governance instrument. Also, as a design choice, decentrality is a feature that, given is costly nature in terms of scalability, needs to be looked at in terms of whether it is actually necessary.[21]

With decentrality also comes transparency. Blockchain is often termed the "trust machine".[22] At the same time, it is called a trustless system, or a system were trust is built in. Let us put the term "trust" that the designers of blockchain technology had in mind to the test with a simple thought experiment. Person A tells his partner B that he is going shopping. B the replies that she trusts A fully. Applying the logic of transparency as trust, B proceeds by installing an app on A's phone to follow his every footstep. The question is, does this measure inspire trust in either A or B? In other words, the definition of "trust" used by blockchain software engineers seems to be entirely different than the common use of the term "trust". Trust and transparency cannot be equalized. If transparency is required, it is a symptom that trust is lacking. Real trust can only be tested if one of the partners of a contract or agreement has faith in the honesty of action of the other party. Full and enforced transparency as a

[18]Hsieh et al. (2018).

[19]Karlstrøm (2014).

[20]McCarthy N Bitcoin Devours More Electricity Than Switzerland [Infographic]. In: Forbes. https://www.forbes.com/sites/niallmccarthy/2019/07/08/bitcoin-devours-more-electricity-than-switzerland-infographic/.

[21]Zwitter and Boisse-Despiaux (2018).

[22]The trust machine. The Economist, www.economist.com/leaders/2015/10/31/the-trust-machine.

governance tool, thereby, potentially erodes trust. The governance effect of trustlessness is a reduction of trust for the benefit of transparency.

Immutability in the blockchain is achieved by cryptographically looking each transaction together with the previous transaction. Thereby, no previous transaction can be altered without breaking the cryptographic chain with all subsequent transactions. This makes the blockchain underline, for example, bitcoin technology and other similar technologies temper-proof. Imagine the deployment of blockchain technology in data associated with digital identity. Illegal actions surrounding personhood would permanently be on somebody's record. This would also mean that if somebody who has been falsely convicted for a crime or somebody who has served his time for the crime has a permanent and undeletable stain on her record. In most Western legal systems, a crime for which a sentence has been served cannot be held against the person. With an immutable ledger, this legal principle might be reduced to mere lip service. Also, while blockchain technology might work perfectly and might be completely tamper proof, humans are still susceptible of making errors and adding wrong information. Since such information cannot be deleted from the blockchain, the ledger becomes an immutable record of our past mistakes.

Having analyzed the underlying principles of blockchain technology as for example deployed with bitcoin technology, it becomes very clear that by implementing blockchain technology we are implicitly introducing new governance principles. "Code is Law" applies in particular to blockchain technology as so many of its design features were created with specific behavior regulating principles in mind. Extending this argument even further, almost all technologies which implicitly follow certain governance-relevant norms introduce these into the daily lives of their user-base. Thereby, these new technologies become carriers of new implicit norms that can cause frictions with existent norms of the applicable legal system of the user.

Taking the conclusion seriously that technologies, such as blockchain and digital ledger technology, impose concrete norms on its users would require the regulator to take certain measures. Most importantly, a government or any regulator that is concerned about the functioning of its normative framework would want to check the compatibility of newly introduced technologies and their underlying norms with its existent laws and principles. Furthermore, the regulator might come to the conclusion that a newly introduced technology will have concrete governance effects that deviate materially from the existent normative and legal framework. In this case the regulator will have to submit the normative and legal consequences of the new technology for approval to the legislator and/or for policy approval to the executive. In essence, new technologies, particularly such that introduced new governance principles, need to be treated like newly introduced laws and/or contracts.

5 Conclusion

Technologies and their inherent design choices create normative structures that affect governance. This chapter aims to illustrate how blockchain technology in particular introduces new norms into a legal framework. We first analyzed the different forms of governance by distinguishing between old and new governance. Both old and new governance represent traditional views on governance that do not take into consideration Cyberspace as a medium that affects the real world in a quite fundamental manner. Furthermore, we introduced Cyber-governance as a form of governance that would, in addition to traditional governance objects and mechanisms, also accept entities that inhabits to digital domain. Of particular note are digital entities such as autonomous software like bots and viruses. Data and machine learning need to be added as resource and means of production. Finally, we supplemented traditional governance by new forms of governance mechanisms, such as code and terms of use. Cyber-governance departs from the assumption that territoriality and individual agency are fundamental pillars of governance mechanisms.

With a view to code that functions as legal norms, Blockchain technology is particularly suited to create governance structures and mechanisms. However, one needs to be aware of the norms that are implicitly introduced into the legal system by a specific blockchain technology. We have looked at the blockchain technology that underlies cryptocurrencies such as Bitcoin. This blockchain introduces a decentralized, transparent, cryptographically locked and thus immutable shared ledger. All these adjectives are design choices that have normative effect on its users, as described above. In summary, design choices have normative powers over the user and over user interaction. If this is indeed the case, then regulators have to actively assess newly introduced digital ledger technology and other technologies for their effect on the normative and legal system.

With the advancements of technology, particularly in the field of machine learning and artificial intelligence, the normative powers of technology will increasingly cause frictions with the legal system in which they are embedded. These frictions are bound to become bigger the more invasive these technologies become and the more they determine user interaction and decision making. This in part has to do with an increasing awareness of software engineers regarding their ethical and legal responsibilities and the governance power they can or need to exert through design choices. The solution is not that software engineers should become lawyers, but that lawyers should become more aware and active in the technological domain.

We need to see technologies as tools that have effects on our governance structures. The more technologies with normative effects are being introduced into a legal framework, the more this framework changes. Blockchain technology and other similar technologies can be the future of "smart law". But they need to be applied in a targeted manner. Else, we will be living with laws comprised of code inaccessible to our legal understanding or influence.

References

Ali A, Qadir J, ur Rasool R et al (2016) Big data for development: applications and techniques. Big Data Anal 1:1–24. https://doi.org/10.1186/s41044-016-0002-4

Bevir M (2010) Democratic governance. Princeton University Press, New Jersey

Bevir M (2013) A theory of governance. University of California Press, Berkeley

Börzel TA, Risse T (2010) Governance without a state: can it work? Regul Gov 4:113–134

Colombi-Ciacchi A (2014) Judicial Governance in private law through the application of fundamental rights. Austrian Law J 1:120–134

Hazenberg JLJ, Zwitter A (2017) Network governance im big data- und Cyber-Zeitalter. Zeitschrift für Evangelische Ethik 61:184–209. https://doi.org/10.14315/zee-2017-0305

Hsieh Y-Y, Vergne J-P, Anderson P et al (2018) Bitcoin and the rise of decentralized autonomous organizations. J Org Design 7:14. https://doi.org/10.1186/s41469-018-0038-1

Karlstrøm H (2014) Do libertarians dream of electric coins? The material embeddedness of Bitcoin. Distinktion J Soc Theory 15:23–36. https://doi.org/10.1080/1600910X.2013.870083

Kooiman J (2003) Governing as governance. SAGE, London

Lessig L (1999) Code and other laws of cyberspace. Basic books, New York

Lessig L (2000) Code is law. On liberty in cyberspace. Harvard magazine

Levi-Faur D (2012) From 'Big Government' to 'Big Governance'? In: Levi-Faur D (ed) The Oxford handbook of governance. Oxford University Press, Oxford, pp 3–18

Lobel O (2012) New governance as regulatory governance. In: Levi-Faur D (ed) The Oxford handbook of governance. Oxford University Press, Oxford, pp 65–82

Majone G (2001) Nonmajoritarian institutions and the limits of democratic governance: a political transaction-cost approach. J Inst Theor Econ 157:57–78

Mayntz R (2003) From government to governance: political steering in modern societies. Summer Academy on IPP, pp 7–11

McGuffin C, Mitchell P (2014) On domains: cyber and the practice of warfare. Int J 69:394–412

Nakamoto S (2008) Bitcoin: a peer-to-peer electronic cash system. www.cryptovest.co.uk

Qadir J, Ali A, ur Rasool R et al (2016) Crisis analytics: big data-driven crisis response. J Int Hum Action 1:12. https://doi.org/10.1186/s41018-016-0013-9

Rhodes RAW (1996) The new governance: governing without government. Pol Stud 44:652–667

Rhodes RAW (1997) Understanding governance: policy networks, governance, reflexivity, and accountability. Open University Press, Philadelphia

Swartz L (2018) What was Bitcoin, what will it be? The techno-economic imaginaries of a new money technology. Cult Stud 32:623–650. https://doi.org/10.1080/09502386.2017.1416420

Van Kersbergen K, Van Waarden F (2004) 'Governance' as a bridge between disciplines: cross-disciplinary inspiration regarding shifts in governance and problems of governability, accountability and legitimacy. Eur J Polit Res 43(2):143–171

Zwitter A (2015) Big data and international relations. Ethics Int Aff 29:377–389. https://doi.org/10.1017/S0892679415000362

Zwitter A (2016) Wer haftet für künstliche Intelligenz, wenn sie Mist baut? Süddeutsche Zeitung, www.sueddeutsche.de/digital/serie-kuenstliche-intelligenz-wie-ein-hund-1.2854646

Zwitter A, Boisse-Despiaux M (2018) Blockchain for humanitarian action and development aid. J Int Hum Action 3:16. https://doi.org/10.1186/s41018-018-0044-5

Blockchain: The Regulatory Challenges for Central Banks and Financial Sector

Gino Giambelluca

Contents

1 Introduction

Why is important for financial authorities to deal with the digital innovation? The main reason is that the digitalization in finance has a direct impact on their statutory objectives: the efficiency and the reliability of payment systems, the smooth functioning of financial market infrastructures, the soundness of the intermediaries, the consumer protection.

Fintech, cyber security, blockchain, e-identity, among the others, are issues more and more in the agenda of the authorities at international and domestic level. In the recent past the financial relationships were basically bilateral. There was from one side a financial intermediary offering its services and on the other side the customer. The new business models of the digitalization, the sharing economy, new technologies like DLT and blockchain broke this paradigm, making the financial ecosystem more complex and fragmented: in many cases it is difficult for both customers and supervisors to understand who is really responsible and for what in the financial chain.

The opinion expressed in this publication are those of the Author. They do not purport to reflect the opinions or views of Banca d'Italia.

G. Giambelluca (✉)
Banca d'Italia, Rome, Italy
e-mail: Gino.Giambelluca@bancaditalia.it

B. Cappiello, G. Carullo (eds.), *Blockchain, Law and Governance*,
https://doi.org/10.1007/978-3-030-52722-8_7

The task of financial authorities today, in front of this revolution, is to maintain the confidence of users and all stakeholders in financial services. This is not an easy task: they have to manage the trade off between innovation on one hand and security on the other. They have to gain the capacity to look beyond the traditional players, not only in financial field, improving their knowledge of new phenomenon and technologies.

More than in the past regulators should resort to high-level principles, soft laws and secondary regulation, easier to change and more suitable to be time to market. But a clear and modern regulatory framework is not enough: authorities are required to improve the cooperation with other institutions—cross-board and cross-sector—and have set-up an open dialogue with the market through innovative methods: innovation hubs, sand-boxes, fintech channels are just an example. Blockchain and its applications in the financial world are also a field of experimentation for this new approach.

2 Blockchain and the Financial Sector: Risks and Opportunities of Stablecoins

The most promising use cases of blockchain in financial sector are concentrated in the field of payments; this technology can trigger a deep transformation of interbank payments, international transactions, remittances, clearing and settlement services, in addition to enabling the creation of new forms of virtual currency. Use of blockchain in payments has several advantages: reduction of complexity, real-time transfer of funds, high transparency, network resilience and other benefits linked to the distributed functions on the chain. Many of the features of the blockchain are in line with the objectives of payment oversight performed by central banks: regular operation, reliability, efficiency, protection of payment services users.

But risks and uncertainties must also be considered. Operational security issues have not yet fully explored. Lack of interoperability among the chains, between the new and the traditional environments, and limits in scalability of the infrastructure should also be taken into account. From a legal perspective, the governance, the legal foundation of the infrastructure, anonymity as well as data protection issues can raise many concerns.

Nowadays, financial authorities are trying to apply their supervision methodologies to analyze and to assess payment infrastructures and applications based on blockchain technologies. The starting point can only be the Principles for Financial Market Infrastructures (PFMI),[1] adopted by financial authorities as an international standard for the supervision of payment systems. Some of the principles, e.g. those related to the legal basis, the governance, the settlement finality, the operational

[1]Bank for International Settlements - Committee on Payment and Settlement Systems, *Principles for Financial Market Infrastructures*, April 2012.

risks, can be applied case by case considering the characteristics of each blockchain infrastructure.[2]

Another example of the regulators' approach is the position taken on the stablecoin initiatives like Libra, recently announced by Facebook. The report of the G7 working group[3] describes risks and opportunities associated to the development of stablecoins initiatives at global level and highlights the challenges and the initiatives to be launched in order to fill the regulatory gaps.

As regard the opportunities, it is recognized that stablecoins initiatives may foster efficiency in international payments. Nowadays it is not so easy to set up international payment schemes because of the number of intermediaries involved, the technical, economic and political and economic constraints. Stablecoins may also help financial inclusion, as long as they can allow people who don't have a payment account to manage more easily their payments.

On the other hand, financial authorities are concerned by the challenges and the risks for public policies and regulations.

3 Guiding Principles in Regulating Stablecoins

Many issues shall be addressed related to legal uncertainty, governance, financial integrity, safety of payments, cyber risks, data protection, consumer and investor protection. Moreover, in the long term impacts on monetary policy and financial stability should be considered.

A well founded, clear and transparent legal basis is one of the prerequisite for any stablecoin arrangement. This is important to ensure the trust of the user in the stablecoin schemes. For instance, it's very important to establish if a stablecoin is a money equivalent or is a property right or is a contractor claim. If a stable coins entails a right against the issuer or against the underlying assets.

Specific issues are related to the cross jurisdictional nature of some stablecoin arrangements, in particular of the global ones: it is fundamental to understand what is the law applicable, what is the competent court in case of claims.

A sound governance is another important condition of any payment scheme or infrastructure. It is important to understand what are roles and responsibilities of each actor involved, what is the risk posed to the payment system of the intervention in the scheme of different subjects, from IT players to third party providers, from credit cards circuits or other financial actors.

The application of highest standards of anti-money laundering (AML) is crucial to ensure the integrity of any virtual currency initiative, including stablecoins. AML

[2]An analytical framework to adapt PFMI to clearing and settlement system based on DLT, is provided by Bank for International Settlements - Committee on Payments and Market Infrastructures, *Distributed ledger technology in payment, clearing and settlement*, February 2017.

[3]G7 Working Group on Stablecoins, *Investigating the impact of global stablecoins*, October 2019.

authorities have recently amended their standards to include the virtual asset transactions,[4] looking for applying AML requirements to virtual asset service providers; in stablecoin schemes based on peer to peer transactions, without the intervention of an intermediary, the application of AML controls is an open issue to be solved.

According to the principle "same business, same risk, same rule", stablecoin initiatives shall be in line with the best international standards aiming at ensuring the safety of payment systems, like the PFMIs mentioned above. Cyber risk is another important point. In recent years financial regulators enhanced their efforts to define a new framework of principles dedicated to cyber security.[5] These principles should be taken into account even in blockchain initiatives, since not all the risks have yet been deeply studied and analyzed.

Last but not least, data protection issues are very sensitives for final users, especially in those initiatives promoted by biggest internet players.

The final part of the G7 report is dedicated to the regulatory framework potentially applicable to stablecoin initiatives. There are already a number of standards and recommendations that may fit with stablecoins schemes, as mentioned above. Many of these are already applicable at international level, but others are not harmonized, like for example the electronic money regulation in Europe. This is the reason why the G7 gave the mandate to the Financial Stability Board to assess which are the regulatory gaps that we have in the field of stable coin and virtual assets and on this basis to adopt, as much as possible, a common approach at the international level.

The final message of G7 financial authorities is that no global stablecoin project should become operational until all the open issues, legal, regulatory and oversight, are adequately addressed.

4 Conclusion

In conclusion, the challenge for authorities in blockchain is like the solution of the Rubrik's cube. They have to find the right balance between multiple dimensions, geographical (national, European and international level) and sectorial (financial vs cross-sector approach). They have also to calibrate their instruments of intervention: not only regulation, but new instruments as well, like cooperation and an open dialogue with all the actors. The final objective is the set-up of a sound ecosystem to foster a sustainable development of digitalization in financial sector.

---

[4]Financial Action Task Force, FATF, *Guidance for a Risk-Based Approach to Virtual Assets and Virtual Asset Service Providers*, June 2019.

[5]CPMI-IOSCO, *Guidance on cyber resilience for financial market infrastructures*, June 2016.

Blockchain-Based Financial Investments and the Role of Regulatory Authorities: The Italian Perspective

Martina Tambucci

Contents

1 Introduction

CONSOB is the national Authority controlling the Italian regulatory market.[1] The role of all type of gatekeepers, such as CONSOB, has indeed being challenged by the advent of distributed ledger technologies (such as the blockchain technology) and the real revolution that these carry. The main feature of a DLT is that it allows the exchange of any type of digital data on a peer-to-peer basis, in the absence of a central entity responsible for the functioning of the whole system. Accordingly, C ONSOB is been playing a pivotal role in qualifying and regulating new financial investments taking the form of so-called tokens developed through new technologies (such as Distributed ledger technology, and blockchain).

The opinion expressed in this publication are those of the Author. They do not purport to reflect the opinions or views of Banca d'Italia.

[1]Consob is the Italian securities regulator, established pursuant to the Law No. 216 of 7 June 1974.

M. Tambucci (✉)
CONSOB, Rome, Italy
e-mail: m.tambucci@consob.it

B. Cappiello, G. Carullo (eds.), *Blockchain, Law and Governance*,
https://doi.org/10.1007/978-3-030-52722-8_8

2 The Italian Normative Framework on DLTs

As regards the Italian normative framework, since 2018 the decree law number 135/2018[2] established a legal definition of DLT. The main elements of this definition are: *(i)* the existence of a ledger which is characterized by being shared, distributed, replicable, accessible simultaneously, architecturally decentralized on a cryptographic basis; *(ii)* the purpose of such ledger is to provide for the recording, validation, update and storage of data with the possibility of verifiability by any participant in the technology; *(iii)* the data remains inalterable and not modifiable.

The decree law also established the legal effects of the Distributed ledger technology (DLT) at national level, making-reference to the EU Regulation on the electronic identification:[3] the use of the DLT is considered as the electronic timestamp in accordance with the mentioned Regulation.

The spreading use of DLT type of technologies give rise to opportunities as well as risks. As known, blockchain (as an example of such technologies) has the potential to increase efficiency and speed for transactions and to reduce the cost of many processes. This is due to its main characteristics such as: decentralization, immutability of data recorded, which in turn implies high security, and transparency, as all the participants share the same information; but, as anticipated, there are also risks in using this new technology that need to be tackled.

In this regard, it is worth referring to the so-called blockchain trilemma which states that it is always possible to achieve the three main attributes of scalability, security and decentralization but at the expense of others, which means—in other words—that it's impossible to maximize all the three properties at the same time. And this is indeed the limit of the blockchain.

Following this premise, the reminder is focused on an analysis of the possible use of this new type of technologies in the finance sector. In order to conduct the analysis, it is useful to unbundle the different phases within the value chain since the issuance of a financial instrument until the so called servicing. This latter refers to, for instance, the know your customer processes as well as the management of corporate actions in connection to financial instruments.

3 The ICOs Phenomenon

The first and most prominent use of DLT has been recorded in the payment and settlement industry. This is probably due to the circumstance that the so-called straight through-processing as a way of organising the business, whose behind logics

[2]Converted into the Law No. 12 of 11 February 2019 (published on the Gazzetta Ufficiale - Serie generale - n. 36 of 12 February 2019.

[3]Regulation (EU) No 910/2014 of the European Parliament and of the Council of 23 July 2014 on electronic identification and trust services for electronic transactions in the internal market.

resemble that of DLT, started to be employed in that context and became typical of the sector. STP is used by financial companies to speed up their transaction processing time and is based on the idea to allow companies to have the same information be streamlined through a process across multiple points.

More recently, a new use of DLT began to spread within the financial sector, that is the phenomenon under the name of Initial Coin Offerings (ICO), which gained great attention by national competent authorities, such as CONSOB and other security regulators.

As regards the ICO nature, there's a definition in the FinTech action plan by the European Commission.[4] In other words, ICOs consist in the massive issuance, by companies and entrepreneurs, of tokens as a tool to raise capital for their projects. Such digital tokens may be used in return for goods or services or securities, commodities or derivatives, depending on the nature of the ICO and the participants' activities.

The FinTech action plan involves both a number of legislations already issued and a number of actions to be taken in the near future. Among them, some represent the most important pieces of legislation having an impact in the context of the blockchain: that concerning cyber security, the regulation above mentioned on the electronic identification, the payment systems directive, the regulation on data protection, and the directives on anti-money laundering. It is interesting to look at the future actions that will be taken at European level and that are part of the mentioned action plan, which includes, *inter alia*, an initial proposal concerning the definition of clear and converging requirements for FinTech companies through the setting of common standards and interoperable solutions. A clear objective is to enable innovative business to scale up across Europe through innovation facilitators as well as to remove obstacles to the use of cloud services.

Besides, there are other interesting aspects of the plan: a study on the feasibility of a blockchain infrastructure at European level (public infrastructure), to develop cross-border services as well as a coherent cyber resilience framework for the European financial sector.

The following data are of help in better grasping the magnitude of the ICO phenomenon: total funds raised by ICOs since 2016 amount to 31.6 billion dollars, 21.6 of which were raised in 2018, while in 2019 total funds raised are around 3.1 billion. Since the final part of 2019, the ICOs phenomenon seems having declined. Possible explanations for that: on the one hand, there is new appetite for stablecoins (a topic that will be dealt with later in the chapter); on the other hand, ICOs might have been curbed by the increasing attention of financial regulators, particularly the U.S. Security and exchange Commission (the SEC).[5] The SEC found most of the

---

[4]Communication from the Commission to the European Parliament, the Council, the European Central Bank, the European Economic and Social Committee and the Committee of the Regions - FinTech Action plan: For a more competitive and innovative European financial sector - Brussels, 8.3.2018; COM(2018) 109 final.

[5]The U.S. Securities and Exchange Commission (SEC) is an independent agency of the United States federal government. The SEC holds primary responsibility for enforcing the federal securities

ICOs launched in the U.S. as no compliant with the rules on the offering of securities. And this has definitely represented a deterrent.

4 The Role and the Initiatives of CONSOB and of Other Security Regulators

Given the above context, it is important to understand the role of CONSOB and, more generally, of all security regulators. First, it has been the ordinary activity of enforcement that has triggered the CONSOB attention on the phenomenon. The Togacoin case that CONSOB investigated in the past is an example (the details are publicly available on CONSOB website).[6] Other cases are mostly frauds. Some of them have been qualified as offers of financial products and in that case, they have been subjected to the applicable discipline at national level.

CONSOB has also provided its cooperation to ESMA[7] in the analysis of ICOs and crypto assets to the benefit of the European Commission. The advice of January 2019 by ESMA[8] to the European Commission is primary focused on the difficulties in applying the disciplines of the financial sector to crypto assets. Moreover, the advice provides a synthesis of the issues regarding the treatment of crypto assets that are not financial instruments.

Besides, CONSOB has also conducted a number of studies on FinTech in collaboration with some Italian Universities. The relevant research papers are published on the CONSOB website. These deal with topics such as: the development of FinTech, the data economy, the digitalisation of the investment advice service, Financial Data Aggregation and Account Information Services, the marketplace lending and the robo-advice.[9]

In March 2019 CONSOB published a call for evidence where it is put forward an ideal regulatory approach for ICOs and exchange systems of crypto assets.[10] On May 2019, Consob also managed a public hearing at the Bocconi University to open a debate with the industry on the same issues.

The final outcome of such activities is a concrete proposal that will have to be taken up by the Government to transform into real legislation applicable at national

laws, proposing securities rules, and regulating the securities industry, which is the nation's stock and options exchanges, and other activities and organizations, including the electronic securities markets in the United States.

[6] http://www.consob.it/web/consob-and-its-activities/warnings/documenti/english/entutela/cns/2019/enct20190128.htm.

[7] The European Securities and Markets Authority (ESMA) is a European Union financial regulatory agency and European Supervisory Authority.

[8] https://www.esma.europa.eu/sites/default/files/library/esma50-157-1391_crypto_advice.pdf.

[9] http://www.consob.it/web/area-pubblica/fintech.

[10] On 2 January 2020 the Consob Final Report on ICOs was published; see http://www.consob.it/documents/46180/46181/ICOs_20200102.pdf/cfd5527f-1b49-4937-8ab5-68ae0e2af99f.

level. When starting such exercise, CONSOB has considered as being relevant, first of all, its task to protect investors against frauds, through determining a correct use of technology and through the imposition of transparency targeted requirements. On one side, it might be useful to subject to supervision the promoters of ICOs, for instance by requiring them specific governance requirements as well as an initial authorization for the internal models to conduct the business. It is also possible to work on the system resilience. New platforms are designed and developed to offer new services.[11] From a security regulator standpoint, it is thus necessary to think of a set of requirements to ensure the resilience of such platforms. The discussion paper by CONSOB goes deeper into the subject, though paying much attention not to encroach on the current EU legislation. Accordingly, the scope of the regulatory proposal is limited to crypto assets that are neither financial instruments nor Packaged Retail Investment and Insurance-based investments (PRIIPs) or Packaged Retail investment products (PRIPs) or Insurance-Based Investment product (IBIPs), which are all regulated at the European level. On the contrary, crypto assets that are financial products, according to the national definition within the Consolidated Law on Finance,[12] may be in scope.

There are indeed a number of benefits linked to the desirable entrance-into-force of such a legal framework. A very first benefit would be to avoid both to regulators and market operators to assess, on a case by case basis, when a crypto-asset is to be offered to the public in respect of specific requirements aimed at protecting the investors. Another benefit would be that of avoiding the application of the domestic discipline to financial products taking the form of tokens, which would be too burdensome or not proportionate for the specificities of crypto assets. Besides, there are also some shortcomings. Having a crystallized legal framework at national level might be difficult in a situation where the environment rapidly changes. In order to avoid such rigidity, CONSOB has decided to support a mechanism of opt-in, that will not make the regulation compulsory. As a consequence, ICO promoters can decide to use an ICO platform that is authorized by CONSOB, but they can also decide not to make use of such platform and the offering remains legitimate even if not recognized and regulated by the authority.

The operators of these ICO platforms would be the gatekeepers and would play a crucial role vis-à-vis the authority. They would be tasked with organizational requirements and their principal responsibility would be the appropriate selection of the offers. They will have to comply with conduct rules and to apply standardized transparency to the benefit of investors. Finally, CONSOB also suggests to introduce requirements to ensure technological safety and business continuity.

[11]This phenomenon goes under the name of "platformisation".

[12]According to Article 1, paragraph 1, point u), in the Consolidated Law on Finance (Legislative Decree No, 58 of 24 February 1998) "financial products" shall mean "[...] *every other form of investment of a financial nature* [...]", and financial instruments (that are nonetheless excluded from the scope of the regulatory approach, as said.

Given this, a question arises as regards who might be the operator of a platforms referred to above. These might be operators of crowdfunding platforms already authorized by CONSOB, as well as other duly authorized entities, on condition that they would comply with similar requirements to those applicable to crowdfunding service providers. Following the example of the legislation passed in France for ICOs and Digital Asset Service Providers, operators of the platforms would also benefit, as per the CONSOB proposal, of an opt-in choice. According to the French legislation, if the promoter of an ICO decides not to request the authorization (visa) to the AMF,[13] it is obliged to disclose to investors the absence of an authorization.[14] Providers of broker-dealing services in the context of the ICO are also subjected to a specific discipline in France, including entities managing exchange systems for crypto assets.[15]

As a way to provide additional comparative elements, it is worth mentioning that in the UK the national Authority has been working a lot on the need to frame a regulation, thus developing the first sandbox at European level, as well as an innovation hub, for the use of new technologies. More precisely, with respect to crypto-assets, the UK security regulator (the FCA) has limited itself to issuing detailed guidance setting out the conditions on which basis different types of crypto assets fall in the regulatory perimeter established for financial instruments[16] by the harmonised European rules.

Malta too has enacted a detailed legal framework, according to which operators are first of all required to assess whether tokens are virtual tokens.[17] In that case, the financial services regulation is not applicable. As a second step, they will have to assess whether tokens different from virtual tokens correspond to the qualification of financial instruments provided for by the Markets in financial instruments directive

---

[13]The Autorité des marchés financiers (AMF) is the securities regulator in France.

[14]Refer to the applicable law and AMF regulation and guidance at: (i) https://www.legifrance.gouv.fr/affichCode.do;jsessionid=7FDC2C8700672159BC437A4252949B5B.tplgfr44s_2?idSectionTA=LEGISCTA000038509541&cidTexte=LEGITEXT000006072026&dateTexte=20191123; (ii) https://reglement-general.amf-france.org/eli/fr/aai/amf/rg/livre/7/titre/1/20200426/notes/fr.html; (iii) https://www.amf-france.org/fr/espace-professionnels/fintech/mes-relations-avec-lamf/obtenir-un-visa-pour-une-ico.

[15]Refer to the applicable law and AMF regulation and guidance at: (i) https://www.legifrance.gouv.fr/affichCode.do;jsessionid=615D63451152DC31A264074FA513B3CF.tplgfr44s_2?idSectionTA=LEGISCTA000039408732&cidTexte=LEGITEXT000006072026&dateTexte=20191123; (ii) https://reglement-general.amf-france.org/eli/fr/aai/amf/rg/livre/7/titre/2/20200426/notes/fr.html; (iii) https://www.amf-france.org/fr/actualites-publications/actualites/prestataires-de-services-sur-actifs-numeriques-le-dispositif-pacte-en-detail.

[16]Guidance on Cryptoassets, Policy Statement PS19/22, UK Financial Conduct Authority, July 2019.

[17]The Virtual Financial Assets Act, Chapter 590 of the Laws of Malta (the VFA Act), the Innovative Technology Arrangements and Services Act, Cap 592 of the Laws of Malta (ITASA), and the Malta Digital Innovation Authority Act, Cap 591 of the Laws of Malta (the MDIA Act), published in 2018.

(MiFID) issued by the European Commission.[18] In case of positive answer, the MiFID discipline kicks in. As a second step, in case tokens are not included in the other two categories, operators have to assess whether they can be considered virtual financial assets. In this case, a tailor-made discipline would apply. To define it, Maltese authorities took into consideration the most important harmonizing legislations at European level (notably on prospectus, market abuse and services in financial instruments) and, on that basis, they elaborated a specific discipline applicable to virtual financial assets.

In the document published by CONSOB there is also a proposal specifically concerning the exchange systems of crypto-assets; again, this is dealt with in terms of opt-in, because it would be up to the operators of such exchanges to decide whether or not to require to be registered by CONSOB and be consequently supervised by the authority.

The operators of such systems could be: the operators of the trading venues which have been already authorized, the operators of crowdfunding platforms and the operators that manage ICOs' platforms and other entities that meet the criteria that should be laid down by CONSOB (once empowered by the level one legislation). The opt-in mechanism, in this case, is based on the possible incentives for operators of such exchanges to ask for registration by CONSOB, which would in turn allow to acquire a quality label with a clear signalling function for investors.

Lastly, in the Final Report published by CONSOB on 2 January 2020,[19] leveraging on many comments submitted by respondents to the public consultation, another category of operators was identified, as those dealing with the custodial services of crypto assets and the settlement of transactions involving the transfer of the ownership of crypto assets. This category, named as digital wallet service providers, is subject to similar rules that would be applicable to operators of exchanges, but targeted to the risks involved by the specific activities carried out. They would also be subject to an initial authorisation and on-going supervision by CONSOB if voluntarily entering the regulated space (opt-in).

5 Stablecoins

To conclude, it is just briefly mentioned the very recent trend of diffusion of so called stablecoins, which, according to a mainstream definition, are a new class of cryptocurrencies that attempt to offer price stability and are backed by a reserve asset. They have jeopardized the debate since the launch of Libra initiative. Given this, one might wonder why stablecoins raise much more appetite compared to that

[18]Reference is made to Directive 2014/65/EU of the European Parliament and of the Council of 15 May 2014 on markets in financial instruments.

[19]http://www.consob.it/documents/46180/46181/ICOs_20200102.pdf/cfd5527f-1b49-4937-8ab5-68ae0e2af99f.

raised by the existing and reknown crypto-currencies (e.g. ether, bitcoin). The first plausible answer is concerned with one of the peculiarities of the latter: crypto-currencies have so far proved to be highly volatile. Contrarily, the idea behind stablecoins—even if they share many features of the other crypto-currencies—is to stabilize the price of the coin by linking its value to a pool of underlying assets.

As such, stablecoins might be more capable of serving as means of payment and storage of value. They could potentially contribute to the development of global payment arrangements, thus threatening the existing legal currencies. Stablecoins have the potential to reduce the efficacy of monetary policies, posing risks for the international monetary system as a whole, as well as threatening the financial stability. Besides, stablecoins create problems in terms of an appropriate detection of money laundering and they are risky also in terms of fair competition. These are the reasons why standard and policy setters are debating stablecoins at length. Just to mention some: the Financial Stability Board, the Financial Action Task Force, which is tasked with anti-money laundering function, and the G7 and G20 as well.

Are VAT Rules Really Inadequate for Distributed Ledger Technology's Transactions?

Michele Ferrari

Contents

1 The Scope of the Chapter

The use of virtual currencies and tokens has dramatically risen recently and regulations in force could appear to do not be able to follow the technology's path. However, when it is time to consider the tax treatment of transactions involving Distributed Ledger Technologies (DLT), it is necessary to refer to existing

M. Ferrari (✉)
Avvocato, Milan, Italy

B. Cappiello, G. Carullo (eds.), *Blockchain, Law and Governance*,
https://doi.org/10.1007/978-3-030-52722-8_9

provisions, case-law and principles of law, as well as to the nature of the activities, the status of the parties involved and the specific facts and circumstances of the case.

In particular, in the present chapter, few Value Added Tax (VAT) implications related to DLT will be analysed, assuming that the transactions are carried out in the European Union (EU). To this extent, it cannot do without referring to the directive 2006/112/EC (VAT Directive), the VAT principles as meant by the case law of the Court of Justice of the European Union (ECJ), the official documents published by the European Commission and by the Tax Revenues of some States.

Thoroughly, when approaching a new topic (as DLT), it should be asked whether: the transaction developed on a blockchain is either a supply of good[1] or a supply of service for consideration;[2] the supply falls within any VAT exemption laid down in the VAT Directive;[3] the supplier is a taxable person.[4] Last but not the least, where the supply is taxable.[5]

---

[1]Article 14 VAT Directive provides that a supply of good shall mean the transfer of the right to dispose of tangible property as owner.

[2]Supply of service is defined in Article 25 VAT Directive on a residual basis and means any transaction which does not constitute a supply of goods. As regards determining whether a supply of services is affected for consideration, the ECJ recalled that it is settled case law that the concept of the "*supply of service effected for consideration*" requires the existence of a direct link between the service provided and the consideration received, see *Bastova*, C- 432/15 and Terra and Kajus (2017).

[3]It is settled case law that VAT exemptions shall be strictly interpreted as exceptions to the general principle according to which VAT is to be levied on supplies, see *Nordea*, C-350/10.

[4]According to Article 9 of VAT Directive a taxable person is anyone, wherever in the world, who performs economic activities whatever the purpose or result, not acting as final consumer. The exploitation of tangible or intangible property for the purposes of obtaining income therefrom on a continuing basis shall in particular be regarded as an economic activity.

[5]In this latter case, territoriality rules will be subject to the qualification given to the supply—good or service—and to the persons involved—taxable persons and/or final consumers. As it is known, in a supply of goods the place of supply depends whether the goods are dispatched/transported or not. If the goods are not dispatched/transported, the place of supply shall be the place where the goods are located at the time when the supply takes place (Article 31 VAT Directive); if the goods are dispatched or transported, the place of supply shall be the place where the goods are located at the time when dispatch or transport of the goods to the customer begins (Article 32 VAT Directive). As well as, in the supply of services, the place of supply depends whether the supply is between taxable persons (B2B) or between a taxable person and a consumer (B2C). In the former (B2B), the place of supply shall be where the receiver has established his business (Article 44 VAT Directive); in the latter (B2C), the place of supply shall be where the supplier has established his business (Article 45 VAT Directive).

Furthermore, it should be taken into consideration that the general rules could be subject to exceptions. For instance, the VAT Directive provides that in certain circumstances the place of supply could be where the consumer has his permanent address or usually resides (as the case may be with supply of electronic services to non-taxable persons provided by Article 58 VAT Directive).

Finally, it should be also considered that European Union is changing the territoriality rules, where the final scope is to tax the supply of goods and services in the place where they are consumed (see *Towards a single EU VAT area - Time to act*: COM(2017) 566 final and COM (2017) 567 of European Commission). In this way, the VAT would be declared and collected in the Member State where the supplier is established (via a one-stop-shop mechanism). This will entail that taxation would cover all cross-border supplies of goods and services (and therefore the supplier,

Given the above, in the following paragraphs, firstly there will be an overview on bitcoins transaction's VAT treatment (*i.e.* any cryptocurrencies) given by the VAT Committee of the European Commission (VAT Committee) and the ECJ; secondly it will follow the VAT implications underlying the DLT's transactions and the experience of some States.

2 Background on Cryptocurrency's VAT Treatment: The European Perspective

Official discussion on cryptocurrency's legal status and VAT treatment at EU levels started in 2014, when the UK delegation asked the VAT Committee to discuss the qualification of bitcoins.

In particular, during the 101st meeting of the VAT Committee,[6] bitcoin was defined as an unregulated decentralized peer-to peer form of digital private money, which can be exchanged for goods or services (where accepted) or traded in its own right.

In order to qualify the VAT treatment of bitcoin, the VAT Committee focused the analysis on the following possible legal status:

- electronic money,[7]
- currency,[8]
- negotiable instrument,[9]

---

and not the customer, would be liable for the VAT on all goods and services purchased from other Member States) so that all supplies of goods and services within the single market, either domestic or cross-border, will be treated the same way.

[6]Working paper No. 811, 29 July 2014.

[7]According to the VAT Committee bitcoin should be distinguished from electronic money, as defined by Article 2 of Directive 2009/110/EC: "*electronically, including magnetically, stored monetary value as represented by a claim on the issuer which is issued on receipt of funds for the purpose of making payment transactions*". According to Article 1(1) of that same directive, only certain categories of electronic money issuers are recognized, mainly credit institutions, electronic money institutions, post office giro-institutions, the ECB and national central banks, and Member States or their regional or local authorities under certain conditions. It seems that in electronic money schemes, the link with traditional money forms is preserved. The VAT Committee referred that no Member State has expressed a view which envisages the option of treating bitcoins as electronic money.

[8]Considering the functions of traditional currencies outlined by the European Central Bank (ECB) (see http://www.ecb.europa.eu/pub/pdf/other/virtualcurrencyschemes201210en.pdf – p. 10), the VAT Committee concluded that bitcoins could not be considered a currency due to the lack of supervision, potential technical problems and high volatility.

[9]It would imply the applicability of Article 135(1)(d) of the VAT Directive, whereby Member States shall exempt "*transactions, including negotiation, concerning deposit and current accounts, payments, transfers, debts, cheques, and other negotiable instruments, but excluding debt collection*". The VAT Committee concluded that, although bitcoins could fall within the meaning of "*other negotiable instruments*" certain concerns may arise as regards negotiability of bitcoin. In this

– a security,[10]
– a voucher[11] or
– a digital product.[12]

Subsequently, during the 104th meeting the VAT Committee[13] focused the analysis on the possibility to consider bitcoin either as *(i)* a negotiable instrument, or *(ii)* a digital product.

Finally, on 22 October 2015 ECJ[14] held that "*bitcoin virtual currency* [...] *cannot be characterised as 'tangible property' within the meaning of Article 14 of the VAT Directive, given that, as the Advocate General has observed in point 17 of her Opinion, that virtual currency has no purpose other than to be a means of payment*"[15] and that "*the transactions at issue in the main proceedings, which consist of the exchange of different means of payment, do not fall within the*

---

respect, the VAT Committee outlined that according to the opinion of the Advocate General (AG) in *Granton Advertising* (C-462/12), "*other negotiable instruments*" shall be seen as instruments which confer the right to claim a sum of money. Bitcoin can be exchanged for currency only to the extent that another private party is willing to buy them on an exchange or in a peer-to-peer transaction.

[10]It would imply the applicability of Article 135 (1)(f) of the VAT Directive, whereby Member States shall exempt "*transactions, including negotiation but not management or safekeeping, in shares, interests in companies or associations, debentures and other securities, but excluding documents establishing title to goods, and the rights or securities referred to in Article 15(2)*". According to the VAT Committee, the holder of bitcoin neither has any rights of ownership against the bitcoin organization nor has any claims against any company or organization, nor any similar right, Lambooij (2014).

[11]At the time of the Working paper was drafted, VAT treatment of vouchers was not harmonized at EU level. Since 1 January 2019 the Voucher Directive (2016/1065/EC) has been implemented (see Working paper No. 983/2019). According to the VAT Committee it is difficult to treat bitcoin as a voucher for VAT purposes. Indeed, bitcoin does not embed the obligation for the supplier to provide goods or services in exchange.

[12]In this respect, Article 7(1) of the VAT Implementing Regulation states that: "*electronically supplied services as referred to in Directive 2006/112/EC shall include services which are delivered over the Internet or an electronic network and the nature of which renders their supply essentially automated and involving minimal human intervention, and impossible to ensure in the absence of information technology*". Also, Article 7(2)(c) considers "*services automatically generated from a computer via the Internet or an electronic network, in response to specific data input by the recipient*" to be an electronically supplied service.

Due to its digital character, bitcoin could fall within the definition of electronically supplied services. Indeed, bitcoin is delivered over the Internet or an electronic network, and it is generated from a computer via the Internet or an electronic network in response to specific data input by the recipient. However, in the VAT Committee's view, while it is undoubtedly so that bitcoin is transferred electronically, the question is whether there is a supply of services, in the terms of the VAT Directive. Notably, the classification of transfers in bitcoin as supplies of services may be controversial in cases where its functioning and purpose is equal to that of a means of payment because for VAT purposes payments are not consumption but measure the consumption (see section 3.1.6, Working paper No. 811/2014).

[13]Working paper No. 854, 30 April 2015.

[14]*Skatterveket v. David Hedqvist*, C-264/14 (*Hedqvist*).

[15]Para. 24 *Hedqvist*.

concept of the 'supply of goods', laid down in Article14 of the directive. In those circumstances, those transactions constitute the supply of services, within the meaning of Article 24 of the VAT Directive.

To this extent it is interesting to ponder the analysis carried out by the Advocate General (AG).[16] Notably, it is firstly considered that "*transfer of legal tender as such is accepted as not constituting a chargeable event for VAT purposes.* [...]". Secondly, it is pointed out that "*Currencies currently used as legal tender* [...] *have no other practical use than as a means of payment. Their function in a transaction is simply to facilitate trade in goods in an economy; as such, however, they are not consumed or used as goods*".

Consequently, the AG argued that "*that which applies for legal tender should also apply for other means of payment with no other function than to serve as such. Even though such pure means of payment are not guaranteed and supervised by law, for VAT purposes they perform the same function as legal tender and as such must, in accordance with the principle of fiscal neutrality in the form of the principle of equal treatment, be treated in the same way*".

In the light of the above, the AG concluded that "*they* [bitcoin] *must be treated in the same way as legal tender*".

Furthermore, in order to determine whether the activity of exchange of bitcoin into traditional currencies is subject to the exemptions laid down in Article 135 (1) from d) to f) of VAT Directive, the ECJ held that "*transactions exempt from VAT under those provisions are, by their nature, financial transactions even though they do not necessarily have to be carried out by banks or financial institutions*".[17]

As to Article 135(1)(e),[18] the ECJ deemed that "*transactions involving non-traditional currencies, that is to say, currencies other than those that are legal tender in one or more countries, in so far as those currencies have been accepted by the parties to a transaction as an alternative to legal tender and have no purpose other than to be a means of payment, are financial transactions*".[19] Afterwards, the ECJ concluded that "*it therefore follows from the context and the aims of Article 135(1)(e) that to interpret that provision as including only transactions involving traditional currencies would deprive it of part of its effect*"[20] and that "*in the case in the main proceedings, it is common ground that the 'bitcoin' virtual*

[16]Para. 14–17 AG's Opinion.

[17]Para. 37 *Hedqvist.*

[18]It provides that "*transactions, including negotiation, concerning currency, bank notes and coins used as legal tender, with the exception of collectors' items, that is to say, gold, silver or other metal coins or bank notes which are not normally used as legal tender or coins of numismatic interest*".

[19]Para. 49 *Hedqvist.*

[20]Para. 51 *Hedqvist.*

currency has no other purpose than to be a means of payment and that it is accepted for that purpose by certain operators".[21,22]

In this latter regard it is remarkable to consider the AG's reasoning in relation to scope underlying the exemption provided by Article 135(1)(e). Notably, it is pointed out that "*the exemption is not limited to currencies used within the European Union*" but "*all of the world's currencies are covered by the exemption. It follows that the objective of Article 135(1)(e) of the VAT Directive is to ensure that, in the interests of the smooth flow of payments, the conversion of currencies is as unencumbered as possible. Exempting from VAT the exchange of legal tender for a means of payment which does not have legal status but which nevertheless is a pure means of payment, such as the bitcoins in this case, is in line with this objective. In so far as means of payment exist which are involved in payment transactions because they fulfil the same payment function in the course of trade as legal tender, the levying of VAT on exchanges of such means of payment would constitute an additional burden on payments*".[23]

It seems that according to the ECJ and the AG the analysis of the bitcoin's legal status (*i.e.* as well as of any cryptocurrency) should be carried out by way of a substantial approach. In particular, if cryptocurrencies are accepted by the operators as means of payments, for VAT purposes they would perform the same function as legal tender and thus they should be treated the same way.

Another important aspect outlined by the AG regards the fact that "*the lack of stable value and vulnerability to fraud of bitcoins cannot justify different treatment*". Indeed, "*regardless of whether, depending on the currency, legal tender is also subject to such risks to the same extent, the only place for considerations of this kind is the governmental supervision of the financial markets. VAT is independent of this, however. It is clear from the case-law that even if a practice is prohibited under supervisory law, its assessment for VAT purposes is unaffected.*[24,25]

---

[21]Para. 52 *Hedqvist.*

[22]For sake of completeness, the ECJ deemed that both the exemptions laid down in Article 135(1)(d) and in Article 135(1)(f) of the VAT Directive could be applied.

[23]Para. 39 and 40 AG's Opinion in *Hedqvist.*

[24]Para. 44 AG's Opinion that recalled *GfBk* (C-275/11), para. 32.

[25]For sake of completeness it should be referred to the Opinion rendered by the European Central Bank (ECB) on 12 October 2016—"*on a proposal for a directive of the European Parliament and the Council amending Directive (EU) 2015/849 on the prevention of the use of the financial system for the purpose of money laundering or terrorist financing and amending Directive 2009/101/EC*". In this respect, according to ECB it would be more accurate to regard cryptocurrencies as means of exchange, rather than as means of payment. Moreover, Article 1, lett. d) Directive 2018/843/EU transposed the ECB's opinion and provided that "*virtual currencies means a digital representation of value that is not issued or guaranteed by a central bank or a public authority, is not necessarily attached to a legally established currency and does not possess a legal status of currency or money, but is accepted by natural or legal persons as a means of exchange and which can be transferred, stored and traded electronically*". In this scenario, it should be wonder which is the purpose of such Directive. In particular, if the scope is related to anti-money laundering and countering the financing of terrorism (see eighth whereas), the substantial nature of cryptocurrencies as means of payment

In the light of the ECJ's conclusions the VAT Committee[26] revisited its point of view accepting the fact that neither the qualification of Bitcoins as negotiable instrument nor as digital products have been accepted.

3 VAT Implications on Transaction Under DLT

Given the ECJ's conclusions, in the following paragraphs it will analyse the VAT implications of the: supplies of goods and services remunerated by way of any cryptocurrencies; mining activity; digital wallets operations; and intermediation provided by exchange platforms.

For all the above topics it will be necessary to wonder whether the transaction is relevant for VAT purposes, whether the transaction falls within the exemptions provided by the VAT Directive and the players involved are VAT taxable persons.

3.1 Supplies of Goods and Services Remunerated by Way of Cryptocurrencies

According to Article 73 of VAT Directive "*the taxable amount* [of a supply of goods or services] *shall include everything which constitutes consideration obtained or to be obtained by the supplier, in return for the supply, from the customer or a third party, including subsidies directly linked to the price of the supply*".

Therefore, if cryptocurrencies are a means of payment, likewise any legal tender, and they are the remuneration of supplies of goods and/or services, these latter will fall within the VAT scope. Consequently, VAT will be levied on the consideration paid for the supply (*i.e.* the value of the cryptocurrency[27] when the transaction takes place).

At this point it is clear that a conversion issue could arise. Nonetheless, the existing mechanism laid down by Articles 230 and 91 of VAT Directive for the conversion into Euros—when the taxable amount of a transaction is expressed in a currency other than that of the Member State in which the VAT is due—could be taken into consideration. To this extent it will be possible to: *(i)* use the exchange rate applicable corresponding to the latest selling rate recorded, at the time VAT becomes chargeable, on the most representative exchange market; *(ii)* use the latest exchange rate published by the ECB at the time VAT becomes chargeable.

---

should not be affected by external laws as so affirmed by the AG's Opinion in *Hedqvist* and the recalled ECJ case-law.

[26]Working paper No. 892, 4 February 2016.

[27]Redmar (2014).

Some concerns could still persist when the conversion regards cryptocurrencies inasmuch as the VAT Directive refers to an official exchange market and to official exchange rates.[28,29]

Nevertheless, according to the VAT Committee such concerns could be allayed by Article 72 of VAT Directive where the exchange rate can be the open market value of the cryptocurrency.

3.2 Transactions Underlying the Consensus Mechanism

DLT allows players in the systems (called "nodes") to transact in a peer-to peer network and stores these transactions in a distributed way across the network. Each transaction is to be verified by way of a "consensus mechanism". The traditional one is "proof of work" (PoW) where miners—anonymous and volunteer workers—solve mathematical puzzle to check the transactions. The miner who first solve the problem is rewarded with new cryptocurrencies. The system also allows to leave a "transaction fee" for the miner, like a tip or gratuity left.[30]

An alternative way of validating transactions is "proof of stake" (PoS) where the success of the validation depends on number of cryptocurrencies.[31] The more cryptocurrencies a validator owns, the more likely the validator can validate the transaction. Such activity is rewarded by transaction fees.

At this point it could be argued whether the activity performed by both the miners and the validators are relevant for VAT purposes.

As to miner activities, there is not a clear view.

According to the VAT Committee,[32] it should explore whether miners receive a transaction fee in return of the activity of the mining activity or not.[33]

In particular in the event miners did not receive a transaction fee there would not be any grounds to consider the validation activity under the VAT scope. However, it should be asked if the new cryptocurrencies automatically generated every time that a transaction request is successfully verified could be the reward for the mining activities, bearing in mind that the VAT Directive does not require that the consideration is obtained directly from the person to whom those services are supplied.

[28]In *Regina v. Ernest George Thompson, Brian Albert Johnson and Colin Alex Norman Woodiwiss* (C-7/78) the ECJ observed that, although doubts may be entertained as to the question of whether krugerrands are to be regarded as legal means of payment, it should nevertheless be noted that, on the money markets of those Member States which permit dealings in these coins, krugerrands are treated as being equivalent to currency.

[29]Section 5.2.2 of Working paper No. 892/2016 and Section 3.6 of Working paper No. 854/2015.

[30]Kroll et al. (2013).

[31]Bal (2018a).

[32]Working paper No. 892/2016, Section 5.2.4.

[33]However, if the service is carried out for the miner's private use, the transaction would be treated as a supply of services for consideration according to Article 26(1)(b) of the VAT Directive.

Indeed, according to Article 73 of the VAT Directive the consideration may be obtained from a third party, which could lead to see new cryptocurrencies created by the system as consideration for the miner.

In the event miners received a transaction fee, the VAT Committee deems that it is totally uncertain that the transaction would be taxable pursuant to Article 2(1)(c) of the VAT Directive. In fact, transaction fees are voluntary and are an incentive to make sure that a particular transaction is verified more quickly by the miner. Therefore, transaction fees and the activity performed by miners could somehow be dissociated.

In this perspective, mining activity could be treated outside the VAT scope.

The above conclusion is supported by some academic[34] according to which the VAT relevance will be excluded on the basis of the principle drawn by *Tolsma* case,[35] in so far as there is not any specific customer for the mining activities and the new cryptocurrencies that miners receive, which are automatically generated by the network itself. Thus, there would not be any legal relationship between a provider (miner) and a recipient (consumer) of a service (mining); there would not be any mutual obligation; and then the reward received by the provider would not be the value actually given in return for the service supplied.

So pointed out, a different solution could be found when cryptocurrencies will shrink—as well as the automatic reward that miners receive—and the remunerations derived from each verification would be insufficient to create enough profit for miners, thus any transaction request could be verified by a miner without him receiving a transaction fee. In this scenario, according to the VAT Committee, it would resemble the more traditional exchange of services for consideration. Consequently, there will actually be a direct link between the fee paid by the cryptocurrency user and the verification activity.

As to validator activities, it seems that particular concerns could not arise. In fact, the validation of the transaction is paid with a fee and thus the remuneration would be considered directly linked to the activity thereof.

If the transactions performed by miners and validators felt within the scope of VAT, it would be pertinent to examine whether mining activity were exempt according to Article 135(1) of the VAT Directive, notably points (e) and (d).

In this respect the VAT Committee argued that Article 135(1)(e) of VAT Directive ("*transactions, including negotiation, concerning currency, bank notes and coins used as legal tender, with the exception of collectors' items, that is to say, gold, silver or other metal coins or bank notes which are not normally used as legal*

[34]Redmar (2014).

[35]In *Tolsma* case (C-16/93), ECJ was asked to determine whether donations in a tin received from passers-by for playing music had to be treated as consideration for a service, since the payments were not stipulated. ECJ held that the playing of music for which no consideration was stipulated did not constitute a supply of services effected for consideration. There was no agreement, *i.e.* no legal relationship, between the parties and there was also "*no necessary link between the musical service and the payments to which it gives rise*", see para. 17.

tender or coins of numismatic interest"), which covers "*transactions concerning*" currency, could be applied for miners' activity (and validator's).

So stated, the VAT Committee briefly analysed whether such services could also be exempt pursuant to Article 135(1)(d) of the VAT Directive ("*transactions, including negotiation, concerning deposit and current accounts, payments, transfers, debts, cheques and other negotiable instruments, but excluding debt collection*"). In this regard, it was pointed out that the services supplied by miners look rather like the activities covered by Article 135(1)(d), that is, payments and transfers. In fact, payments and transfers cannot be seen as a supply of a currency as such, but as services which allow for the supply of a currency to take place. In the words of the ECJ in *SDC* case (C-2/95), "*a transfer is a transaction consisting of the execution of an order for the transfer of a sum of money*",[36] and also according to the AG, payments and transfers must comprise the execution of cash and non-cash payments to a particular third-party recipient and this bears a substantial resemblance to miner's activities.

Given that in *Hedqvist* the ECJ put cryptocurrencies (bitcoin) and traditional currencies at the same level for VAT purposes, the VAT Committee argued that should assume that transactions concerning payments and transfers of legal tender currencies are not distinct from those concerning payments and transfers in bitcoin.

To be covered by the exemption, it is not required that a transaction constitutes payment or transfer, but it must present a sufficient degree of connection with such payment or transfer.

In the VAT Commission's view, the role played by miners could be reminiscent of the facts analyzed by the ECJ in *Nordea* case, where a company (SWIFT) provided with a worldwide electronic messaging service which allowed payment operations to take place, by connecting financial institutions and other corporate clients. The ECJ found that the services provided by SWIFT were not covered by the exemption, regardless of how necessary these inputs were, and that SWIFT's activities "*do not by themselves perform any of the functions of the financial transactions referred to in the VAT Directive, that is to say those which have the effect of transferring funds or securities, and do not therefore possess the character of such transactions*".[37]

The VAT Committee observed that some could see miners as a mere contact point between bitcoin users intending to send and receive a transfer, in line with the services provided by SWIFT. However, unlike the services provided by SWIFT, miners would not only act as mere transmitters of information, but actually would perform an activity which is crucial for the sustainability of the bitcoin system, the accuracy of the content of the transactions and avoiding the problem of double spending.

Therefore, whilst SWIFT's responsibility was found to be limited to technical aspects and the mere passing-on of information with them having no access to the

[36]Para. 53, *SDC*.

[37]Para. 43. *Nordea*.

content of the messages transmitted, the VAT Committee argued that mining activities could constitute the actual transfer of funds. Moreover, such activity could fall within the scope of VAT but subject to the exemption provided by Article 135(1)(d) of VAT Directive.

Another issue could regard whether miners and validators are VAT taxable persons acting as such, pursuant to Article 9(1) of the VAT Directive, where a taxable person means "*any person who, independently, carries out in any place any economic activity, whatever the purpose or results of that activity. Any activity of producers, traders or persons supplying services, including mining and agricultural activities and activities of the professions, shall be regarded as 'economic activity'. The exploitation of tangible or intangible property for the purposes of obtaining income therefrom on a continuing basis shall in particular be regarded as an economic activity*".

The European VAT applies a global concept of "*taxable person*". Indeed, "*anyone*" could refer to an individual, a legal person (private or public limited companies), cooperation, joint ventures, consortia and partnerships. Taxable person can be treated as such even when lacking legal personality,[38] as well as "*any activity*" comprises any activity of producers, traders or persons supplying services, including mining and agricultural activities and activities of the professions.

Finally, according to the VAT Directive, an activity has an independent[39] character when it is exercised by a person who is not organically integrated into an undertaking or an administration (thus, excluding activities conducted in a judicial or in a public administrative capacity); that person has appropriate organizational freedom with regard to the human and material resources used in the exercise of the activity in question and the economic risk inherent in that activity is borne by him.[40]

Considering that to perform the validation activity miners have to dispose of some powerful hardware able to unravel mathematical problems, the VAT Committee observed that a direct relationship may exist between the hardware tools and the capacity to find solutions to complex calculations. This could be seen as an indication that miners carried out an economic activity.

Similar reasonings could be done for validators.

However, even if it is likely to consider both miners and validators VAT taxable persons, it should be borne in mind that VAT is levied provided that the validation transaction is considered relevant for VAT purposes.[41]

---

[38]Terra and Kajus (2017).

[39]The requirement that a taxable person acts in an "independent" capacity excludes, according to Article 10 of the VAT Directive, employees from an obligation to charge value added tax on services provided to their employers.

[40]Terra and Kajus (2017). See also *Gmina Wrocław* (Case C-276/14).

[41]Lastly, if miners/validators were considered VAT taxable persons and the validation activity felt within the VAT scope, the territoriality topic would have to be analysed. In this respect, it should wonder whether the presumptions provided for electronic services (see Article 58 VAT Directive and Article 24(a) of Implementing Regulation to VAT Directive) could transposed.

3.3 Transactions Underlying Digital Wallets

Digital wallets are software platforms generally provided by third parties that can be stored offline in the user's own personal computer or stored and accessed through online connection. The digital wallets also allow users to transact among each other by sending and receiving virtual currency and it could happen that digital wallet providers asked fees in exchange for such services.

At this point, it should argue whether the services rendered by digital wallet providers fall within the scope of VAT Directive. To this end two requirements have to be considered: whether there is consideration and the supply of service is rendered by a VAT taxable person.[42]

Regarding the consideration, it is known that from the settled case-law of the ECJ[43] a supply of services is affected for consideration within the meaning of Article 2(1)(c) of the VAT Directive only if there is a direct link between the services supplied and the consideration received.

In this regard the VAT Committee assumed both the case where the fee is not paid and the case where the walled providers ask a fee to their client.

In the former, the transaction would fall outside the scope of VAT. Nonetheless, the VAT Committee noted that if the supply of services free of charge is carried out by the digital wallet provider for his private use or for that of his staff or, more generally, for purposes other than those of his business, the transaction should be treated as a supply of services for consideration pursuant to Article 26(1)(b) of the VAT Directive.

In the latter, from the above-mentioned settled case law, the fees would constitute the remuneration for the service supplied by the digital wallet provider.

Again, if the transaction falls within the VAT scope, it will be necessary to ask whether the service is exempt pursuant to Article 135(1)(e) of VAT Directive. Considering the financial transactions of such exemption, it is reliable to consider the services supplied by digital wallet providers exempt. Indeed, as noted by the VAT Committee, the services at stake directly "*concern*" a means of payment (*i.e.* making available the cryptocurrencies to users) and create rights and obligations in relation to that means of payment.

At this point it should ponder whether digital wallet providers are VAT taxable persons acting as such, according to Article 9(1) of the VAT Directive.

The vast scope of the provision leads to consider the digital wallet providers as taxable persons. Moreover, according to VAT Committee the development and exploitation of software platforms in exchange for a fee could constitute an economic activity.

Indeed, if digital wallet providers are rewarded and there is a direct link between that consideration and the services provided, they are supplying services that fall within the VAT scope and they are acting as VAT taxable persons.

---

[42]See Section 5.2.3 of Working paper No. 892/2016.

[43]See *Loyalty Management UK and Baxi Group* in C-53/09 and *Tolsma* in C-16/93.

Lastly, in the event wallet provider's transactions were relevant for VAT purposes it should wonder where such service is to be VAT relevant. Assuming that the wallet provider's client is a final client it should argue whether the special provision envisaged for electronically supplies in Article 58 VAT Directive and Article 7 of the Implementing Regulation to VAT Directive can be taken into consideration.

If the wallet provider's client is a taxable person, the common territoriality rules will be applied. However, assuming that the wallet providers were considered an interface between the clients' transactions, it should consider whether the combine provisions of Article 28 VAT Directive and Article 9(a) of the Implementing Regulation to VAT Directive could be applied. Indeed they set forth that "*where electronically supplied services are supplied through a telecommunications network, an interface or a portal such as a marketplace for applications, a taxable person taking part in that supply shall be presumed to be acting in his own name but on behalf of the provider of those services unless that provider is explicitly indicated as the supplier by that taxable person and that is reflected in the contractual arrangements between the parties*".

As well as, given that the service could be rendered everywhere, it should wonder if the presumptions laid down in Article 24(a), (b), (c), (d), (e), (f) of Implementing Regulation to VAT Directive could be transposed in the case at hand.[44]

3.4 Intermediation Provided by Exchange Platforms

Services consisting in the exchange of bitcoin for traditional currency and vice versa were found to be exempt pursuant to Article 135(1)(e) of the VAT Directive by the ECJ.

However, the VAT Committee[45] outlined that in other cases the services supplied by bitcoin exchange platforms to buyers and sellers of the virtual currency are related to intermediation. In such circumstances, exchange platforms aim at enabling trade directly between bitcoin users by offering a virtual market-place; and the platform may charge a fee for making use of its trading tool.

In order to examine whether the services provided by exchange platforms acting as an intermediary fall within the scope of VAT it is crucial to verify if there is consideration (in the event the service is rendered free of charge, it will be out of scope of VAT); and whether the supply of services is effected by a taxable person acting as such.

The VAT Committee concluded affirming that given the development and exploitation of online exchange platforms constitute an economic activity, the mentioned service would be considered taxable. However, the exemption envisaged by Article 135(1)(e) of the VAT Directive would not be applicable.

[44]See https://eur-lex.europa.eu/legal-content/EN/TXT/?uri=CELEX:02011R0282-20200101.

[45]Section 5.2.5. Working paper 892/2016.

4 Initial Coin Offerings: Legal Status of Tokens and VAT Implications

As known, Initial Coin Offerings (ICO's) consist of the creation of digital tokens by start-up companies and their distribution to investors in exchange for fiat currency or mainstream cryptocurrencies (Bitcoin or Ether).[46] Start-up companies raise, thus, capital for the financing of commercial and development projects where tokens are sold for cryptocurrencies or legal money.[47] The usual arrangement is that the business, instead of offering equity participation through shares, sells token (new cryptocurrencies) to purchasers and then uses the money to build the business or to develop the new project.[48]

Moreover, once the tokens are issued, they can be resold in secondary markets on exchange platforms or directly between individuals, even before the project or the new business is developed.

In the following paragraphs, it will analyse the VAT implications under ICO's 'transactions'.

4.1 *ICO's as VAT Taxable Persons*

In order to treat ICO's as a taxable person, it has to be referred to Article 9 of VAT Directive.

However, given the aforementioned vast scope of the rule, it seems that ICO's can be considered taxable persons. Indeed, according to the ECJ,[49] initial investment expenditure incurred for the needs of, and with the view to carrying on, an enterprise should be considered an economic activity.[50] Therefore, considering that preparatory acts are economic activities, even when the intended economic activities never materialize, the acquisition of operating assets to launch the ICO's could be regarded as economic activity as well.

Furthermore, considering that who launches the ICO's bears the risk of not being able to sell the tokens at all or only being able to sell them at a price below the purchase amount, ICO's could fall in the notion of VAT taxable person.

[46]OECD (2019), *Initial Coin Offering (ICOs) for SME Financing*, www.oecd.org/initial-coin-offerings-for-sme-financing.htm.

[47]Bal (2018b).

[48]Fairpo (2018).

[49]*Rompelman* (C-268/83) and *INZO* (C-110/94).

[50]Terra and Kajus (2017).

4.2 *The Uncertain Legal Status of Tokens*

Tokens can be encompassed in the broad term of cryptocurrency.[51] Besides, they differ from cryptocurrency coins. In fact, tokens cannot operate independently but they require another platform, such as Ethereum, to exist and operate. In addition, being a means of exchange, tokens may be outfitted of several functionalities.

Tokens can be divided into three main categories:

- utility tokens, in this case they will be exchanged for services or goods once such services or goods are ready to be marketed;
- equity tokens, which are generally similar to equity shares in a company: they permit the investors to earn "dividends" (the reward is based on the successful performance of the company) and they could carry the right to vote on major company proposals;
- debt tokens, which are similar to short-term loans and they embody the right to variable or fixed interest during a specified time period.

All three types of tokens have in common that they serve as a means of financing: offerors issue digital tokens to collect funds to finance their future project.[52]

However, considering the differences in both structure and purposes, it is clear that the correct treatment of tokens has to be carried out by a case-by case analysis.

Firstly, considering the intangible nature of tokens (*i.e.* as a digital product), their sale should be considered an electronically supplied service.[53]

Another possibility is to treat tokens as negotiable instruments. Such interpretation would imply the applicability of Article 135(1)(d) of the VAT Directive.

However, looking through the tokens' nature, it seems that they are not aimed at serving a direct means of payment. Indeed, as outlined by some academic,[54] tokens could operate as a way of transferring money, bearing in mind that the ultimate objective of the offeror is to obtain funds to finance future projects. Nevertheless, tokens do not give their holder an unconditional right to be paid in currency. Moreover, they can be exchanged for currency (*i.e.* sold on secondary markets) only to the extent that another party is willing to buy them.

Furthermore, tokens could fall within securities. Such interpretation would imply the applicability of Article 135(1)(f) of the VAT Directive, which exempts "*transactions, including negotiation but not management or safekeeping, in shares, interests in companies or associations, debentures and other securities*". The term "*other security*" is not defined in the VAT Directive. However, as previously recalled, in *Granton Advertising* the ECJ pointed out that an instrument would only qualify as a security if the transfer of the instrument implied the acquisition

[51]Bal (2018b).

[52]Ibid.

[53]In case of the client is final consumer, Article 58 VAT Directive could be applicable.

[54]Bal (2018b).

of a right of ownership over the issuer or claim against the issuer and the instrument could be exchanged for money or goods.

The purchaser of debt or equity tokens assumes a position similar to that of a debt or shareholder. He could acquire some rights in respect of the offering company. Thus, debt and equity tokens could actually fall within the definition of "*other securities*".[55]

So affirmed, if tokens are considered similar to securities, an ICO's could be treated in the same way as a share issue. In this respect, the ECJ[56] clarified that the issuing of shares is not an economic activity as it is made with the aim of raising capital and not providing services.

Since traditional means of financing (debt and share issue) can be either exempt or outside the scope of VAT, it would seem discriminatory to subject ICO's (as an alternative way of financing) to VAT.

Finally, utility tokens could be treated as vouchers and in particular they could fall within multi-purpose vouchers.[57]

Recently, during the meeting on 12 April 2019, the VAT Committee[58] was asked to consider the similarities with the Voucher Directive. In this regard it pondered that tokens are digital assets that can be used as virtual currency, as financial instruments similar to securities ("financial tokens") or as instruments representing goods and services ("utility tokens").

Given their hybrid nature, the VAT Committee outlined that doubts could arise as to which tax rules are applicable and that various different instruments may be considered to be tokens but at EU and international level, the difference between currency tokens, investment tokens and utility tokens is not clear.

Moreover, as to utility tokens, they could be comparable to vouchers. However, as long as there is no EU regulation to define the notion of utility tokens, the VAT Committee deemed that it is not possible to know with certainty their essential characteristics (in fact, it is recognised that tokens can be hybrid instruments).

In this respect the Policy Department of the European Parliament carried out a study on Cryptocurrencies and blockchain, where utility tokens are defined as digital instruments that "*grant their holders (future) access to specific products or services. They can be used to acquire certain products or services, yet they do not constitute a general- purpose medium of exchange, simply because they can generally only be used on the token platform itself*".

It seems that utility tokens have a hybrid nature as they can be compared to digital coins, and they also have an investment component, as they are traded, and hence

---

[55]In this regard, it should be noted that according the European Securities and Markets Authority (ESMA), where crypto-assets qualify as transferable securities or other types of MiFID financial instruments, a full set of UE financial rules are likely to apply to their issuer (or firms providing investment services/activities to those instruments. See, https://www.esma.europa.eu/sites/default/files/library/esma50-157-1391_crypto_advice.pdf.

[56]*Kretztechnik* (C-465/03).

[57]See Article 30(a)(3) and Article 30(b)(2), VAT Directive.

[58]Working paper No. 983, 13 November 2019.

sold at a profit, in the community of token holders. They are mostly used in a form to ease payment across borders, or to provide access to a product on the blockchain. In other terms, they confer rights to use or consume certain products developed by the issuing company and deposited on the blockchain, but they can also be traded being an autonomous source of profit without relation to any entitlement to goods or services embedded in the token.

5 The Experience of Some States. An Overview in Germany, United Kingdom, Malta, Switzerland and Italy

5.1 Germany

On 27 February 2018, the German Ministry of Finance clarified some questions concerning the treatment of cryptocurrencies for tax and regulatory purposes. The Ministry of Finance confirmed the opinion given by the Federal Financial Supervisory Authority (BaFin) considering virtual currencies as financial instruments. To this extent, BaFin deemed that the legal classification applies to all currency schemes, regardless the software an encryption technology they use.[59]

So stated the Minister of Finance[60] argued that "mining" is a non-taxable transaction. Indeed the transaction fee, which miners can receive from other users of the system, is paid on a voluntary basis and is not directly related to the services provided by the miners; receiving new bitcoin from the bitcoin system cannot be classified as payment for mining services because there is no exchange of services, as that requires an identifiable beneficiary.

With regard to digital wallets, the Federal Ministry of Finance determined that if they are offered for a fee, they qualify as other services supplied by electronic means which are taxable and liable to taxation, if the place of performance is in Germany.

Lastly, the Ministry of Finance stated that operations on trading platforms cannot be exempt from VAT. However, if the operators of such platforms buy and sell bitcoin and other virtual currencies as intermediaries in their own name, they may be exempt from VAT.

---

[59]Bal (2018b). Monitor, 2018 (Volume 29), No. 2, published online on 15 March 2018, IBFD.

[60]Gesley J (2018) Germany: Federal Ministry of Finance Publishes Guidance on VAT Treatment of Virtual Currencies. In: BITRSS Crypto and Bitcoin World News. https://bitrss.com/news/89216/germany-federal-ministry-of-finance-publishes-guidance-on-vat-treatment-of-virtual-currencies.

5.2 *United Kingdom*

On 20th December 2019, HMRC published guidelines for business[61] regarding the tax treatment for transactions carried out by way of crypto-asset exchange tokens. HMRC specified that such guidelines do not apply to the issue of tokens under initial coin offerings or other similar events and that they only deal with the tax treatment of exchange tokens (for example, bitcoin), addressing in a future guidance the tax treatment on security tokens and utility tokens.

According to HMRC, crypto assets are cryptographically secured digital representations of value or contractual rights that can be transferred, stored and traded electronically.

HMRC does not consider crypto assets to be currency or money. This statement reflects the position previously set out by the *Cryptoasset Taskforce report*[62] where three types of crypto assets have been identified:

- exchange tokens, that are intended to be used as a method of payment;
- utility tokens, that provide the holder with access to particular goods or services on a platform usually using DLT;
- security tokens, that may provide the holder with particular interests in a business, for example in the nature of debt due by the business or a share of profits in the business.

According to HMRC, the tax treatment of all types of tokens is subject to the nature and the use of the token itself. Nonetheless, for VAT purposes, it is pointed out that bitcoin and similar crypto assets should be treated as follows:

- exchange tokens received by miners for their exchange token mining activities will generally be outside the scope of VAT on the basis that:

  the activity does not constitute an economic activity for VAT purposes since there is an insufficient link between any services provided and any consideration;
  there is no customer for the mining service;
  when exchange tokens are exchanged for goods and services, VAT will not be due on the supply of the token itself;

[61]See: https://www.gov.uk/government/publications/tax-on-cryptoassets/cryptoassets-tax-for-businesses. HMCR also published a guideline for individuals; see https://www.gov.uk/government/publications/tax-on-cryptoassets/cryptoassets-for-individuals. In this latter, HMRC points out that the guideline does not consider the tax treatment of crypto-assets held for the purposes of a business carried on by an individual.

[62]The Cryptoassets Taskforce report lays out the UK's policy and regulatory approach to cryptoassets and distributed ledger technology in financial services. See: https://www.gov.uk/government/publications/cryptoassets-taskforce.

– charges (in whatever form) made over and above the value of the exchange tokens for arranging any transactions in exchange tokens will be exempt from VAT, if the conditions outlined in the Vat Finance Manual (VATFIN7200) are met.[63]

Finally, given the *Hedqvist* judgement, HMRC affirmed that a supply of any services requiring to exchange "*exchange tokens*" for legal tender (or other exchange tokens) and vice versa will be exempt from VAT under Item 1, Group 5, Schedule. 9, of the Value Added Tax Act 1994.

5.3 *Malta*

On first November 2018, Malta Virtual Financial Regulations Act and the Virtual Financial Assets Act[64] (VFAA) came into force. The VFAA set forth new class of digital assets, known as DLT assets along with ancillary services and product offerings relating to DLT assets, such as Initial Coin Offerings, virtual financial assets, exchanges, and virtual financial asset agents, and service providers.

On the same date, Malta Commissioner for Revenue (Malta Revenue) issued important guidelines on stamp duty and VAT[65] treatment for DLT assets' transactions.

Particularly, according to VFAA and Malta Revenue, DLT assets can be classified as follows:

– Coins: that refer to DLT assets designed solely as a means of payment and are meant to serve as an alternative to legal tender;
– Tokens: that are divided in:

financial tokens that are similar to equities, debentures, units in collective investment schemes, or derivatives and including financial instruments;
utility tokens whose utility, value or application is solely restricted to the acquisition of goods or services within the DLT platform or in relation to which they are issued or within a limited network of DLT platforms;
hybrid tokens that could contain the features of both financial and utility tokens.

So stated Malta Revenue analysed the VAT treatment of DLT assets' transactions.

Regarding Coins, given the *Hedqvist* case, the Malta Revenue considered the cryptocurrencies a means of payment as alternative to legal tender. Moreover, whether the exchange of cryptocurrencies for other cryptocurrencies or for fiat

[63]See Item 5, Schedule 9, Group 5 of the Value Added Tax Act 1994.

[64]See http://www.justiceservices.gov.mt/DownloadDocument.aspx?app=lom&itemid=12872&l=1.

[65]https://cfr.gov.mt/en/vat/guidelines_to_certain_VAT_Procedures/Documents/Guidelines%20-%20DLTs%20VAT.pdf.

money is a supply of services for consideration, such service could fall within the VAT exemptions.[66]

As to walled providers, Malta Revenue pointed out that if wallet providers require the payment of fees (for allowing coin users to hold and operate a cryptocurrency and create rights and obligations in relation to the means of payment), the service would be relevant for VAT purposes, but it will not be VAT exempt.

In relation to miners, Malta Revenue considered the mining activities out of VAT scope, as there would not be any direct link between the compensation received and the service rendered as well as there would not be any mutual performance between the supplier and the receiver.

On the other hand, whether miners receive payment for other activities, according to the Malta Revenue there would be a chargeable event for VAT purposes. In this case, in so far that such service would be deemed to take place in Malta, Maltese VAT would be applicable at the standard rate.

As to financial tokens, the Malta Revenue outlined some concerns.

In particular, where a financial token is simply issued to raise capital, it is noted that the issuing itself would not give rise to VAT implications in the hands of the issuer, since the raising of finance does not constitute a supply of goods or a supply of services for consideration and thus it would be out the VAT scope.

Regarding the utility tokens, the Malta Revenue deemed that they would have the characteristics of vouchers.

Finally, as to ICO's, Malta Revenue pointed out that, whether investors place their money at the ICO's stage against tokens—that are issued as a means of collecting funds for the development of a future project—such initial offering may not necessarily constitute a chargeable event for VAT purposes. To this extent it is argued that it may be that at such point, any specific good or service will be identified, any corresponding price for a supply could be fixed. As well as it would not be possible to determine whether the project undertaken were realized and the investors have received a return.

According to Malta Revenue, such transactions would be out of VAT scope. Similarly, there would not be any transaction in the scope of VAT if the money placed by the investor served to acquire a security (equity, debenture, etc.).

Where, on the other hand, the tokens issued gave rights to identified goods or services for a specified consideration, a chargeable event for VAT purposes could arise and its proper VAT treatment would have to be examined.

5.4 *Switzerland*

On February 16, 2018 the Swiss Financial Market Supervisory Authority (FINMA) published "*Guidelines for enquiries regarding the regulatory framework for coin*

[66]Vat Act, item 3(4), Part Two, 5th Schedule.

offerings (ICOs)"[67] where it is noted that there is not any universally recognized classification of digital tokens, neither in Switzerland nor elsewhere in the world.

According to FINMA[68] digital token generations can be divided as follows:

- payment tokens that are comparable to "*cryptocurrencies*", and they are intended to be used as a means of payment for acquiring goods or services or as a means of money or value transfer;
- utility tokens that provide access to a digital application or service;
- asset tokens that represent assets such as debt or equity claim on the issuer, shares in real values, companies, income, or a right to dividends or interest. In terms of economic function, the token must be considered as a share, a bond, or a derivative financial instrument;
- hybrid tokens that are tokens that are deemed to be both securities and means of payment.

On fifth December 2019, the Canton of Geneva published a document "*Guide: Token Generation in the Canton of Geneva*"[69] where, among other topics, there is an interesting VAT analysis on the different types of tokens.

As to payment tokens, they are treated as a means of payment. It should be noted that insofar as these tokens are considered out of scope, VAT on expenses directly and exclusively related to the generation of these tokens should not be deductible.

As to utility tokens they are considered as pre-payment of services under common law (*i.e.* right of access, right to a service). As such, if the prepaid services are clearly identifiable and known at the time the tokens are generated, that generation would be treated as a taxable service in the place of business of the recipient of said service.

On the other hand, if the services are not clearly identifiable and known, the generation of the tokens could constitute a means of payment.

As to Asset tokens, they are treated as contractual relationships (similar to financial instruments) and not as shares/participations under company law. In this respect, FTA does not express an opinion on this subject and seems to consider such tokens as excluded from the scope of VAT. However, in order to give a qualification and thus to determine the VAT treatment, the underlying asset and the rights related to tokens should be taken into consideration.

As to Hybrid tokens, it is outlined that VAT treatment should be determined on a case-by-case basis.

---

[67] See https://www.finma.ch/en/news/2018/02/20180216-mm-ico-wegleitung/.

[68] On August 27, 2019, the Federal Tax Administration (FTA) published a working paper entitled: "*Cryptocurrencies and initial coin/token offerings (ICO/ITO) as the subject of wealth, income, and profit tax, withholding tax, and stamp duties*".

[69] See https://www.ge.ch/document/guide-digital-token-generations-canton-geneva.

5.5 *Italy*

On 28 September 2018, the Italian Tax Revenue (Italian Revenue) published an answer to a tax ruling (No. 14/E/2018) in relation to the tokens' tax treatment as per Income Tax and VAT perspective. In that case, it was launched an ICO's where tokens entitled the purchaser to use services for the diagnosis for infertility at the issuing company' s own laboratories, against payments in cryptocurrencies; tokens would have been used by the original purchaser or they would have been sold to third parties, against payments in cryptocurrencies.

Under the VAT perspective, the Italian Revenue encompassed the tokens within the utility token category and given the entitlement to benefit of certain services affirmed that they could be treated as voucher.[70] However, considering that from 1 January 2019, the Voucher Directive would have been entered into force, the Italian Revenue concluded that it will be necessary to verify whether tokens can fall within the specific rules implemented by that Directive.

Considering the specific structure of the operation analysed, it seems that the interpretation provided by the Italian Revenue is reliable. However, it is crucial to point out that an extensive application of such interpretation could entail few concerns.

Precisely, as to utility tokens the VAT Committee[71] outlined that the arguments that could lead to utility tokens qualifying as a voucher are only that they can be exchanged with goods or services and they can be used only in a limited network.

On the other hand, the arguments that could lead utility tokens to being excluded from being treated as a voucher are that:

- redemption of the rights embedded in the token is not its only purpose. In fact, while a voucher, which can no longer be redeemed, is deprived of its value, as it is strictly linked to the goods and services embedded in it; the utility token can continue to be traded in a secondary market, as the instrument has multiple functions further to that of being considered the consideration for a supply of goods or services;
- a utility token that is not redeemed seems to be able to be transformed into a currency token or an investment token and then be traded in a secondary market;
- there may be a lack of sufficient detail of the goods supplied or the services provided, or of the identity of the potential suppliers taking part in the chain, as otherwise needed;
- in certain situations, they operate as cryptocurrencies and therefore could be considered to be payment services.

For sake of completeness, on 20 April 2020 the Italian Revenue published another answer to a tax ruling (No. 110/E/2020) where tokens are issued by an ICO's that is developing a platform (running on blockchain technology) that will

[70] Perno (2018) and Gavioli (2018).

[71] Working paper 983/2019.

allow the users to sign, encrypt and exchange commercial documents in digital format. In particular, from the facts it is drawn that:

- a network of servers will be created, and such network will perform validation activities for transactions by way of a "consent protocol" that uses the "proof of stake" (PoS) method. The validators (so-called validator nodes) shall use the software of the company and they will be provided with a minimum number of tokens that shall be bound to guarantee the validation activity;
- transactions on the platform shall take place only through tokens specifically generated by the company;
- a consortium formed by the validation nodes will have the purpose, *inter alia*, to purchase in its own name and on behalf of the consortium members the necessary tokens. These tokens will then be sold to the consortium members;
- the validator nodes can purchase (through the consortium) the tokens issued by the company until a certain date; afterwards, tokens will only be purchased at the "digital exchange" or through direct exchange with other persons.

Finally, the company specified that the tokens do not constitute a financial instrument, do not imply for the purchaser any rights related to the company.

So pointed out, the company asked the Italian Revenue the correct VAT treatment of token transfers from the company to the consortium. According to the company, given the hybrid nature of the tokens, they could be classified *(i)* as "utility tokens", to the extent that they can be used to make use of the platform and be treated as vouchers pursuant to Article 6, *quater*, para. 2, of Presidential Decree No. 633/1972, *(ii)* as a "payment token", insofar as they are exchanged as a means of payment to purchase goods or services on the market and be treated as money transfers pursuant to art. 2, para. 3, letter a) of Presidential Decree No. 633/1972 (VAT out of scope).

The Italian Revenue did not agree with the company's interpretation. In fact, it excluded that the qualification of the tokens are "payment tokens", as at the time of issue they would not have the function of a virtual currency which, as stated by the Court of Justice in the *Hedqvist* judgment, has "*no other purpose than that of a means of payment*" (see para. 24 of C-264/14).

As far as the classification of tokens as vouchers is concerned, the Italian Revenue did not provide any particular reasonings. However, it pointed out that the tokens should be qualified as utility tokens since following to their purchase it is possible to use the services on the company's blockchain, use the software and act as a validator. Notably, according to the Italian Revenue, the buyer (the consortium) pays a commission to the company to obtain the token utilities needed to perform the validation activity.

In the light of the above, the Italian Revenue considered that the company provides a generic supply of service relevant for VAT purposes (according to Article 3, para. 3, of Presidential Decree No. 633/1972 and subject to the ordinary VAT rate of 22%). In particular, the company is paid with a commission in order to allow the access and the use of the platform and to let carry out the activity of validator.

Regarding the exchange of cryptocurrencies[72] into other traditional currencies, the Italian Revenue affirmed that such activity is relevant for VAT purposes, but it falls within the exemption provided by Article 10, para. 1, no. 3, Presidential Decree 633/1972.[73] This interpretation is in line with the EJC's case law.

Careful academics[74] noted that it would be essential to clarify the VAT treatment underlying DLT's transactions, namely: the supply of new cryptocurrencies to miners (which seems to fall within the VAT exemptions envisaged by Article 10, para. 1, no. 3, Presidential Decree 633/1972); the management of wallets (which seems to be subject to VAT applying the ordinary rate) and the issuance and trade of tokens.

6 Use of DLT to Label VAT Fraud

The current set-up of the system, where different legislations and collection systems exist across the UE, gave rise to a vast number of frauds. In the report published in September 2019 of European Commission it is calculated that the current missing VAT across the EU was approximately € 137 billion in 2017. The two principal fraud mechanism are the missing trader intra-community and the extra-community frauds, notably a supplier in a chain of transactions takes advantage of a temporary discontinuance in the VAT compliance obligations and fails to account for VAT, collect VAT money from its customers and then disappears.

DLT may bring substantial support in order to label VAT frauds. According to a recent report of the European Commission,[75] a blockchain system can be used to register all transactions and support collection of VAT charges, implementing multi-directional smart contract between the buyer, the seller, the Revenue, the buyer's bank and the seller's bank. Particularly, in this way the blockchain system would produce digitalized invoice level data and introduce an automatic taxation by splitting the payment made via banking system.

According to the aforementioned report, one major implication of the new system is that the input-output VAT clearing would have to be done by the Revenue and not by the firms submitting VAT tax returns. Moreover, the Tax authority would remit to the seller part of the output VAT transferred by the buyer's bank.

---

[72]Regarding the qualification of cryptocurrencies, it should refer also to: Law Decree 90/2017 (that transposed Directive 2018/843/EU); Final Report of Consob "*Le offerte iniziali e gli scambi di crypto-attività*", published on 2 January 2020; *Tribunale Amministrativo Regionale per il Lazio*, judgement no. 01077/2020, published on 27 January 2020.

[73]See also answer to the tax ruling No. 72/2016.

[74]Antonacchio (2019). Giorgi (2019).

[75]Allessie D et al., *Blockchain for digital government: An assessment of pioneering implementations in public services*, 2019.

In the view of careful academic,[76] a such system may arise concerns in term of VAT direct payment. Indeed, SME's may use the VAT paid by their customers as a cash flow advantage, given that VAT usually only needs to be paid at later point in time, or that it can be offset against the VAT that they have been paying to their suppliers. Notwithstanding this cash flow advantage would disappear, as the VAT would no longer be in the hands of the supplier, the customer will receive the VAT paid to the supplier instantly from the tax authorities, if that customers is able to reclaim the VAT.

7 Conclusions

From the above analysis, it is drawn that at EU level there is a great uncertainty on both the qualification of cryptocurrencies and of tokens. As to the legal status of cryptocurrencies it cannot be ignored that ECB and then Directive 2018/843/EU considered more accurate to regard cryptocurrencies as means of exchange, rather than as means of payment (as the ECJ held in the *Hedqvist* case). At this point, few concerns may arise. More precisely, given the scope of the aforesaid Directive 2018/843/EU, it should argue whether such qualification could affect the VAT treatment and whether two different qualifications provided could co-exist, to the extent that they met distinctive needs (Directive 2018/843/EU's scope seems to be anti-money laundering and countering the financing of terrorism; VAT Directive's scope is to tax either supplies of goods or services for consideration that are relevant for VAT in accordance with the principles of neutrality and equal treatment, regardless of their lawfulness).

In this respect, according to the AG's Opinion (given in *Hedqvist* case) it seems that the substantial nature of cryptocurrencies as means of payment should not be affected by external laws. It is clear that this type of uncertainty can only be allayed by the EU laws and by the ECJ's case law.

Akin reasonings could be carried out for tokens. Indeed, as set out by OECD, "*token classification and taxonomies are being discussed by regulators and the industry in an effort to understand what regulation should apply to them. Tokens could be considered as financial instruments, securities, commodities, non-cash payment facilities or managed investment schemes, depending on the characteristics*".[77]

It seems that in the lack of a specific law, only following to a correct understanding of the nature of the specific token and of the broader framework of relations between the parties involved, it will be possible to achieve to a correct legal qualification and thus to the relative tax treatment.

[76]van der Bosch et al. (2018).

[77]*OECD (2019), Initial Coin Offering (ICOs) for SME Financing*, page 49:

Last but not the least, it should argue where all these transactions are taxable. Given that, for instance, miners, validators, wallet providers and cryptocurrency's users can be everywhere (in EU or in the world), it should be asked if the existing presumptions provided for the electronically services supplied could be eventually transposed in the case at hand.

All these uncertainties lead to the conclusion that it is time that a "*new block*" should be added in the chain of the VAT Directive's rules.[78]

References

Antonacchio F (2019) Initial coin offering: riflessi fiscali, antiriciclaggio e di tutela dei mercati finanziarti, connessi all'emissione di criptovalute (o cripto-assets). Rivista di Diritto Tributario

Bal A (2018a) International - Blockchain, initial coin offerings and other developments in the virtual currency market - IBFD. Financ Capital Mark 20

Bal A (2018b) International – VAT treatment of initial coin offerings. Int VAT Monit 29

Fairpo A (2018) VAT and intangibles: VAT in a blockchain world. Tax J

Gavioli F (2018) Cessione di token digitali: i profili fiscali. Pratica Fiscale e Professionale

Giorgi S (2019) Cripto-attività, tra poliformismo e dubbi qualifatori in materia fiscale. Rivista di Diritto Tributario

Kroll JA, Davey IC, Felten EW (2013) The economics of bitcoin mining, or bitcoin in the presence of adversaries. In: Proceedings of WEIS. p 11

Lambooij M (2014) Retailers directly accepting bitcoins: tricky tax issues? Deriv Financ Instrum 16:138–144

Perno C (2018) Trattamento tributario dei token in sede di Initial coin offering. Il Fisco:47–48

Redmar W (2014) Bitcoin and EU VAT. Int VAT Monit 254–257

Terra B, Kajus J (2017) A guide to the European VAT Directives 2017. IBFD

van der Bosch T, Diederichsen D, Demetrius C (2018) International - blockchain in global finance and tax - IBFD. Financ Cap Mark 20

[78]In this regard, see the public consultation launched by the European Commission in order to the EU Regulation proposal on crypto-asset: https://ec.europa.eu/info/law/better-regulation/have-your-say/initiatives/12089-Directive-regulation-establishing-a-European-framework-for-markets-in-crypto-assets. In the third quarter of 2020 a response could arrive.

Blockchain and Comparative Law

Cristina Poncibò

Contents

1 Introduction

The chapter contains a preliminary exploration of the notion and functioning of blockchain technology (hereinafter 'blockchain') in the light of comparative law and specifically the theories of legal formants[1] and transnational law and global law.[2] The chapter argues that blockchain networks can be fruitfully conceptualized according to the categories of comparative law.[3] In particular, transnational law refers to any law which transcends state laws.[4] The conceptual framework of such a theory includes, for example, the shift from regulation to co-ordination, the hybridization of private and public regimes, the relationship between soft law and hard law, and, finally, the establishment of regimes capable of legislating and enforcing their

[1]Sacco (1991).

[2]Siems (2018), pp. 303–331; Michaels (2016); Husa (2015), p. 55.

[3]Michaels (2016); Husa (2015), p. 55; Calliess and Zumbansen (2012).

[4]Jessup (1956), p. 2.

C. Poncibò (✉)
Law Faculty, University of Turin, Turin, Italy
e-mail: cristina.poncibo@unito.it

B. Cappiello, G. Carullo (eds.), *Blockchain, Law and Governance*,
https://doi.org/10.1007/978-3-030-52722-8_10

norms.[5] Here the point is that public and private blockchains, while very different,[6] show to have all these characteristics that are proper of transnational law regimes.

Blockchain technology enables the creation of decentralized currencies, self-executing digital contracts and intelligent assets that can be controlled over the Internet. This technology also enables the development of new governance systems with more democratic or participatory decision-making, and decentralized (autonomous) organizations that can operate over a network of computers without any human intervention.[7] These applications have led many to deem that the blockchain will shift the balance of power away from centralized authorities in the field of communications, business, and even politics or law.[8]

Blockchains, in fact, consist of a series of nodes, miners and programmers that affect the overall architecture of the chain of blocks, acting in cooperation on the networks. In essence, such a system comes ex ante to the regulation of user conduct, through a series of system settings, similarly to what could happen in the physical world through architectural choices that affect the physiognomy of buildings and the structuring of roads. Thus, it is self-effective because it finds its effectiveness in the very fact of its existence and efficiency.

Having in mind this, we argue, they are private regimes that operate in the digital environment and, consequently, they tend to rely on self-produced rules (i.e. the code) and, thus, are conceptually in search of autonomy from domestic legal systems. Additionally, we underline that the code and the law are subject to a process of hybridization. Our point is that blockchains are governed by different forces: code, law, but also market and social norms. We also note that smart contracts play a central role within these digital networks not only to support trade, but also to govern the blockchains.

Thus, the aforementioned argument (i.e. the conceptualization of blockchains in terms of transnational law regimes) obviously has relevant consequences. Analyzing blockchains as private regimes helps us to highlight three fundamentals of this emerging technology.

Firstly, blockchain networks are discussed here as private powers of the digital environment, grounding on the architecture and using the language of the web, namely coding and, precisely, *the lex cryptographia*.[9] In particular, the chapter questions the well-known expression 'the code is law' with the view of clarifying its boundaries and considering its relationship with state-based law.

Secondly, blockchains have a transnational dimension. This is to say that comparative lawyers may consider the code as a case of global law by assuming that computer scientists use the common language of math and algorithms across legal systems.

---

[5]Calliess and Zumbansen (2012), 96 fs.

[6]Konashevych (2019).

[7]Lianos et al. (2019).

[8]Finck (2018) and De Filippi and Wright (2018).

[9]De Filippi and Wright (2018).

Finally, our arguments show that smart contract plays a regulatory function in governing blockchains. Specifically, we argue that, in blockchain ecosystems, contracting is not merely a transaction tool, but also a fundamental part of the architecture and governance of the system. Put it differently, we argue that smart contracts are contributing to govern the networks by definitively bridging the technical and the legal perspectives.

In conclusion, our analysis confirms the process of hybridization of law and code that characterizes contemporary legal systems, while stressing the need to acknowledge these changes and deal with them to cope with the challenges posed by innovation to the law.

2 Blockchains as Transnational Law Regimes

Legal scholars widely explored the crisis of State as a source law and, consequently, the emergence of various forms of (self)-regulation coming from particular 'social subsystems' of an economic and technological matrix.[10] In particular, Teubner discussed the topic to elaborate the concept of an autopoietic system that is capable of reproducing and maintaining itself.[11] In essence, these are forms of self-regulation that stand alongside the State to respond to the irrepressible need for rapidity and efficiency in managing the transnational private activities that are specific to a global society.[12] Following the plots of this approach, it is easy to note that law making is moving from states—institutionally appointed to legislate—to private regulators. This process of private regulation occurs by the agreements entered into by global players, such as multinationals companies and the world standardization organizations, just to mention a few.[13] Private regulation is central also in the Internet as we note bellow.[14]

Given this background, the chapter points out that blockchains may be fruitfully conceived as global private regimes according to Teubner's theory. It is also important to note that they show very peculiar characteristics with respect to the classical theory of transnational law.[15]

Firstly, they belong to the digital world, rely on the *Lex Cryptographia*, and allow nodes to operate without borders and across national borders (see the Section 'Global Law'). In this regard, it may be useful to clarify that blockchains operating in the digital world are organized into three most common forms.[16] First,

[10]Michaels (2016); Husa (2015), p. 55; Calliess and Zumbansen (2012).

[11]Teubner (1992).

[12]Teubner (2004), p. 59.

[13]Teubner (2004).

[14]Lessig (1999b).

[15]Michaels (2016); Husa (2015), p. 55; Calliess and Zumbansen (2012).

[16]Konashevych (2019).

there are public blockchains that are purely peer-to-peer, decentralized and permissionless. In such a case, any miner can access the network to add, verify or validate data without restrictions at any time. Secondly, we can observe private blockchains, namely a chain of block that is permissioned and controlled by a central authority, which grants permission to pre-selected people who can add and verify records. Additionally, it is also possible to distinguish consortium blockchains that are also formed as permissioned and where a group of nodes governs all transactions. An author believes, for example, that private blockchains, where the requirement of decentralization fails, cannot be conceptually configured as real blockchains.[17]

Secondly, digitalisation and its more recent developments—blockchains—have had far from secondary consequences with respect to space, time and emancipation. On the one hand, this has strengthened the 'a-spatial dimension' of economic-social relations. In this sense, it is possible to argue that transnational blockchains create a set of jurisdictions other than state without a territorial basis. It makes little sense to try to replicate in this case the forms of regulation of States, making an emerging and decentralized law rather necessary, but converging towards common rules for mutual coordination. On the other hand, blockchain ideology determined the removal of the hierarchy in intersubjective relationships that are occurring in a sort of 'a-temporality'. It promotes an emancipatory right from below, non-state, whose purpose is coordination and not subordination. It is a right that arises in the context of self-determination and is conceived as autonomous, not hierarchical, and governed by contract.

Notwithstanding the variety of their forms and structures, blockchains as global private regimes of the digital world are generally developed rules and practices expressed in the language of informatics (i.e. the code). We mean that the code is produced freely, autonomously in the network and it is based on cooperation and autonomy. These are experiences that are currently limited, niche proposals, even if today they represent a new organizational model. Thus, the code has been adopted by the actors of the networks (coders, miners), who, despite being deprived of a central authority, are capable of regulating the activities of the actors of blockchains.[18]

On such basis, the chapter stresses that the aforementioned process of 'emptying' state sovereignty towards sector social subsystems has found in the evolution of digital technology, that is to say blockchains, its greatest propulsive support. The process shows in recent times a more intense acceleration due to the 'digital revolution', which created an instant connection method between the various users of the global blockchains networks. For example, for Teubner, modern law has failed as a regulator of social behavior and as a composer of conflicts. He believes that the origin of the crisis of law must be sought in the inadequacy of law itself (and in particular of positive law) to face the complexity of society in terms of social

[17] Konashevych (2019).

[18] Teubner (2004) and Wright and De Filippi (2015).

structures and systems interacting with each other.[19] This analysis offers an extraordinary tool for understanding the blockchain phenomenon. Indeed, the law is unable to deal with blockchains.

In light of the foregoing considerations, it is clear that the structure of blockchains poses an extremely complex task for the researcher in comparative law, who is called to examine the dynamics of the very different legal formants of the blockchain.

3 Legal Formants and the Blockchain

With reference to our case, the retreat of the directive action of the states is confirmed by the rise of forms of a regulation which is internal to the dynamics of the blockchains and, sometimes, comes directly from the evolution of the technique. A precise confirmation of this perspective can be found in the context of cyberspace, the creation and development of which represents an almost exclusive expression of the technology.[20] Clearly, such direction subverts the traditional conception of the law, as an expression of the sovereignty of the state and of the effectiveness of the 'proper' legal norm, finding in the programming code the main disciplinary factor of these networks.

The new 'law' evokes the image of a self-produced law that would be more democratic that the old 'law'. A similar mystification regards the representation of a sort of 'crypto-legal system'. In the case of blockchains, the snapshot of a soft and polycentric network is placed on the top-down portrait of a private regime symbolically represented by a horizontal network of nodes. Thus, the problems underlying the discipline of the blockchains are part of a wider context that has seen the process of economic and commercial globalization determine the decline of political power as the main source of regulation of human conduct.[21] For the philosopher Severino, technology is not handmaiden of the forces that govern the world, but itself governs the destiny of humanity. Indeed, technology continues its path knowing that it will not encounter any obstacles and no impassable limits (Irti and Severino 2001 and 2006).[22] In his words: "The great forces of the Western tradition have the illusion then of availing of the technique to achieve their purposes: the power of technique has become in fact, or has already started to become, their fundamental and primary purpose".[23]

Unlike the law which—as traditionally understood—constitutes the expression of a specific ideological system and tends to achieve a precise model of society, technology is conceptually neutral and devoid of a teleological perspective. It is

---

[19]Teubner (2004).

[20]Lessig (1999a).

[21]Brownsword et al. (2017).

[22]Irti and Severino (2001).

[23]Severino (2009), pp. 8–9.

placed on an eminently 'functional' plan and operates the same as a mechanistic criterion.[24] In essence, it is exhausted in its own functioning, allowing the explanation of certain behaviors and inhibiting others, whose selection must be considered the result of an evaluation performed on the basis of rules of economic efficiency.

In this sense, technology constitutes an essential tool for the emergence of globalization, allowing to overcome the legal fragmentation deriving from the diversity of individual national laws. Interestingly, it is not implemented in a normative way, but on a functional basis.[25]

Here, an analogy with the theory of legal formants of a system[26] only hold to a certain point in our case, but it helps us in understanding basic blockchain governance structure. The 'legal formants' of blockchain systems are the code, the law, when available and relevant, the social norms and the market forces.[27]

The first tool is the most interesting for the purposes of this paper: Lessig indicated the term 'architecture' in his studies about the governance of the web (Lessig 1996). It represents a criterion and form of organization of the environmental context in which the behavior of several individuals who operate therein are expressed and developed, and whose configuration and structuring, from an eminently 'technical' point of view, in the sense of allowing or inhibiting the performance of certain actions.[28]

With reference to blockchains, by grounding on Lessig's framework, two authors developed the idea that the widespread deployment of blockchains will lead to the expansion of a new subset of laws, which they called *lex cryptographica* or code (as before mentioned) consisting of 'rules administered through self-executing smart contracts and decentralized (autonomous) organizations'.[29]

In this context, it is possible to understand Wright and De Filippi's statement—code is law—regarding the governance of blockchains.[30] To clarify, the authors have taken up Lessig's thoughts on the fundamental role of the technology (i.e. informatics in our case) in governing the web and applied such ideas to blockchains.[31] In this sense, it is possible to say in a provocative way that blockchains are crypto private regime of the digital world interacting with the law of the real world.

Thus, one may argue that the core developers of the blockchain are like the legislative power of the blockchain system. Actually, they have the power to develop the code and add it to the core repository, but they do not have the power to put it into effect. Instead, full nodes have that power. An author notes: "Full nodes are like the

---

[24]Tien (2004).

[25]Creutzfeldt et al. (2020).

[26]Sacco (1991).

[27]Lessig (1999a).

[28]Lessig (1999a).

[29]Wright and De Filippi (2015).

[30]De Filippi and Wright (2018).

[31]Lessig (1999a).

judicial branch of blockchains. While the legislative branch can make as many laws as they want, the judicial branch can choose not to implement those laws if it finds them to be unlawful".[32]

The second formant is law, which continues to play an important role, being able to direct the disciplinary scope of the other factors, stimulating, directly or indirectly, above all the market structures and the configurations of the technique.

The third tool consists of social norms, which, although devoid of the character of coercibility, are capable of affecting the behavior of affiliates, through a mechanism of psychological conditioning that manifests itself in social reprobation towards those who violate those rules, based on ethical, civil and moral aspects of a given human consortium.

The third instrument is the market, which requires a flexible regulation system that self-generates on a customary basis, on the basis of competitive criteria based on the demand-offer relationship, and which, due to its global dimension, is capable of conditioning the economic and regulatory policies of States indirectly and, consequently, guiding the conduct of social groups and individuals.

Thus, the aforementioned legal formants, although operating autonomously, can interact, by converging—albeit in different ways—in the disciplinary result, thus tracing possible functional connections between them, which find in the regulation of blockchains one or more of their own elective areas.[33]

Interestingly, as noted before, the computer programmer is the source of the code, the legislator of blockchains. Moreover, there is no doubt that there is a substantial 'concentration' of the latently directive power among those who define the architecture of the web, consisting in the elaboration of the technical rules, and of the (substantial) application of the same, without any guarantee that allows to limit their scope to respect super-individual rights.[34] This because coding and standards are increasingly included in blockchains and manage the networks. Therefore, the problem that arises relates to the democracy of the process of elaborating the code and, in particular, to the correct expression of the control power that resides therein. Clearly, those involved in the design could structure it in such a way as to allow the breach of fundamental rights and freedoms.[35] Thus, it is possible to argue that, not surprisingly, blockchains as transnational law regimes seem capable to develop their own set of legislative and adjudicative solutions by relying on the architecture and the code. The formulation of such architecture is left to the decisions taken by programmers in the absence of an authority.[36]

In fact, the technical rules are endowed with self-executive capacity (and, therefore, also self-sanctioning), in the sense that they find immediate application, with the further consequence of not being open to interpretation, in consideration of the

[32]Maddrey (2018), p. 3.

[33]Lessig (1999b).

[34]Teubner (2012).

[35]Teubner (2012).

[36]Walch (2019).

main characteristics of the specific case. The entire disciplinary system operates automatically and ex ante, because of the rigid mechanistic schemes of the binary system, presenting itself, in its degenerative perspective, as potentially functional to the breach of fundamental freedoms, for example. These considerations highlight the risk of sliding the self-regulation of the blockchains as global private regimes of the Internet towards the drift, not already or not only of the arbitrariness, but of the functionality to the global affirmation of a technocracy. A system dedicated to the use of multimedia code for the pursuit of particular economic interests, ultimately dictated by the utilitarian and speculative logics of the market.

In this latter context, the relationship established between the law of state source and the architecture of blockchains is particularly interesting, given that, on the one hand, the former can impose the adoption of certain technical choices, which affect the structural configuration of the web, indirectly regulating the conduct of network users.

On the other hand, the latter acts in a virtual system whose environmental contours are entirely the result of a design that is capable ex ante and independently of regulating the behavior of users of the network. Thus, it achieves objectives potentially coinciding with those pursued by the political-institutional power.[37]

Consequently, the code implies an evident control power of the chains of blocks, representing the means by which they can allow or inhibit certain actions by users, substantially orienting their behaviour in a way that may be functional to the disciplinary purposes of a private regime.[38]

Thus, the importance and indispensability of the directive role of state legislation emerges which—by limiting the operating margins of the implicit principle of technological neutrality—would impose the transparency of the architectural configuration processes of the blockchain.

4 Global Law

The issues related to the regulation of the web have given rise to an intense legal debate, where authors have invented expressions such as *lex electronica* or *lex informatica*,[39] which until recently were the above mentioned *lex cryptographia*.[40]

All expressions advanced the idea that the normative activity should be oriented towards the imposition of eminently technical solutions, the whole of which should condition and, therefore, govern the conduct of the users of the network, without going into detailed positive regulations, consequently solving the root problem of the uniformity of the different national legal systems.

[37] Solum and Chung (2004).

[38] Lessig (1999a), p. 511.

[39] Reidenberg (1998) and Lessig (1999a).

[40] De Filippi and Wright (2018).

Here our point is that, for a comparative lawyer, the *lex cryptographia* could be conceptualized as 'a global law without a state'[41] that is commonly shared by coders and blockchains across borders.[42] What follows is that the global dimension of the code (that is based on informatics and math) that allows the connection and the simultaneous exchange of data between users located all over the world and is subjected to different disciplines clashes with the localistic nature of state regulations. Accordingly, we observe the rise of a paradoxical situation, whereby the activity of a blockchain user could be legitimate in the territorial context of a given State, but at the same time be prohibited and sanctioned in another jurisdiction.

For the sake of clarity, we mean that these networks operate across national borders so that they tend to remain scarcely regulated under domestic and supranational laws, with the exception of blockchains where cryptocurrencies are traded.[43]

Our argument (i.e. the code is a global law) would find its own justifying rationale in considering at least three aspects of the *lex cryptographia*, strictly connected to the fact that it consists in eminently technical solutions.

The first profile that is taken into consideration relates to the determination of the jurisdictional context in which the rules of conduct can be applied with effective results. In this regard, it is a peaceful fact that most of the digital activities are transnationally based, occurring between users or between users and websites located in different parts of the planet, and individually submitted to the authority of different countries. Thus, laws could provide for divergent disciplines, considering the fact that they should be implemented in territorial contexts subject to the sovereignty of other states.

In addition, the *lex cryptographia*, which consists of rules and options of a technological nature, pertains to the configuration of the digital world and the setting of network protocols and software, and it does not meet the jurisdictional limit of the national physical borders. The realm (or improperly the jurisdiction) in which such rules apply is the entire global network, so that they would allow to overcome the structural fragmentation of state-derived standardization.[44]

The second qualifying profile of the concept relates to the flexibility of the technical provisions which would allow the laws to better adapt to the disciplinary need for transnational activities, increasing the level of certainty of the applicable regulatory regime, thus, promoting the development and extension of flows of online information and, in particular, of digital market.

This objective, which in a strict sense in the legal context is pursued through the deregulation of economic activities and the expansion of the areas of intervention of contractual autonomy, leaves the task of developing transactional regulation criteria to commercial practice. Therefore, blockchains recognize a wide margin of personalization of the various system configurations on behalf of the user or of the technical

---

[41]Teubner (2004).

[42]Cassese (2003) and Teubner (1997).

[43]Finck (2018).

[44]Reidenberg (1998), p. 578; Finck (2018).

options that govern the operation of network protocols and software, restricting or expanding the access and circulation of digital information.

The third profile of the *lex cryptographia* that is taken into consideration concerns the enforcement regime of the rules of the code. In real environments, the law—in particular with regard to sanctions—finds later application in the conduct they want to repress. However, this fact renders them substantially ineffective in the context of the blockchains, both because they are often not executable towards a person who has his physical headquarters in a jurisdictional area under the authority of another State, and because of the difficulty of identifying the user who has committed a specific offence.

On the contrary, *lex cryptographica* would present the possibility of adopting technical solutions that in advance (*ex ante*) are able to assess the conformity of the actions that the user can perform with a specific legal system, allowing or inhibiting them in a preventive way.[45] Furthermore, and consequently, these are rules that are capable of self-execution, operating automatically, without the need for a third-party authority to intervene ex post to ensure their application.

Interestingly, the emergence of the code makes us remember the lex mercatoria of the medieval socio-economic context and its subsequent developments. This was intended as a set of common rules, emerging from practice, and aimed at creating a disciplinary system capable of increasing the sense of trust and security in commercial operators. The lex mercatoria overcomes the localistic fragmentation of regulatory statutes—as such functional to the development of international transactions.[46] Put it differently, the lex mercatoria *ex machina* (i.e. *lex cryptographica*) leads us to draw comparisons with the medieval age, a return to the ancient and medieval model of jus commune among merchants from different places. That is to say, we may observe a sort of digital medievalism.[47]

This considered, it is undeniable that the blockchains are characterized by an intense profile of disciplinary uncertainty, caused by the non-existence of a uniform regulation applicable with homogeneity. In other words, the state of ineffectiveness of national laws tends to result in the substantial anarchy of blockchains that claim to be able to assure the efficiency of cross-border transactions (with regard to the lex mercatoria) through modern technologies that increase speed and eliminate the physical barriers inherent to determining the spatial context of operation.

In the face of this, legal scholars considered that a solution cannot be reasonably identified in the use of traditional disciplinary instruments of state matrix, but in the recognition of the regulatory potential that resides in the same technique. Particularly, the code governs the blockchain system, which impose rules of conduct on users, suitable to rise to the rank of substantial sources of regulatory production.[48]

[45]De Filippi and Wright (2018).

[46]Berman and Kaufman (1978).

[47]Grossi (2017), p. 101.

[48]De Filippi and Wright (2018).

In other words, it is believed that precise rules of conduct for users can derive from the preparation of technical choices aimed at affecting the functioning of the network. The rules here mentioned were capable of governing the flows of information and data, summed up in a lex computer capable of overcoming the particularisms deriving from the legislation of state source and of ensuring a global self-regulation of the blockchains with a wide margin of flexibility and sharing.

The basic theoretical principle on which the *lex cryptographica* is based is that by which coding, in addition to allowing a huge implementation of commercial activities through the acceleration and intensification of information flows, presents in itself characteristics suitable for avoiding—through the adoption of planning measures—a regime of anarchy, dissolved by any objective regulation of behavior.[49] The various architectural models of the blockchains could also be subject to promotion by national legislators, through the adoption of regulatory measures aimed at using coding for the pursuit of specific political and institutional.[50]

In summary, these are technological solutions based on the self-discipline of the blockchain, which by focusing on the architectural approach of the digital environment, allow the enucleation of a series of rules of conduct suitable to govern the action of the subjects of the network in advance. Substantially, blockchain operates in a uniform way and also opens up forms of self-empowerment for users, called to cooperate on how to manage their rights and on the levels of protection they need to be provided.

From the foregoing observations it emerges that the fragmented nature of national laws constitutes in itself an irremediable limit for an efficient discipline of these networks, whose a-temporal and a-spatial connotations (as before mentioned) make it substantially detached from any attempt at regulation, which can be considered endowed with the characteristics of effectiveness and transactional uniformity.

These considerations are at the basis of the reflections of legal scholars, which has identified in the *lex cryptographica* the most suitable tool for regulating blockchain networks across borders. They argue that it has a high degree of flexibility, which makes it compatible with the structural and functional peculiarities of the network.[51]

Therefore, in such a context, the chapter argues that domestic legislators should trace the principles and guidelines aimed at protecting the fundamental rights of the users, but through a minimalist approach. In summary, we suggest that regulatory flexibility by the state and the customization of technical tools should essentially converge towards forms of accountability to protect fundamental rights within these global private regimes of the digital environment.

[49]Finck (2018).

[50]Finck (2018).

[51]De Filippi and Wright (2018).

5 Regulatory Contract Law

Our point is that the rules governing blockchains have been adopted by private self-regulation and, specifically, by coordination among users. Additionally, it appears that the coordination is pursued by relying on a quite peculiar example of regulatory contract law.[52]

This situation inevitably leads to a subversion of the constant conception of the sources of law, which, from the original setting according to which the legal system finds its validity exclusively in compliance with the procedures for the formation of standards, comes to recognize its main factor of innovation. In such a context, the contract takes over the role traditionally reserved to the law in the direction of socio-economic phenomena by assuming a regulatory function.[53]

Private autonomy is the humus from which norms sprout: this is par excellence in the hypothesis of contractual norms, but this concerns customary norms, as ascribable to the same subjects who observe them. As an author observes with respect to the lex mercatoria, contract law is the medium for excellence for trading across borders.[54] In particular, scholars have clearly recognised the role of contractual governance from an historical perspective.[55]

Here the point is that the reliance on contract and contracting in governing blockchains remains, in any case, a common and central element to the networks.[56] Alongside the contract, which assume particular forms in blockchains, there are additional factors, such as conventions, customs, effectiveness.[57] In the words of an author, in blockchains "the legal framework is essentially pushed down to the level of the contract". The goal is "not lawlessness and anarchy, but that legal frameworks become more granular and personalized to the situation".[58]

Specifically, blockchains grounds on the concept of rough consensus. In particular, Lessig notes "We reject kings, presidents and voting. We believe in rough consensus and running code".[59] Now, in blockchains, 'consensus' means that the nodes on the network agree on the same state of the chain, in a sense making it a self-auditing ecosystem. Specifically, consensus protocols allow a blockchain to be updated, while ensuring that every block in the chain is true as well as keeping participants incentivized.

Thus, nodes, developers and others govern blockchains by agreement. This 'rough consensus' is primarily used, for example, to achieve the necessary

[52]Collins (2012).

[53]Cutler and Dietz (2017).

[54]Ferrarese (2006).

[55]Cutler and Dietz (2017), p. 9.

[56]Taskinsoy (2019).

[57]Bobbio (1942), p. 101.

[58]Swan (2015).

[59]Lessig (2005), p. 55.

agreement on a single data value or a single state of the network among distributed processes or multi-agent systems, such as cryptocurrencies.

Interestingly, consensus decision-making is a creative and dynamic way of reaching agreement between all members of a group. Instead of simply voting for an item and having the majority of the group get their way, a group using consensus is committed to finding solutions that everyone actively supports, or at least can live with.

This consensus is algorithmic because it represents a process in computer science used to achieve agreement on a single data value among distributed processes or systems. Interestingly, users agree because they rely on the code itself, namely the technology.

In brief, consensus mechanisms are protocols that make sure all nodes (a device on the blockchain that maintains the blockchain and, sometimes, processes transactions) are synchronized with each other and agree on which transactions are legitimate and are added to the blockchain.

In this sense, it is possible to note that smart contracts play a fundamental role within the blockchain, and specifically they represent a new means of transacting among nodes and developers, and, more important, contribute to a new paradigm of coordination among nodes, miners and coders with respect to traditional forms of governance and management.[60] Legal scholars pointed out that a smart contract is a computer program that directly controls the transfer of digital currencies or assets between parties under certain conditions. These programs are stored on blockchain technology and, upon the circumstances of the case, they may (totally or partially) contain binding obligations and amount to a binding contract.[61]

Indeed, some scholars imagine a future where commerce will take place exclusively using smart contracts, thereby avoiding current activities such as contract drafting, judicial intervention, opportunistic behavior and the inherent ambiguities of written language. Others highlight the elimination of reliance upon trust-based intermediaries made possible by hosting self-executing contract code on distributed systems, and the potential for commercial activity to take place between the decentralized autonomous organizations (DAOs) without any need for human interaction or intervention.[62]

It is clear that the physiognomy of law is changing around the wishes of the new sovereigns, the programmers exposing such an algorithmic consensus in trading, and managing the blockchains. Therefore, the clear features of the law (hinged in the state legal systems) fade into soft law, the a-typical nature of contract law, the flexibility of rules created and managed privately, and the dismissal of the paradigm of validity and the rise of the criterion of effectiveness.

As a result, the law as the product of a process of political integration in the context of a democratic-pluralistic state system is subject to the right of a contractual

[60]Davidson et al. (2018).

[61]Di Matteo et al. (2019).

[62]Werbach (2018).

matrix born in a-territorial and digital blockchains. The subrogation takes place primarily through the direct occupation of the spaces of political law, both in the sense of overlap with existing norms and as colonization of virgin territories. In the hypothesis of the overlap, there is a sort of de facto de-application of rules belonging to the state, supranational or international hard law, in favor of the (auto) rules produced by the code programmers.

First, the existing law results to be inadequate or inconsistent with the priorities of the new digital horizon, an inadequacy that we can define as political and which results in a provision of political law.

The second hypothesis concerns the 'beauty of speed'[63] or to the image of the digital blockchain as hyperactive time; scientific-technological evolution is driving a race with impetuous rhythms, which redraws the boundaries of the economy, politics and society. Hard law rules are not suitable for the new rhythms and the coders impose their own understanding of economy and society.

It is the right of the dictatorship of the present, where the normative force of the fact only tells us that the status quo is legitimate. In the light of the concept of law explained above, it is always a question of law, albeit an undemocratic law, without aspirations of justice, but rather dominated by efficiency aimed at effectiveness.

Therefore, the terrain of the clash with the law opens up: recognizing the effectiveness as a source of law does not mean to accept its rampant subordination to technology. While blockchains users may reach a disenchanted awareness of the status quo, they cannot ignore the defense of the law as being democratic, emancipated and anchored to constitutional values. In other words, effectiveness arises as a criterion of legitimacy in blockchains, thus creating a legal vacuum and corroding the spaces of the law.[64]

The question is whether we should recognize the obsolescence of the law in the face of disruptive innovation. The question is whether coders, private subjects, are entitled to attribute or deny a right regardless of democratic legitimacy and refractory to any control from the state.[65]

Indeed, we observe the rise of contract law that is flexible, rapid and transnational by nature and particularly the fundamental role of such a 'software and contract' (i.e. the smart contract) of the governance of blockchains. This process could also be understood given that the contract is able to manage a set of horizontal relationships of users, while abandoning vertical relationships among them.

Indeed, discussing the decentralization of blockchains does not mean thinking of a right that comes from below, created through a democratic and equal sharing and sharing in legal production. This is rather the result of a fragmented and shattered right, prey to the subjects who have the power to appropriate it for their own use and consumption: developers, coders, and programmers. The history of the Internet

---

[63]Marinetti (1909).

[64]Bobbio (1942).

[65]Teubner (2004).

would seem to confirm this assumption. The Internet, the network born to be a space of freedom, ended up being an oligopoly of data.

In any case, it is clear that the medium (technology, coding) is becoming the aim, the end of communication. In the light of this reflection, the famous phrase 'the medium is the message' immediately becomes understandable: the means transforms the messages it conveys, and often, in the post-modern era, becomes the end.[66]

This also implies that, by virtue of coding, the contract occurring within blockchains takes on completely different connotations with respect to the conception of this institution that belongs to the real world. In some cases, it will not even be possible to speak of a contract, but of the mere automatic execution of a contract already concluded.[67]

In his book, Werbach outlines four different 'trust architectures'. The first is peer-to-peer trust. It corresponds to morals and reputational systems according to which people come to trust each other. The second is leviathan trust, which corresponds to institutional trust. You can see this working in our system of contracts, which allows parties that do not trust each other to enter into an agreement because they both trust that a government system will help them resolve disputes. The third is intermediary trust. A good example is the credit card system, which allows untrusting buyers and sellers to engage in commerce. The fourth trust architecture is distributed trust. This trust applies to the security system that is blockchain.

To clarify, what blockchain does is shift some of the trust in people and institutions to trust in technology. You need to trust the cryptography, the protocols, the software, the computers and the network. In brief, you need to trust them as a whole, because there are often single points of failure.

The medium (the blockchain) transforms the bargaining rules, as we know them. Nodes enter contracts without trusting, nor even knowing, the other party or parties. The code executes contracts in an automatic way with no flexibility at all.

Furthermore, the courts and tribunals ensure the force of the law in the real environment. In blockchains, the enforcement is incorporated into the writing of a code that makes the contractual clauses executable algorithmically. In doing so, the programmer jointly exercises functions that, in the real world, are comparable to both legislative and jurisdictional ones.

6 The Interplay of Law and Code

Our analysis is both descriptive and normative with respect to blockchain. The sections above underline how there is an undoubted attempt on behalf of 'global technology' to engulf the old state-owned law and highlight how there is currently no prevalence of a model. Instead, we can see the coexistence of two regulatory

[66]McLuhan (1994).

[67]Werbach (2018).

structures (law and technology), which appear to be destined to interplay in the future.

Also important is the analysis carried out so far which highlights the need to think about the question not so much in terms of opposition between law and code, but more in terms of interaction and, perhaps, cooperation.

Our reconstruction clashes with the two main positions in scholarship that are usually opposing each other. One focuses on the liberal conception of the blockchain (namely, cyber-libertarianism), while the other applies a paternalistic conception to blockchains (namely, cyber-paternalism). In the first case, the code would be the only regulatory source of the blockchains, while in the second case, the law should be imposed in order to prevail over the code through the regulation of the networks. In other words, the law should limit the environment of these digital private regimes, while clashing against its transnational dimension, just to provide an example.

Otherwise, the foregoing considerations tend to establish a regime between code and state rules, tending to interact in governing blockchains. The intensification of such interplay is at present the only way to develop blockchain technology with the aim of promoting its implementation from infancy to a mature technology. It especially has a potential for managing private and commercial transactions across borders that surely deserves our efforts. Having considered the above, the chapter favors the adoption of regulatory interventions characterized by an intense margin of flexibility and self-regulation within the networks, while fixing principles also by the law. Otherwise, the enthralling rhythm of technological evolution—which constantly finds more complex and faster forms for the circulation of information flows—and the accentuation of the profiles of a-territoriality and a-temporality of the blockchain will tend to marginalize the scope of the state and supranational law even more.[68] In our view, the law should assume an indispensable role: it must protect the respect of our shared fundamental values within blockchains and when they interplay with the real world. As an author notes, human dignity is not negotiable also within digital private regimes.[69] In this respect, the code risks to favour the affirmation of merely commercial interests—similarly, to what happened with the lex mercatoria.[70] The chapter points out this intense mixture of legal and extra-legal tools for regulating blockchains and the difficult search of a point of equilibrium in these transnational law regimes to promote the evolution of the blockchain and, at the same time, the protection of fundamental values of our societies. In the words of an author, "Technology is now deeply intertwined with policy. We are building complex socio-technical systems at all levels of our society. (...) Surviving the future depends in bringing technologists and policymakers together".[71]

[68]Irti (2009), p. X.

[69]Teubner (2004), pp. 126–127.

[70]Teubner (2004), p. 126.

[71]Schneier (2019).

7 Conclusion

Our conclusion follows: the blockchain subverts the traditional configuration of comparative law that is based on a territorial conception of the law.[72] Indeed, scholarship in philosophy[73] and social sciences[74] has revealed the decline in the role of territory as an organizing principle (i.e. the doctrine of 'deterritorialization').

In this chapter, we argue that alongside the legal systems, other 'normative regimes' have come into existence in digital environments: they flow from a set of independent normative sources, such as the code, and ultimately the social norms of the nodes, the miners and the core developers.[75] Thus, code developers, nodes and thinkers (i.e. legal scholars) are capable of playing part (or all) the functions of legal formants beyond the rigid limits of the law in a formal sense.[76] Our claim is that comparative law is called to explore these new legal spaces.[77] Indeed, it must be noted that the creation of blockchains that allow the simultaneous interaction of a number of users located all over the planet has inevitably contributed to the development of these transnational law regimes of the digital environment.

We observe the elevation of technology, as noted in the introduction, to the rank of global authority, producer of its own rules intended to favor the efficiency of international commerce and capable of orienting (*rectius*: determining) the economic and social policy decisions of states, towards affirmation of special interests.[78] A question follows on whether our case could be considered an example of global law.[79]

This process, which has already been in place for some time, has marked the retreat of the directive action traditionally carried out by national laws—the fragmented nature of which represents an obstacle to the functionality of transnational blockchains. Clearly, the affirmation of blockchains and their rules—is weakening the control capacities of national politics and has challenged the regulatory functionality of the legislation in a formal sense. It is therefore true that state law is not very flexible for efficient international commerce, the validity of which is subordinated to its derivation from a hierarchy of sources of law, legitimated by a political constitution, which governs the bodies responsible for enacting it and it related training procedures.[80]

In blockchains, that are characterized by the above-mentioned a-spatial and a-territorial dimension of the digital world, a new lex mercatoria has emerged,

---

[72]Siems (2018), pp. 303–331; Michaels (2016); Husa (2015), p. 55.

[73]Deleuze and Guattari (1972).

[74]Teubner (2012).

[75]Schrepel (2019).

[76]Sacco (1991).

[77]Hofmann and Botzem (2010), p. 18.

[78]David (1976) and Galgano (2005).

[79]Siems (2018), p. 331.

[80]Galgano (2005).

which operated in a reality characterized by fragmented jurisdictions: the *lex cryptographica*. In other words, the case here considered confirms the trend towards 'deterritorialization', a term which is meant to refer specifically to detachment of regulatory authority from a specific territory.

The chapter conceived blockchain networks in terms of transnational law regimes at the crossroad of the digital and the real environments. In particular, blockchains overcome their discontinuity from the legal systems by relying on the code, the forces of the market and the enucleation of common rules (i.e. social norms, such as forking). The latter, through their repeated observance, were elevated to the rank of uniform 'norm' destined to find application on a universal scale, exceeding the limits set by the 'particular' law of the national systems.[81] Having noted the above, the fascinating expression the 'code is law' demonstrates how technological architectures contain normative languages, that are linked to math and algorithms of self-organization that establish and control the rules of blockchains.[82]

Therefore, the distinctive profiles of blockchain as transnational regimes also emerged in their 'digital' and 'global connotation' as opposed to the local character of the state-based law. Moreover, blockchain relies on the concept of a 'software and contract' (i.e. smart contract) because of its rapidity, and adaptability to changes in reality in contrast with the rigidity of the laws. Indeed, contracting within blockchains open up forms of agreement (rectius of personalization) in defining specific regulatory structures and sanctions.[83]

Additionally, the code deals with the shortcomings of law with regard to blockchains: the slowness in the regulatory processes of technology is an example. Innovation runs too quickly compared to the legislators' ability to come up with a solution.[84]

The consequence of this is the aforementioned process of interplay between law and code, which represents a great challenge for legal scholars. It also represents a food for thoughts for comparative law scholars questioning whether the code may represent a case of global law.[85] Finally, the chapter highlighted how the contract plays a central role in managing international commercial transactions and contributes to governing blockchain networks. Of course, the contract takes on new connotations because of the 'medium' blockchains, so much so that this institution seems to be distorted with respect to its traditional definition and regulation in national systems. In particular, the reliance on the notion of 'rough consensus' and the new architecture of trust just provides an example of how much blockchain users are redesigning our common understanding of contracts and contracting.

[81] Irti (2009).

[82] De Filippi and Wright (2018).

[83] Galgano (2005).

[84] Schrepel (2019).

[85] Twining (2000).

References

Berman HJ, Kaufman C (1978) The law of international commercial transactions (Lex Mercatoria). Harv Int Law J 274:221–277
Bobbio N (1942) Custom as a normative fact. Giappichelli, Torino
Brownsword R, Scotford E, Yeung K (2017) The Oxford handbook of law, regulation and technology. Oxford University Press, Oxford
Calliess R-P, Zumbansen (2012) Rough consensus and running code. Hart, Oxford and Portland
Cassese (2003) The global legal space. Laterza, Roma-Bari
Collins H (2012) Regulating contracts. Oxford University Press, Oxford
Creutzfeldt N, Mason M, McConnachie K (eds) (2020) Routledge handbook on socio-legal theory and methods. Routledge, London
Cutler AC, Dietz T (2017) The politics of private transnational governance by contract. Routledge, London
David R (1976) International trade law: a new task for national legislators or a new lex mercatoria?, in Riv. dir. civ., 577
Davidson S, De Filippi P, Potts J (2018) Blockchains and the economic institutions of capitalism. J Inst Econ 14(4):639–658. https://doi.org/10.1017/S1744137417000200
De Filippi P, Wright A (2018) Blockchain and the law. The rule of code. Harvard University Press, Cambridge
Deleuze G, Guattari F (1972) Anti-OEdipus. Minuet, Paris
Di Matteo L, Cannarsa M, Poncibò C (2019) The Cambridge handbook of smart contracts, blockchain technology and digital platforms. Cambridge University Press, Cambridge
Ferrarese MR (2006) Boundless law. Legal inventiveness and spaces in the global world. Laterza, Roma-Bari
Finck M (2018) Blockchain regulation and governance in Europe. Cambridge University Press, Cambridge
Galgano F (2005) Globalization in the mirror of law. Il Mulino, Bologna
Grossi P (2017) The invention of law. Laterza, Rome-Bari
Hofmann J, Botzem S (2010) Transnational governance spirals: the transformation of rule-making authority in internet regulation and corporate financial reporting. Crit Policy Stud 4(1):18–37
Husa J (2015) A new introduction to comparative law. Hart, Oxford
Irti N (2009) The legal order of the market. Laterza, Roma-Bari
Irti N, Severino E (2001) Dialogue on law and technique. Laterza, Rome-Bari
Irti N, Severino E (2006) The questions of the jurist and the answers of the philosopher (a dialogue on law and technique). Contr impr 665
Jessup P (1956) Transnational law. Yale University Press, New Haven
Konashevych O (2019) Why 'permissioned' and 'private' are not blockchains. https://doi.org/10.2139/ssrn.3496468. Accessed 20 Mar 2020
Lessig L (1996) Reading the constitution in cyberspace. Emory Law Rev 896
Lessig L (1999a) The law of the horse: what cyberlaw might teach. Harv Law Rev 113:501–546. https://doi.org/10.2307/1342331
Lessig L (1999b) Code and other laws of cyberspace. Basic Books, New York
Lessig L (2005) Commons on the wires. In: Hartley J (ed) Creative industries. Blackwell, Malden MA, Oxford, pp 55–69
Lianos I, Hacker P, Eich S, Dimitropoulos G (2019) Regulating blockchain. Techno-social and legal challenges. Oxford University Press, Oxford
Maddrey N (2018) The three branches of blockchain governance, medium. https://medium.com/digitalassetresearch/the-three-branches-of-blockchain-governance-75a29bf98880. Accessed 20 Mar 2020
Marinetti FT (1909) Manifesto of futurism
McLuhan M (1994) Understanding media: the extensions of man. MIT, Boston

Michaels R (2016) Transnationalizing comparative law. Maastricht J Eur Comp Law 23 (2):352–358. https://doi.org/10.1177/1023263X1602300208

Reidenberg JR (1998) Lex Informatica: the formulation of information policy rules through technology. Tex Law Rev 76:553–593

Sacco R (1991) Legal formants: a dynamic approach to comparative law. Am J Comp Law 39 (1):1–34

Schneier B (2019) We must bridge the gap between technology and policy making. Our future depends on it, World Economic Forum. https://www.weforum.org/agenda/2019/11/we-must-bridge-the-gap-between-technology-and-policy-our-future-depends-on-it. Accessed 20 Mar 2020

Schrepel T (2019) Is blockchain the death of antitrust law? The Blockchain Antitrust Paradox. Geo Law Tech Rev 3:281. https://doi.org/10.2139/ssrn.3193576

Severino E (2009) Il destino della tecnica. Bur, Milan

Siems M (2018) Comparative law. Cambridge University Press, Cambridge

Solum L, Chung M (2004) The layers principle. Internet architecture and the law. Notre Dame Law Rev 815

Swan M (2015) Blockchain: blueprint for a new economy. O'Reilly Media, Sebastopol

Taskinsoy J (2019) Blockchain: a misunderstood digital revolution. Things you need to know about blockchain. https://doi.org/10.2139/ssrn.3466480. Accessed 20 Mar 2020

Teubner G (1992) Law as an autopoietic system. The European University Institute Press

Teubner G (1997) Global law without a state. Dartmouth

Teubner G (2004) Global private regimes: neo-spontaneous law and dual constitution of autonomous sectors? In: Ladeur KH (ed) Public governance in the age of globalization. Ashgate, Aldershot, pp 71–87

Teubner G (2012) Constitutional fragments. Societal constitutionalism and globalization. Oxford University Press, Oxford

Tien L (2004) Architectural regulation and the evolution of social norms. Yale J Law Technol 7 (1):1–22

Twining W (2000) Globalisation & legal theory. Butterworths, United Kingdom

Walch A (2019) Deconstructing decentralization: exploring the core claim of crypto systems. In: Brummer C (ed) Crypto assets: legal and monetary perspectives. Oxford University Press

Werbach K (2018) The blockchain and the new architecture of trust. MIT, Boston

Wright A, De Filippi P (2015) Decentralized blockchain technology and the rise of Lex Cryptographia. https://doi.org/10.2139/ssrn.2580664. Accessed 20 Mar 2020

Part III
Smart Contracts and Dispute Resolution

Smart (Legal) Contracts, or: Which (Contract) Law for Smart Contracts?

Giesela Rühl

Contents

1 Introduction

The law applicable to smart contracts is a neglected topic. At times it is even discarded as irrelevant or unnecessary. In fact, many authors claim that smart contracts especially when stored and executed with the help of blockchain

This chapter further develops the topics covered by the Author in Rühl (2019a), p. 147 ff. as well as Rühl (2019b).

G. Rühl (✉)
Humboldt University of Berlin, Berlin, Germany
e-mail: giesela.ruehl@hu-berlin.de

B. Cappiello, G. Carullo (eds.), *Blockchain, Law and Governance*,
https://doi.org/10.1007/978-3-030-52722-8_11

technology make contract law and, in fact, the entire legal system obsolete.[1] "Code is law" is the frequently cited catchphrase.[2] In the following chapter I will challenge this view and argue, first, that smart contracts need contract law just as other, traditional contracts, and, second, that the applicable contract law can—at least in most cases—be determined with the help of the traditional rules of private international law.

The chapter is organized in two parts: In the first part (Sect. 2) I will look at the relationship of smart contracts and the rules of contract law. And in the second part (Sect. 3) I will shed light on the rules of private international law and their application to smart contracts. However, before getting started several clarifications are in order: *First*, I will not embark on the difficult—and probably impossible—endeavour to define the term "smart contract". There are a multitude of definitions out there.[3] And there is no agreement as to which is the right one. For the purpose of the following chapter suffice it to note that a "smart contract" is first and foremost a piece of software that controls, monitors, or documents the execution of some legal obligation that has been created elsewhere.[4] *Second*, I will not discuss whether and under what conditions smart contracts amount to "contracts" in legal terms. The reason for this is that the answer depends on the very topic of my chapter, namely the applicable law: A contract under German law is not necessarily the same as a contract under Italian, French or English law. And chances are that different requirements have to be met before a smart contract can, if at all, be qualified as a contract. *Third*, I will only discuss which *contract* law applies to smart contracts. In contrast, I will not deal with the question which property law determines the third-party effects that may or may not result from a smart contract. By the same token, I will not deal the question of which public or regulatory, for example, data protection laws govern smart contracts. *Fourth,* I will only look at the applicable contract law from a European perspective, more specifically from a European Union perspective. I will, therefore, only discuss which contract law will apply to smart contracts if courts in EU Member State have to determine the applicable law. *Fifth*, even though smart contracts are usually discussed in one breath with blockchain technology and cryptocurrencies I will not confine my analysis accordingly. This is because smart contracts do not have to run on blockchains. Nor is their use limited to the transfer and the use of Bitcoin, Ripple and the like. In fact, they can literally be applied to execute and support almost any kind of transaction, including the transfer of real-world assets such as movable and immovable property. The following chapter will, therefore, use blockchain-based smart contracts as well as the transfer of cryptocurrencies, if at all, as examples for how smart contracts can be put to use. *Finally*, I will only focus on the relationship between the immediate parties of a

[1]See Sect. 2.

[2]The catchphrase can be traced back to Lessig (1999, 2000).

[3]See for an overview Braegelmann and Kaulartz (2019), pp. 1 ff; Low and Mik (2020), pp. 1 ff; Mik (2019), pp. 70 f.

[4]In a similar vein Szabo NJ (1994); Filippi and Wright (2019), pp. 74 ff; Lim et al. (2016).

smart contract whereas I will not shed light on the relationship to other parties. In particular, I will not dwell on the question which law applies to the blockchain infrastructure as such and to the relationship between the parties involved in the setting up and the running of a blockchain, the so-called "nodes".[5]

2 Smart Contracts and Traditional Contract Law

The question of how people can trade with each other independently of national laws is a question that has kept philosophers, economists and lawyers busy for centuries.[6] In recent years, the discussion has been fuelled by the emergence of smart contracts. They promise nothing less than automatic execution of legal obligations and, hence, the end of external enforcement mechanisms such as lawyers and courts. Some authors even go so far to argue that smart contracts, especially when stored on and executed on a blockchain, do not require any legal system to operate. *Kai Schiller*, author of the German blog blockchainwelt.de, for example, notes:

> Smart contracts enable the execution of trustworthy transactions and agreements between anonymous parties and without the need for a ... legal system ...[7]

And a Russian colleague, *Alexander Savelyev* adds:

> ... smart contracts do not need a legal system for their existence: they may operate without any overarching legal framework. De facto, they represent a technological alternative to the whole legal system.[8]

A closer look, however, reveals that smart contracts are not—and should not—be independent of the law.[9] In fact, while it might be true that smart contracts do not need a legal system to operate and to execute legal obligations, there can be little doubt that smart contracts depend on a legal system to determine whether there is any enforceable legal obligation to begin with. This is because the smart contract itself—as a piece of code—does not have the means of knowing whether an enforceable legal obligation has been validly created. It does not even have the means of knowing whether the parties who decide to make use of a smart contract

[5]For an overview of the choice of law problems associated with the blockchain technology, notably cryptocurrency systems Dickinson (2019), pp. 93 ff; Lehmann (2019), pp. 93 ff; Martiny (2018a), p. 553; Zimmermann (2018), p. 566.

[6]Kronman (1985).

[7]Schiller (2018).

[8]Savelyev (2017), p. 132.

[9]In a similar vein Cardozo's Blockchain Project, (2018) p. 9 ("smart contracts ... will not operate in a legal vacuum"). Filippi and Wright (2019), p. 78 ("do not operate in a vacuum"); Lim et al. (2016) ("... smart contracts do not exist in a vacuum"); Martiny (2018a), p. 559; Mik (2017), p. 287 ("... smart contracts must ... remain compatible with their jurisdiction-specific legal framework"); Möstlein (2019), p. 285 ("..., legal jurisdictions will always prevail over digital jurisdictions"); Vos (2019).

have validly agreed to do so. All that a smart contract can do is to do what it has been told to do. However, the mere power to do something, does not mean that doing it, is right or legal. Code is not law. And it should not.

Take the following—frequently cited—example for a smart contract: A rents an apartment from B. They agree that B will be entitled to lock the door to the apartment if A does not pay the rent. In addition, they agree to enforce their agreement with the help of a smart contract that will automatically lock the door if A fails to pay. Now, many will say that the smart contract of my example will ensure that A will pay the rent on a regular basis. And this may well be true. The problem, however, is, that under some laws, for example German law, the use of a smart contract in my example is invalid because a landlord is not allowed to evict the tenant only because he fails to pay the rent. He will have to terminate the contract first—which he may only do if the tenant has not paid the rent for at least two months.[10] And even then he will have to go to court to have the tenant evicted the rationale clearly being protection of the tenant as a weaker party. The example, thus, shows that smart contracts need a legal system to determine whether they are valid or invalid, legal or illegal. They need a legal system as a normative point of reference.

The decisive question, therefore, is not whether smart contracts are subject to law at all, but rather to which law they are subject. Which law determines whether a contractual obligation has been validly created? Which law determines whether a contractual obligation may be enforced with the help of a smart contract?

3 Smart Contracts and Private International Law

Traditionally, the question of which law applies to a contract is determined by the rules of private international law. As a field of law that looks back on almost 1000 years of history[11] and that is, today, firmly anchored in the legal systems of almost all states,[12] it assigns cases that have a connection to different states to a specific legal system with the help of choice of law rules. The literature on smart contracts, however, has largely ignored private international law and decided to simply assume that a certain national law applies. Or it is argued that smart contracts especially when stored and enforced with the help of blockchain technology are hard to assign to a particular legal system because blockchain transactions are, as a matter of principle, conducted simultaneously on computers scattered around many different jurisdictions.[13] In a contribution for the Oxford Business Law Blog, *Mateja Durovic*, for example, writes:

---

[10] Cf. §§ 543(1) and (2) No 3 of the German Civil Code.

[11] See Siehr (2017), pp. 1390 ff.

[12] See, for example, the national reports to be found in Basedow et al. (2017).

[13] Note, however, that there are many different types of blockchains with very different characteristics, capabilities and functions. See only Filippi and Wright (2019), pp. 13 ff. and 33 ff.

> What makes the regulation of smart contracts particularly complex is their cross-border nature, given that they are generally operated by different computers located in different jurisdictions. This may make it more difficult to identify the law ... applicable to the contract.[14]

The interesting question, therefore, is whether private international law is able to deal with smart contracts? Are the traditional rules that determine the applicable contract law able to assign smart contracts to a particular legal system? Are they able to determine the applicable law if smart contracts are operated on different computers located in different jurisdictions with the help of blockchain technology? In the remainder of this chapter I will argue that the answer is yes and that at least the European rules of private international law are well equipped to deal with the vast majority smart contracts. However, before I turn to the details a few words on the need for private international law are in order.

3.1 *When to Apply: The Case for Private International Law*

3.1.1 Connection to a Foreign Country

Private international law always comes into the picture when there is a reason to think about the applicable law because a case has a connection to a foreign country.[15] If there is no such connection domestic law will naturally apply. But when exactly is this requirement met? When exactly is a case connected to a foreign country? Is it sufficient that a smart contract is operated on a blockchain that involves actors ("nodes") scattered across various jurisdictions? As a matter of principle, the answer should be yes. After all, there is broad agreement that no high demands are to be placed on the connection to a foreign country. In the context of contracts, it is, for example, sufficient if parties from different states are involved or if the contract is concluded or performed abroad.[16] According to the majority view even the use of a foreign language will trigger the need to think about the applicable law.[17] As a consequence, it should also be taken as a sufficient connection to a foreign country if a smart contract is processed with the help of a cross-border blockchain.[18] Note,

[14]Durovic (2018). In a similar vein Djazayeri (2016), at E. III. ; Woebbeking (2019), p. 109, note 38.

[15]Note, however, that there is a discussion whether private international law simply does not apply if there is no connection to a foreign country—or whether the rules of private international law apply, but will necessarily lead to domestic law. As regards the Rome I Regulation, the majority view seems to be that the connection to a foreign country is a requirement for application of the Rome I Regulation because the European legislature, by virtue of Article 81 of the Treaty on the Functioning of the European Union (TFEU), is only allowed to regulate cross-border cases. See for a more detailed discussion Magnus (2018), pp. 507 ff; von Hein (2018), para. 9 f.

[16]Martiny (2018b), para. 23; Weller (2015), para. 19.

[17]Martiny (2018b), para. 23; Weller (2015), para. 19.

[18]Rühl (2019a), p. 154 para. 13.

however, that this finding does not mean that the use of blockchain technology or the location of the "nodes" will actually result in the application of a foreign law.[19] It only means that there is a reason to check whether this is so.

3.1.2 Uniform Substantive Law

The connection to a foreign country, however, is only a necessary, but not a sufficient condition for the application of private international law. In fact, despite a connection to a foreign country there is no need to determine the applicable law with the help of private international law where uniform substantive law applies.[20] With regard to international contracts uniform substantive law is usually to be found in international treaties such as the United Nations Convention on Contracts for the International Sale of Goods of 11 April 1980 (CISG).[21] It contains internationally unified substantive law for international sales contracts and directly applies to contracts for the sale of goods concluded between parties having their seat in different contracting states (Article 1 CISG).[22] A smart contract that meets these requirements will, therefore, be directly governed by the provisions of the CISG with no need to resort to national law with the help of private international law. National law will only reenter the stage if gaps in the CISG have to be filled (Article 7 (2) CISG) or if application of the CISG is excluded by law or by agreement of the parties (Articles 2 and 6 CISG). According to Article 2 lit. a) CISG, for example, the Convention does not apply to the sale of goods for personal, family or household use and, hence, to consumer contracts.

Sales law, however, is not the only field where international treaties laying down uniform substantive law can be found. In addition, they are also frequently encountered in transport law.[23] In fact, many contracts for the carriage of goods or persons are governed by the Convention on the Contract for the International Carriage of Goods by Road (CMR) of 19 May 1956, the Convention for the Unification of Certain Rules for International Carriage by Air of 28 May 1999, or the Convention concerning International Carriage by Rail (COTIF). In addition, European regulations such as the Air Passenger Rights Regulation of 2004[24] and the Passenger

[19]See for the details Sect. 3.2.

[20]Ferrari (2017a), pp. 1772 ff. See for a more detailed discussion of the dogmatic explanation why uniform substantive law supersedes private international law von Hein (2018), para. 14.

[21]See for an overview Ferrari (2017b), pp. 338 ff.

[22]Buchleitner and Rabl (2017), p. 13; Rühl (2019a), p. 151 para. 8. See for a discussion about whether the CISG may apply to contracts relating to the sale of bitcoin as well as contracts of sale for bitcoin Martiny (2018a), p. 561.

[23]See for an overview Damar (2017), pp. 1726 ff.

[24]Regulation (EC) No 261/2004 of the European Parliament and of the Council of 11 February 2004 establishing common rules on compensation and assistance to passengers in the event of denied boarding and of cancellation or long delay of flights, and repealing Regulation (EEC) No 295/91, OJ 2004 L 46/1.

Rights Regulation of 2007[25] may come into the picture. If and to the extent a smart contract falls into the scope of one of these instruments there is, again, no room for national law and, hence, no need for private international law. The latter will, again, only become relevant to the extent that the above-mentioned treaties and regulations contain gaps.

3.2 *Where to Look: The Sources of Private International Law*

If and to the extent that the applicable law has to be determined with the help of private international law the next question that arises is: which rules of private international law? The answer depends on who is or who will potentially be charged with the task of determining the applicable law:[26] Courts located in the European Union will usually look to the Rome I Regulation[27] and the uniform choice of law rules to be found therein.[28] However, it is not a matter of course that the Rome I Regulation can actually be applied.

3.2.1 European Law: Rome I Regulation

According to Article 1(1) the Rome I Regulation only governs the determination of the applicable law if the case relates to a contractual obligation in civil and commercial matters.[29] With a view to smart contracts this requirement obviously triggers the question of whether they amount to "contractual obligations"? Unfortunately, there is as of yet no case law that would deal, let alone answer, this question.[30]

[25]Regulation (EC) No 1371/2007 of the European Parliament and of the Council of 23 October 2007 on rail passengers' rights and obligations, OJ 2007 L315/14.

[26]Note that this does not mean that the following considerations only matter when a smart contract actually comes before a court. Since parties are acting and negotiating "in the shadow of the law" they will be essential for all parties who wish to know what rights and obligations may come with a smart contract.

[27]Regulation (EC) No 593/2008 of the European Parliament and of the Council of 17 June 2008 on the law applicable to contractual obligations (Rome I) OJ 2008 EU L 177/6. See for an overview Garcimartín Alférez (2017), pp. 1553 ff; Lando and Nielsen (2008), p. 1687. As well as the contributions in Ferrari and Leible (2009).

[28]Note, that according to the majority view the Rome I Regulation is only binding for state courts, but not for arbitral tribunals. See for a more detailed discussion Mankowski (2011), pp. 30 ff.

[29]See for exceptions Article 1(2) Rome I Regulation.

[30]Note that the term "contractual obligations" is European in origin and in nature. It is, therefore, to be interpreted autonomously and without reference to national law. For the same reason the question whether a smart contract amounts to a contractual obligation in the meaning of Article 1 (1) Rome I Regulation has to be distinguished from the question of whether a smart contract amounts to a contract under English, French, German or Italian law. See for a detailed discussion Rösler (2017).

However, according to the CJEU the term "contractual obligation" covers all obligations freely assumed by one (private) party towards another[31] irrespective of whether they are mutual or unilateral.[32] When applied to smart contracts, this definition naturally raises the problem that smart contracts, as pieces of software, usually do not create obligations themselves. Rather they control, monitor, or document the execution of—freely assumed—obligations that have been created elsewhere. It, therefore, seems save to say that the Rome I Regulation does not apply to smart contracts as such, but "merely" to the obligations that they help to control, monitor, document or execute.[33] The situation may, however, be different if the obligation itself is brought about through algorithms and if the obligation is fully embodied in the code. In this case one can argue that the smart contract itself contains a freely assumed (mutual or unilateral) obligation in the meaning of Article 1(1) Rome I Regulation. But this should remain the exception for the time being. In any event, it should not matter whether the Rome I Regulation applies to the smart contract as such or "merely" to the legal obligations it helps to execute: At the end of the day it is the Rome I Regulation that determines the applicable contract law.

3.2.2 Exceptions: International Treaties and Denmark

That courts in the EU will usually apply the Rome I Regulation to determine the law applicable to smart contracts (or the obligation they help to execute) does not mean that they will always (have to) do so. Two exceptions deserve to be mentioned: *First*, according to Article 25 Rome I Regulation, nothing in the Rome I Regulation prejudices the application of international treaties that lay down choice of law rules for international contracts. Courts in Member States that are party to applicable international treaties will, therefore, have to apply the choice of law rules to be found in these treaties. With a view to smart contracts the 1955 Hague Convention on the law applicable to the international sale of goods[34] may come into the picture. It is in

---

[31] ECJ, C-359/14 and C-475/14 – ERGO Insurance ./. If P & C Insurance, ECLI:EU:C:2016:40, para. 44 ("freely consented"). See also ECJ C-26/91 – Handte ./. TMCS, ECLI:EU:C:1992:268, para. 15 ("freely assumed"); ECJ C-51/97 – Réunion européenne SA ./. Spliethoff's Bevrachtingskantoor BV, ECLI:EU:C:1998:509, para. 17; ECJ C-334/00 – Tacconi ./. Wagner, ECLI:EU:C:2002:499, para. 12; ECJ C-265/02 – Frahuil ./. Assitalia SpA, ECLI:EU:C:2004:77, para. 24. See for a detailed presentation Wilderspin (2017), pp. 472 ff.

[32] ECJ C-27-02 – Engler ./. Janus Versand GmbH, ECLI:EU:C:2005:33, para. 50 ff.; ECJ C-180/06 – Ilsinger ./. Schlank & Schick GmbH, ECLI:EU:C:2009:303, para. 59f.

[33] Rühl (2019a), p. 153, para. 11. In a similar vein Martiny (2018a), pp. 559 f; Zimmermann (2018), pp. 568 f.

[34] Full text available at <https://www.hcch.net/en/instruments/conventions/full-text/?cid=31>.

force, among others, in France and Italy,[35] and lays down uniform choice of law rules for international sales contract. Courts in France and Italy will, therefore, not resort to the Rome I Regulation to determine the applicable law, but to the 1955 Hague Convention if a smart contract qualifies as sales contracts in the meaning of that Convention. *Second*, according to Recital 46 the Rome I Regulation does not apply in Denmark. This is because Denmark does not participate in the adoption of any measures taken under Chapter 4 of Title V TFEU ("Judicial cooperation in civil matters").[36] Danish courts will, therefore, apply rules of national—or international—private international law, notably the rules of the Rome Convention,[37] to determine the law applicable to smart contracts. As regards substance, however, the Rome Convention resembles the Rome I Regulation.[38]

3.2.3 Brexit: Application of the Rome I Regulation in the UK

Application of the Rome I Regulation will also be challenged by the recent departure of the UK from the EU. In fact, since the UK has left the EU on 1 February 2020 the Rome I Regulation no longer applies in the UK by virtue of its membership in the EU. However, pursuant to the Withdrawal Agreement concluded between the UK and the EU[39] it continues to apply up until 31 December 2020.[40] And after that date the Rome I Regulation will remain applicable in the UK by virtue of Sections 2 and 3 of the European Union (Withdrawal) Act 2018 as amended by the European Union (Withdrawal Agreement) Act 2020. Courts in the UK will, therefore, rely on the Rome I Regulation irrespective of both the UK's membership in the EU and the UK's future relationship with the EU.[41] As a consequence, the Rome I Regulation will not only be applied by courts inside, but also by (some) courts outside the EU.

[35] See the status table available at <https://www.hcch.net/en/instruments/conventions/status-table/?cid=31>.

[36] Protocol No. 22 to the Treaty of Lisbon, OJ EU 2012 C 326/299.

[37] Rome Convention of 19 June 1980 on the law applicable to contractual obligations, OJ EC 1980 L266/1.

[38] See for a discussion of the differences Lando and Nielsen (2008), pp. 1687 ff.

[39] Articles 67, 68 and 126 Agreement on the Withdrawal of the United Kingdom of Great Britain and Northern Ireland from the European Union and the European Atomic Energy Community, OJ EU 2019 C384 I/01. See also Section 1a European Union (Withdrawal Act) 2018.

[40] Articles 67, 68 and 126 Withdrawal Agreement (n 38). Note, that according to Article 132 of the Withdrawal Agreement the transition period could have been extended through adoption of a single decision before 1 July 2020. However, the EU and the UK chose not to do so.

[41] See Sections 2 and 3 European Union (Withdrawal) Act 2018. See for a more detailed discussion of the consequences of Brexit for private international law Rühl (2018), pp. 99 ff; Rühl (2020a), p. 443; Rühl (2020b), pp. 21 ff.

3.3 *How to Proceed: The Rome I Regulation and Smart Contracts*

In the light of the above courts in the EU and in the UK—with the exceptions noted above—will usually turn to and apply the Rome I Regulation to determine the law applicable to smart contracts (or the legal obligation they help to execute). Parties who wish to find out which law governs their smart contracts will, therefore, likewise have to look to the Rome I Regulation.[42] What does this mean?

3.3.1 Principle of Party Autonomy

Application of the Rome I Regulation means, first and foremost, that the applicable law will be determined through the principle of party autonomy.[43] One of the cornerstones of European private international law[44] and embodied in Article 3 of the Rome I Regulation, it allows parties to submit their contract to the national law[45] they want and without requiring any territorial or other connection to the chosen law.[46] As regards smart contracts the principle of party autonomy is, therefore, able to establish a connection to a particular legal system even if the smart contract operates in a completely virtual and, as the case may be, completely decentralised environment. For the parties this is good news:[47] They will know which law applies to their contract, i.e. they can easily determine whether their contract is valid or invalid. And, more importantly, they may choose themselves, which contract law they wish to apply. They may choose the contract law that offers the best legal environment for their smart contract.

The decisive question, therefore, is how the parties of a smart contract can choose the applicable law? Since a choice of law can hardly be represented in algorithmic

---

[42] Parties who expect that courts outside the EU will hear a case will, of course, look to the private international law rules that these courts will apply.

[43] See for a more comprehensive presentation Heiss (2009); von Bar and Mankowski (2019), § 1 paras. 60 ff; Muir Watt (2017), pp. 1336 ff; Mills (2018), pp. 326 ff.

[44] Recital 11 Rome I Regulation. Note, that the principle of party autonomy is broadly recognized and applied by virtual all states around the globe. See for a recent account Basedow (2015), pp. 115 ff.

[45] Note that Article 3 Rome I Regulation does not allow the choice of a non-state law, such as, for example, the Principles of European Contract Law, the UNIDROIT Principles of International Commercial Contracts or some form of lex cryptographica. See for a more detailed discussion von Bar and Mankowski (2019), § 1 paras. 183 ff; Mills (2018), pp. 491 ff.

[46] See, however, the limitations to be found in Article 3(3) and (4) Rome I Regulation.

[47] Spink A et al., *Cryptoassets and smart contracts: The UKJT Legal Statements*, 25 November 2019, pp. 36 ff. ("very simple legal solutions to the conflict of laws issue"). In a similar vein Vos G, *Future Proofing for Commercial Lawyers in an Unpredictable World, Annual COMBAR lecture*, 12 November 2019, para. 39. ("The real prize will be to persuade the coders to include a simple English law and UK jurisdiction clause in their algorithmic engagements.").

fashion—“if this, then that”—a choice of law will have to be declared otherwise.[48] The most straightforward way of doing this is an express choice. It can be part of the contract which is executed with the help of the smart contract, or it can be enshrined in a separate declaration, notably a Ricardian contract. A Ricardian contract combines traditional (natural language) and digital—smart—contracts by recording a document both in human and machine-readable format and by linking it to some safe storage or other system.[49] What is more important for the purpose of this chapter, however, is that a Ricardian contract also allows the parties to agree on terms that cannot be directly incorporated into the smart contracts. A Ricardian contract may, therefore, turn out to be the perfect vehicle for a choice of law clause.

A choice of law, however, does not have to be express. According to Article 3 (1) Rome I Regulation it may also be implied. A smart contract or the contract that it serves to execute may, for example, be so obviously tailored to a particular legal system that it can be assumed that the parties wanted the contract to be governed by this law.[50] Yet, the problem with an implied choice is that Article 3(1) Rome I Regulation requires that it is ‘clearly demonstrated’ by the terms of the contracts or the circumstances of the case which means that there must be evidence that the parties actually had the intention to choose the applicable law.[51] In the context of smart contracts such an intention will often be missing because many people, and especially coders, do not know that they can actually choose the applicable law. In this case courts will have to turn to Article 4 Rome I Regulation.

3.3.2 Principle of the Closest Connection

Article 4 Rome I Regulation is one of the longest and one of the most complex provisions of the Rome I Regulation. It provides that a contract is governed by the law of the closest connection. However, to actually find that law, Article 4 needs eight specific choice of law rules, two residual choice of law rules and one escape clause.[52]

---

[48]Rühl (2019a), p. 156.

[49]See the proposal to establish a global, non-profit Ricardian Contract Repository by Oliver Goodenough from Vermont Law School.

[50]Rühl (2019a), p. 19.

[51]See for a more detailed discussion von Bar and Mankowski (2019), § 1 paras. 120 ff; Mills (2018), pp. 327 ff.

[52]See for a detailed presentation von Bar and Mankowski (2019), § 1 paras. 120 ff; Magnus (2009), pp. 27 ff; Remien (2016), pp. 211 ff; Wilderspin (2017), pp. 472 ff.

3.3.2.1 Article 4(1) Rome I Regulation: Specific Contracts

In the absence of a choice of law, determination of the applicable law will always have to start with Article 4(1) Rome I Regulation. The provision contains specific choice of law rules for a number of contracts: In view of contracts for the sale of goods Article 4(1) lit. a Rome I Regulation, for example, provides that the law of the seller's habitual residence applies. Regarding contracts for the provision of services Article 4(1) lit. b Rome I Regulation stipulates that the law of the service provider's habitual residence governs. And as far as contracts relating to immovable property are concerned Article 4(1) lit. c and d Rome I Regulation calls for application of either the country where the property is located or the law of the common habitual residence of the parties. When applied to smart contracts Article 4(1) Rome I Regulation will, therefore, draw a straight line to the applicable law if the smart contract in question (or the contract it helps to execute) may be classified as a contract in the meaning of Article 4(1) lit. a to h Rome I Regulation. Whether this is the case will, of course, depend on the smart contract in question and is, therefore, impossible to say in the abstract. However, as a matter of principle, smart contracts can be used to execute or support almost any type of contract. In particular, they may be used to monitor payment obligations. There is, hence, a good chance that a smart contract will actually fall into the scope of one of the contracts listed in Article 4 (1) lit. a to h Rome I Regulation.[53]

However, even if one of the specific choice of law rules of Article 4(1) Rome I Regulation is applicable, this is not the end of the story. According to the escape clause to be found in Article 4(3) Rome I Regulation a court may refuse to apply the law indicated in Article 4(1) Rome I Regulation and apply the law of another state instead. Yet, in order to do so it must be clear from all the circumstances of the case that the contract is "manifestly more closely connected" with that state. It is, therefore, not enough that the contract has some connection to some other state. Rather it is required that the connection is much stronger than the connection to the state whose law is applicable by virtue of Article 4(1) Rome I Regulation.[54] The mere fact that a smart contract may have connections to a large number of countries because it is processed on a blockchain will, therefore, usually not amount to a manifestly closer connection that will allow departure from Article 4(1) Rome I Regulation.[55]

[53]Examples may include contracts for the sale of goods against payment of Bitcoin or Ripple which will should be governed by Article 4(1) lit. a) Rome I Regulation. See for a more detailed discussion Dickinson (2019), para. 5.10; Martiny (2018a), pp. 559 ff; Zimmermann (2018), p. 569.

[54]Martiny (2018c), para. 287; von Bar and Mankowski (2019), § 1 paras. 353 ff.

[55]Rühl (2019a), pp. 159 f.

3.3.2.2 Article 4(2) Rome I Regulation: Characteristic Performance

Article 4(1) Rome I Regulation will go a long way to determine the law applicable to smart contracts. But there are arguably a number of smart contracts that do not fall under this provision. Take, for example, smart contracts for the sale of cryptocurrencies: They do not amount to contracts for sale of goods in the meaning of Article 4(1) lit. a Rome I Regulation because cryptocurrencies are not tangible.[56] And they do not qualify as contracts concluded within a multilateral trading system in the meaning of Article 4(1) lit. h Rome I Regulation either because Bitcoin, Ripple and are not considered to be financial instruments.[57] In these and other cases, that do not fall under Article 4(1) Rome I Regulation, the residual choice of law rule of Article 4(2) Rome I Regulation comes into the picture. It calls for application of the law of the country where the party required to effect the characteristic, i.e. the non-monetary performance has its habitual residence and, thus, allows for a fairly straightforward determination of the applicable law. Applied to the above-mentioned sale of cryptocurrencies it leads to the law of the seller's habitual residence. However, just like Article 4(1) Rome I Regulation, application of Article 4 (2) Rome I Regulation is subject to the escape clause of Article 4(3) Rome I Regulation. Should it turn out, that a smart contract is manifestly more closely connected to some other state, courts may decide to apply the law of that state. However, as explained above, Article 4(3) Rome I Regulation has to be applied in a restrictive fashion and is, hence, limited to clear cases.

3.3.2.3 Article 4(4) Rome I Regulation: Closest Connection

The specific choice of law rules to be found in Article 4(1) Rome I Regulation and the characteristic performance rule enshrined in Article 4(2) Rome I Regulation will help to determine the applicable law in the bulk of cases relating to smart contracts. Where both provisions fail, for example, because the smart contract is an exchange contract or because several parties without common habitual residence have to effect the characteristic performance, the residual choice of law rule of Article 4(4) Rome I Regulation will apply. It calls for application of the law of the closest connection, however, without giving any indication as to how this law has to be determined. So, what are courts supposed to do when faced with a contract that is not covered by Article 4(1) and (2) Rome I Regulation?

According to the ECJ determination of the law of the closest connection requires courts to proceed in two steps: In a first step they must "conduct an overall

[56]Martiny (2018a), pp. 558 ff; Zimmermann (2018), p. 569. Note, that cryptocurrencies may also be used as means of payment. Contracts for the sale of goods against payment of Bitcoin or Ripple should therefore, be covered by Article 4(1) lit. a) Rome I Regulation. See for a more detailed discussion Dickinson (2019), p. 98; Martiny (2018a), pp. 559 ff; Zimmermann (2018), p. 569.

[57]See for a detailed discussion Dickinson (2019), p. 111.

assessment of all objective factors characterizing the contractual relationship".[58] In a second step courts must then "determine which of those factors are ... most significant".[59] When applying Article 4(4) Rome I Regulation courts will, therefore, have to gather all existing connections of the contract in question and determine the relative weight of these connections as compared to other connections. In so doing, courts will not only have to consider traditional connecting factors like the habitual residence of the parties, the nationality of the parties as well as the place of formation and the place of performance of the contract. Rather they will also have to consider other connecting factors like the language of the contract or the currency in which the contract price has to be paid. As a matter of principle, however, the range of factors that can and have to be considered is not limited.[60] With a view to blockchain transactions it has, therefore, been argued, that courts should also look to the location of the (majority) of "nodes".[61] However, since the location of the "nodes" seems arbitrary and may also be subject to change it remains to be seen whether courts will follow this analysis when applying Article 4(4) Rome I Regulation to blockchain-based smart contracts.[62]

3.3.2.4 Remaining Problems

There is no denying the fact that Article 4 Rome I Regulation is a very complex provision. However, when applied to smart contracts it will, at the end of the day, be possible to say which law applies. This is because Article 4 Rome I Regulation mostly relies on a connecting factor, namely the habitual residence of one of the parties, which is able to link even completely virtual smart contracts to a particular national law:[63] After all, even parties who enter into smart contracts and use blockchains will usually have a habitual residence. And usually it will be possible to determine where this habitual residence is.

This finding, however, should not create the impression that Article 4 Rome I Regulation would never result in any problems when applied to smart contracts. For example, there may be smart contracts that do not easily fit into the traditional categories that characterize Article 4(1) and (2) Rome I Regulation. In a similar vein, it may happen that the habitual residence of the relevant party cannot—or only with difficulty—be determined because the smart contract is processed

---

[58]ECJ C-305/13 – *Haeger & Schmidt GmbH v. Mutuelles du Mans Assurances IARD*, ECLI:EU:C:2014:2320, para. 49. See for a detailed discussion of the circumstances that may be taken into account Martiny (2018c), paras. 307, 320 ff.

[59]Ibid., paras. 307, 320 ff.

[60]See for a comprehensive discussion Ibid., paras. 307, 320 ff.

[61]See, for example, Dickinson (2019), pp. 115 f who argues that the relationship between the participants in the Bitcoin cryptocurrency system have the closest connection to China because this is where the majority of "miners" is located.

[62]Equally sceptical Zimmermann (2018), p. 566.

[63]In a similar vein (with a view to contracts for the transfer of Bitcoin) Lehmann (2019), p. 125.

anonymously—or pseudonymously—via a blockchain.[64] In all of these cases the applicable law will have to be determined in accordance with Article 4(4) Rome I Regulation. And, naturally, this will neither be an easy task nor will it always lead to entirely convincing or foreseeable results. Parties who wish to avoid unpleasant surprises are, therefore, reminded that they may, before and after conclusion of a contract, choose the applicable law in accordance with Article 3 Rome I Regulation. Unnecessary legal uncertainty can, thus, be avoided.

3.3.3 Protection of Weaker Parties, Notably Consumers

The preceding analysis shows that Articles 3 and 4 Rome I Regulation are fairly well equipped to deal with most smart contracts. However, according to Articles 5 to 8 Rome I Regulation both provisions are modified if one party is perceived to be weaker than the other. A discussion of the Rome I Regulation would, therefore, be incomplete without a look at these provisions. Yet, since Articles 5 to 8 Rome I Regulation are at least as complex as Article 4 Rome I Regulation, the following remarks will focus on Article 6 Rome I Regulation and, hence, on the protection of consumers.[65]

3.3.3.1 Party Autonomy and Preferential Law Approach

As discussed earlier in this chapter the Rome I Regulation first and foremost relies on the principle of party autonomy to determine the applicable law.[66] In the context of consumer contracts, however, unlimited application of this principle may cause problems:[67] Since professionals engage in the same kind of transaction on a day-to-day basis they have a cost-justified incentive gather information about alternative laws and to select the law that is most congenial to their interests. Occasionally contracting consumers, in contrast, face severe informational costs and, therefore, will usually forego the acquisition of information about the applicable law and, hence, not be able to assess the quality level of the chosen law. Professionals do, therefore, have an incentive to choose a law with a very low level of consumer protection. And this, in turn, may set a dynamic in motion that will lead to a market for lemons, i.e. a market for inefficient choice of law clauses which may, again in the worst case, result in a complete break-down of the market.

---

[64]With a view to the pseudonymous transfer of cryptoassets such as Bitcoin via blockchain, see Ibid., p. 114. Note, however, that the same author later, at 124 f., claims that it is "easy" to apply Article 4 Rome I Regulation to the contract underlying the transfer of Bitcoin.

[65]See for a more detailed presentation of Articles 5 and 8 Rome I Regulation Rühl (2019a), pp. 161 ff.

[66]See Sect. 3.3.1.

[67]See for a detailed discussion of the rationale of consumer protection in private international law Rühl (2011), pp. 569 ff.

It goes without saying that any such development is not desirable. Article 6 (2) Rome I Regulation, therefore, curtails the effect of choice of law clauses in consumer contracts.[68] Specifically, it provides that a choice of law may not deprive consumers of the mandatory provisions of the law of their habitual residence. As a consequence, the chosen law will only apply if and to the extent that it provides for more protection than these provisions. If, in contrast, the chosen law provides for less protection, the contract is governed by a law mix, consisting of the chosen law and the mandatory provisions of the consumers' habitual residence. Article 6 (2) Rome I Regulation, thus, effectively establishes a minimum level of consumer protection and, hence, helps to avoid a race to the bottom.

On the other hand, however, there is no denying the fact that Article 6(2) Rome I Regulation makes the determination of the applicable law more complex and, hence, less foreseeable: Instead of simply applying the law chosen by the parties, courts have to undertake an issue-by-issue comparison between the chosen law and the mandatory law of the consumer's habitual residence. In addition, Article 6(2) Rome I Regulation effectively bars professionals from using the same set of terms and conditions when contracting with consumers from different countries. The provision, hence, increases the transaction costs associated with the conclusion and performance of cross-border consumer contracts. However, while all this may be true, it is nothing that applies to smart contracts only. In fact, Article 6(2) Rome I Regulation has long been criticized for being overly complex and for sacrificing legal certainty and ease of application over the protection of consumers. Its application to smart contracts, thus, only highlights already existing—and well known—difficulties associated with the preferential law approach without adding new or special ones. One may nevertheless find comfort in the fact that, according to Article 6(1) lit. b) Rome I Regulation, the preferential law approach only applies when the professional directs his professional activities to the country where the consumer is habitually resident.[69] The reach of the preferential law approach is, hence, limited to professionals who actively seek to contract with foreign consumers.

3.3.3.2 Closest Connection and Consumers' Habitual Residence

The situation looks a little bit better when the parties have not chosen the applicable law. In this case, Article 6(1) Rome I Regulation calls for application of the law of the consumers' habitual residence. The provision, thus, avoids the risk, associated with the preferential law approach embodied in Article 6(2) Rome I Regulation, that different laws have to be applied to the same contract. At the same time, it resorts to a connecting factor, namely the consumers' habitual residence, that will make the determination of the applicable in most cases law possible even if the contract in

[68] See for a more detailed presentation Ragno (2009), p. 151 ff; Wilderspin (2017), pp. 464 ff.

[69] In addition, the contract eventually concluded must fall into the scope of such activities. See for a more detailed discussion of these—complex—requirements Rühl (2016), pp. 67 ff.

question is fully or partly executed with the help of a smart contract. Nonetheless, it should not be overlooked that application of the law of the consumers' habitual residence will make contracting with foreign consumers more complex because professionals will have to adjust their terms and conditions to different laws depending on where the consumers they are contracting with are habitually resident. But just as with the preferential law approach this is nothing that applies to smart contracts only. And there is nothing that would indicate that smart contracts would pose special problems in that regard. This holds also true because application of Article 6(1) Rome I Regulation—just like application of Article 6(2) Rome I Regulation—is limited to professionals who actively seek to contract with foreign consumers.

3.3.3.3 Remaining Problems

Article 6 Rome I Regulation is without any doubt a difficult and controversial provision. And while most of the complexities associated with its application also affect traditional contracts, there may be problems that will hit smart contracts particularly hard. Take, for example, smart contracts that are concluded and executed anonymously via a blockchain such as Bitcoin or Ripple. Will Article 6 Rome I Regulation apply in these situations? Will it apply in situations where the professional does not know and, arguably, has no way of knowing whether he or she is contracting with a consumer?[70] According to the ECJ Article 6 Rome I Regulation does not apply if a consumer (consciously) creates the impression through his or her own conduct that he or she is acting for professional or commercial purposes or if the consumer conceals that he or she is acting for private purposes.[71] Application of Article 6 Rome I Regulation will, therefore, be excluded if the use of a particular blockchain signals that the user is acting for professional purposes. If, in contrast, the use of a particular blockchain cannot be understood to send out any such signal, for example, because the blockchain is open for both professionals and consumers and its use, therefore, neutral as regards the contractual purpose, it is unclear whether Article 6 Rome I Regulation may apply.

By the same token, it is unclear whether Article 6 Rome I Regulation may apply if a smart consumer contract is concluded anonymously via a blockchain. In contrast to Article 4(4) Rome I Regulation which calls for application of the law of the closest connection if the habitual residence cannot be determined, there is no such gap-filler in Article 6 Rome I Regulation. As a consequence, it is unclear how courts are supposed to proceed when a smart contract falls into the scope of Article 6 Rome I Regulation, but the consumers' habitual residence is unknown. One may, however,

[70] According to the definition to be found in Article 6(1) Rome I Regulation a consumer is a natural person who concludes a contract for a purpose which can be regarded as being outside his or her trade or profession.

[71] ECJ C-464/01 – *Johann Gruber v. Bay Wa AG*, ECLI:EU:C:2005:32, para. 51.

find comfort in the fact that these cases will not be too numerous because "anonymity" rarely means actual anonymity but mostly pseudonymity. In most cases it will, therefore, be possible to determine who is behind a transaction and where that person is habitually resident.

3.4 *Beyond Contract: Other (Non-contractual) Aspects of Smart Contracts*

As discussed earlier in this chapter the Rome I Regulation only determines the law applicable to contractual obligations. Naturally, however, smart contracts may also give rise to problems that are not contractual in nature. The question which law applies to these problems will then have to be determined by the private international law rules applicable to these problems. Non-contractual obligations, for example, will fall into the scope of the Rome II Regulation,[72] while property law issues will be governed by the domestic private international law rules of the Member States.[73] In many cases, however, the private international law rules relating to other, notably non-contractual problems will refer to back to the Rome I Regulation. Take, for example, the Rome II Regulation. According to Articles 10(1) and 11(1) Rome II Regulation non-contractual obligations that arise out of unjust enrichment or *negotiorum gestio* and have a close connection to a contract will be governed by the applicable contract law. And according to Article 12(1) and 4(3) Rome II Regulation the same holds true for obligations arising out of *culpa in contrahendo* or torts closely connected with a contract. In the end, it will therefore, very often be the provisions discussed in this chapter that will decide about the applicable law.

4 Conclusion

Smart contracts are said to change the way we trade goods and services. And they are said to pose numerous challenges for the law. In this chapter I have tried to show, that the determination of the applicable contract law is not one of them. To be sure, smart contracts, especially if they are processed with the help of blockchain technology, may have connections to a large number of jurisdictions. And they may give rise to new questions and problems. However, since the applicable choice of law rules of the Rome I Regulation resort to connecting factors, namely party choice and habitual residence, which work reasonably well in a decentralized virtual

[72]Regulation (EC) No. 864/2007 of the European Parliament and of the Council of 11 July 2007 on the law applicable to non-contractual obligations (Rome II), OJ EU 2007 L 199/40. See for a more detailed discussion in Dickinson (2017), pp. 1562 ff.

[73]See d'Avout (2017), pp. 1428 ff.

environment,[74] it will usually be possible to assign a smart contract to a particular legal system. This finding will, of course, not be welcomed by those who consider smart contracts as a way out of any legal system and who use blockchain technology specifically to evade traditional legal orders. Yet, as long as private international law does not allow parties to choose a non-state law or no law at all, this expectation of the parties will not be honoured by national courts.

A completely different question is, of course, whether the law applicable by virtue of the Rome I Regulation offers a suitable legal framework for smart contracts. However, we can expect that parties will increasingly make use of their right to choose the applicable law in accordance with Article 3 Rome I Regulation and, hence, make a judgment about the quality of the applicable law by voting "with their feet". In the long run, private international law will, therefore, not only determine the law applicable to smart contracts and thereby foster legal certainty. It will reveal which law is best equipped to meet the challenges of digitalization in the eyes of the parties and thereby encourage legislatures and judges to compete for application of their laws.[75] Some countries, including the UK,[76] Germany,[77] Italy[78] and the Netherlands[79] have already started to think about whether their respective national laws provide a good legal environment for smart contracts. Private international law and especially the principle of party autonomy will, hence, be the driver for law reform and—hopefully—better laws for smart contracts.

References

Basedow J (2015) The law of open societies: private ordering and public regulation in the conflict of laws. BRILL, Leiden

Basedow J, Rühl G, Ferrari F, de Miguel Asensio PA (eds) (2017) Encyclopedia of Private International Law. Edward Elgar Publishing, Cheltenham/Northhampton

Braegelmann T, Kaulartz M (2019) Einleitung. In: Braegelmann T, Kaulartz M (eds) Rechtshandbuch Smart Contracts. C.H. Beck, Munich, pp 1–12

Buchleitner C, Rabl T (2017) Blockchain und Smart Contracts: Revolution oder alter Wein im digitalen Schlauch? Ecolex 1:4–17

Cardozo's Blockchain Project (2018) Smart contracts and legal enforceability, p 9

[74]Equally optimistic Dickinson (2019), pp. 97 and 137; Zimmermann (2018), pp. 568 f. 573. In a similar vein Lehmann (2019), p. 125.

[75]See for a more detailed discussion of regulatory competition in contract law Rühl (2013), pp. 61 f.

[76]See UK Jurisdiction Task Force (2019), p. 135 ff. Spink A et al. (2019). Vos (2019), paras 13 ff. and 56 ff.

[77]See Federal Ministry for Economics Affairs and Energy, *Blockchain Strategy of the Federal Government*, 2018.

[78]See Italian Law no. 12 of 11 February 2019, converting into law, with amendments, Law Decree no. 135 of 14 December 2018 on urgent simplification measures for businesses and publication, G.U. 12/02/2019, no. 36.

[79]See Dutch Advisory Committee on Blockchain, *Dutch Blockchain Research Agenda*, 2018.

d'Avout L (2017) Property and propriety rights. In: Basedow J, Rühl G, Ferrari F, de Miguel Asensio PA (eds) Encyclopedia of Private International Law. Edward Elgar Publishing, Cheltenham/Northhampton, pp 1428–1436
Damar D (2017) Transport law (uniform law). In: Basedow J, Rühl G, Ferrari F, de Miguel Asensio PA (eds) Encyclopedia of Private International Law. Edward Elgar Publishing, Cheltenham/Northhampton, pp 1726–1738
Dickinson A (2017) Rome II Regulation (non-contractual obligations). In: Basedow J, Rühl G, Ferrari F, de Miguel Asensio PA (eds) Encyclopedia of Private International Law. Edward Elgar Publishing, Cheltenham/Northhampton, pp 1562–1574
Dickinson A (2019) Cryptocurrencies and conflict of laws. In: Fox D, Green S (eds) Private and public law implications of cryptocurrencies. Oxford University Press, Oxford, pp 93–138
Djazayeri A (2016) Rechtliche Herausforderungen durch Smart Contracts, jurisPR-BKR 12/2016, Anm. 1
Durovic M (2018) Law and autonomous systems series: how to resolve smart contract disputes – smart arbitration as a solution. In: Oxford Law Faculty. https://www.law.ox.ac.uk/business-law-blog/blog/2018/06/law-and-autonomous-systems-series-how-resolve-smart-contractdisputes
Dutch Advisory Committee on Blockchain (2018) Dutch blockchain research agenda
Ferrari F (2017a) Uniform substantive law and private international law. In: Basedow J, Rühl G, Ferrari F, de Miguel Asensio PA (eds) Encyclopedia of Private International Law. Edward Elgar Publishing, Cheltenham/Northhampton, pp 1772–1779
Ferrari F (2017b) CISG. In: Basedow J, Rühl G, Ferrari F, de Miguel Asensio PA (eds) Encyclopedia of Private International Law. Edward Elgar Publishing, Cheltenham/Northhampton, pp 338–346
Ferrari F, Leible S (eds) (2009) Rome I Regulation: the law applicable to contractual obligations in Europe. Sellier, Munich
Filippi PD, Wright A (2019) Blockchain and the law: the rule of code. Harvard University Press, Cambridge
Garcimartín Alférez F (2017) Rome Convention and Rome I Regulation (contractual obligations). In: Basedow J, Rühl G, Ferrari F, de Miguel Asensio PA (eds) Encyclopedia of Private International Law. Edward Elgar Publishing, Cheltenham/Northhampton, pp 1553–1562
Heiss H (2009) Party autonomy. In: Ferrari F, Leible S (eds) Rome I Regulation: the law applicable to contractual obligations in Europe. Sellier, Munich, pp 1–16
Kronman AT (1985) Contract law and the state of nature. J Law Econ Organ 1:5–32
Lando O, Nielsen PA (2008) The Rome I Regulation. Common Mark Law Rev 45:1687–1725
Lehmann M (2019) Who owns bitcoin? Private law facing the blockchain. Minnesota J Law Sci Technol 21:93–136
Lessig L (1999) Code: and other laws of cyberspace. Basic Books
Lessig L (2000) Code is law. On Liberty in Cyberspace. Harvard Magazine January/February 2000. https://harvardmagazine com/2000/01/code-is-law-html
Low KF, Mik E (2020) Pause the blockchain legal revolution. Int Comp Law Q 69:135–175
Lim C et al. (2016) Smart Contracts: Bridging the Gap Between Expectation and Reality. In: Oxford Law Faculty. https://www.law.ox.ac.uk/business-law-blog/blog/2016/07/smart-contracts-bridging-gap-between-expectation-and-reality
Magnus U (2009) Article 4 Rome I Regulation: the applicable law in the absence of a choice. In: Ferrari F, Leible S (eds) Rome I Regulation: the law applicable to contractual obligations in Europe. Sellier, Munich, pp 27–50
Magnus R (2018) Der grenzüberschreitende Bezug als Anwendungsvoraussetzung im europäischen Zuständigkeits-und Kollisionsrecht. Zeitschrift für europäisches Privatrecht (ZEuP) 26:507–540
Mankowski P (2011) Rom I-VO und Schiedsverfahren. Recht der internationalen Wirtschaft (RIW) 57:30–44
Martiny D (2018a) Virtuelle Währungen, insbesondere Bitcoins, im Internationale Privat-und Zivilverfahrensrecht. Praxis des Internationalen Privat-und Verfahrensrechts (IPRax) 38:553–565

Martiny D (2018b) Art. 1 Rom I-VO. In: Münchener Kommentar zum BGB, C.H. Beck, Munich
Martiny D (2018c) Art. 4 Rom I-VO. In: Münchener Kommentar zum BGB, C.H. Beck, Munich
Mik E (2017) Smart contracts: terminology, technical limitations and real world complexity. Law Innov Technol 9:269–300
Mik E (2019) Smart contracts: a Requiem. J Contract Law 36:70–94
Mills A (2018) Party autonomy in private international law. Cambridge University Press, Cambridge
Möstlein F (2019) Conflicts of laws and Codes. Defining the Boundaries of Digital Jurisdictions. In: Hacker P, Lianos I, Dimitropoulos G, Eich S (eds) Regulating Blockchain: Techno-Social and Legal Challeges. Oxford University Press, Oxford, pp 277–288
Muir Watt H (2017) Party autonomy. In: Basedow J, Rühl G, Ferrari F, de Miguel Asensio PA (eds) Encyclopedia of Private International Law. Edward Elgar Publishing, Cheltenham/Northhampton, pp 1336–1341
Ragno F (2009) The law applicable to consumer contracts under the Rome I Regulation. In: Ferrari F, Leible S (eds) Rome I Regulation: the law applicable to contractual obligations in Europe. Sellier, Munich, pp 151–170
Remien O (2016) Closest connection and escape clauses. In: Leible S (ed) General principles of European private international law. Kluwer Law International B.V., Alphen aan den Rijn, pp 211–224
Rösler H (2017) Interpretation, autonomous. In: Basedow J, Rühl G, Ferrari F, de Miguel Asensio PA (eds) Encyclopedia of Private International Law. Edward Elgar Publishing, Cheltenham/Northhampton, pp 1006–1015
Rühl G (2011) Consumer protection in choice of law. Cornell Int Law J 44:569–601
Rühl G (2013) Regulatory competition in contract law: empirical evidence and normative implications. Eur Rev Contract Law 9:61–89
Rühl G (2016) The consumer's jurisdictional privilege: on (missing) legislative and (misguided) judicial action. In: Ferrari F, Ragno F (eds) Cross-border litigation in Europe: The Brusses I Recast Regulation as a Panacea? Wolters Kluwer, Milano, pp 67–96
Rühl G (2018) Judicial cooperation in civil and commercial matters after Brexit: which way forward? Int Comp Law Q 67:99–128
Rühl G (2019a) Smart Contracts und Internationales Privatrecht. In: Braegelmann T, Kaulartz M (eds) Rechtshandbuch Smart Contracts. C.H. Beck, Munich, pp 147–168
Rühl G (2019b) The law applicable to smart contracts, or much ado about nothing? In: Oxford Business Law Blog. https://www.law.ox.ac.uk/business-law-blog/blog/2019/01/law-applicable-smartcontracts-or-much-ado-about-nothing
Rühl G (2020a) Im Schatten des Brexit-Abkommens: Perspektiven für das Internationale Privat- und Verfahrensrecht'. Neue Juristische Wochenschrift (NJW) 7:443–447
Rühl G (2020b) Private international law post-Brexit: between plague and cholera. Revue de Droit Commercial Belge/Tijdschrift voor Belgisch Handelsrecht (RDC/TBH) 1:21–26
Savelyev A (2017) Contract law 2.0: 'Smart' contracts as the beginning of the end of classic contract law. Inf Commun Technol Law 26:116–134
Schiller K (2018) Was sind smart contracts? | definition und Erklärung. In: Blockchainwelt. https://blockchainwelt.de/smart-contracts-vertrag-blockchain/
Siehr K (2017) Private international law, history of. In: Basedow J, Rühl G, Ferrari F, de Miguel Asensio PA (eds) Encyclopedia of Private International Law. Edward Elgar Publishing, Cheltenham/Northhampton, pp 1390–1401
Spink A et al. (2019) Cryptoassets and smart contracts: the UKJT legal statements
Szabo NJ (1994) Smart contracts. http://www.fon.hum.uva.nl/rob/Courses/InformationInSpeech/CDROM/Literature/LOTwinterschool2006/szabo.best.vwh.net/smart.contracts.html
UK Jurisdiction Task Force (2019) Legal statement on cryptoassets and smart contracts. p. 135 ff
von Bar C, Mankowski P (2019) Internationales Privatrecht, Volume 2, C.H. Beck, Munich
von Hein J (2018), Art. 3 EGBGB. In: Münchener Kommentar zum BGB, C.H. Beck, Munich

Vos G (2019) Cryptoassets as property: how can English law boost the confidence of would-be parties to smart legal contracts? In: Joint Northern Chancery Bar Association and University of Liverpool Lecture. https://www.judiciary.uk/wp-content/uploads/2019/05/Sir-Geoffrey-Vos-Chancellor-of-the-High-Court-speech-on-cryptoassets.pdf

Weller M (2015) Article 1 Rome 1. In: Calliess GP (ed) Rome Regulations. Wolters Kluwer, Alphen aan den Rijn

Wilderspin M (2017) Contractual obligations. In: Basedow J, Rühl G, Ferrari F, de Miguel Asensio PA (eds) Encyclopedia of Private International Law. Edward Elgar Publishing, Cheltenham/Northhampton, pp 472–479

Woebbeking MK (2019) The impact of smart contracts on traditional concepts of contract law. J Intellect Prop Inf Technol Electron Commer Law 10:105–113

Zimmermann A (2018) Blockchain-Netzwerke und Internationales Privatrecht – oder: der Sitz dezentraler Rechtsverhältnisse. Praxis des Internationalen Privat-und Verfahrensrechts (IPRax) 38:566–573

Smart (Legal) Contracts: Forum and Applicable Law Issues

Paolo Bertoli

Contents

1 Smart Contracts: What They Are, What They Are Not, and What They May Become

Smart contracts represent an uncertain instrument, both from a technological and from a legal standpoint, and any analysis thereof requires an understanding of the instruments that are the subject matter of the analysis. There is no generally accepted definition of smart contracts, under both a technical or technical perspective and in legal theory or comparative law.

In general terms, smart contracts can be seen as a set of codified functions allowing a computer machine to process a code, *i.e.*, a protocol that elaborates in a predetermined way the information that it has gathered or that were inserted into it (if required conditions are met, certain actions are executed), and whose main aim is to produce certain legal effects between the parties involved, predetermined by such parties.[1]

Some scholars associate smart contracts to the formalized expression and automated execution of legally binding contracts, with the use of a code to perform contractual obligations, with protocols that facilitate, verify, execute and/or embody

[1]Clusit (2018), p. 28.

P. Bertoli (✉)
Insubria University, Como, Italy
e-mail: paolo.bertoli@uninsubria.it

B. Cappiello, G. Carullo (eds.), *Blockchain, Law and Governance*,
https://doi.org/10.1007/978-3-030-52722-8_12

the terms of a contract. The embedding of legal terms in hardware and software serves the scope of preventing breaches or controlling assets by digital means.[2]

Therefore, the term smart contract generally refers to instruments that envisage the translation and transposition into computer code not only of the rules that form what may roughly be called (para) contractual regulation, but also the real word-circumstances on the basis of which a contract is to be performed automatically (in whole or in part).[3]

Smart contracts are thus agreements that can be formed online (as is very common nowadays), but their distinctive feature is that their performance is enabled and guaranteed by a network of decentralized, co-operating computer nodes.[4]

Italian legislation defines smart contracts as "a computer program that operates on technologies based on distributed ledgers and whose performance automatically binds two or more parts on the basis of effects predefined by such parties".[5]

Smart contracts are, at least partly, self-executing agreements. A widespread and highly ideological conception behind smart contracts is to have contracts that are automatically enforced without any need for a third party, thus reducing intermediation, transaction and litigation costs.[6]

A widespread, but wrong, example of smart contract is the humble vending machine. In order to explain how smart contracts are self-executing, scholars compare them to a vending machine: if the machine is operating properly when you insert the money, the contract for the sale will be executed automatically. A physical device within the machine is encoded with a seller's offer. The machine will only dispense soda if the terms of the agreement are met.[7] However, this is a misunderstanding. First, a vending machine is not a contract, but an offer made to the world at large. A contract is formed with whoever selects one of the available options and inserts the required amount. Second, it is unquestionable that the vending machine can automate both the formation and performance of a sale of good. The same could be said of many e-commerce websites, such as Amazon or Spotify, which automate contract formation and, whenever the contractual subject matter is digital, also the performance of the contract. However, neither the vending machine nor websites are or enforce contracts. They only dispense goods (or digital content) in response to payment. Indeed, contrarily to smart contracts, they are incapable of embodying (and hence automating) all terms of a transaction, including the real-world circumstances that, once satisfied, set in motion the performance of the contract.[8]

---

[2] Mik (2017), p. 269 ff.

[3] Di Ciommo (2018), p. 291 ff.

[4] Mik (2017), p. 269 ff.

[5] Law decree 14 December 2018 No. 135, as amended by Law 11 February 2019 No. 12 (Article 8-*ter*).

[6] Cf. de Caria (2017), p. 108. de Caria (2019), p. 731 ff. Perugini and Dal Checco (2015).

[7] Raskin (2017), p. 305 ff.

[8] Mik (2017), p. 269 ff.

To the contrary, the distinctive features of smart contracts are generally considered to be: (i) self-enforceability, meaning that once concluded, their execution is no longer dependent on the will of its parties or third parties and (ii) self-sufficiency, meaning that they do not need intermediaries. They are also "trust-less", in the sense that the truth of an event is established by means of 'distributed consensus', *i.e.*, confirmation by a majority of nodes in a decentralized network and the chain is trust-less because it confirms a certain state of affairs without the need to trust third parties confirming it, with the aim of tamper proof enforcement that cannot be stopped or modified by the parties.[9]

Smart contracts are presently best suited to automatically execute two types of transactions found in many contracts: (i) ensuring the payments of funds upon certain triggering events and (ii) imposing financial penalties if certain objective conditions are not met. In each case, human intervention, in particular the judicial system, is not required once the smart contract has been deployed and is operational, thereby reducing the execution and enforcement costs of the contracting process.[10]

Smart contracts are used for instance in the field of loan contracts. In case of payment defaults, smart contracts can automatically block the keys that are required to enter the respective apartment, so that the tenant no longer has access to it. Similarly, rented or leased cars can be blocked in the case of payment defaults. These systems are called "starter interrupt devices". As another example, in insurance contracts, for instance, automated payments can be effected for flight delays.[11]

There is a general trend, including—as seen—in the Italian legislation, to confuse smart contracts with the block-chain technology and to believe that smart contracts are solely based on a block-chain technology. Block-chain is a technology based on network users sharing a common data-base so that their transactions can be managed through a chain of operations that take place between different nodes in a network.[12] Indeed, some authorities define smart contract as computer code that automatically executes all or parts of an agreement and is stored on a blockchain-based platform.[13] In actual practice, however, only a somewhat modest fraction of the automated operations carried out on the Internet use the block-chain, while all other smart contracts are entered into and performed through other means that any way ensure the decentralization of the performance.[14]

As noted, smart contracts scholars have been focused so far are those that allow to automate the process of performing (certain) contractual obligations. It has been noted that the block-chain technology could push itself to create contracts that not

[9]See Rinaldi (2019).

[10]Levi SD, Lipton AB An Introduction to Smart Contracts and Their Potential and Inherent Limitations. https://corpgov.law.harvard.edu/2018/05/26/an-introduction-to-smart-contracts-and-their-potential-and-inherent-limitations/, p. 3.

[11]Möslein (2018).

[12]Bertoli (2018), p. 583 ff.

[13]See Di Ciommo (2018), p. 301.

[14]See Ibid., p. 301. Pardolesi and Davola (2019), p. 195 ff.

only automate the performance of a contract, but also its negotiation and conclusion.[15]

2 The Code Is Not the Law

At the very end, the issue is whether smart contracts, whatever form they take, are actually newly shaped regulations arising from private autonomy or are just a "fancy name" to indicate mere protocols to transfer data or may be able to interact with block-chain technology, but that do not constitute new and separate legal instruments.[16]

The concept of smart contracts has developed from the idea or ideology of creating transnational contracts that are fully detached from domestic legal systems. In this connection, it has submitted that contracts that are executed in the digital world do not need "conflict of law provisions, since there are no collisions of various legal systems", everything happening on the internet.[17] In this vein, "Code is Law" was the paradigm presented by Lawrence Lessig when discussing smart contracts. The idea behind this theory or concept is that the development of the technology led or may lead to a scenario where it is not the law anymore, but instead the software to regulate the users' behaviour.[18]

In the light of the foregoing, many authors still claim that smart contracts do not need a central authority or an external enforcement mechanism because they are immune from human intervention.

The present author strongly disagrees with such theories. There is a fundamental methodological flaw in the assertion according to which the code is the law. This assertion, indeed, is based on a reversal of the proper legal methodology: an automated code or computer protocol can have legally binding effects only if and the extent the applicable law so prescribes or allows. So, before one looks at the code, one needs to look at the law. The code can be the law if and to the extent the law says so. In turn, this calls for the necessity of a proper choice-of-law and choice-of-court analysis of any legally binding instruments, whether they are smart or automatically or partly automatically enforceable contracts.

The ideas underlying the "code is the law" proposition resemble very much certain thesis circulated mainly in the 1980s and 1990s about *lex mercatoria* and international commercial arbitration forming an autonomous transnational legal order, detached from any domestic legal system. As discussed by many (including the present author) elsewhere, if *lex mercatoria* and international commercial arbitration can detach from domestic legal systems in some of their practical dynamics,

[15]Savelyev (2017), p. 9.

[16]Pardolesi and Davola (2019), p. 305 ff.

[17]de Caria (2017), p. 113.

[18]Lessig (2000). Hassan and De Filippi (2017).

their creation and existence depends on domestic legal systems, which allow them to be created, deploy and (if need be) be enforced through State monopoly of coercive powers. The same seems true with respect to smart contracts.[19]

Smart contracts, in other words, constitute autonomous and self-sufficient legally-binding agreements if and to the extent that they translate an already reached agreement into digital code, subject to the limitation provided for by the law applicable thereto.[20] Obviously, smart contracts will always require the will of the parties in order to become effective, just any other contract. Such will is manifested when an individual decides to enter into such an agreement or, in case of electronic agents, when an individual decides to use an agent for the conclusion of certain agreements and decides to be bound by their actions.[21]

The conception that it is impossible to breach a smart contract because the code is immutable and self-executing, whether accurate in all respects or not, does not *per se* limit the possibility and need of judicial assistance and overview over such instruments. Just to make an example, given that as noted smart contracts are entered into upon the parties' consent, disputes may inevitably arise as to issues surrounding the parties' consent. Indeed, there are issues that can be resolved only by judges, *e.g.*, whether a party was negligent/diligent, whether there were defects in the consent to enter into the agreement, whether there was a force majeure circumstance.[22] Therefore, the issue is not whether smart contracts are subject to the law, but rather which law they are subject to.

3 Forum Issues in Smart Contracts

Given that smart contracts are agreements reached via agreement of the parties (either off or on-line) that use computer protocols to ensure in whole or in part their performance, the existing private international law instruments seem well suited to address the choice-of-court and choice-of-law issues they pose.[23]

As to the former, the Brussels I-*bis* Regulation notably allows parties, regardless of their domicile, to agree that a court or the courts of a EU Member State are to have jurisdiction to settle any disputes which have arisen or which may arise in connection with their smart contract. The relevant agreements must be: (i) in writing or evidenced in writing; (ii) in a form which accords with practices which the parties have established between themselves; or (iii) in international trade or commerce, in a form which accords with a usage of which the parties are or ought to have been

---

[19]For a reconstruction of the debate see Marrella (2003). Boschiero (2005), p. 83 ff.

[20]de Caria (2017), p. 113. Cappiello (2020).

[21]Savelyev (2017), p. 9.

[22]Chamber of Digital Commerce Smart Contracts Whitepaper. In: Chamber of Digital Commerce. https://digitalchamber.org/smart-contracts-whitepaper/. Finocchiaro (2018), p. 441 ff.

[23]See Pretelli (2018), p. 17 ff. For an analysis, including *de jure condendo*, see Cappiello (2020).

aware and which in such trade or commerce is widely known to, and regularly observed by, parties to contracts of the type involved in the particular trade or commerce concerned (Article 25(1)). When such contracts are entered into digitally, as it may frequently happen, any communication by electronic means which provides a durable record of the agreement shall be equivalent to "writing" (Article 25 (2)). The EU Court has recently clarified in this respect that the method of accepting the general terms and conditions of a contract for sale by "click-wrapping", concluded by electronic means, which contains an agreement conferring jurisdiction, constitutes a communication by electronic means which provides a durable record of the agreement, where that method makes it possible to print and save the text of those terms and conditions before the conclusion of the contract.[24]

Absent any choice of law, in the case of the sale of goods, jurisdiction would rest in the place in a Member State where, under the contract, the goods were delivered or should have been delivered and, in the case of the provision of services, in the place in a Member State where, under the contract, the services were provided or should have been provided (Article 7(i)(b)). In case of sale, including of digital content, the principles elaborated by the EU Court grant jurisdiction to the Courts of the place of final destination of the goods; in case of services, jurisdiction rests in principle with the place where the beneficiary of the service is located, if the service is performed on-line, with no relevance of the place where the relevant serves are located.[25]

Rules of jurisdiction in the Regulation vary in case of consumer smart contracts, *i.e.*, contracts concluded by a person, the consumer, for a purpose which can be regarded as being outside his trade or profession. The protective jurisdictional discipline in the Regulation applies if the relevant consumer (smart) contract: (i) is a contract for the sale of goods on instalment credit terms; (ii) is a contract for a loan repayable by instalments, or for any other form of credit, made to finance the sale of goods; or (c) in all other cases, has been concluded with a person who pursues commercial or professional activities in the Member State of the consumer's domicile or, by any means, directs such activities to that Member State or to several States including that Member State, and the contract falls within the scope of such activities (Article 17). The latter case, which is the most frequent one including in case of smart consumer contracts, requires a so-called targeting approach of the activities of the professional side of the contract. The EU Court clarified that in order to determine whether a trader whose activity is presented on its website or on that of an intermediary can be considered to be 'directing' its activity to the Member State of the consumer's domicile it should be ascertained whether, before the conclusion of any contract with the consumer, it is apparent from those websites and the trader's overall activity that the trader was envisaging doing business with consumers

[24]Judgment of 21 May 2015, case C-322/14, *Jaouad El Majdoub* v. *CarsOnTheWeb.Deutschland GmbH*, ECLI:EU:C:2015:334.

[25]See in particular judgments of 25 February 2010, case C-381/08, *Car Trim GmbH* v *KeySafety Systems Srl*, ECLI:EU:C:2010:90; 9 June 2011, case C-87/10, *Electrosteel Europe SA* v *Edil Centro SpA*, ECLI:EU:C:2011:375.

domiciled in one or more Member States, including the Member State of that consumer's domicile, in the sense that it was minded to conclude a contract with them.[26] The Court clarifies that the following matters are capable of constituting evidence from which it may be concluded that the trader's activity is directed to the Member State of the consumer's domicile: (i) the international nature of the activity; (ii) mention of itineraries from other Member States for going to the place where the trader is established; (iii) use of a language or a currency other than the language or currency generally used in the Member State in which the trader is established with the possibility of making and confirming the reservation in that other language; (iv) mention of telephone numbers with an international code; (v) outlay of expenditure on an internet referencing service in order to facilitate access to the trader's site or that of its intermediary by consumers domiciled in other Member States; (vi) use of a top-level domain name other than that of the Member State in which the trader is established; and (vii) mention of an international clientele composed of customers domiciled in various Member States. On the other hand, the mere accessibility of the trader's or the intermediary's website in the Member State in which the consumer is domiciled is insufficient. The same is true of mention of an email address and of other contact details, or of use of a language or a currency which are the language and/or currency generally used in the Member State in which the trader is established.[27] On the other end, the foregoing provision does not require the existence of a causal link between the means employed to direct the commercial or professional activity to the Member State of the consumer's domicile, namely an internet site, and the conclusion of the contract with that consumer. However, the existence of such a causal link constitutes evidence of the connection between the contract and such activity.[28]

4 Choice of Law Issues in Smarts Contracts

Similarly, choice of law issues relating to smart contracts seem not to be particularly dissimilar to those that are posed by traditional contracts. First, Rome I Regulation allows parties to a smart contract to choose the applicable law, without requiring any territorial link. Where all other elements relevant to the situation at the time of the choice are located in one or more Member States, the choice of an applicable law other than that of a Member State shall not prejudice the application of provisions of EU law, where appropriate as implemented in the Member State of the forum, which

[26]Judgment of 7 December 2010, case C-144/09, *Pammer* v *Reederei Karl Schlüter GmbH & Co. KG*, ECLI:EU:C:2010:740.

[27]Judgment of 7 December 2010, case C-144/09, *Pammer* v *Reederei Karl Schlüter GmbH & Co. KG*, ECLI:EU:C:2010:740.

[28]Judgment of 17 October 2013, case C- 218/12, *Lokman Emrek* v *Vlado Sabranovic*, ECLI:EU: C:2013:666.

cannot be derogated from by agreement.[29] For all cases when the smart contract is concluded in a traditional fashion (either off or on-line), and computer protocol assist the performance of the contractual obligations, the choice can be expressed in the agreement. To the contrary, for the (futuristic) scenario that the smart contract is exclusively concluded via block-chain technology or represented in algorithmic fashion, the choice of law may be difficult to be directly incorporated into the contract, and may thus have to be expressed in a separate declaration. Choice of law can also be implied, i.e., clearly demonstrated by the terms of the contracts or the circumstances of the case. Implied choice may be hard to establish in smart contracts, given their frequent international character and possible anonymity. As it has been pointed out, "this is nothing special—and nothing that can only occur when parties conclude a smart contract".[30]

Article 4 Rome I Regulation contains rules to determine the applicable law in absence of choice by the parties. The applicable law in contracts for the sale of goods is that of the country where the seller has his habitual residence and in contracts for the provision of services is that of the country where the service provider has his habitual residence (para. 1, which also sets forth rules for other types of contract, all expression of the characteristic performance criterion). Accordingly, sales and service smart contracts will be subject to the law of the place where the seller or the service provider is habitually resident, similarly to traditional contracts.

Where the contract is not covered by paragraph 1 or where the elements of the contract would be covered by more than one of the types of contracts of paragraph 1, the contract shall be governed by the law of the country where the party required to effect the characteristic performance of the contract (usually, the non-monetary performance) has his habitual residence. Where it is clear from all the circumstances of the case that the contract is manifestly more closely connected with a different country, the law of that other country shall apply. In case the habitual residence of the relevant party cannot be determined because the smart contract is processed anonymously via a block-chain, the law of closest connection will be determined in accordance with Article 4(4) Rome I Regulation by taking into account all the circumstances of the case. Again, these rules do not seem to pose issue specific to smart contracts, at least as long as they are concluded in a traditional fashion (either off or on-line).

Moreover, Articles 5 to 8 Rome I Regulation contain specific choice-of-law rules for carriage contracts, consumer contracts, insurance contracts and employment contracts. They modify the rules contained in Article 3 and 4 in order to protect weaker parties and apply the law of the habitual residence of the weaker party, unless parties have agreed otherwise. Therefore, these articles rely on connecting factors which allow the straightforward determination of the applicable law even if the contract in question is a smart contract.[31]

---

[29]See Bertoli (2005), p. 455 ff.

[30]Rühl (2019).

[31]See Ibid. Ruhl (2018), p. 201 ff.

References

Bertoli P (2005) Corte di giustizia, integrazione comunitaria e diritto internazionale privato e processuale. Giuffré, Milano
Bertoli P (2018) Virtual currencies and private international law. Rivista di diritto internazionale privato e processuale 54:2
Boschiero N (2005) La lex mercatoria nell'era della globalizzazione: considerazioni di diritto internazionale pubblico e privato. Sociologia del diritto
Cappiello B (2020) Dallo "smart contract" computer code allo smart (legal) contract. I nuovi strumenti (para) giuridici alla luce della normativa nazionale e del diritto internazionale privato europeo: prospettive de jure condendo. Rivista del commercio internazionale
Clusit (2018) Blockchain & Distributed Ledger: aspetti di governance, security e compliance. https://clusit.it/blog/blockchain-distributed-ledger-aspetti-di-governance-security-e-compliance/
de Caria R (2017) A digital revolution in international trade? The international legal framework for blockchain technologies, virtual currencies and smart contracts: challenges and opportunities. In: Modernizing international trade law to support innovation and sustainable development. U NCITRAL 50th anniversary congress. United Nations, pp 105–117
de Caria R (2019) The legal meaning of smart contracts. Eur Rev Priv Law 6:731–752
Di Ciommo F (2018) Smart contract and (non-) law. The case of the financial markets. Law Econ Yearly Rev 7
Finocchiaro G (2018) Il contratto nell'era dell'intelligenza artificiale. Rivista trimestrale di diritto e procedura civile 72:441–460
Hassan S, De Filippi P (2017) The expansion of algorithmic governance: from code is law to law is code. Field Actions Sci Rep 17:88–90
Lessig L (2000) Code is law. On Liberty in Cyberspace. Harvard Magazine. https://harvardmagazine.com/2000/01/code-is-law-html
Marrella F (2003) La nuova lex mercatoria: principi Unidroit ed usi dei contratti del commercio internazionale. CEDAM, Padova
Mik E (2017) Smart contracts: terminology, technical limitations and real world complexity. Law Innov Technol 9:269–300. https://papers.ssrn.com/sol3/papers.cfm?abstract_id=3038406
Möslein F (2018) Conflicts of laws and codes: defining the boundaries of digital jurisdictions. SSRN
Pardolesi R, Davola A (2019) "Smart contract": lusinghe ed equivoci dell'innovazione purchessia. Il Foro Italiano
Perugini ML, Dal Checco P (2015) Smart contracts: a preliminary evaluation. SSRN
Pretelli I (2018) Improving social cohesion through connecting factors in the conflict of laws of the platform economy. In: Pretelli I (ed) Conflict of laws in the maze of digital platforms. Schulthess, Éditions Romandes, Zürich
Raskin M (2017) The law and legality of smart contracts. Georgetown Law Tech Rev 1:304
Rinaldi G (2019) Smart contract: meccanizzazione del contratto nel paradigma della blockchain. www.academia.edu/39741128/Smart_contract_meccanizzazione_del_contratto_nel_paradigma_della_blockchain
Ruhl G (2018) The unfairness of choice-of-law clauses, or: the (unclear) relationship of Art. 6 Rome I regulation and the unfair terms in consumer contracts directive. Common Mark Law Rev 55:201–224
Rühl G (2019) The law applicable to smart contracts, or much ado about nothing? Oxford Law Faculty. https://www.law.ox.ac.uk/business-law-blog/blog/2019/01/law-applicable-smart-contracts-or-much-ado-about-nothing
Savelyev A (2017) Contract law 2.0:'Smart'contracts as the beginning of the end of classic contract law. Inf Commun Technol Law 26:116–134

Integrating Smart Contracts with the Legacy Legal System: A US Perspective

Oliver R. Goodenough

Contents

1 Introduction

Contracts help to solve some of the basic challenges of cooperation for humans. One of the insights of economics, since the time of Adam Smith, is that a great deal of human productivity comes from cooperation and collaboration. In the eighteenth Century that astounding Scottish polymath published the foundational book for economics: *An Inquiry into the Nature and Causes of the Wealth of Nations*. He opens Chapter 1 of *The Wealth of Nations* by pointing out the importance of the division of labor in human prosperity:

The greatest improvement in the productive powers of labour, and the greater part of the skill, dexterity, and judgment with which it is anywhere directed, or applied, seem to have been the effects of the division of labour. (Smith 1776)

He uses the example of the benefits of specialization for the manufacture of a pin to illustrate how productivity increases with specialization and the application of technology:

O. R. Goodenough (✉)
Vermont Law School, South Royalton, Vermont, USA
e-mail: OGOODENOUGH@vermontlaw.edu

B. Cappiello, G. Carullo (eds.), *Blockchain, Law and Governance*,
https://doi.org/10.1007/978-3-030-52722-8_13

To take an example, therefore, from a very trifling manufacture; but one in which the division of labour has been very often taken notice of, the trade of the pin-maker; a workman not educated to this business (which the division of labour has rendered a distinct trade), nor acquainted with the use of the machinery employed in it (to the invention of which the same division of labour has probably given occasion), could scarce, perhaps, with his utmost industry, make one pin in a day, and certainly could not make twenty. But in the way in which this business is now carried on, not only the whole work is a peculiar trade, but it is divided into a number of branches, of which the greater part are likewise peculiar trades. One man draws out the wire, another straights it, a third cuts it, a fourth points it, a fifth grinds it at the top for receiving the head; to make the head requires two or three distinct operations; to put it on, is a peculiar business, to whiten the pins is another; it is even a trade by itself to put them into the paper; and the important business of making a pin is, in this manner, divided into about eighteen distinct operations, which, in some manufactories, are all performed by distinct hands, though in others the same man will sometimes perform two or three of them. (Smith 1776)

If you scale up this kind of process, and add on the gains of trade that make this specialization possible, you get the modern, complex economy where human productivity has climbed exponentially and where want is receding, even in poor countries. The challenge of sustainability of resources in the face of so much activity is, of course, a real consequence of these gains, and one that urgently needs solutions. Nonetheless, the problems of success are generally preferable to the problems of failure, and those sustainability solutions will, in their turn, require our collaboration and cooperation to achieve.

As game theory helps us to model, however, collaboration and cooperation do not always come easily. In many game forms, defection and predation offer short-term advantage at the cost of long-term collaborative gains (Gintis 2000; Dixit and Skeath 2004). Game theory has identified many such structures, such as the first-mover problem, the Prisoners Dilemma, and the Stag Hunt game (Skyrms 2004; Goodenough 2007). For cooperation to prosper, the pathways to defection need to walled off in some way, sometimes by (i) altering the pay-off structure by means such as adding penalties to defection, and other times by (ii) creating execution structures that have enough automaticity to be reliable and resistant to defection once set in motion.

Classical contracting follows the former strategy. The parties lay out a pathway of behavior that they anticipate will create a mutually beneficial collaboration or exchange. Goods and money may change hands; rights and duties may be created, transferred or extinguished; labor and ideas may be contributed to some joint effort. To become a contract, a prose statement is developed that describes the expected events of execution. And then thanks to *legal recognition, recourse and enforcement,* the pay-offs from defection are to a large degree removed, through damages, penalties and specific performance. This change in probable pay-offs increases the reliability of the expected behavior sufficiently to allow the players to move forward with the necessary level of confidence in each other's behavior.

Reliable execution structures, by contrast, can be created directly into the physical world. A classic example is the soda or candy vending machine—the armored case of the machine and its dispensing design makes it hard to break into. A money/credit card recognition device assures payment. And the recognition value of the brand on the machine increases reliability. While law helps the machine do its job, it requires no legally enforceable "contract" to create reliability—that is baked into the structure itself (Goodenough 2007).

2 Smart Contracts and Computable Contracts

"Smart contracts" look a lot like vending machines. In fact, Nick Szabo, widely regarded as one of the foundational thinkers of what has become cryptocurrency, used just that example in his short foundational paper on smart contracts, "Formalizing and Securing Relationships on Public Networks," first published in 1997. He explains:

Within a limited amount of potential loss (the amount in the till should be less than the cost of breaching the mechanism), the machine takes in coins, and via a simple mechanism, which makes a freshman computer science problem in design with finite automata, dispense change and product according to the displayed price. The vending machine is a contract with bearer: anybody with coins can participate in an exchange with the vendor. The lockbox and other security mechanisms protect the stored coins and contents from attackers, sufficiently to allow profitable deployment of vending machines in a wide variety of areas. (Szabo 1997)

He goes on to posit a whole domain of "contracts embedded in the world."

Building on this approach, the designers of blockchain systems have developed what they call "smart contracts." These started out as relatively simple sets of if/then instructions for the transfer of cryptocurrency on the occurrence of some event or set of events (Levi and Lipton 2018; Cohn et al. 2017). In this they resembled relatively simple escrow arrangements or letters of credit. In these early stages, the critics of this approach said, with some justification, that smart contracts are neither smart nor contracts (e.g. Cohn et al. 2017, p. 276). Those businesses and researchers who have investigated the means for encoding more *complex* relationships of event and consequence have sometimes referred to their work as "computable contracting" or even "computational law" (e.g. Surden 2012; Love and Genesereth 2005; LSP Working Group 2019).

The past few years, however, have seen an increase in the contractual expressivity of languages growing out of the smart contract tradition, with Ethereum's Solidity as an important early example (Solidity 2020). There has also been movement from the computable contracting side, which had aspired to greater capacity than the original smart contract scripts had permitted, toward building more complexity through a stack of smart contracts. Convergence is likely (LSP Working Group 2019).

One holdover from the smart contracting tradition, however, is the deeply held belief that smart contracts could exist largely outside any traditional or legacy legal system. Just as the cryptocurrencies themselves were digital artifacts that were, at least in their supporters' eyes, independent of government control, so too were the smart contracts, since they were able to provide extra-legal execution assurance. The crypto-libertarians who make up a significant part of blockchain world view this as a feature, not a bug (e.g., Staples et al. 2017).

While the automaticity of a "smart contract" may be part of its attraction, it does not necessarily remove it from scrutiny by traditional courts and regulators. The crypto-libertarians argue that a virtual currency, existing on a truly dispersed network of nodes, will resist direct interference by nation states and other legal authorities. This view is naive. The states don't have to control the network—they just have to control the transaction parties. If a court can assert physical jurisdiction over a human party or a human executive of a corporate party, then it can force that human to take actions on the network to make payments, reverse transactions, cough up taxes, or otherwise conform the electronic transaction to the state-mandated outcome. The song made famous by Clash (1979) has resonance here: "I fought the law. and the law won."

And as "smart contracting" bleeds over into more sophisticated "computable contracting," law stops being an impediment and starts being a necessity. A complex contract, with terms more developed than "if X happens, transfer coins Y to party Z" lives in a context of execution and performance that involves the physical world, and will benefit from having recourse to legal enforcement to reinforce its reliability. The two streams of reliability—physical execution constraints and external enforcement through law—are converging again.

3 Ricardian and Mixed Text/Code Contracts

The "Ricardian Contract" is one example of this convergence. As originally envisioned by Ian Grigg (2004, 2015), this was intended to be a contract whose expression was both executable by a computer and understandable by a human reader. As the concept has grown, the term has also come to be applied to mixed text/code contracts, where part of the arrangement is set out in executable software and part is set out in a natural language original. While the mixed format is probably a way-station on the journey to a more fully realized computable contract, it will be an important intervening step. And such mixed format agreements will, by necessity, have some interaction with the legacy world of law.

4 The Legal Framework for Smart and Computable Contracts

Except for a fringe of anarchic transactions between anonymous actors dealing through code-based interactions that either never touch down in the physical world or remain hidden from traditional governments, smart and computable contracts will not be able to live solely in their own autonomous world independent of law, courts and tax collectors. Their automaticity, reliability and clarity of execution may diminish the role of the traditional justice system in most instances, but these advantages will not fully eliminate that role. And so there needs to be some kind of accommodation between the two—and that accommodation is in progress. The remainder of this paper will explore two elements in that accommodation process in the United States: (i) the recognition in the legacy legal system for contracts expressed in whole or in part in code, and (ii) the legal treatment of a "repository" for prose versions of standard clauses, such as most "boilerplate" provisions on choice of law and forum, notices, etc.

A last precursor to this exploration is a reminder that the law of these encoded contracts will not always look like the current law applied to natural language agreements. That law has evolved over the past centuries to meet the needs and capacities of word-based formulations of event and response. It is worth noting that these, too, are "computational" in the formal meaning of that term (Flood and Goodenough 2015). When the automobile replaced the horse as the primary means of personal transportation, the well-developed principles of *horsemanship* needed to be drastically revised—if not outright abandoned—to develop the principles of *driving*. In the same way, while many of the goals of contract law will remain the same, the way in which those goals are met in a digital framework may look quite different from the rules for paper-based agreements.

5 Legal Recognition of Contracts Expressed in Code

A simple starting point for contracts expressed in code is whether the law will even *recognize* them as enforceable instruments. Many traditional laws require bargains, at least of a certain value or duration, to be *in writing*. This is based on a legacy concept that writing is the most formal and permanent mode for expression and recordation of information. Times have changed, however. I am composing this "paper" through a keyboard attached to a digital machine which can display words on a screen. You may be reading it through similar means. The expectation that tangible pieces of paper with writing on them are the apex form of recordation, even with respect to natural language statements, needs to be questioned, and the laws that saw writing as such an apex for embodying an agreement need to be changed.

In the United States, we were lucky to have had this principle addressed over two decades ago in the Uniform Electronic Transactions Act (UETA). It was proposed by the National Conference of Commissioners on Uniform State Laws (Uniform Law Commission) in 1999 and has since been adopted (with mostly minor variation) on a state level (where most American contract law exists) in 47 of the 50 states, as well as the District of Columbia and the US Virgin Islands. The holdout states are Illinois, New York and Washington, although they do have somewhat similar legislation, thanks in part to E-SIGN, discussed below. At this writing, Washington is considering adoption (Uniform Law Commission 2020).

The provisions of UETA were quite forward looking when it was drafted (Uniform Law Commission 2020). They were based, at least in part, on the UNCI TRAL Model Law on Electronic Commerce (UNCITRAL - United Nations Commision on International Trade Law 1996, 1999; Uniform Law Commission 2019; Boss and Kilian 2008; Blythe 2012). The UNCITRAL model has either been adopted or provided inspiration in a number of countries. The European Union has issued directives and regulations supporting electronic commerce as well, most recently eIDAS (Electronic Identification, Authentication and Trust Services), promulgated in 2014 (European Union 2014, see generally Smits 2017). The member states have chosen to implement these ideas in a variety of ways, beyond the scope of this paper. The core take-away is that UETA has international ancestry, siblings, and cousins.

The core provision of UETA is Section 7, which, in its model version, provides:

"SECTION 7. LEGAL RECOGNITION OF ELECTRONIC RECORDS, ELECTRONIC SIGNATURES, AND ELECTRONIC CONTRACTS.

(a) A record or signature may not be denied legal effect or enforceability solely because it is in electronic form.
(b) A contract may not be denied legal effect or enforceability solely because an electronic record was used in its formation.
(c) If a law requires a record to be in writing, an electronic record satisfies the law.
(d) If a law requires a signature, an electronic signature satisfies the law.

Definitions are set out in Section 2 of the act. Pertinent definitions include:

. . . .

(5) "Electronic" means relating to technology having electrical, digital, magnetic, wireless, optical, electromagnetic, or similar capabilities.

. . . .

(7) "Electronic record" means a record created, generated, sent, communicated, received, or stored by electronic means.

(8) "Electronic signature" means an electronic sound, symbol, or process attached to or logically associated with a record and executed or adopted by a person with the intent to sign the record.

. . . ."

Taken together, these provisions remove many of the formal barriers that might have hindered giving legal recognition to a code-embodied contract (Cohn et al. 2017). The arrangement still needs to constitute a contract when evaluated by other legal criteria, but at least the use of software in its formation and recordation is no impediment to that recognition.

In addition to resolving these formal questions, UETA also goes a long way toward recognizing automated transactions:

> **"SECTION 14. AUTOMATED TRANSACTION.**
> In an automated transaction, the following rules apply:
>
> (1) A contract may be formed by the interaction of electronic agents of the parties, even if no individual was aware of or reviewed the electronic agents' actions or the resulting terms and agreements.
> (2) A contract may be formed by the interaction of an electronic agent and an individual, acting on the individual's own behalf or for another person, including by an interaction in which the individual performs actions that the individual is free to refuse to perform and which the individual knows or has reason to know will cause the electronic agent to complete the transaction or performance.
> (3) The terms of the contract are determined by the substantive law applicable to it."
>
> In the definitions:
>
> "(2) "Automated transaction" means a transaction conducted or performed, in whole or in part, by electronic means or electronic records, in which the acts or records of one or both parties are not reviewed by an individual in the ordinary course in forming a contract, performing under an existing contract, or fulfilling an obligation required by the transaction."

UETA is complemented by a federal law, the E-SIGN Act (see, generally, Williston and Lord 2012 §4:4). In a reverse of the normal pattern, ESIGN's federal provisions recognizing electronic signatures gives way to UETA's broader enactment for states and transactions where UETA applies.

The drafters of UETA were intentionally platform-neutral in their approach. In early 2019, the Uniform Laws Commission approved a *Guidance Note Regarding the Relations between the Uniform Electronic Transactions Act and Federal ESIGN Act, Blockchain Technology and "Smart Contracts"*. This was prompted by the enactment, in a few states, of some UETA supplements that specifically mentioned Blockchain. The legislative intent of these mentions was to make these states appear attractive for blockchain commerce. The Note expresses concern that these modifications might be interpreted as restricting other approaches.

Recently, a variety of states enacted or considered legislation that amends the Uniform Electronic Transactions Act (UETA) to specifically address "blockchain" or "smart contracts." Such amendments directly contravene the technology-neutral principles that have enabled the UETA to remain effective over the course of nearly two decades of technological change. In fact, rather than improve the UETA, these blockchain or smart contract amendments undermine the efficacy of the UETA going forward (Uniform Law Commission 2019).

The Note expresses further concern that in their simplest form as mere execution scripts, smart contracts may not, in fact, meet the general idea of contracts, involving at least two parties and some meeting of the minds over a course of conduct. That said, to the extent they do rise to the level of a "contract" in the legal sense, UETA should ensure that the use of code in all or part of the specification of the obligations will not deprive them of legal recognition.

Although a full review of UETA is outside the province of this paper, those interested in smart and computable contracting may wish to study it in greater detail. Practice oriented and scholarly treatments include Williston and Lord (2012 §4:5), Dively (2000), Boss (2001), and Norwood (2006). The application of UETA to blockchain and smart contracting is explored further by Cohn et al. (2017), and the international context around UNCITRAL in Boss and Kilian (2008) and even more broadly in Blythe (2012).

In litigated cases involving electronic contracting, the provisions of UETA and E-SIGN have been applied broadly to support legal recognition and enforcement for transactions entered into and recorded using electronic means (Williston and Lord 2012 §§4:4 and 4:5 and the cases referenced therein, Cohn et al. 2017; Owens 2018).

The law has also sparked several commercial ventures that provide platforms for electronic signatures on traditional natural language contracts exchanged and executed via the Internet. One of these, the U.S. based company, DocuSign Inc. had achieved a pre-Covid-19 market capitalization level in early 2020 of more than $14 billion by helping to remove some of the friction in classic text-based contract formation (Market Watch 2020). The potential financial worth of code-enabled contracting would appear to be even greater once the practice matures. The distancing requirements of the Covid-19 crisis have made e-commerce solutions even more attractive in many contexts.

6 Mixed Format Contracting

UETA also resolves some of the concerns around recognizing mixed-format contracting. The portion of the agreement embodied in code will be deemed a "writing." The remaining challenge is: will the law allow a contract to exist with parts in more than one location? Happily, under traditional US law, the doctrine of "incorporation by reference" allows such a division. A contract formed in one writing can make reference to material set out in other writings and "incorporate" that other text into what is interpreted and applied as a unified contract. Similar concepts exist in many other legal systems.

The fourth edition of the Treatise *Williston on Contracts* sets out the principle from a US perspective:

As long as the contract makes clear reference to the document and describes it in such terms that its identity may be ascertained beyond doubt, the parties to a contract may incorporate contractual terms by reference to a separate, noncontemporaneous document including a separate agreement to which they are not parties and including a separate document which is unsigned. (Williston & Lord §30:25 at pp. 296–301, references omitted)

If this is accomplished, "that other document, or the portion to which reference is made, becomes constructively part of the writing, and in that respect the two form a single instrument" (Id at p. 304).

Taking the UETA position that an electronic expression of a contract counts as a writing and can be the "signed" portion of the agreement, making reference in that electronic contract to provisions in a traditional writing portion will be an effective way of marrying the two sets of provisions, provided that the reference is specific and clear enough. A challenge for mixed format contracts will be satisfying these requirements for clarity of reference.

As a practical matter, incorporation by reference can be applied to give legal "depth" to blockchain-based "smart contracts." As discussed above, currently most smart contracts are simple scripts that embody execution but which make no specification about non-execution matters like choice of law and venue. If a dispute arises and the traditional mechanisms of the law are invoked around a specific smart contract, many questions central to that process will be left up in the air. An entry level example is the choice of the law that should be applied. As we have seen, while many jurisdictions recognize electronic contracting generally and blockchain contractual evidence specifically; others do not. Selecting and effectively specifying a smart contract-friendly jurisdiction would be a very useful step in making use of a mixed format contract.

The blockchain field could benefit from the development of short boilerplate attachments that would specify desirable answers for these kinds of questions and that could be linked up in a smart contract and incorporated by reference. More complex *standard* terms could be handled similarly. In order to satisfy the specificity requirements of incorporation by reference, the other critical element would be some kind of broadly recognized repository or repositories for the attachments and a standardized means for making reference to such a repository.

7 Elements of a Repository[1]

Practically, such an effort would require three steps:

[1]The discussion of a Blockchain Text Repository in this chapter draws, in part, on material included in a proposal prepared by the author for use by the Digital Ledger Governance Association, Inc. (DLGA), and those portions are used with the permission of the DLGA.

- Establishing a widely used format for such an identifier.
- Establishing a secure repository for the clauses themselves, so that specific versions, with their identifier, can be accessed reliably by users and, in the case of a dispute, by the forum.
- Populating the repository with intelligent and usable options that could be readily used by smart contract creators.

Some fields of use are particularly susceptible this approach, particularly those where high volume and repeat players already support standardized forms with little negotiation of boilerplate terms. These areas include finance, transportation contracts, intellectual property licensing, and supply chain verification.

A short hash-based format could be used for the identifier. Such a format could start with a generic identifier, recognized in custom as suggesting both the incorporation step and the registry. If the registry were called the Blockchain Term Repository, for instance, the identifier could be "#BTR". Then there should be a short designator for the origin of the suggested clause, much like a financial ticker symbol. If the terms were promulgated by Stanford's CodeX center, for instance, the designator could be "SCX". The promulgation of suggested terms under a particular sourcing label would need to be subject to some security/curation to ensure that attribution is correct.

A short identifier for the version itself could then follow. If, for instance, it invoked California law (a UETA State), that could be mentioned in compressed form, along with a short characterization, such as "BOILERPLATE" and a version number. This element would be up to the clause provider to determine. Putting these together, the identifier could be:

#BTR.SCX.CA.BOILERPLATE.4

Obviously, a number of different approaches could be adopted as the standard; this approach is provided by way of illustration.

Adoption and use would be facilitated by a secure repository that would record the identifier together with the standard text that it is meant to represent. There could, in theory, be several such repositories, with examples perhaps attached to a particular chain or software approach. The host of such a repository should be a respected neutral party with a reasonable expectation of organizational durability. Possible examples include a trade association, a foundation with interest in blockchain, a university, or a governmental agency. The repository itself would require some thought in its implementation. For instance, it should include a way to register and verify the source of each entry, along with local storage for the entries and some kind of periodic posting to a distributed ledger that can provide long-term verification. Good coding will be necessary. An alternative approach could be to piggyback onto an existing repository, such as GitHub.

The population of the repository could either be done via some central, curated body, or could be left to bottom-up proposals, with the goal of allowing the most useful to emerge through industry use. The bottom-up approach would probably create a more diverse and successful set of options, although some light curation will be necessary to eliminate nonsensical proposals, mis-identification of sources, or attempts at sabotage. As to format, the content of particular entries could include:

- The hash identifier described above.
- A statement of the text or other matter to be the contents incorporated into the smart contract by reference to the hash identifier
- A field in which the source of the text can provide ancillary material about itself, its intentions with the text, and legal references and citations which may be useful.

The contents, once posted, would be put in the public domain.

Topics that could be addressed through a BTR attachment could include such traditional boilerplate matters as:

- Choice of law
- Choice of Dispute Resolution Forum
- Arbitration/Courts
- Location/Venue
- Remedies
- Injunction
- Indemnification
- Damages
- Amendments/Complete Agreement

Any blockchain-specific considerations could also be addressed (e.g., the smart contract would be subject to the rules and actions of the chain on which it is recorded).

Where to direct notices is not included on this list. This area could raise privacy and identity concerns that would require additional care as a repository is established, and any repository project should seek additional input before suggesting a standard. More complex issues like representations and warranties or bankruptcy and defaults could also be incorporated via models posted to the repository as common, standardized approaches emerge.

8 Conclusions

The use of executable code to specify and then perform contractual agreements is growing rapidly. Such approaches include the relatively simple scripts often called "smart contracts" as well as more developed examples frequently labeled "computable contracts." Although some proponents of digital contracting have argued that the automaticity of machine-execution will remove such agreements from legal review, the more realistic view is that interaction with the legacy legal system is likely to remain a feature of contracting.

To make that interaction productive, law must integrate itself with the new formats and challenges of computational contracting. One entry level requirement is recognition of the format itself. In the United States, UETA provides such recognition across a broad range of issues arising from the use of electronic means for contract formation and recordation.

A second issue is treatment of mixed-format or Ricardian contracts. In the near term, we can expect the widespread use of natural language text to supplement the code-embodied portions of an agreement. Such a mixture can be legally permissible in the United States under the doctrine of "incorporation by reference." To be effective, the reference from the "signed" portion to the other material must be sufficiently explicit so that both the intention and the target text can be reliably understood. Developing a standardized approach for such a reference and one or more recognized repositories for material to be incorporated will help ensure both informed use and legal recognition.

References

Blythe SE (2012) An e-commerce law for the world: the model electronic transactions act. Xlibris, Bloomington

Boss A, Kilian W (eds) (2008) The united nations convention on the use of electronic communications in international contracts: an in-depth guide and sourcebook. Wolters Kluwer, Frederick

Boss AH (2001) The uniform electronic transaction act in a global environment. Idaho Law Rev 37:275

Clash (1979) I fought the law. Original music and lyrics by Curtis S (1958). Official video of the Clash version. Available at https://www.youtube.com/watch?v=AL8chWFuM-s

Cohn A, West T, Parker C (2017) Smart after all: blockchain, smart contracts, parametric insurance and smart energy grids. Geo Law Technol Rev 1:273–304. Available at https://perma.cc/TY7W-Q8CX

Dively MJH (2000) The new laws that will enable electronic contracting: a survey of the electronic contracting rules in the uniform electronic transactions act and the uniform computer information transactions act. Duq Law Rev 38:209–254

Dixit A, Skeath S. (2004) Games of strategy, 2nd edn. W.W. Norton, New York

European Union (2014) Regulation (EU) No 910/2014 of the European Parliament and of the Council of 23 July 2014 on electronic identification and trust services for electronic transactions in the internal market and repealing Directive 1999/93/EC, available at https://eur-lex.europa.eu/legal-content/EN/TXT/?uri=uriserv%3AOJ.L_.2014.257.01.0073.01.ENG

Flood M, Goodenough O (2015) Contract as automaton: the computational representation of financial agreements. OFR Working Paper, No. 15-04, revised (2017), available at https://www.financialresearch.gov/working-papers/files/OFRwp-2015-04_Contract-as-Automaton-The-Computational-Representation-of-Financial-Agreements.pdf

Gintis H (2000) Game theory evolving. Princeton University Press, Princeton

Goodenough O (2007) Values, mechanism design, and fairness. In: Zak PJ (ed) Moral markets: the critical role of values in the economy. Princeton University Press, Princeton, pp 228–257. Available at https://ssrn.com/abstract=933012

Grigg I (2004) The ricardian contract. Available at http://iang.org/papers/ricardian_contract.html

Grigg I (2015) On the intersection of ricardian and smart contracts. Available at https://iang.org/papers/intersection_ricardian_smart.html

Levi SD, Lipton AB (2018) An introduction to smart contracts and their potential and inherent limitations, Harvard Law School Forum on Corporate Governance https://corpgov.law.harvard.edu/2018/05/26/an-introduction-to-smart-contracts-and-their-potential-and-inherent-limitations/

Love N, Genesereth M (2005) Computational law. Available at http://logic.stanford.edu/publications/love/computationallaw.pdf

LSP Working Group (Goodenough O Principle Author) (2019) Developing a legal specification protocol: technological considerations and requirements. Stanford CodeX Publication. Available at https://law.stanford.edu/publications/developing-a-legal-specification-protocol-technological-considerations-and-requirements/

Market Watch (2020) DocuSign. https://www.marketwatch.com/investing/stock/docu

Norwood JM (2006) A summary of statutory and case law associated with contracting in the electronic universe. DePaul Bus Commer Law J 4:415–450

Owens L (2018) 7 landmark electronic signature legal cases. Electronic Signature and Records Assoc. Available at https://esignrecords.org/2018/01/28/7-landmark-electronic-signature-legal-cases/

Skyrms B (2004) The stag hunt and the evolution of social structure. Cambridge, Cambridge

Smith A (1776) An inquiry into the nature and causes of the wealth of nations. Variously reprinted including Prometheus, Amherst, New York (1991)

Smits JM (2017) Contract law a comparative introduction, 2nd edn. Elgar Cheltenham

Solidity (2020) Solidity. Available at https://solidity.readthedocs.io/en/v0.6.6/

Staples M, Chen S, Falamaki S, Ponomarev A, Rimba P, Tran AB, Weber I, Xu X, Zhu J, (2017) Risks and opportunities for systems using blockchain and smart contracts. Data 61 (CSIRO), Sydney. https://assets.ctfassets.net/sdlntm3tthp6/resource-asset-r297/58dd59299229647cf4196a69a796b3ce/0d843b74-ef95-4611-89de-6d18bbc53473.pdf

Surden H (2012) Computable contracts. UC Davis Law Rev 46:629–700. Available at https://lawreview.law.ucdavis.edu/issues/46/2/articles/46-2_surden.pdf

Szabo N (1997) Formalizing and securing relationships on public networks. Reprinted at https://nakamotoinstitute.org/formalizing-securing-relationships/

UNCITRAL – United Nations Commission on International Trade Law (2020) UNCITRAL model law on electronic commerce (1996) with additional article 5 bis as adopted in 1998. Available at https://uncitral.un.org/en/texts/ecommerce/modellaw/electronic_commerce

UNCITRAL – United Nations Commission on International Trade Law (2020) UNCITRAL model law on electronic commerce (1999) UNCITRAL model Law on electronic commerce with guide to enactment 1996 with additional article 5 bis as adopted in 1998. United Nations, New York. Available at https://uncitral.un.org/sites/uncitral.un.org/files/media-documents/uncitral/en/19-04970_ebook.pdf

Uniform Law Commission (2019) Guidance Note Regarding the Relation Between the Uniform Electronic Transactions Act and Federal Esign Act, Blockchain Technology and "Smart Contracts," Electronic Transactions Act. Uniform Law Commission, available at https://www.uniformlaws.org/viewdocument/guidance-note-regarding-the-relatio?CommunityKey=2c04b76c-2b7d-4399-977e-d5876ba7e034&tab=librarydocuments

Uniform Law Commission (2020) Electronic Transactions Act. Uniform Law Commission, available at https://www.uniformlaws.org/committees/community-home?CommunityKey=2c04b76c-2b7d-4399-977e-d5876ba7e034

Williston S, Lord RA (2012) Williston on contracts, 4th edn. West, St. Paul

About Smart Contract Dispute Resolution

Amedeo Santosuosso

Contents

1 Blockchain, a Technology Among Several Others

Blockchain is the way universally used to describe the distributed register or ledger technology. It shares several features and aspects with a series of other technologies, among the others, cryptocurrencies, bitcoin, smart contracts, Internet, Internet of thing and AI. Some very brief clarifications on these interconnections might offer a reasonable background for a better understanding of our focus: dispute resolution.

Cryptocurrencies At its origin, it is well known, blockchain's history is intertwined with bitcoins. However, it is nowadays definitively clear that current developments of blockchain and its wide use in public institutions, educational entities and among professionals exclude a full overlap of blockchain with any cryptocurrency. An example, among many others, from the civil law litigations area might help. In the field of descent and distribution the major disputes relate to the actual and concrete proof of the deceased's will and rights involved. If all the documents concerning the rights enjoyed by the decedent were in blockchain registers, many disputes might be avoided and those interested in the property could have access to more reliable and

A. Santosuosso (✉)
Pavia University, Milan, Italy
e-mail: a.santosuosso@unipv.it

B. Cappiello, G. Carullo (eds.), *Blockchain, Law and Governance*,
https://doi.org/10.1007/978-3-030-52722-8_14

verifiable data than the systems currently allow. Similarly, in the field of labor law and people recruitment, the technology of distributed registers would allow to check the truth of previous work experiences of a candidate for a job, with great savings of time and human resources. An interested experience is offered by *Recruit Technologies*, which, in collaboration with *Ascribe.io*,[1] has developed cryptographic certificates of authenticity of titles and curricula based precisely on a blockchain technology.

The Internet Blockchain is essentially tied to the Internet on whose shoulders it travels. The Internet is made up of a plurality of protocols which, when combined, create different levels of communication (one of which is the well-known TCP/IP). Blockchain technology uses application protocols capable of both transmitting data and storing information and performing some computational processes, in a way that does not depend on any centralized operator. The main aspect is, therefore, the use of the Internet, but with two significant variations: the first, consisting of the fact of using the network as a place in which not only to transmit, but also to store and process data (i.e. the chained blocks) and, the second, to set up an equal and non-hierarchical network, based on a consensus mechanism and a decentralized virtual mechanism that manages and validates data and carries out computational activities. Centralized services, which also exist in a blockchain and interact with it, operate independently of the underlying peer network.

Smart Contracts Blockchain and smart contracts have an area where they overlap each other, while each of them has its own larger part beyond the overlap. Indeed, even though it is, in some sense, the natural environment of smart contracts, blockchain has a huge quantity of other different applications, e.g. voting, certification and more (see above). Conversely, smart contracts embedded in blockchain belong to the larger family of computable contracts, i.e. contracts which are directly written as a software (they totally skip the phase of writing down in natural language and then translating in a computable language). Indeed, computable contracts exist and are widely developing outside the blockchain environment. The development of a Legal specification protocol dedicated to smart contracts on the Internet is a clear example of this.[2]

Internet of Things As for the correlation between the Internet of Things (IoT) and blockchain, IBM and Samsung have developed a system called ADEPT[3] (decentralized autonomous peer-to-peer telemetry), in which a technology similar to blockchain provides the backbone for a decentralized IoT network, functioning as a ledger to manage a massive amount of devices. ADEPT is not the only project that has tried to combine blockchain technology and IoT, as evidenced by the existence

[1]See https://www.ascribe.io and https://github.com/ascribe.

[2]See the Legal Specification Protocol project by Professor Oliver Goodenough and Codex Center at Stanford University, USA.

[3]https://www.ibm.com/downloads/cas/QYYYV9VK visited March 14, 2020.

of numerous startups who are trying to use the potential of technology in combination with IoT.

Artificial Intelligence Blockchain and smart contracts do not belong, strictly speaking, to the field of AI, even though they have some obvious links.

2 Contract or Software? The Controversial Nature of Smart Contracts

A closer look at the *nature* of smart contracts, might help in focusing the issue of this chapter.

At the moment the search for a unique definition of smart contract appears stuck on the crucial (perhaps sterile) dilemma whether they are still contracts.

The character of the smart contract is represented by the fact that the parties reach an agreement on the contractual clauses and on the timing, taking advantage of the *if-this-then-that* logic, that is, *if* a presupposition occurs (*this*), *then* it achieves a result (*that*). For the rest, a smart contract might be self-executing, in the sense that it has some (we will see below in what limits and under what circumstances) ability to enforce its clauses and enter into execution without any support of an external party (e.g., the payment of a sum of money in the event of contractual breach: upon the occurrence of the condition of breach the sum agreed as a penalty will be automatically paid from one party's account to that of the other).

This intertwining of software technologies with traditional legal wording (will of the parties, agreement, content of the contract) is at the origin of the question: is the smart contract still a contract (even if a new type) or is it an IT entity (software, code, network), which has nothing of the traditional contract, neither in its structure nor in the form of expression of the binding nature of the parties will. Markus Kaulartz, a Tech lawyer (according to his self-definition) working for CMS (a group of lawyers operating internationally in the new technology sector), in a speech at the Humboldt University on Smart contract Dispute Resolution, states verbatim that "a smart contract basically is not a contract. It is only software that performs an obligation under predefined conditions"[4] with some exceptions.

The statement, net of a somewhat simplistic tone for a lawyer (executing an obligation still looks something legal!), reflects the dual appearance of the smart contract, a duplicity that, in my view, is not only between traditional contract and software, but also (and perhaps mostly) between the natural language traditionally used by the parties (as it has always happened) and the parties agreement which is expressed in a formal language (such as that of the code and the software through

[4]See Kaulartz M Blockchain Arbitration. In: YouTube. https://www.youtube.com/watch?time_continue=30&v=N4jtK4HaKfQ.

which the agreement is formalized in the blockchain or other technological environment).[5]

It can be preliminarily noted that the statement according to which the smart contract is not a contract implies and assumes an idea of a contract that is immutable over time, blocked at its latest definition before the advent of IT and the Internet, while we shouldn't forget that the contract (in the many different connotations it assumes in the different languages and cultures) is probably the most flexible and open tool to changes over time that the legal history of humanity knows. Thus, it seems reasonable the point of view of who says that today

> in many ways, smart contracts are no different than today's written agreements. To execute a smart contract, the parties must first negotiate the terms of their agreement until they reach a 'meeting of the minds'. Once agreed upon, parties memorialize all or parts of their understanding in smart contract code which is triggered by digitally signed blockchain-based blocks transactions.[6]

3 If Things Go Wrong

The scenario that opens up when things do not go well (e.g. a party does not fulfill the contract) is more revealing on the nature of the smart contract than many theoretical discussions. Even people who strongly maintain smart contracts are not contracts have to admit that smart contracts are useful and necessary only when simple facts and few legal arguments are to be assessed. The only residual risk of disputes should regard only programming errors (there are always bugs!) and other minor things, disputes whose solution is arbitration. Conversely "complicated cases and where legal assessments are necessary, must be treated with AI techniques".[7]

Therefore, the crucial point in order to have a useful smart contract is that facts are well defined and legal arguments are not complex. This means, just to make an example, that an insurance contract covering let's say the risk of loss of the crop due to drought implies the "natural" risk of disagreement between the parties about the severity of the drought, its incidence on the crop, the real entity of damages and more. However, the same contract might be replaced with a smart contract where the insurance coverage is linked to the extent of rains how reported by an authoritative and agreed weather forecast entity in a specific area (e.g. AccuWeather).

Doing so a significant change happens in the concept of risk and in the object of the contract. There is clearly a shift from the risk of the crop loss to a parameter (the measurement of the rains) which the parties agree to consider linked to the loss of crop. The possibility that the same intensity of the rain can cause a higher or lower

---

[5]The issue goes beyond the topic of smart contracts and blockchains and rather concerns the relationship between computation and law, see Santosuosso (2020), chap. 8.

[6]Filippi and Wright (2019), p. 74.

[7]See Kaulartz M Blockchain Arbitration. In: YouTube. https://www.youtube.com/watch?time_continue=30&v=N4jtK4HaKfQ.

loss of crop in a specific field is a sort of sub-risk the parties accept in view, the client, of getting a prompt and unquestionable payment of a sum of money and, the insurance company, of having less disputes and litigations and their related costs of legal assistance.

At the end, a contract where the insurance company agrees to pay a sum of money in relation to an agreed parameter, can be a computable (reasonably self-executing) contract. And this may be true for any kind of contract where the *if* is a parameter and the *then* are legal consequences clearly foreseen by legislation and/or clearly agreed in the contract. We might say that a smart contract would be comfortable in the world of Frederick Schauer rules, where only written and with non-general and open content rules deserve the quality of 'rule'.[8]

Having this in mind we can finally approach the issue of Smart Contract Dispute Resolution.

4 Smart Contract Dispute Resolution

The point is that we have to realistically accept that, even though the contract is carefully parametrized in its clauses and is self-executing at a high degree, some litigation may happen, for several reasons, from bugs which may always happen to unexpected and unforeseen events. A fully self-executing contract is not a frequent entity in complex matters, and this means that an efficient and reliable system of dispute resolution is a crucial point in order to have a fully development of smart contracts potentiality.

A UK initiative starts from a similar view of the current system. According to Sir Geoffrey Vos, smart contracts will finally be able to take off only when market participants and investors have confidence in them. Traditional investors have yet to be convinced that their legal rights can be protected when trading in cryptoassets and entering into smart contracts.[9] This is the consideration on which a public consultation on blockchain and smart contracts was launched in May 2019 in the United Kingdom. It is a very pragmatic assumption that, although with an approach certainly putting the state at the center (if seen with the eyes of the great supporters of these technologies), reflects the widespread awareness that the balance between state and international regulations and blockchain is still to be found. The dilemma has been summarized as follows:

Regulating too soon could provide valuable guidance as to the legitimate uses of blockchain technology but could also stamp out potential benefits. Regulating too

[8]Schauer (1991).

[9]The LawTech Delivery Panel, Legal statement on cryptoassets and smart contracts, UK Jurisdiction Taskforce, November 2019, available at https://35z8e83m1ih83drye280o9d1-wpengine.netdna-ssl.com/wp-content/uploads/2019/11/6.6056_JO_Cryptocurrencies_Statement_FINAL_WEB_111119-1.pdf visited 21 March 2020 (see the Introduction, p. 4, and the Foreword by Sir Geoffrey Vos, Chancellor of the High Court).

late may dissuade the most risk-averse actors from exploring blockchains because of legal uncertainty while simultaneously allowing socially objectionable aspects of technology to emerge.[10]

The supporters of the very particular and different nature of smart contracts highlight three characterizing aspects. In the first place, the risk of litigation is poor, as smart contracts are programs codes determined by events, which execute the rules of the code: deterministic contracts contain sufficient information to determine a result without the need for external information (such as, for example, a transfer order of funds from one wallet to another on a certain date). Furthermore, and in theory, a smart contract does not need intermediaries, lawyers, judges, banks, insurance companies, in summary it does not need to resort to the authority of a third party. Finally, where conflicts arise, the remedy is arbitration.

However, even arbitration, as it has emerged in blockchain/smart contract practice, has its shortcomings. Firstly, the concept and legal value of arbitration change according to the environment (if internal to blockchain or off-chain "real world") and the jurisdictions. Some arbitrations in blockchain environment look like oracles, in the sense that the solution is given by a vote without any explanation. On the other side, the difference in jurisdictions is relevant in arbitration given in general legal systems, where the arbitration may be expensive and taking a long time. For instance, the Italian civil law has two kinds of arbitration, where the let's say higher (*arbitrato rituale*) has the same legal value of a decision given by a court and very high costs; the less formal option (*arbitrato irrituale*) has the nature and value of a contract that leaves to the interested party the only choice to initiate an enforcement procedure in a public court, addressing the same problems that arbitration in smart contracts intends to prevent. At that point having signed the contract through an automatic or IT system is a meager satisfaction.

Thus, we might conclude that the dispute resolution system is perhaps the bottleneck for a full development of computable contracts, both embedded in blockchain or not.

5 When a Smart Contract Is Embedded in a Blockchain: A Deeper Exploration

The core of the contractual structure in a blockchain is made up of three main elements: account, available assets and contract. By *account*, we mean an address that can identify a person, entity or group of people who will interact with the ledger in question, the so-called ledger. The *assets* include both tangible goods and services, invoices and exchanged units of value. More generally, the goods can be defined as the set of values exchanged and owned by one or more parties, who possess the cryptographic key that allows to give rise to the contract. The last

[10]Filippi and Wright (2019), p. 57.

requirement is represented by the actual *contract*, intended as a logical sequence of actions that mediates the transfer of currency and data between the parties.

The accounts send updates to the ledger, which consist of authorized transactions, thus changing their status. The transactions, before being aggregated and sequenced in a block, are sent to verify their integrity and data integrity. All ledger transactions are digitally signed by an account holder on the network. The ledger has three key properties, which differentiate it from traditional network traffic: (a) *authentication*, as an attacker cannot disguise himself using the account of a part of the transaction, if the party is not; (b) *integrity*, as the receipt of the transaction cannot be changed after the fact; (c) *non-malleability*, as any changes to the transaction will invalidate the issuer's signature, thus also invalidating the transaction.

Each clause is discussed and approved by both parties before being placed on the chain. Once approved, it is inserted in the first block and, at that moment, undergoes the transformation from natural language into encrypted language capable of being understood by the system. The operations that the parties perform are as follows: enter, through their cryptographic keys, both the clauses they intend to enter into the contract and the operations that the system will carry out automatically, in the event of violation of one of the aforementioned clauses. Thanks to the *if/then* sequence, if the system records the occurrence of the fact referred to in a certain clause (if), the contract will progress; if, on the contrary, the content of the clause is violated, the contract will automatically carry out the remedies provided by the parties themselves or by law. Thanks to the backup system, it will not be possible to find yourself in a situation where one party boasts the existence of some clauses and the other party boasts different clauses of the same contract. Just like the technologies that are used every day, from cell phones to computers, the blockchain is also equipped with a data saving system.

In addition to the rescue system, the contract is also duplicated, so that, in the event of its modification, it is always clear which is the original shared by the parties themselves. A copy of the entire register is stored on each node-device of each participant, so that each information record contains both the copy of the transactions and the corresponding data in a predetermined format, and the block containing the transactions carried out in chronological order, protected then by a Hash code. To understand this operation, you can imagine a tree diagram: from a single starting point, represented by the agreement of the parties, several roads branch out, of which only one leads to the conclusion and full execution of the contract, while the others are all possible ramifications of different situations that can occur.

6 Disputes Arising from Smart Contracts: The JUR Proposal

On this reality, and on the consideration that in the general legal system the time and resources that a party must spend to obtain the execution of a contract (if the other party is in default) are much higher than that used to achieve the contractual agreement and its drafting, JUR bases its proposal. JUR, a young reality in the blockchain and smart contract field, formulates an interesting scheme:

Thanks to blockchain, justice can shift from a centralized system to a decentralized one, while smart contracts will transform a slow and expensive process into one that is inexpensive, reliable, fast and affordable. Jur mixes these two technologies to deliver a dispute resolution system on a global scale, where decentralization is the fundamental value in order to create transparency, quality and incorruptibility. [...] Jur was born when CEO and co-founder Alessandro Palombo realized that replacing traditional contracts with smart contracts was not enough for the intended purpose of changing the law system. Sure, you can create self-automated contracts with smart contracts, but a judiciary decision by a court is always necessary for having it enforced into the real legal system. That meant that the innovative potential contained within smart contracts was nullified.[11]

The system designed by JUR distinguishes the different levels at which a smart contract is self-executing and realistically recognizes that, in many cases, the contract will be only partially self-executing or even depend on subjective evaluations, with the consequence that the use of a dispute resolution system offering guarantees is an essential condition for the application development of smart contracts.

The proposal can be summarized as follows: (a) the judgment is not decentralized and requires that one or three arbitrators issue a written decision (the arbitrators earn the same amount regardless of their decision); (b) on the decision, the system performs a decentralized and blind peer review; (c) the referee being assessed remains anonymous; (d) three auditors, randomly selected, evaluate the decision and earn or lose tokens and reputation depending on whether they vote for or against the majority; (e) the referee being evaluated receives or loses reputation points in accordance with the reviewers' vote.

According to the proposers, in this way, an ecosystem is created that guarantees the quality of the judgments and the presence of an impartial judge. Everything happens within the blockchain system without recourse to public authorities. The idea is "to fill the market gap with an elegant solution that reduces the complexity of the current global legal system. In order to offer a truly innovative and affordable service, the platform is powered by a token utility, the JUR token, the token of justice".

[11](2020) Jur's debut: the token of justice (JUR) is on public sale from 28th August. In: Medium. https://medium.com/jur-io/jurs-debut-the-token-of-justice-jur-is-on-public-sale-from-28th-august-ab0ffd8cbb59.

7 A Slow, Expensive Database?

We do not know if blockchain technology will solve its problems and keep the promise we spoke of at the beginning of this chapter or if it will only prove to be a slow, expensive database.[12] What is certain is that blockchain is increasingly intertwined with a complex of constantly evolving technologies. An efficient dispute settlement system can be one of the decisive aspects.

References

Filippi PD, Wright A (2019) Blockchain and the law: the rule of code. Harvard University Press, Cambridge

Santosuosso A (2020) Intelligenza artificiale e diritto. Perché le tecnologie di IA sono una grande opportunità per il diritto. Mondadori Università, Milano

Schauer F (1991) Playing by the rules: a philosophical examination of rule-based decision-making in law and in life. Clarendon Press, Oxford

Song J (2018) Why blockchain is hard. Medium. https://medium.com/@jimmysong/why-blockchain-is-hard-60416ea4c5c

[12] "Just like 'cloud' means someone else's computer and 'AI' means a tweaked algorithm, 'blockchain' in this context means a slow, expensive database": Song (2018).

Smart Contracts, ODR and the New Landscape of the Dispute Resolution Market

Pietro Ortolani

Contents

1 Introduction

Like any complex phenomenon, dispute resolution can be observed through different lenses. We can look at it from a public law perspective, scrutinizing the nature and the limits of the power that adjudicators exert, be them State judges, or private arbitrators. Conversely, we can analyze it from the vantage of private law, focusing on the role of private autonomy, the importance of party impulse, and the relationship between procedural remedies and individual substantive rights. Taking one step back, however, it is also possible to observe the dispute resolution landscape in its entirety, as a market where different actors offer competing services, according to the pattern of monopolistic competition.[1] Looking at dispute resolution from this point of view, State court litigation and commercial arbitration are two of the many options that users are presented with, and invited to choose from; dispute resolution, in fact, is an ever-growing market, as the recent proliferation of international commercial courts demonstrates.[2] In this type of market, competing "products" undergo a process of progressive differentiation, aimed at enhancing their attractiveness in

[1]Chamberlin (1962).
[2]Bell (2018), pp. 193–216.

P. Ortolani (✉)
Radboud University, Nijmegen, The Netherlands
e-mail: p.ortolani@jur.ru.nl

B. Cappiello, G. Carullo (eds.), *Blockchain, Law and Governance*,
https://doi.org/10.1007/978-3-030-52722-8_15

the eyes of the users. Technology can be an important differentiating factor, maximizing the efficiency of a given dispute resolution service and, as a consequence, highlighting its desirability, as opposed to the available alternatives. In light of this, it is particularly interesting to investigate the potential impact of new technologies (and, in particular, of blockchain technologies) on dispute resolution, while observing the latter as a market. The aim of this short contribution, hence, is to highlight the different ways in which technology may alter (or disrupt) the dispute resolution market, with a particular focus on Online Dispute Resolution (ODR).

2 The Persistence of Non-Deterministic Lawyering

The narrative of blockchain technologies and smart contracts "taking over" the law, and progressively making all legal services obsolete, is so simplistic as to be almost comically inadequate. While on the one hand smart contracts follow a technologically deterministic logic, on the other hand a contract functions, as an intellectual construct, precisely because it is *not* deterministic. The existence of a margin for interpretation,[3] one would be tempted to conclude, is inherent to how law works. Therefore, if it is true that not all aspects of a commercial transaction can be translated into an if-then logic, then the resolution of disputes arising out of a contract will normally require human intervention. Lawyers die hard, despite the rise of the *lex cryptographica*:[4] counsels, judges and arbitrators seem to resolutely resist obsolescence. And yet, if we scratch the surface, things are more complex than they may initially seem.

Over the course of five years of research on the topic of blockchain and dispute resolution,[5] I have made a bet of sorts. First, I observed the meteoric rise of Bitcoin, and the ever-growing amount of transactions verified on the Bitcoin blockchain. While many of those transactions were of a purely speculative nature, niches of users do deploy Bitcoin as a currency, within specific communities.[6] It is reasonable to assume that a certain minority of those transactions, unavoidably, will result in a dispute. My initial hypothesis, hence, was that the increase of transactions denominated in Bitcoin would be followed, a few months or years down the line, by a specular increase in the amount of Bitcoin-related court cases. In other words, I expected a rise in the number of litigations where a plaintiff requested the enforcement of a contract denominated in Bitcoin. The assumption underpinning my hypothesis, of course, was that the degree of automation inherent to the Bitcoin

[3]See Santosuosso's chapter in this volume.

[4]Filippi and Wright (2019), pp. 193–204.

[5]Ortolani (2016a), pp. 595–629.

[6]Ortolani (2016b), pp. 569–627.

protocol would prove insufficient to prevent or resolve disputes; court cases, hence, would unavoidably start cropping up.[7]

To put it bluntly, my initial hypothesis was wrong. I started counting US court cases mentioning the word "Bitcoin", but I failed to observe the rise in litigation that I was expecting. As my research on the topic shows,[8] if there has been an increase in Bitcoin-related civil and commercial litigation, it has been a very timid one. Thus, I started asking myself why: how was it possible that such an important volume of transactions would result in almost zero disputes? Had dispute resolution really been made obsolete, after all? An answer, of course, is that the majority of users buy Bitcoin for merely speculative purposes. However, this answer is only partially satisfactory: Bitcoin is used (or at least, it has been used, for a certain period of time) to purchase goods and services too. In sum, things did not quite add up. I started looking for alternative hypotheses.

3 Escrow Mechanism and the Potential of Self-Enforcing ODR

An important part of the answer was hidden in Satoshi Nakamoto's white paper.[9] One sentence, in particular, struck me as highly instructive, if somewhat mysterious: "routine escrow mechanisms could easily be implemented to protect buyers". Despite its enormous impact, this aspect of the white paper has remained largely overlooked: from the very beginning, the Bitcoin white paper takes dispute resolution into account. Implicitly, the paper makes a reference to a specific type of adjudication, based on an escrow wallet. Nakamoto's paper, in a nutshell, contains a specific proposal concerning self-enforcing ODR, and the solution that it proposes has been adopted within the Bitcoin community, as well as on other blockchains.

Whenever cryptocurrencies are used to conclude e.g. a sales agreement, the funds are normally not transferred directly from the wallet of the buyer to the wallet of the seller. Typically, the funds are stored on a multi-signature wallet, which essentially works like a lock with two keyholes. Buyer and seller are both provided with a key, but one key is not enough to unlock the funds stored in the wallet. If the transaction runs smoothly and the goods are delivered to the buyer, the parties will agree to use both of their keys, and free the funds in favor of the seller. However, if a dispute arises, the parties have the possibility of appointing an adjudicator, who will hold a third key, and will conduct a (rather rudimentary) dispute resolution procedure. At the end of this procedure, he or she will give the key to the winning party. Therefore, not only is this adjudicator able to make an award: he or she will be able to

[7]In a similar vein see Rabinovich-Einy and Katsh (2019).

[8]Ortolani (2019), pp. 289–310.

[9]Nakamoto (2008).

effectively enforce the award, ensuring that the prevailing party receives the disputed funds.

The importance of this development can hardly be overstated. Traditionally, enforcement is the monopoly of the State: it is, more precisely, part of the State's monopoly over the use force. Now, within the niche of escrow-based dispute resolution, that monopoly largely comes to an end. Whenever the disputed assets are tokenized, self-enforcement of dispute resolution outcomes becomes a tangible possibility. Bitcoin, in other words, was just the beginning: it was a proof of concept, showing that self-enforcing ODR is possible. As blockchain technologies become ripe for exploitation, Nakamoto's intuition can percolate into different forms of dispute resolution, and we are currently witnessing the development of a number of promising projects, whose level of sophistication goes far beyond multi-signature escrow wallets.

What will this mean, for the dispute resolution market? Possibly, the market will undergo a process of fragmentation and increasing specialization. On the one hand, "traditional" arbitration (leading to *res judicata*) will continue to play a key role: self-enforcement may prove unsuitable for complex (and often cross-border) commercial transactions, as the mechanism of escrow (and the need to keep the funds stored until the contract has been performed) may be difficult to reconcile with high-value contracts. In this context, blockchain technologies can be used as case management tools, and there is certainly a lot of room for improvement and modernization, in these respects. Besides "traditional" arbitration, however, other types of private adjudication systems are currently being developed, often operating on the basis of game-theoretical incentives. This is a new type of out-of-court adjudication, which does not necessarily qualify as arbitration from the point of view of domestic law and of the 1958 New York Convention, but which can nevertheless have a fundamental practical effect. These systems can, in particular, meet a demand for dispute resolution that has so far remained almost completely ignored: the one arising out of low-value, high-volume transactions.

4 Conclusions: A Wider Offer of Dispute Resolution Services?

To go back to my initial contention against smart contracts "making lawyers obsolete", we should rethink the argument in more nuanced terms. For the time being, we are faced with a layered landscape, where different dispute resolution systems coexist and potentially compete: first of all, some simple disputes may be avoided through the deterministic enforcement of smart contracts. Besides that, whenever a certain amount of human interaction and "non-deterministic lawyering" is necessary, different options may be available, with a varying degree of technological embeddedness. In a nutshell, there may be more alternatives than State court litigation, or "traditional" arbitration.

Technology, thus, unleashes a process of progressive specialization of different dispute resolution fora and mechanisms, each of them covering a niche in an expanding, variegated market. The consequences of the use of different mechanisms, of course, may vary drastically: if, on the one hand, both litigation and "traditional" arbitration are meant to produce *res judicata* effects, private adjudication based on a blockchain-based escrow system may not prevent the *de novo* re-hearing of the case, at a later stage. Be it as it may, the use of blockchain technologies in dispute resolution seems to open unprecedented possibilities. In the near future, the demand for dispute resolution may be met in a richer, more nuanced and comprehensive fashion.

References

Bell GF (2018) The new international commercial courts-competing with arbitration-the example of the Singapore international commercial court. Contemp Asia Arb J 11:193

Chamberlin EH (1962) The theory of monopolistic competition: a re-orientation of the theory of value, vol VIII. Harvard University Press, Cambridge

Filippi PD, Wright A (2019) Blockchain and the law: the rule of code. Harvard University Press, Cambridge

Nakamoto S (2008) Bitcoin: A Peer-to-Peer Electronic Cash System. 11

Ortolani P (2016a) Self-enforcing online dispute resolution: lessons from bitcoin. Oxford J Legal Stud 36:595–629

Ortolani P (2016b) The three challenges of stateless justice. J Int Dispute Settlement 7:596–627

Ortolani P (2019) The judicialization of the blockchain. In: Hacker P, Lianos I, Dimitropoulos G, Eich S (eds) Regulating blockchain: techno-social and legal challenges. Oxford University Press, Oxford

Rabinovich-Einy O, Katsh E (2019) Blockchain and the inevitability of disputes: the role for online dispute resolution. J Disp Resol 47

Blockchain, Smart Contracts and New Certainties: What Future for Notaries?

Michele Nastri

Contents

1 Preliminary Remarks

The world of cryptocurrencies, and of the Blockchain in general, arrived at courts all over the world. The reason is clearly exposed in a paper published in the "Harvard Journal of Law & Technology" about the first case on this issue examined by the United States Antitrust court: "*where there is money there is power, and where there is power there is abuse of power*".[1]

This observation would be enough to stop thinking about the Blockchain as a benevolent artificial intelligence ready to solve all of our problems.

In fact, every technology follows its rules, which depend on the tools it uses and on the process organization set by its designers.

Thus, technologies aren't neutral, since all of them depend on some human decision, and they set some rules to human actions.

The law should regulate social life by protecting both individual rights and the community as a whole. Its aim is to balance interests, and its rules should prevail

[1]Stylianou (2019).

M. Nastri (✉)
Notary, Naples, Italy
e-mail: mnastri@notariato.it

B. Cappiello, G. Carullo (eds.), *Blockchain, Law and Governance*,
https://doi.org/10.1007/978-3-030-52722-8_16

over the rules of technology. Because of their function in social life, the creation of legal obligations is complex and structured. For this reason, legal obligations are stricter than technological rules—which in principle should be considered as a good thing.

This also applies to the Blockchain, which, rather than a technology, is a set of technologies organized in a process, or more correctly, in a range of processes or declinations. It thus becomes evident that technology control is a source of power, and that the protection of individual rights is required in this context too.

It is wrong to say that the Blockchain creates disintermediation: actually, the mediation doesn't disappear, it's just condensed. The Blockchain reduces the number of intermediate entities, and thus their influence on transactions costs, but the choices are concentrated during model creation and modification, with possible concentrations of power.

Furthermore, the chain is not self-sufficient, and some unavoidable questions must be taken into account:

- The protection of privacy, but not of absolute anonymity: this is the main problem of cryptocurrencies, also in an anti-money laundering (AML) perspective;
- The verification of the digital identity, along with the guarantee of security and privacy;
- The problem of document storage: the Blockchain contains strings of data, and therefore is not a very effective technology for document storage, which is an important requirement for the protection of the rights, especially in civil law legal systems.

2 A "Lay" Approach to the Blockchain

However, the Blockchain presents some features that make it suitable to use it as an alternative to traditional systems. Being basically an interoperable technology, it makes database sharing easier, while meeting the need to track online transactions; therefore, it can serve scalable solutions and can be used in unregulated contexts.

Nevertheless, a preliminary process and purpose analysis is needed to assess if the use of the Blockchain is preferable to other solutions, and it should take into-account elements such as:

- The subjects;
- The objects of the transactions;
- The privileges of some stakeholders, as the power to direct, modify or nullify some activities and results;
- The rights involved.

In short: a feasibility assessment, followed by a cost-benefit analysis.

3 Legal Professions, Notaries and the (Alleged?) Role Crisis

Such an approach can also apply to the disintermediation of legal professions. Legal professions serve as a connection between the world of law and actual practices.

Lawyers guarantee fair conditions for the access to justice.

Notaries, through the preliminary assessment and control of the legal relationships between private parties, provide preventive justice thus reducing the trials.

Both of these professions are not strictly necessary for the activities in which they are involved: in some legal systems, notaries don't perform the same functions as they do in civil law countries, and in some others it is not mandatory to have a defense lawyer during a process, or at least not always.

In theory, disintermediation may be considered as a possibility; but is it possible to reduce or abolish the functions of legal professions without compromising the protection of individual rights?

At present, and considering the risks of false disintermediation, I would say no.

Another element to be considered is the function of documentary evidence.

In civil law legal systems, a written document, whether public or authenticated, has a higher probative force: in these systems, the role of the notary is particularly useful.

Furthermore, only public or authenticated documents can be stored in public registers, as the quality of documents stored in a public register influences the quality of the register itself (trash in/trash out).

Figures of mediators ensuring that the documents meet minimum requirements to be considered legally valid documents are, at the moment, an essential element for the civil law legal systems.

We should also consider the set of functions performed by public officers and notaries for the public interest:

- Certification functions, like the verification of personal identities, but also the identification, quality assessment (for instance, real estate compliance) and ownership verification of the assets subject to the transaction (real estate, companies, shareholdings);
- The legality audit, that guarantees the compliance of the negotiation to the will of the parties, and also to the law. Such mediation between law and the will of people is also a cultural one, and it guarantees the protection of the contractual relationship;
- The tax liability;
- The protection of legality through anti-money laundering tasks;
- The implementation of public registers;
- The performance guarantee through controls and civil, tax, penal and disciplinary liability.

4 Blockchain and Public Registers

Talking about the Blockchain means talking about registers (ledger), hence the comparison to public registers comes naturally.

The assessment of its use must take-into-account the functions of public registers, starting with the need of a central authority.

In civil law legal systems, public registers protect individual rights (from the right to a name, to real or intellectual property, to the business system etc.) and, consequently but not secondarily, the public interest in the proper performance of contractual relationships.

In common law legal systems, this function is only rarely performed by public registers, and it is replaced by right protection systems, usually by way of compensation rather than restoration of the right.

The quality of a public register depends on the trustworthiness of its content, which is guaranteed by:

- Provenance and quality checks of the information submitted (by accepting only public or authenticated documents);
- The public management of the register;
- The power of public authorities to perform authoritative changes within judicial or administrative activities;
- The storage of deeds and documents in the public registers.

Let's think about the Italian land registry system (which is quite similar to the corresponding systems in civil law countries): it is divided in real estate public registers and cadastral registers, that are both managed by the *Agenzia delle Entrate* (Revenue Agency). The real estate registers certify the ownership of the rights on the assets. The cadastral registers identify the assets and are used for tax purposes.

This system, including only public or authenticated documents (notarial, administrative or judicial deeds) is completely digital since 2010 and it is constantly updated to the previous day. The transmission of documents has also a fiscal function.

The system relies on the existence of a central authority and of strict rules for data access and management, and its effectiveness has been acknowledged worldwide: it was awarded one of the first places in the Doing Business Ranking of the World Bank.[2]

Any change in this system should therefore guarantee, in principle, equal or higher performance levels, and would also imply to change complex systems of rules as the Civil Code—in particular, the regulations concerning the form of contracts, contractual evidence and real estate public registers–, the Code of Civil Procedure—in particular signature verification, complaint of forgery–, and more

[2]See the 2018 Doing Business report, available at https://www.doingbusiness.org/content/dam/doingBusiness/media/Annual-Reports/English/DB2018-Full-Report.pdf.

rules on real estate public registers,[3] cadastral rules, planning laws,[4] energy certification regulations,[5] relevant tax legislation,[6] and anti-money laundering regulations.[7]

Moreover, methods as the creation of legal sandboxes seem not suitable to the purpose, since they would imply the exclusion of assets or rights from this system, undermining its trustworthiness.

It would be therefore unrealistic to think about changing the land registry system into a system that doesn't involve central authorities and doesn't allow any judicial authority to modify the registers.

Yet, it is possible to use the features of interoperability and scalability of the Blockchain to improve those sectors that are not (or not properly) covered by the public registers, and therefore:

- Create interconnections between existing public registers (for instance, between parish and civil registers on one hand, and land registers on the other);
- Create public registers that won't be subject to a single authority, but that will be the union of several public registers, for instance on a transnational level (like the project of interconnecting via the Blockchain the European security institutes);
- Create interconnections between public registers, including those having totally or partially the same function, hold by different authorities, like in the case of the biological testament—in the form of the so called *Dichiarazione Anticipata di Trattamento* (DAT, i.e. Advance Treatment Declaration)—which is stored in the DAT registers that are managed centrally by the State and locally by the Regions;
- Use the Blockchain to create new registers in totally or partially unregulated contexts. There could be an application in the real estate sector which could be useful to integrate (without replacing) the land registers: we are talking about building rights, provided by national and regional regulation and by the resulting planning rules, such as those building rights that are totally or partially independent from the ownership of a building area, and that are therefore tradable separately.

5 Notaries and Blockchain

If we think about enhancing human activities through new technologies, we can find several applications for the Blockchain that could improve the notarial activity.

[3]See in particular law n. 52/1985.

[4]See law n. 47/1985, and legislative decree n. 380/2001.

[5]See legislative decree n. 192/2005.

[6]Such as stamp and registration duty, mortgage tax, cadastral duty, inheritance and gift tax.

[7]See legislative decree n. 231/2007.

The *Albo Unico delle professioni* (AUP, Professional Register): all the professionals must be found in the professional register (Decree of the President of the Republic 137/2012) in order to grant public and transparent access to the related information (such as the termination of the membership). In a completely digital relationship with the public administration, the professional qualification (like lawyer, or engineer) can be a discriminating factor for the access to data and activities. So, an application has been created that collects, through a permissioned Blockchain, different professional registers, while guaranteeing the updating, security and interoperability of these registers. Integrating this system in the SPID (Public System of Digital Identities) and in other digital identity systems would allow a controlled access to digital resources (this could apply to several digital processes, or to the submission of the project for a new building to the municipality).

Another application field could be the settlement of assets in case of inheritance: for the heirs, obtaining the settlements of deposits, policies and investments from banks, post offices and insurance companies, even with the intervention of the notary for the writing of affidavits or certificates of inheritance, requires to get an expensive, onerous and uselessly duplicate documentation. A permissioned blockchain involving municipalities and notaries, as well as financial and insurance mediators who hold the assets belonging to the inheritance could not only simplify and speed up the settlement, but also allow the finding of unknown assets.

In inheritance or trust issues, the multi-signature uses the traditional function of the notary as a depositary of documents and assets. The notary must guarantee the access to a wallet containing an asset or the possibility to obtain a certain resource. For instance, in successions, this system could allow the notary to execute the last will and testament at the same time of the publication of the testament; while in contracts, after having ascertained the occurrence of an event or the fulfilment of an obligation, the notary could unlock subsequent events such as the payment of an amount. Anyway, notaries and their digital structures could perform security functions, storing emergency access credential in case the ones provided to the owners are unavailable.

Asset tokenization. An asset is, in this case, an active legal position derived from a notarial deed. Its circulation requires more effective systems than credit assignment (historically this same need originated negotiable instruments), or equity (shareholdings). The need is to allow the circulation of such legal positions also in a virtual asset market through a digital process of tokenization, creating a specific object (token) meant to circulate on designated platforms. Possible applications are asset positions, such as the one generated by a deferred price (the so-called new promissory note), or by a loan (so-called new securitization), but also the issue and circulation of equity (shareholdings), financial instruments and negotiable instruments. A change in regulations could also allow to promote equity crowdfunding, that currently is only possible through mediators,[8] managing dedicated portals, which didn't bring great results so far. Based on the notarial deeds reporting the

[8]See legislative decree n. 58/1998, art. 100 *ter*.

shareholders' resolution about the sale of shareholdings, as well as financial and negotiable instruments, it would be possible to issue representative tokens and to assign them to the participating investors.

6 Smart Contracts and Notaries

Finally, there are the smart contracts. There has been much talk about them, while they still lack a univocal definition from a juridical and operational point of view. The acknowledgement of smart contracts in Italian legislation (Law-Decree 14/12/2018, n. 135 amended by law 11/2/2019, n. 12) was rather inaccurate and lacks guidelines for the application, thus making more difficult to classify them. In fact, these laws just regulate the executive phase of smart contracts, leaving out its full classification in the contract legislation (and therefore the evaluation of its necessary elements: parties, agreement, cause, object, form). The consequences of this legislation suggest a reflection on some general categories of the legal system.

A mention should be made about the form, that points directly to the protection of individual rights: the smart contract is written, and it operates not only through a technical mediation containing unwritten rules (i.e. the operating rules of the machines), but mostly using a different language from the natural one, which is the processing language. This raises the issue of the knowability of the content of the smart contract and of the contractual rule binding the individual.

At present we could use these technologies to improve the activities we already perform as notaries, and we are also considering the usefulness of smart contracts in the executive phase of the contract, in order to speed up some traditional activities—such as the escrow—and make them safer. We are thinking about a platform providing notaries with a tool that would allow them to interpret the information contained in an input document written in natural language in order to extract useful data for the automatic creation of smart contracts. Smart contracts should be created based on the a.i. interpretation of documents written in natural language (notarial deeds), in order to perform executive functions of the contract legislation, such as real estate businesses with a payment plan or a retention of title agreement, or a contract providing the fulfilment of pecuniary obligations through a smart contract, or a deposit of the price with the notary.

In time, after fixing the form of smart contract and having integrated the smart contract model in the legal system, it would be possible to integrate some notarial functions in smart contracts, for instance when the effectiveness of a notarial deed depends on the occurrence of an event integrated in the smart contract, or if a smart contract requires a signature authentication, or if the notarial deed itself is a smart contract, or finally, if the notary performs the function of oracle in a smart contract, by certifying data or events.

Reference

Stylianou K (2019) What can the first blockchain antitrust case teach us about the crypto-economy? Harv J Law Technol. https://jolt.law.harvard.edu/digest/what-can-the-first-blockchain-antitrust-case-teach-us-about-the-crypto-economy

Part IV
The "Sustainable" Applications of Blockchain

Introduction to Distributed Ledger Technologies for Social, Development, and Humanitarian Impact

Giulio Coppi

Contents

1 Blockchain and Sustainable Development Goals (SDGs): Where Is the Lie

The humanitarian and development sectors are probably the most abused by blockchains and Distributed Ledger Technologies (DLTs) apologists in terms of SDG-washing. The DLT arena is swinging constantly from megalomania to chronic multidimensional complex of inferiority against other traditional actors such as banks, finance brokers, and money transfer systems. As DLTs struggle to prevail and become mainstream, justifying its potential to solve the most wicked challenges of our age proved to be much easier than facing the issues limiting their competition in adoption, technical improvements, and capacity to scale. This does not mean that all attempts at harnessing DLTs "for good" are coming from a bad place. As it

G. Coppi (✉)
Digital Specialist for Field Operation, Norwegian Refugee Council, Oslo, Norway

B. Cappiello, G. Carullo (eds.), *Blockchain, Law and Governance*,
https://doi.org/10.1007/978-3-030-52722-8_17

always happens, the sector is populated by very different people motivated by countless reasons and while some only see the "unbanked" as an untapped business target, others are definitely hoping to make a difference against the cynical business model of existing financial systems.

Unfortunately, some uncritical and often venture-capital fueled media coverage given to DLTs doesn't really help in understanding who belong to what side of this spectrum,[1] nor does some random UN-endorsed content promoting use cases (i.e. the SDG Coins) that aren't.[2] Respectable works analyzing the topic in an ethical and rigorous way[3] remain in a niche and require basic understanding of who the authors are to weed out the bad content. Overall, filtering out what DLTs cannot do for the SDGs is the easiest approach: When any headline announce how this technology is going to eradicate poverty or end conflict,[4] sometimes it is lazy clickbait to hide a rundown of projects. More often, it is just plainly not true.[5] Beyond the hype, however, there is indeed something happening. DLTs surely are not a silver bullet, but it seems more and more safe to affirm that some innovative components of distributed technologies can be used together with other solutions to accomplish important and previously unattainable goals.[6]

For this very reason, I prefer to use the term "DLTs" rather than "blockchain". Although this has waned in recent times, for years the sector has seen a fiery debate on what "blockchains" actually means,[7] a discussion that has too often hijacked intellectual resources from more relevant priorities. Less dogmatic and more open to mixed and innovative approaches, the term DLTs is a catch-all that allows to explore decentralized technologies without being bogged down by requirements such as

[1]Wintermeyer L (2019) Blockchain At The United Nations Leading Solutions To The Global Crisis. In: Forbes. https://www.forbes.com/sites/lawrencewintermeyer/2019/09/26/blockchain-at-the-united-nations-leading-solutions-to-the-global-crisis/.

[2]SDG investing: advancing a new normal in global capital markets (2017) Background paper for an expert group meeting of the Financing For Development Business Sector Steering Committee. https://www.un.org/esa/ffd/wp-content/uploads/2017/03/SDG-Investing-Report_170306.pdf.

[3]See i.e. Zwitter and Herman (2018).

[4]Karayaneva N (2019) Will Blockchain Make Poverty Obsolete? What Is The Root Of All Evil? In: Forbes. https://www.forbes.com/sites/nataliakarayaneva/2019/05/02/will-blockchain-make-poverty-obsolete-what-is-the-root-of-all-evil/.

[5]For an example of bad faith reporting (and undignified language for people affected by crisis), see Rueda M (2020) Nonprofits turn to cryptocurrency to help needy Venezuelans. In: The Inquirer. https://www.inquirer.com/news/nation-world/venezuela-crisis-givecrypto-cryptocurrency-bitcoin-eos-20190522.html. I personally contributed with an interview, the reporter discarded anything critical and framed a fictitious "bitcoin saviour" story out of thin air.

[6]See i.e. Tillemann T et al. (2019) The Blueprint for Blockchain and Social Innovation. In: New America. http://newamerica.org/digital-impact-governance-inititiative/blockchain-trust-accelerator/reports/blueprint-blockchain-and-social-innovation/.

[7]See i.e. Popejoy J (2019) Why IBM's Blockchain Isn't a Real Blockchain. In: Cointelegraph. https://cointelegraph.com/news/why-ibms-blockchain-isnt-a-real-blockchain.

immutability or consensus protocol.[8] For the scope of this paper, DLTs is an 'umbrella term to designate multi-party systems that operate in an environment with no central operator or authority, despite parties who may be unreliable or malicious'.[9]

2 Canvassing the DLTs for SDGs Landscape: A Guidance Framework

This introduction paper aims to canvas the existing SDG-inspired initiatives and to identify a few of those that are actually running DLTs software and measuring impact. This is easier said than done: Unfortunately, the blockchain fever that hit the world around 2017\2018 on the wave of an unstoppable investment frenzy driven by pyramid schemes known as initial coin offerings (ICOs)[10] and boosted by the pump and dump[11] that charmed thousands of people in entering the blockchain market, also left behind countless shells of do-gooder projects launched, funded, and soon abandoned.

To avoid falling into the startup hype trap and true to my legal studies background, I gave myself a set of rules to select the projects worth engaging with. This has holistically grown into an informal framework building on 4 core pillars: Solidity, Delivery, Scope, Governance. This is not the place to discuss this framework, suffice to say that interesting initiatives need to show sufficient proof of having a hard coded system with good documentation and an adequate development team; its efforts must have translated into concrete applications used in real life contexts over a decent period of time; the project must have a clear intention to contribute to one or more SDGs expressed through a publicly available strategy (i.e. "we transfer money thus we target poverty" is not enough); and finally, the project must be either backed by or in partnership with at least one actor with good reputation and experience in targeting relevant SDGs.

Sometimes, however, such in depth analysis is not needed as just a few words on the project website could give away the real level of dedication to the SDGs. More often than not, bootstrapped startups patched-up after a round of seed funding or a hackathon, will throw online a greenwashed website with positive messaging about the problem of their choosing. The resulting mix of buzzwords with terms randomly

[8]Rosic A (2017) Proof of Work vs Proof of Stake: Basic Mining Guide. In: Blockgeeks. https://blockgeeks.com/guides/proof-of-work-vs-proof-of-stake/.

[9]Rauchs et al. (2018).

[10]Frankenfield J (2019) Initial Coin Offering (ICO). In: Investopedia. https://www.investopedia.com/terms/i/initial-coin-offering-ico.asp.

[11]Dhir R (2019) How a Pump-and-Dump Scheme Works. In: Investopedia. https://www.investopedia.com/terms/p/pumpanddump.asp.

taken from social impact, sustainable development, and humanitarian vocabulary shows the lack of research on the subject. These are three different completely different applications, responding to mostly separate legal frameworks and regulatory environments, despite being frequently used as synonym in newspapers. Nowadays, it is commonly accepted that any corporate actor or business has some form of impact on society, regardless of its positive or negative nature. Companies striving to deliver positive social impact can be driven by a narrow vision of social impact, a mix of ethical and financial considerations known as the Economic, Societal and Governance (ESG) factors. These are commonly measured by their material impact on the business investment, rather than on people.[12] This is, of course, not the correct interpretation under the UN Guiding Principles on Business and Human Rights.[13] The broadest connotation of social impact includes "all impacts on humans and on all the ways in which people and communities interact with their socio-cultural, economic and biophysical surroundings."[14] Incidentally, it is within this broader vision that the idea of "Tech for Good" was originally created, as an "intentional design, development and use of digital technologies to address social challenges."[15]

As subdomains of social impact, we then find international development and humanitarian action. In a simplistic way, development aims to provoke or facilitate positive change within communities through the strengthening of Human Rights, while humanitarian action intervenes to stop or mitigate the negative consequences of natural or man-made disasters by applying the framework provided by International Humanitarian Law. The former generated so much expertise and knowledge in the sector, to deserve a whole movement for itself. Called Information and Communications Technology for Development (ICT4D), it is the practice of utilizing technology to assist poor and marginalized people in developing communities.[16] The use of technological tools in humanitarian response is less pervasive due to the sensitivity of the contexts, where advanced tools are often associated with military actors or can be weaponized by them.

---

[12]Zhou, Jianying M (2019) Explaining the differences between ESG, SRI & Impact Investing to Clients. In: Investopedia. https://www.investopedia.com/financial-advisor/esg-sri-impact-investing-explaining-difference-clients/.

[13]Guiding Principles on Business and Human Rights: Implementing the United Nations 'Protect, Respect and Remedy' Framework (2011) UN. https://www.ohchr.org/Documents/Publications/GuidingPrinciplesBusinessHR_EN.pdf.

[14]Vanclay (2003).

[15]Roberson J (2018) What is Tech for Good? In: Hacker Noon. https://hackernoon.com/what-is-tech-for-good-533c65b73e72.

[16]Information and Communication Technologies for Development. CRS https://www.crs.org/our-work-overseas/ict4d.

3 DLTs and Social Impact

In the early days of DLTs, it was hard to find out which projects were targeting societal challenges, but today several online platforms dedicated to this technology are exploring their application in the social sphere.[17] The Blockchain Impact Ledger[18] was among the first online platforms created to fill this gap and research done on their collection of projects highlighted how three main SDGs cluster up most initiatives. SDGs 8 (Decent Work and Economic Growth), 11 (Sustainable Cities and Communities) and 16 (Peace, Justice, and Strong Institutions) are the most populated one, with the latter firmly in the lead.[19] Upon further analysis, most of the initiatives targeting SDG 16 can be filed under two main categories: public sector innovation and fintech hubs. The list of actors engaging in public innovation through DLTs includes a few countries (i.e. Estonia, Georgia, the Netherlands and Switzerland) pioneering a streamlined way of deploying DLTs solutions across the public sector, in some cases even at different administrative levels. Other countries are mostly trying to use DLTs to stimulate their fintech ecosystem, by creating regional or national hubs (i.e. Switzerland, Barbados, Malta, Singapore, Japan, South Korea and China). Of course, these lists are highly dynamic and subject to interpretation as almost none of these countries have adopted pure forms of blockchain.[20]

Some other interesting projects target the SDG 11. In Nepal, the Sikka project pioneered by World Vision International created a digital asset transfer platform designed for financially marginalized rural populations in need. Differently from most DLT solutions focused on assets transfer, Sikka was not born out of a desire to disrupt the existing financial or banking system, but rather in the spirit of compliance with national legislation. To keep providing assistance without infringing the Nepalese laws prohibiting mobile money and e-currencies (seen as a threat to tax collection and a mean of corruption), the promoters developed a way to tokenize the assistance provided to communities affected by a tragic earthquake, to allow feature-phone based 'shopping', and to streamline reimbursements to vendors.[21] Other examples include Helperbit[22] (an Italian Bitcoin-based platform that aims to

[17]See i.e. Blockchain for SDGs, available at https://blockchain4sdg.com/.

[18]Goldstein D, Tillemann T (2020) Blockchain Impact Ledger. In: New America. http://newamerica.org/digital-impact-governance-inititiative/blockchain-trust-accelerator/reports/blockchain-impact-ledger/.

[19]Gregori B (2019) Blockchain and Social Impact Research: Preliminary Findings. In: New America. http://newamerica.org/digital-impact-governance-inititiative/blockchain-trust-accelerator/around-the-blockchain-blog/blockchain-and-social-impact-research-preliminary-findings/.

[20]Cullell L (2019) Is e-Estonia Built on Blockchain Technologies? In: Hacker Noon. https://hackernoon.com/e-estonia-is-not-on-blockchain-22iy2gx6.

[21]Sikka project website. https://www.sikka.me/.

[22]Helperbit project website: https://app.helperbit.com/.

brings transparency in charity and insurance sectors)[23] and Moeda (a community-based token that started in Brazil, but now expanding worldwide and focusing also on SDGs 1 and 10).

The SDG 8 had an initial explosion of attention from startups and major corporate actor alike,[24] as core DLTs features seemed to be the easiest and most natural fit for supply chain and procurement processes. Some of the best-known projects include Provenance, which aims to allow shoppers to have full view over the supply chain behind long chain products,[25] and Everledger, that deployed DLTs-powered systems for verifiable sourcing in the jewelry industry.[26] Many other initiatives were not as successful in improving existing systems or proving their social impact. As many in the field stressed from the early days of DLTs, certifying what happens along the official milestones of a supply chain is the easiest part. The highest risk for human rights violations happens in the shadow,[27] where technology rarely applies.

A previous speaker mentioned the use of DLTs in conjunction with geodata for SDG 7 (Affordable and Clean Energy). Similar uses of mixed technologies are being experimented on SDGs 11 (Sustainable Cities and Communities), 12 (Responsible Consumption and Production), 13 (Climate Action),[28] 14 (Life below Water), and 15 (Life on Land) were highlighted in a report by HSBC on green bonds.[29] The report shows improvements in connecting smart devices (Internet of Things—IoT), Big Data, Artificial Intelligence and geodata to track investment impact and automatically release interests for investors through smart contracts. Aside from being one of the few reasonable arguments in favor of radical interconnectivity, it is also the use case with the lowest risk of having some negative or harmful impact on people, to the point that the International Federation of the Red Cross and Red Crescent (IFRC) was exploring the introduction of smart contracts as part of their

[23] Both Sikka and Helperbit—two projects mentioned in the previous section—were actually deployed in the aftermath of earthquakes, although their main implementation wasn't part of the disaster response. As such, they sit in between social impact, development and humanitarian aid.

[24] See i.e. Maersk Press Release (2019) TradeLens blockchain-enabled digital shipping platform continues expansion with addition of major ocean carriers Hapag-Lloyd and Ocean Network Express. https://www.maersk.com/news/articles/2019/07/02/hapag-lloyd-and-ocean-network-express-join-tradelens.

[25] See Provenance website. https://www.provenance.org/.

[26] See Everledger website.

[27] See i.e. the critique by Cullell LM (2019) Blockchain, Human Rights, and the Supply Chain. In: Blockchain For SDG - Blog and Forum for Blockchain and the SDG. https://blockchain4sdg.com/blockchain-human-rights-and-the-supply-chain/.

[28] For other initiatives advocating for DLTs-based solutions for climate action, please see the website of the Climate Chain Coalition: https://www.climatechaincoalition.io/use-cases-and-pilots.

[29] HSBC (2019) Blockchain. Gateway for Sustainability Linked Bonds. https://www.sustainablefinance.hsbc.com/mobilising-finance/blockchain-gateway-for-sustainability-linked-bonds.

forecast-based financing strategy aimed at releasing humanitarian funds right before a natural disaster strikes.[30]

4 DLTs in Development and Humanitarian Applications

So far, there is only one project that could be defined as purely humanitarian and it focuses on deconfliction,[31] the set of processes and procedures agreed by parties to a conflict to allow safe humanitarian access to disputed areas, or the safety of protected sites such as hospitals.[32] The overwhelming majority of DLTs applications for aid is compatible with both humanitarian and development applications, and just as the humanitarian use case just mentioned, they mostly target a variety of basic needs covered by SDG 1 (No Poverty), 2 (Zero Hunger), 3 (Good Health and Wellbeing), 6 (Clean Water and Sanitation), and—although in a less evident way—SDG 11 (Sustainable Cities and Communities). World Food Program Innovation Accelerator started what is possibly the most famous project in this field, Building Blocks, facilitating the access to assistance in specific shops by refugees registered in Jordan with the United Nations High Commissioner for Refugees through biometrics and blockchain.[33] In 2018, the WFP partnered with UN Women to allow Syrian women who participate in the organization's Cash for Work Programme to withdraw cash at a supermarket in a Jordanian refugee camp or make purchases directly, thus adding SDG 5 (Gender Equality) to its scope.[34]

The Islamic Development Bank recognized and supported the IFRC for proposing an online blockchain application for traceability and transparency of Islamic social financing, with a special focus on water and sanitation (SDG 6).[35] Due to the broad and unusual set of partnerships generated, this project also targets SDG 17 (Partnerships for the Goals). Finally, UNICEF has built part of its innovation efforts around DLTs, by developing solutions to make better systems for government payments to schools in South Africa,[36] to improve connectivity in schools

[30]DREF (2019) Forecast-Based Action (FbA) by the DREF. In: International Federation of Red Cross and Red Crescent Societies. https://media.ifrc.org/ifrc/fba/.

[31]Parker B (2018) What is humanitarian deconfliction? In: The New Humanitarian. https://www.thenewhumanitarian.org/analysis/2018/11/13/what-humanitarian-deconfliction-syria-yemen.

[32]The White Flag protocol: https://standard.whiteflagprotocol.net. See also Coppi G, Fast L Blockchain and distributed ledger technologies in the humanitarian sector. In: ODI. https://www.odi.org/publications/11284-blockchain-and-distributed-ledger-technologies-humanitarian-sector.

[33]See Building Blocks' website: https://innovation.wfp.org/project/building-blocks.

[34]UN Women Jordan Press Release (2018) UN Women and World Food Programme harness innovation for women's economic empowerment in crisis situations. In: UN Women | Jordan. https://jordan.unwomen.org/ja/news/stories/2018/september/un-women-and-wfp-blockchain.

[35]IFRC Press Release (2018) IFRC blockchain application wins global islamic finance competition. In: IFRC Innovation. http://media.ifrc.org/innovation/2018/02/12/ifrc-blockchain-application-wins-global-islamic-finance-competition/.

[36]Fabian (2018).

(Project Connect),[37] and by receiving, holding and disbursing donations of cryptocurrencies ether and bitcoin, through their newly-established UNICEF Cryptocurrency Fund.[38] Their ambitious projects touch on SDGs 4 (Quality Education), 16 (Peace, Justice, and Strong Institutions) and 17 (Partnerships). This latest initiative has been welcomed with mixed reaction. On one side there is shared curiosity and eagerness to explore new avenues for making innovation sustainable, but on the other many question the decision of entering what is considered a speculative financial market, and raise issues linked to UNICEF's ethics, role and mandate that reflect on the sector as a whole.[39]

5 Challenges in Adopting DLTs for SDGs

5.1 Access

DLTs have become less expensive compared to their early days, through a bigger variety of commercial offerings. Despite this, access barriers are still very relevant in terms of overall cost for a relatively niche product. Even just the initial investment required to canvas the market and identify the most appropriate and affordable solutions, let alone the required system design, development, hosting, maintenance, and data protection is out of reach for most charities, civil societies, and public actors. Even though prices will likely continue to decrease, this is unlikely to stop being a problem, as DLTs will remain a "nice-to-have" in the digital portfolio of a non-corporate actor with limited resources. In addition to this, despite the skyrocketing number of DLTs engineers, their skillset remains too expensive to attract and retain in the nonprofit or public sector. Continued limitations in the access to human and technological resources mean that public organizations engaged for the SDGs will have to rely on solid partnerships with corporate, finance, and tech actors, thus making SDG 17 the gateway to all the others.

5.2 Scope

Customized DLTs-powered solutions, just like any other emerging technology, are hardly deployable in crisis-affected and low-resources environments because of the

[37]Hydary M (2019) Reducing the Digital Divide Using Blockchain. In: UNICEF. https://www.unicef.org/innovation/stories/reducing-digital-divide-using-blockchain.

[38]UNICEF Press Release (2019) UNICEF launches Cryptocurrency Fund. In: UNICEF. https://www.unicef.org/press-releases/unicef-launches-cryptocurrency-fund.

[39]Andrada N (2019) 8 Digital Principle Issues with UNICEF's Ethereum Cryptocurrency Donations. In: ICTworks. https://www.ictworks.org/uncief-ethereum-cryptocurrency-donations/.

sensitivity of the specific environment, the high levels of risks, and the challenges in bringing on the spot the resources needed to design, develop and maintain the system. Furthermore, this process would require extremely intensive engagement from everyone involved, only to bring an extremely tech solution to a non-tech problem such as armed violence, poor governance, or natural disaster. Very often, the advantages offered by tailor-made DLTs won't make the cut in the priority list of a social actor. The best chance DLTs have, is again to rely on better framework for partnerships and cooperation between different actors (SDG 17), and the mainstreaming of DLTs as 'invisible' backend component to commercial off-the-shelf options already operating in low-resources, volatile, or crisis affected contexts.

5.3 Change Management

As our research has shown,[40] most actors involved in the SDGs are open to using DLTs but very few envision to change the way they work to reflect a more decentralized or even distributed model. DLTs were designed to replace the need for trust between people with trust in the connecting protocol despite the hostile environment surrounding it. Despite this, current versions of most DLTs deployed in the aid field show that organizations don't trust the platform any more than they trust external counterpart or local populations, which may result in more bottlenecks as existing control and validation mechanisms are plainly extended on top of the DLT system.

5.4 Governance

Implementing a DLT system as part of traditional governance system can prove to be extremely complex. Most permissionless and public DLT protocols are designed to be hard to modify. Any changes proposed by the developers need to be validated by a strong majority of node controllers to avoid what is known as hard fork splitting the chain in two parallel and irreconcilable chains. Also, any non-updated node will either join one of the two chains, or suddenly go dark. Although this problem becomes less relevant in private permissioned organizations, most of the instances currently being piloted are based on public chains. The governance system hard coded into the DLT protocol will need to be accepted as-is by everyone within all organizations participating in the system, with potential frictions emerging from the lack of leeway for democratic processes.

[40]Coppi G, Fast L Blockchain and distributed ledger technologies in the humanitarian sector. In: ODI. https://www.odi.org/publications/11284-blockchain-and-distributed-ledger-technologies-humanitarian-sector.

5.5 Downstream Predatory Strategy

Many DLTs explicitly state their goal of remove intermediaries from transactive processes with the aim of increasing efficiency and reducing costs. In practice, however, the systemic inequity of the current system makes so that any DLT hosted or operating from the so-called Western world will be removing intermediaries on the receiving end, while keeping almost intact the system at home. A Europe-based organization will transfer funds from a Europe-registered bank through the blockchain directly to an individual in a country with weaker local governance and regulations which has been hit by a disaster. In this case, the sender is not removing intermediaries but rather reducing the role of local actors and impoverishing the local financial ecosystem by not contributing to local business, financial investments, and taxes. This project is creating dependency from foreign assets, and doing harm against already vulnerable communities.

5.6 Regulatory Environment

Most actors willing to harness any DLTs for SDG-related operations will have to deal with regulatory environment challenges. In many countries there is no specific regulatory or normative environment covering DLTs, which creates important liability risks for anyone navigating blindly. In some other cases, there may be such guidance but due to the complexity and nuances of DLTs it might prove almost impossible to be certain of how to act to be in perfect compliance. This is especially true, for example, when implementing public immutable chains while having to respect GDPR-like rules.

5.7 Obsolescence

When mentioning the obsolescence problem, many think about how quantum technology could make most cryptographic systems deployed to secure DLTs completely useless. This is indeed a risk, and previsions about its timing vary widely. However, even without quantum, DLTs themselves are constantly evolving and outdating their own protocol and processes. As mentioned above DLTs are extremely conservative and tend not to evolve too often. When they do, all nodes who want to stay in the "living" side of the system need to quickly update their system and harmonize it with the others. This requires constant focus on discussions happening in the core development teams, which in the case of public chains is outside of the organization itself, in addition to adequate internal skills to steer the organization through this upgrade process. This also means that even having the resources to access a DLT may prove to be not enough, if there is a lack of capacity to ensure constant technical support.

6 What to Expect in DLTs for SDGs

What I expect and hope to see happening from my own limited point of view is a normalization of this technology. It will be a good sign when there will be no more discussion on the potential of this solution as a standalone innovation, but rather a return to a more nuanced analysis of how DLTs are part of the world we are used to deal with every day. To prove they have win, DLTs need to disappear in the background just as the clearinghouse role of credit did in the past. An invisible hand that changes the way we live, buy, move, without the need for us to know exactly how it works. This will also mean that DLTs have succeeded in integrating with existing standards, and among themselves.

At the moment, all DLTs have a scaling problem that also includes environmental considerations. The struggle of DLTs in going to scale has so far been one of the factors impeding them from seriously challenging traditional financial and transaction systems. This has also hampered efforts to improve commercial availability of DLTs protocols as well as much their needed hardware components. It is almost impossible as of today to imagine that anyone—regardless of their education or tech savviness—could switch to DLTs for replacing entirely any of their daily processes. As such, DLTs are not yet off-the-shelf, intuitive systems ready to take over the commercial market. In conclusion, DLTs need to make disappear their technical complexity in the backend, and become commercially competitive in the frontend to ensure mass adoption, traction, and finally impact. It might be that, in the end, the only possible application standing will actually be a blockchain-powered solution to track the SDGs themselves.[41]

References

Fabian C (2018) Un-chained: experiments and learnings in Crypto at UNICEF. Innov: Technol Gov Glob 12:30–45. https://doi.org/10.1162/inov_a_00265

Rauchs M, Glidden A, Gordon B et al (2018) Distributed ledger technology systems: a conceptual framework. SSRN

Vanclay F (2003) International principles for social impact assessment. Impact Assess Proj Apprais 21:5–12

Zwitter A, Herman J (2018) Blockchain for Sustainable Development Goals:# Blockchain4SDGs-Report 2018. In: Blockchain4SDGs workshop. Rijksuniversiteit Groningen, www.rug.nl/research/portal/publications/blockchain-for-sustainable-development-goals%28ba0b265f-ac42-4005-96ca-fb8f688862fd%29.html

[41]Sadien N (2018) A Blockchain Powered Solution to Track the SDGs. In: New America. http://newamerica.org/digital-impact-governance-initiative/blockchain-trust-accelerator/around-the-blockchain-blog/blockchain-powered-solution-track-sdgs/.

Blockchain, Earth Observation and Intelligent Data Systems: Implications and Opportunities for the Next Generation of Digital Services

Anna Burzykowska

Contents

1 Introduction

The 2018 ESA White Paper on "Blockchain and Earth Observation" refers to the blockchain technology (and other forms of distributed ledgers) as a revolutionary tool for the future growth of the global digital economy.[1] Blockchain's main potential lays in replacing monolithic and centralised data management structures by a distributed system, in which people and organisations can participate in trustworthy, secure, transparent networks that enable a direct collaboration (peer-to-peer). It offers the vision of a data ecosystem where information and digital value exchange can be conducted in a verifiable and privacy-preserving way, and with full and automatic traceability of all transactions (data processing and value chains).

The blockchain industry is currently at the center of the European agenda for the so-called "Deep Tech" industries which span all key cutting-edge disciplines such as Artificial Intelligence (AI), quantum computing, computer vision, robotics,

[1] EO science for society (2019) Blockchain and Earth Observation: a white paper. https://eo4society.esa.int/2019/04/09/blockchain-and-earth-observation-a-white-paper/.

A. Burzykowska (✉)
Science Applications and Climate Department, European Space Agency, Frascati, Italy
e-mail: Anna.Burzykowska@esa.int

B. Cappiello, G. Carullo (eds.), *Blockchain, Law and Governance*,
https://doi.org/10.1007/978-3-030-52722-8_18

nanotech, and, indeed, blockchain. As a result, the conceptual applications of distributed ledgers, their business potential, and implementation feasibility have grasped the interest of governments, investors as well as the rapidly accelerating community of developers and users of distributed applications (DApps). The report released by McKinsey in 2019 has nevertheless stated that while many prototypes have been built between 2017 and 2019, "the blockchain applications have not yet seen the application at scale".[2] This is why blockchain is often referred to as an emerging technology, one that, much as AI, will develop to the full maturity in the next five years (possibly faster). Nevertheless, even today, at this early stage of adoption, there are important characteristics of the blockchain-based data architectures that call for a deeper insight into the driving forces that enable these first pilot applications, and the foresight into the future driven by the hypothetical use case scenarios that will be revealed in the 2020 decade, once the technology proves added value and becomes mainstream.

This chapter focuses on the two application areas where the blockchain technology (distributed ledgers) intersects with the Earth Observation (EO) technology: blockchain-based land registries and data value chains for natural resources management. They both have made important progress in the past two-to-three years and made a direct impact on our understanding of how the digital representation of physical assets and transactions can transform the economic environment around the land administration and management. In this context Earth Observation technology provides the network of sensors that can connect the physical environment to various (centralized and decentralized) digital ledgers. This concept is known as a Digital Twin though which it is possible to apply EO-based imagery to derive information corresponding to the physical representation of natural and man-made objects. Blockchain, on the other hand, is a technology through which this information can be recorded (conveyed) and shared across the product value chain (for management, processing and sharing of data). One of the blockchain objectives is to provide transparency and traceability of this data chain and connect various sources of data together: EO data, logistics data, socio economic data, financial data, trade data, etc. The emerging distributed end-to-end platforms provide new solutions to certify where the data is coming from, who collected it, how it was processed, what happened to it as it went through the value chain, and provide accountability of all of the transactions and processing steps. In data science it is referred to as a Verifiable Claims Data Model through which the data shared across the parties to the distributed network is linked, cryptographically secure, privacy respecting, and machine-verifiable.[3] Such machine-readable information, is further considered a foundation for a new data retrieval and processing model, called federated learning (or decentralized AI), which is reflecting the availability massive, multisource and

[2]Higginson M et al. Blockchain development and the Occam problem. In: McKinsey. https://www.mckinsey.com/industries/financial-services/our-insights/blockchains-occam-problem.

[3]'Verifiable Credentials Data Model 1.0: Expressing Verifiable Information on the Web,' W3 consortium website at https://www.w3.org/TR/verifiable-claims-data-model/.

real-time data through a range of sensors currently being deployed (i.e. satellite sensors, Internet of Things sensors), which coupled with blockchain and Artificial Intelligence analytics is expected to underpin the next generation of information services.[4]

This chapter focuses on the few selected case studies that show the potential for the convergence of EO and blockchain platforms to demonstrate the cutting-edge thinking about how EO technology can be used to advance development of blockchain applications, how blockchain can be incorporated into EO product and service design, and what sorts of new tools and methods can be built on blockchain and EO cross over. These case studies are flagship blockchain initiatives related to land tenure, agriculture and forestry value chains where several important proofs-of-concept have been developed to shed more light concerning the feasibility and lessons learnt from these first implementations.

2 Earth Observation and the Cadastral Intelligence

It may not be immediately evident to an average consumer of weather news or public services such as water or air quality, or flood early warning, however our lives are powerfully supported by the stream of information provided via the European public satellite infrastructure. Europe today is at the forefront of the information revolution enabled by the Copernicus Programme conceived through a collaboration between the European Union and the European Space Agency. The Copernicus is, and will remain for decades to come, the biggest system providing globally the key data about the state of our planet and thus supporting various policies from land management, to forest management, to marine or civil protection and agriculture revealing information about, for example, physical extent of forests, agricultural fields and land plots, type of harvest, yield, productivity, water use, precipitation, etc.

The Copernicus data are routinely coupled with an increasing number of commercial imaging systems (aerial/satellite/drone platforms) that are capable to map every square kilometer of the planet with a resolution ranging from meters to few tens of centimeters and enabling location-based services as well as a range of mapping products based on precise cartographic measurements. This operational availability of new imaging technologies allows to leapfrog the long standing obstacles related to identifying, surveying and mapping the boundaries of land parcels. The technology is sufficiently advanced to enable a rapid word-wide adoption of digital cadaster—an important challenge given that only 30% of global populations have today secure and accurate systems available to them for the adjudication of ownership or use of land rights. The remaining two thirds of global

[4]EO science for society (2019) Blockchain and Earth Observation: a white paper. https://eo4society.esa.int/2019/04/09/blockchain-and-earth-observation-a-white-paper/.

populations, mainly in developing countries, sustain legal void as well as data gap concerning their land and property rights.

Poor land administration and lack of formalization of the land ownership is a well-known challenge to international development and often results from policy, regulatory, governance and cultural barriers. They are often driven by the complexity of traditional (often) shared land ownership structures which are difficult to formalize in a statutory tenure. Nevertheless, there is a consensus that having access to up-to-date geographic information about the land is a key prerequisite for the establishment of the national land tenure system, including the cadaster and certification of land titles.

A typical basis for the cadastral surveys is based on photogrammetry—aerial (or satellite) imagery acquisition and processing followed-up by ground surveys to geocode and check the actual location of legal boundaries of land parcels. The resulting cadastre is a parcel-based system which contains geographically-referenced information and unique, well-defined units of land. These units are defined by formal boundaries marking the extent of land. Each parcel is given a unique parcel-number.[5]

Today, many rural communities are carrying out the titling and digitization of land parcel information in a participatory, or community-driven process. In countries where digitization does take place, land owners are given an option to collectively support official surveyors to identify the location and size of their specific land plots reflecting the community's customary rights. In such cases cadastral survey, especially for agricultural parcels, is conducted using remote sensing imagery (i.e. VHR (Very High Resolution) imagery) as a base on which it is possible to outline the parcels: manually on-screen or by walking the field boundaries with a handheld GPS (Global Positioning System).[6] Increasingly the communities take advantage of the availability of smartphones: in a mobile application satellite imagery serves as a background image for on-screen digitization of parcel boundary acquired directly from the smartphone phone (or a tablet) equipped with the GPS. Such participatory processes which is collecting field boundary information in the field and on the spot is making digitization of individual parcels more inclusive, cheaper and more efficient.

One example of such land mapping and adjudication is a project implemented by the European Space Agency (ESA) with IFAD (International Fund for Agricultural Development, an UN Agency) to demonstrate the feasibility of imaging technologies for land parcel identification and to assist the government of Madagascar in providing small farmers with land ownership certificates based on the use of VHR satellite imagery. This offered the rural farmers the first opportunity to formalize their land ownership. To simplify the designation and exchange of land titles, a detailed image database was provided to enable the classification and delineation of land concessions and properties. Maps were produced for three districts in Haute Matsiatra

[5]Kresse and Danko (2012).

[6]Davidse (2015).

which good approximation of the location and size of specific land plots (see Fig. 1). In other countries, such as Kenya and Tanzania, it is also sufficient to produce a digital imagery map in which it is possible to record the accurate dimensions of any land parcel so long as its boundaries are clearly visible on the photographs.[7] There are also important technical advancements taking place concerning the automated delineation of the land parcels using VHR imagery, automated object recognition and machine deep learning techniques.[8]

3 Blockchain Revolution

Blockchain technology is considered to be another breakthrough in creating modern land registers. The countries such as Sweden, Georgia, Ukraine and Rwanda as well as Ghana and Kenya are currently launching initiatives to test the use this technology as the basis for their land registers and to incentivize collection of land ownership information, with Sweden leading the pack.

The key reason to adopt blockchain-based database as a basis for the national land registries is rooted in the fact that blockchain technology offers a means to enhance the transparency, security, accessibility and efficiency of land register and associated land transactions. In theory, a blockchain-based permanent, public "ledger" (a database) can contain all land records including details of the tenure and/or transfer of ownership, and as such can be accessed digitally by multiple parties (individual owners, public administration, banks, insurance companies, asset brokers, etc.), shared without restrictions among them and updated in real time. Such ledger due to the immutable character of the blockchain data structures, cannot be falsified or tampered with. Once deployed operationally the public and shared character of the ledger can also—in theory—eliminate the need for an extensive bureaucracy to manage and validate (or certify) the records, for example, via notary services. The "smart contract" functionality is proposed here to improve not only the speed of operations for clearing of settlements but also to simplify the legal process associated with various certifications and third-party verifications (i.e. via title companies, escrow companies, inspectors, appraisers, and notaries). As a result, according to the experts, land transactions can be effected in days rather than months, with a significant reduction in transaction fees.[9]

Many commentators agree that such decentralized data structure is aimed to connect different sectors of the economy in completely innovative ways. In Sweden, for example, the proposed blockchain land tenure model entails creation of a shared

---

[7]Ibid.

[8]Crommelinck et al. (2019).

[9]ICA-IT (2016) The Land Registry in the blockchain A development project with Lantmäteriet (The Swedish Mapping, cadastre and land registration authority). http://ica-it.org/pdf/Blockchain_Landregistry_Report.pdf.

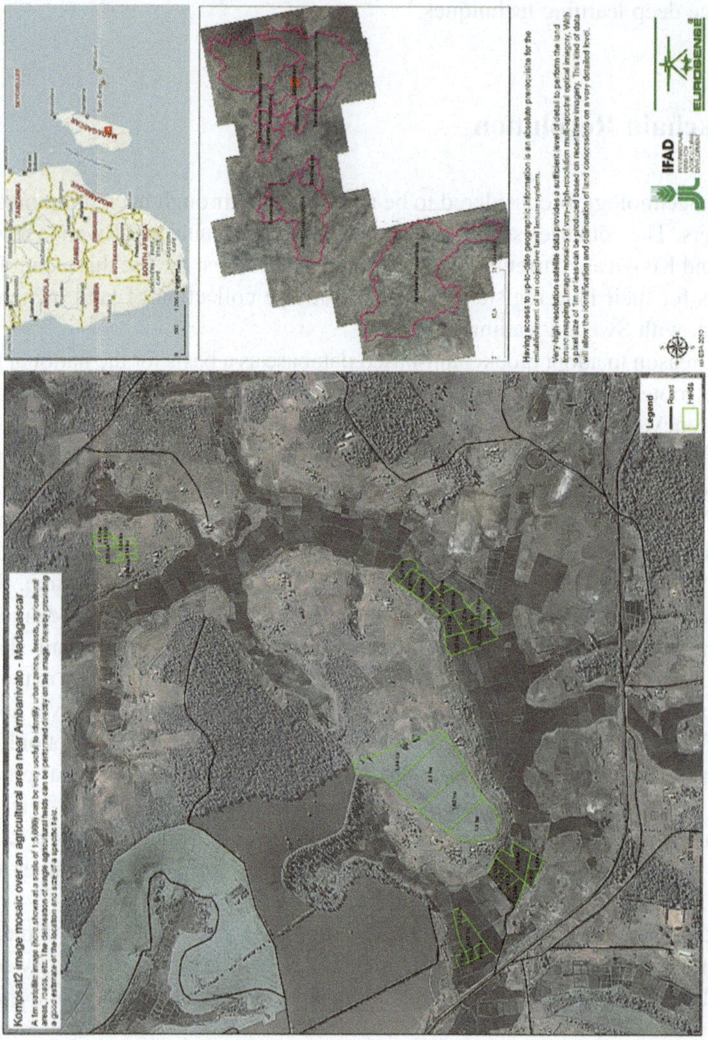

Fig. 1 Field delineation of three districts in Haute Matsiatra based on 1 m-resolution satellite data to support ongoing land reform in Madagascar (Plan Local d'Occupation Foncière). Credit: Eurosense for ESA/IFAD

database in which information about the land property is digitized, put into the distribute ledger and made available for reference in order to facilitate transactions related to a particular property. The banks, buyers, sellers and the national land registry agency (Lantmateriet) can have access to this database and can substantiate/ verify the veracity of any given transfer of ownership, agreement (and other documents) through their unique digital signature (hash on the blockchain). The premise is that they would operate on consensus, therefore if any new record, like a property transaction, is added to the blockchain, it has to be confirmed by the nodes operating within the network.[10] In this sense, for example, the banks participating to the transactions can also ensure, for example, that the buyer has enough funds in their account before authorizing the purchase of the assets.[11] This unlocks a new potential in credit availability and is considered a fundamental shift in sharing data across industries, as well as auditable value exchange.

Today, Sweden is the most advanced in terms of the application of the technology in land management, followed by Georgia. In Sweden, a blockchain developer—ChromaWay has partnered in 2016 with a consultancy group Kairos Future and the Landmateriet—national cadastral agency to test the applications for property transactions and land titles. The application of the technology via a prototype platform demonstrated the increase of transparency and speed of transactions, and has shown the overall feasibility, however the known hurdles include the legality of digital signatures therefore as of 2019 the application is still in the proof-of-concept stage.[12] Another blockchain company called Bitfury has provided to the Georgian National Agency for Public Registry the Land Register solution based on its Exonum platform which achieved an operational use of blockchain-based databases for land title registration with close to hundred thousand transactions already completed. As Georgian land tenure system is akin to private, permissioned ledger, therefore it was easier to deploy, operationally nevertheless it does not yet fully replaced the legacy of centralised systems.[13] Interestingly, both examples feature (or plan for) the smart contract functionality in their respective land registers, in order to execute, amongst other things, escrow services.[14] This raises important legal questions related to the binding force and enforceability of smart legal contracts (or the so called computational contracts)[15] and the need for their legal and regulatory clarity. A thorough understanding of the legal matters and governance models related to the application of blockchain technology to land titling and registry is currently at the core of the discussions on further roll out of these solutions to other countries. From

---

[10]Kriticos S Keeping it clean: Can blockchain change the nature of land registry in developing countries? In: World Bank Blogs. https://blogs.worldbank.org/developmenttalk/keeping-it-clean-can-blockchain-change-nature-land-registry-developing-countries.

[11]Dasgupta (2017).

[12]Allessie et al. (2019).

[13]Ibid.

[14]Ibid.

[15]Walters (2018).

the perspective of the users, they are expected to be agnostic concerning the blockchain (or other technology) back-end that powers the system. The interaction with the applications would not require any special skills other than being comfortable with digital transactions.

In summary, for the most part, the application of blockchain based land register is deemed feasible at scale in the countries where cadaster has been fully established and digitized, and where the records of property transactions, which include information on the ownership and title of a specific land plot, exist. However, the majority of developing countries do not have their land tenure digitized (in a form of cadastral maps and land registers) or the ownership rights properly established (beyond for example traditional or informal land tenure) and enforced by attribution of formal and unique land titles. The availability of secure and functioning land tenure regulations and databases is therefore considered to be a stepping stone for sustainable development. It has been officially recognized as one of the Sustainable Development Goals, SDG Indicator 1.4.2 which calls for the increase of the "*proportion of total adult population with secure tenure rights to land, with legally recognized documentation and who perceive their rights to land as secure, by sex and by type of tenure*". If, therefore, the delineation of land plots and digitization of cadaster (including regular updating of cadastral records) and digitization of land registers can go hand in hand, the opportunities for improvements of the national land governance, and administration via the state-of-the-art land information systems are significant, if not groundbreaking. This is where the convergence of Earth Observation (geospatial information) and blockchain comes into play.

4 EO and Blockchain Crossover

Cadastral surveying, as mentioned before, based on remote sensing measurements can create digital representation of boundaries for the property—or a precise geographical description the borders of the land plot.[16] Once cadaster is established it can take form of traditional centralised land information system, or, thanks to the blockchain data structures, it is possible to create a decentralised platform for land tenure data registration, validation and exchange. Both alternatives serve the same objective—to allow citizens to formalize their land tenure to document their land or property rights in an official and legally binding way through deeds or title certification. In this case, the function of land registers is to provide a proof of authenticity of data, while EO and photogrammetry techniques guarantee that geodetic/geographic information about given land plots are credible and up-to-date.

There are several blockchain companies that are currently developing end-to-end solutions for decentralized land tenure informatics systems which is enabled by the establishment of the cadaster and national land registers. In Rwanda the national

[16]Dale and Binns (1995).

Land Management and Use Authority (RLMUA) and the Rwanda Information Society Authority (RISA) partnered with the blockchain start up Medici Land Governance "*to help Rwanda's government incorporate blockchain and other technologies into its existing systems, developing a paperless system that relies on electronic signatures and digital lodging of surveys for the administrative processes that affect land rights and transfers*".[17] The blockchain solution offered by MLG—Open Index Protocol—is, as of 2019, also developed in Zambia, Liberia, Mexico (and Wyoming, USA). It involves the use of drone-based imagery and other remote sensing technologies as well as a range of GPS tools to capture the location of property assets for extracting parcels, and digitizing existing paper maps on the acquired imagery. Another example is a Ghanaian startup Bitland which proposed the distributed digital ledger to boost the integrity of the land records in Western Africa region. It is currently working in the Ghana's Ashanti Region on a pilot basis and the implementation is supported by land and agriculture surveys via remote sensing (formal account of the results from the pilot phase have not been yet published).[18] Early applicability of blockchain for land governance supported by international donors, such as the World Bank and the UNDP (United Nations Development Programme), was also tested in Honduras and India.[19] Moreover, in November 2019 Inter-American Development Bank (IDB) announced it has contracted Sweden's ChromaWay to develop a land titling and registry platform in Bolivia, Peru and Uruguay.[20]

Overall, the movement to modernize the land tenure systems in developing countries, including via blockchain innovation, revealed a large number of pre-requisites for such transition, some of them being digital identity, accurate data, digital banking and the ability to deliver information services electronically. Moreover, evidence shows that the availability of a secure land tenure is not only relevant for asset valuation, but also a factor which dramatically influences the extent to which farmers are prepared to invest in improvements in agriculture production and sustainable land management. This is because land owners are often agriculture producers who are interested in optimizing their farm operations: from boosting production to reaching the markets in a more efficient way. For them the spin off from well-functioning decentralised digital land registers means not only reducing the risk of land expropriation, but also possibility of unlocking the access to finance, and opening opportunities offered by the digital data-driven economy.

[17]Associated Press (2018) Medici Land Governance, an Overstock Subsidiary, Signs MOU With Government of Rwanda to Implement Paperless Blockchain Land Governance and Property Rights Management. In: AP NEWS. https://apnews.com/Globe%20Newswire/ed58061703257ca18f3ff58132ecd668.

[18]https://www.reuters.com/article/us-africa-landrights-blockchain/african-startups-bet-on-blockchain-to-tackle-land-fraud-idUSKCN1G00YK.

[19]Eder (2019). Oprunenco and Akmeemana (2018).

[20]IADB Project RG-T3356, Distributed Ledger Technology (Blockchain): The Future of Land Titling and Registry, https://www.iadb.org/en/project/RG-T3356.

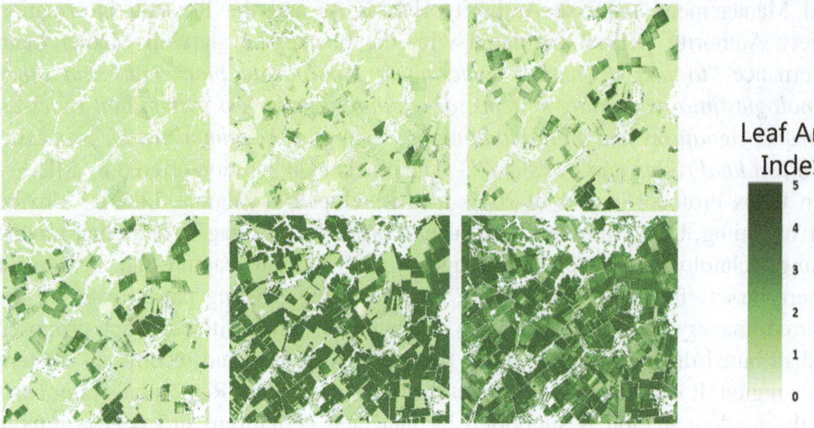

Fig. 2 Example of operational crop monitoring throughout the season based on Sentinel 2 data. Credit: Sentinel 2 for Agriculture project, national demonstrator in Ukraine

5 The Next Generation of the Agriculture Value Chains

Today, thanks to the Copernicus satellite EO system, there is a suite of matured and certified satellite-based operational services available to the farmers to enable data-driven farm production management, or to improve agriculture productivity and market access.[21] These EO-based information services can provide regular information about biomass production levels per plot, farm or agricultural holding, performance of crops (yield prognosis), early warning, assessment of water productivity (i.e. assessment of the amount of water used for the production of agricultural produce "crop per drop", performance of irrigation schemes, compliance with allocated water rights permits), optimization of fertilizer use for precision agriculture, monitoring of organic or sustainable farming practices, and so on (see Figs. 2 and 3). Nevertheless, despite an unprecedented improvement in data access policies (in particular the full, free and open licensing scheme for Sentinel EO data), there are still many obstacles that hold back the global uptake of such information especially in those parts of the world with a limited access to the internet, or where data infrastructures are not digitised.[22] Overcoming this digital divide will open completely new opportunities for EO services.

The blockchain innovation has certainly revived the interest in digitalisation of processes and businesses across the agriculture sector. It has also revealed the need for timely, accurate, transparent and reliable data records to underpin the value chain and exchange. As a result, several blockchain companies dynamically address the

[21]It is worth noting that UAVs are not an immediate substitution of the satellite imagery because only one third of all countries have regulatory environment in place allowing UAV operations.

[22]EO science for society (2019) Blockchain and Earth Observation: a white paper. https://eo4society.esa.int/2019/04/09/blockchain-and-earth-observation-a-white-paper/.

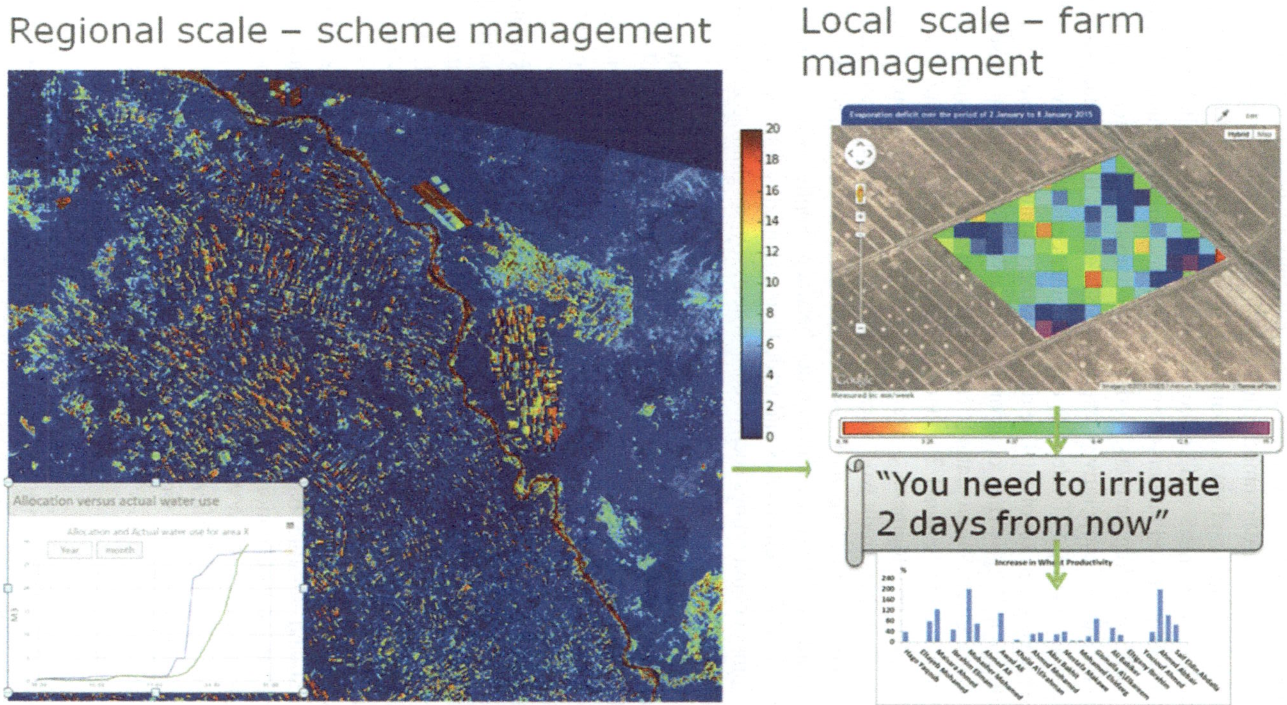

Fig. 3 Satellite Earth Observation (EO) technologies provide a low cost methodology to plan irrigation development. It helps in selecting target areas for irrigation development by quantifying water stress and identifying under-performing areas in both rainfed and irrigated agriculture. Credit: Eleaf for EO4SD Agriculture Cluster

emerging market for agricultural insurance & food and commodities traceability services. GrainChain, for example, offers a software system that integrates internet-of-things (IoT) data, market data, and farmers data into a blockchain platform for transactions in the agriculture commodity markets. In a pilot study in Honduras it has developed a coffee supply chain tracking service which focuses on brokering contracts between the farmers and coffee buyers, along with a digital wallet that enables remote and unbanked farmers to enter, for the first time, a financial exchange system with multiple trading partners. Today, the solution brings together involved banks, insurers, vendors, cooperatives, exporters and farmers to one platform via a smart contract functionality.[23] Trade in Space is another company innovating in this market by the means of fusion of satellite data into smart contracts to enable peer-to-peer commodity trading. The company's TradeWinds platform based on Hyperledger is currently demonstrating services for Brazilian coffee producers and commodity traders using Sentinel 2 imagery for production monitoring. The long term vision for such developments is meant to unlock new income sources for the farmers, and increase their credit worthiness based on the land management practices and yield prognosis (future income). As a result, the individual farmers can be empowered to enforce the pricing transparency between suppliers and commodities processing (value adding) enterprises and trade their commodity futures. The future target market aims at commodities such as corn, wheat, soy, sorghum, coffee, cotton, and livestock and features innovative start-up companies like GrainChain, Bext360, AgriLedger, AgriDigital, Tradein Space, or large corporations such as Starbucks which decided to put the entire supply chain on the blockchain, as well as Unilevel and Nestle that committed in 2019 to the full supply chain transparency via supply chain food provenance blockchain founded by the WWF and the Boston Consulting Group Digital Ventures.[24]

It is evident that for many forthcoming smart contract-enabled business applications, there is a critical need for trusted datastreams and certified information (highly processed data) to enter the code-executed transaction record, in order to further the operation and/or smart contract execution. Today a large majority of blockchain platform developers rely on IoT sensors deployed in the field for detailed information related for example to yield (actual harvest in kg per ha) or quality of the crop. Nevertheless there is a growing body of examples where remote sensing techniques (ground, aerial and satellite based) are used to digitize the production areas (i.e. coffee or palm oil plantations) to provide information concerning the overall grow and state of production. WWF's OpenSC blockchain platform is, for example, providing monitoring and verification services using combination of satellite imagery, live video monitoring and worker biometric data for sectors ranging from palm oil to fisheries. The recently released report by the UN Food and Agriculture

[23]Nelson D (2019) GrainChain's Smart Contracts Unite Honduras Coffee Business. In: CoinDesk. https://www.coindesk.com/grainchain-supply-chain-coffee-honduras.

[24]Young K (2019) Transitioning an Agriculture Supply Chain to Blockchain. In: iRoast. https://iroasts.coffee/blockchain/. WWF OpenSC Blockchain https://opensc.org/case-studies.html.

Fig. 4 Deforested areas within land parcels derived from time-series analysis of Sentinel-1 radar and optical Sentinel-2 and Landsat imagery. Example from Santa Cruz, Bolivia. Black lines: land title database courtesy of INRA Bolivia. Credit: EO4SD Agriculture Cluster (Satelligence for ESA/IDB, 2017)

Organisation (FAO) provides an up-to-date overview of other important case studies addressing the use of blockchain and Earth Observation for agriculture including the blockchain-enabled micro-insurance solutions. The FARMS project (Financial and Agricultural Risk Management for Smallholders) stands out as an example of a "virtual platform" integrated with satellite data (EO based drought index) and mobile money solutions to address the agriculture insurance market. The FARMS pilot, led by ICS (a Dutch-based NGO), strives to deliver transparent secure transactions and information dashboards as well as automated payment via drought coins/vouchers.[25] Experts indeed tend to agree that decentralisation can be considered a remedy for a low uptake of the insurance products by smallholder farmers and one of the low-hanging fruits for the technology uptake at scale.

Another important application area on the crossover of blockchain and EO is related to land administration and monitoring of concession licenses, i.e. verification of compliance with certification requirements and standards in order to screen for production norms and requirements (i.e. land use before a reference date, protected zones delineation to prevent clearance of natural vegetation or primary forest for agriculture activities, monitoring and tracking of the actual crops sown and harvested, etc.). An example of operation EO monitoring practice is presented in Fig. 4 which shows a time-series analysis of Sentinel-1 radar and optical Sentinel-2

[25] Sylvester (2019).

and Landsat imagery revealing a decade of deforestation caused by the convergence of the forest into agriculture areas within individual land parcels. The application of blockchain technology to these data services can further improve the traceability and efficiency of the wood supply chain by complementing this information with additional data on the industry practices and logistics to enable wood certification or, conversely, deforestation-free commodities supply chain like soy or beef.[26] These kinds of information platforms can include information about forest inventory, harvesting plans, dates, real-time information sharing of harvesting activities, pulp mill production rates, tracking of processing products, etc. Such capability is also interesting, for example, in the context of the EU Common Agriculture Policy where the national Paying Agencies link farm operations and their compliance to certain farm management practices with the subsidy payouts. Today this reporting is based on the mix of the farmers declarations and on-the-spots checks however in the near future the monitoring will move towards automated data processing based on remote sensing techniques, in situ data and machine learning therefore the full traceability of the data value chain will gain significance given the billions of euros of subventions at stake. Such vision for the EU-led transformation to digital agriculture was highlighted in May 2019 in the EU Declaration of Cooperation on "A smart and sustainable digital future for European agriculture and rural areas" which aims, i.a., to support research, development and innovation actions aimed at achieving improved food traceability through the use of blockchain technologies in agriculture and throughout the food system.

6 Need for Further Research and Development

Earth Observation techniques coupled with the growing blockchain capability can significantly improve the accessibility, transparency, security and traceability of information necessary to implement digital systems integrating resource management, supply chain management and financial, as well as production, economic, or customer information for a variety of market sectors. While EO services have achieved necessary maturity over the last decade, in the context of the distributed ledgers there is still a need to study deeper the use case scenarios involving adding data content (i.e. spatially referenced and updated land parcel information with associated land use/cover information, land productivity information) to the blockchain-enabled land registers, commodities trading value chains, and other emerging distributed applications (DApps) for forestry, agriculture or other sectors. The objective is to reveal what kinds of information layers can operate in the framework of blockchain-driven services, what are the critical information needs,

[26] Murray L, Alström F (2019) Blockchain in Forest Products. In: Accenture. https://www.accenture.com/us-en/blogs/chemicals-and-natural-resources-blog/blockchain-in-forest-products-improving-wood-certification-processes.

for what timescales, at which levels of resolution and content details. As blockchain network cannot be used to store data (it can only carry the land transaction details, not the object of the transaction, such as documents or geodetic information records), therefore it is paramount to clarify what observations (or data points) can be included in the blockchain transaction "block" (i.e. in a form of statistical or predefined metrics such as biophysical values assigned to the given land plot). This will require addressing the need for standardization and certification of EO data product and information services across the entire data value chain to ensure the credibility of EO services and traceability of this information, including original EO data, to the source.

Finally, one most widely quoted challenge for a wide adoption of blockchain platforms is related to the data ecosystem which it is fueled by. If inaccurate data is entered to the platform it will be maintained in the system. This is also why the EO sensor networks can play an important role in this new technology domain by providing objective, accurate and up-to-date data representing the state of the natural environment, or the movement of goods (or a single source of through validated across different interoperable sensor networks). Other commonly cited technological, legal and regulatory challenges pertain to scalability, interoperability, operational security & cybersecurity, identity verification, and data privacy.[27] Concerning a legal and regulatory framework for the implementations of blockchain solutions the open questions remain concerning the legality of smart contracts, the legal and technical protection measures concerning handling of the sensitive data in this ecosystem, including intellectual property rights as well as data licensing, data rentals and data ownership structures within the blockchain ecosystems.

7 Conclusion

There is a large potential of the convergence of different data collection technologies enabled by decentralized data structures (blockchain and other distributed ledgers) which has captured an attention of the developers, governments, investors, users, and legislative and regulatory bodies. The blockchain has been understood to outperform other technologies in terms of data protection and privacy, security, accountability and transparency of transactions involving multiple parties, and a range of implementations have demonstrated the dawn of new era for handling combined information about global value chains. At the same time, the technology poses new types of challenges. These stem from the fact that blockchain may be seen as incompatible with the existing organizational (centralized), legal, regulatory,

[27]Natarajan H et al. (2017) Distributed Ledger Technology (DLT) and blockchain: Fintech note no. 1. In: World Bank Documents. http://documents.worldbank.org/curated/en/134831513333483951/Distributed-Ledger-Technology-DLT-and-blockchain-Fintech-note-no-1, p. 1.

economic and even societal models. Moreover, there are still outstanding questions about the blockchain transactions and how to express legal contracts in the form of computational code (smart contracts). The blockchain ability to track all the data processing related to transactions has been deemed a challenge for the existing data privacy and protection laws and will require new legal regimes to be implemented to reap full benefits of this technology. Nevertheless as these questions are set to be clarified by the legal and policy experts in the coming years, it is increasingly evident that a steady trend in which distributed ledgers are embraced by the wider community of public and private users is also primed to transform and augment the way we consume and exchange data in the digital age.

References

Allessie D, Sobolewski M, Vaccari L (2019) Blockchain for digital government. Publications Office of the European Union, Luxembourg. https://publications.jrc.ec.europa.eu/repository/bitstream/JRC115049/blockchain_for_digital_government_online.pdf

Crommelinck S, Koeva M, Yang MY, Vosselman G (2019) Application of deep learning for delineation of visible cadastral boundaries from remote sensing imagery. Remote Sens 11:2505. https://ris.utwente.nl/ws/portalfiles/portal/150662968/remotesensing_11_02505.pdf

Dale PF, Binns BO (1995) Cadastral surveys and records of rights in land: based on the 1953 study by Bernard O. Binns. FAO. www.fao.org/3/V4860E/V4860E00.htm

Dasgupta A (2017) The game changer of geospatial systems—blockchain. Geospatial World. www.geospatialworld.net/article/blockchain-geospatial-systems/

Davidse J (2015) Semi-automatic detection of field boundaries from high-resolution satellite imagery. Wageningen University. https://www.stars-project.org/en/knowledgeportal/msc-theses/joel-davidse/

Eder G (2019) Digital transformation: blockchain and land titles. OECD Global Anti-Corruption & Integrity Forum

Kresse W, Danko DM (2012) Springer handbook of geographic information. Springer Science & Business Media

Oprunenco A, Akmeemana C (2018) Using blockchain to make land registry more reliable in India. LSE Business Review. www.undp.org/content/undp/en/home/blog/2018/Using-blockchain-to-make-land-registry-more-reliable-in-India.html

Sylvester G (2019) E-agriculture in action: blockchain for agriculture (opportunities and challenges). The Food and Agriculture Organization of United Nation. http://www.fao.org/3/ca5427en/ca5427en.pdf

Walters EJ (2018) Data-driven law: data analytics and the new legal services. CRC Press

Justice for All: Jur's *Open Layer* as a Case Study, Towards a More Open and Sustainable Approach

Alessandro Palombo and Raffaele Battaglini

Contents

1 The Rise of the Decentralized Dispute Resolution Systems

The contribute that the blockchain technology and smart contracts could give to the dispute resolution space is debated among many legal professional communities. The idea is that developing blockchain-based adjudication protocols could simplify

This work is expression of a joint conceptual planning, however Alessandro Palombo, Ph.D., wrote Sects. 1, 2, and 3, while Raffaele Battaglini, LL.M., wrote Sects. 4 and 5. The authors would like to express their profound gratitude to Luigi Cantisani, LL.M., and Michele D'Asaro for their precious help while writing this chapter.

A. Palombo (✉)
Jur AG, Zug, Switzerland
e-mail: ale@jur.io

R. Battaglini
Battaglini-De Sabato Law Firm, Turin, Italy
e-mail: battaglini@battaglinidesabato.com

B. Cappiello, G. Carullo (eds.), *Blockchain, Law and Governance*,
https://doi.org/10.1007/978-3-030-52722-8_19

the resolution of disputes between private actors and make proceedings more efficient.

Hence, we need first to clarify how blockchain and smart contracts can be used to resolve disputes. Blockchain and smart contracts are strictly connected, since the latter became popular as a result of the success of the Ethereum blockchain, even though the notion of 'smart contract' is decades old.[1]

With the advent of the blockchain technology, smart contracts are experiencing a sort of second life:[2] a blockchain-based network based on the principle of decentralization, intended for issuing and transacting digital currency, empowered by the possibility or storing documents and complex agreements in a tamper-proof hashed form, constitutes the perfect context for implementing a technology such as smart contracts, which is meant for providing automated transactions.

This connection has been achieved for the first time by the Ethereum's blockchain, which was welcomed as a versatile innovation, potentially applicable in many fields, for many purposes: issuing and trading securities, raising funds, tracking the supply chain; electronic voting; etc.

Given the potentialities of smart contracts for automating transactions and many kinds of operations, it is easy to understand why they are fundamental assets for building decentralized dispute resolution systems (hereinafter: "DDRS"). After all, each dispute resolution method consists of more or less complex proceedings. Proceedings are systems of rules according to which, given certain premises, to the accomplishment of a certain action by one of the parties the system must give an output. That sounds like a perfect scenario for smart contracts implementation and to digitize old-fashioned procedures or even creating brand new ones.

---

[1]Szabo NJ (1994) Smart Contracts. http://www.fon.hum.uva.nl/rob/Courses/InformationInSpeech/CDROM/Literature/LOTwinterschool2006/szabo.best.vwh.net/smart.contracts.html.

[2]The concept of "smart contract" was first introduced in 1994 by Nick Szabo. In 1995, the Author defined smart contracts as "*as a set of promises, specified in digital form, including protocols within which the parties perform on the other promises*". Smart contracts became popular as a result of the success of the Ethereum blockchain in 2015. The legal issue to be discussed is when a smart contract can be considered legally binding, in other words when a smart contract becomes a smart legal contract. Very briefly, smart contracts concerning basic sale contracts based on *facta concludentia* and transactions not requiring formalities can be considered a transposition of a valid legal contract. However, we would like to highlight the importance of connecting traditional legal contracts to smart contracts for the purpose of having a solid legal basis empowered by automation, to achieve "smart legal contracts". In its recently published consultation paper, the UK Jurisdiction Taskforce said: "*A smart contract may or may not have legal ramifications as it is merely computer code, whereas a "smart legal contract" refers to a smart contract that either is, or is part of, a binding legal contract*" (available at https://www.lawsociety.org.uk/news/stories/cryptoassets-dlt-and-smart-contracts-ukjt-consultation/). Such a paper illustrates three models for smart contracts and smart legal contracts: the "Solely Code Model" which is code standing by itself (*i.e.* without being housed within any form of natural language contractual architecture), the "Internal Model", *i.e.* a contract written in a document comprising natural language and code and the "External Model", *i.e.* a contract entirely in natural language but including an agreement for certain aspects of the contract to be performed using a program designed for this purpose.

One could argue that smart contracts are in itself a dispute resolution method—or at least a way to prevent proper disputes—since they can gather information and determine the outcome of a certain transaction (e.g. unlocking a sum of money, represented in tokens, stored and locked on a blockchain-based escrow). In many cases, assessing that certain conditions governing the pending transaction have actually been met requires the smart contract to rely on external sources. The technical solution comes in the form of the so-called "oracles", namely middleware meant to connect the smart contract to external sources of information to acquire more data so that the smart contract can fill the gap, assess, and deliver a legal solution to the case.

While an implementation like the oracles certainly reinforces the ability of smart contracts to provide automation, this work is meant to promote the idea that when it comes to resolve complex disputes arising out from complex transaction, there is no better oracle than human intervention, especially in those cases where the evaluation of certain elements passes through a subjective and non-automatable judgment (consider the case of a smart contract called to assess whether the article written by the freelancer is well-written according to the instructions provided by the customer or is completely inadequate and therefore not worthy of economic remuneration).

Technologies available today are not sufficient to provide assessments of elements that require subjective evaluation, as well as a full understanding of the notion of fairness and good faith in contractual relationships. Possibly, in the future, human activity will be completely excluded from these evaluation processes thanks to the evolution of artificial intelligence technology. But until that day comes, it will make perfect sense to design smart contract-based ecosystems that involve not only oracles in the form of middleware, but also—and above all—oracles in the form of human activity. In light of the above, a DDRS could be described as an adjudication protocol based on blockchain and smart contracts in which the human being gets involved in a decentralized way to fill the gaps of smart contracts and help resolving disputes.

As a matter of fact, many DDRS came to light thanks to certain start-up companies' projects. This section aims to provide an extensive overview of these projects, whose stage of development is difficult to determine. Hence, this work relies solely on what is publicly available on the websites of these companies.

The Kleros project started in 2017, with the objective of "assessing equity" in crowdsourcing online dispute resolution, providing the jurors an economic incentive based on an optimized version of ancient Greek Pinkaion coin and designed as a layer operating on the Ethereum platform.

Parties who choose the Kleros dispute resolution system must initially decide the type of court (specific for subject matter and experience) and the number of jurors who will analyze the dispute. Then, Kleros randomly selects jurors within the selected court's jury pool who have opted to be chosen and will initially be compensated for their availability by the counterparties, regardless of their judgement. Once the available elements have been evaluated, Kleros, through the jury of experts already selected—which is entitled to collect further data from the "real world" in order to correctly decide on the merits of the dispute—will issue a verdict based on the majority of the voters, thus transferring a sum in escrow to the winning party.

Subsequently, Kleros will compensate each juror in tokens if the choice of the juror is consistent with the majority or will penalize them in the opposite case through an internal redistributive mechanism. In other words, the jurors are motivated to vote by game theory-based economic incentives, which are expressly illustrated in Kleros's White paper.[3] Furthermore, this same document advertises the mechanism as "arbitration" although, it is not an adequate replacement for commercial arbitration *strictu sensu*.

Mattereum provides a platform for the creation of smart contracts that can solve a wide range of legal issues, but whose initial focus is the legal transfer of rights and physical assets on a blockchain through the use of smart contracts. To do this, Mattereum uses a decentralized legal system called the "Smart Property Register" which, through the automation of a Ricardian smart contract,[4] ensures property rights, as well as transfers of ownership and the resolution of disputes managed by "technically competent mediators".[5] Although Mattereum mentions the New York Convention in its working paper, no explanation is provided therein on how the project is aiming to meet the requirements for the recognition and enforceability of the arbitral awards under such a treaty. The specifications of this dispute resolution methods are not known at the moment.

Oath currently provides smart contracts with an integrated dispute resolution mechanism that is modelled on the common-law jury system and is referred to as "Smart Arbitration".[6] However, the choice of terminology is misleading, because it is not a digitized version of commercial arbitration *strictu sensu*, it is instead a mechanism in which the dispute is referred to a jury, whose members are part of one single community. Admission to the jury pool is approved by the Oath Community itself. A random selection mechanism based on algorithms assigns a team of jurors to the dispute opened on Oath.

Sagewise does not actually offer an autonomous dispute resolution method, but rather merely offers a software development kit that allows parties to send a contract to a designated dispute resolution system. The planned system is designed to anticipate problems that may arise later, for example relating to the quality of the code of the smart contract itself, and in general to address all issues that require dispute resolution. In other words, there is a "Dispute Resolution Mode" within the smart contract that remains blocked until a certain event triggers it, and that can be

---

[3]Kleros Short Paper v1.0.7, available at https://kleros.io/whitepaper_en.pdf.

[4]Grigg (2004).

[5]Mattereum protocol, available at https://mattereum.com/upload/iblock/784/mattereum-summary_white_paper.pdf.

[6]OATH Protocol Blockchain Alternative Dispute Resolution Protocol, available at https://www.oathprotocol.com/files/OATH-Whitepaper-EN.pdf.

used for many types of issues (issuance of security tokens, supply chains, financial services, digitized assets, consumer marketplace).

2 Jur's Ecosystem and Dispute Resolution Mechanisms

Jur AG is a legal tech company based in Switzerland that is working on a decentralized legal ecosystem based on the blockchain technology in order to automate contract creation, formation, execution, enforcement, and dispute resolution.[7]

Jur aims at creating an all-inclusive ecosystem for managing the whole life-cycle of the contractual relationships that include: (i) a framework to allow professionals to create legal contract templates supported by smart contracts to automate specific provisions of the business transactions; (ii) a marketplace for such smart (legal) contracts that facilitates the dissemination and creation of new high-quality contracts; (iii) an integrated blockchain-based dispute resolution system.[8]

This ecosystem has been designed with the ambition of establishing an alternative to traditional contractual relationships management methods, as a response to the possible inefficiencies of traditional justice systems administered by state authorities, and it is driven by principles of free market, efficiency and economic incentives.

Originally, Jur's project was designed as an online dispute resolution method based on blockchain to solve micro, small, medium sized claims. So, it was more focused on the dispute resolution side rather than on the creation and management of automated contracts based on the smart contract technology. A reflection of such a genesis can be observed today within the Jur Beta Platform which can be used by the parties to manage a contractual relationship provided that they have JUR tokens, which is the crypto-asset that fuels the Jur's ecosystem as better explained in Sect. 3 of this work.

As of today, the parties can:

- upload a traditional hand-signed paper-based contract to the platform;
- indicate key performance indicators to which one or both parties must adhere so that the contractual obligations can be considered fully and perfectly executed;
- indicate a resolution proof, i.e. a real-world related tool that proves that the contractual obligations have all been correctly executed;
- deposit the sum due from one party to the other, represented in JUR tokens, through an escrow smart contract;
- set the duration of the contract;
- accept or reject the setup proposed by the other party and composed of paper-based contract, key performance indicators, resolution proof and escrow smart

[7]More information available at www.jur.io.

[8]Jur Whitepaper V2.0.2, available at https://jur.io/wp-content/uploads/2019/05/jur-whitepaper-v.2.0.2.pdf.

contract deposit. In this regard, the escrow smart contract creates a bond between the electronic wallets of the two parties only when the party receiving the proposal accepts the proposal;

- the possibility for either party to initiate a dispute to decide on the allocation of the deposited sum upon the occurrence of a breach of contract.

In case the parties start a dispute, this would happen on the so-called "Open Layer", the DDRS developed by Jur and already working, although some features still need to be completed. The Open Layer is fully illustrated in Sect. 4 of this work.

The Jur Beta Platform can be used by a limited number of early adopters who have purchased the JUR tokens (more on this topic in Sect. 3) at the moment and usually under the guidance of the Jur company. Nevertheless, it is worth mentioning that a first purchase and sale of real assets, not crypto assets, took place on Jur Beta Platform. Specifically, it was the sale and purchase of a used car between two Austrian citizens.[9]

Moreover, the current version of Jur Beta Platform offers a very limited set of features compared to the will to build an ecosystem, as described in the Jur White Paper.

The final version of Jur Platform aims to offer the following features:

- the "Jur Editor", i.e. an a tool that allows users to create smart (legal) contracts either starting from a blank document or using templates made available by other users
- the "Jur Marketplace" which is meant to facilitate the sale of smart legal contract templates created by users of the platform;
- three dispute resolution mechanisms graduated according to the value of the disputes, namely:
    - the "Court Layer", i.e. digitized commercial arbitration meant for high-value disputes and designed according to the international legal framework that governs commercial arbitration in order to render arbitration awards final, recognisable and enforceable under the New York Convention;
    - the aforementioned "Open Layer", mostly suited for low-value disputes, where the decision-making process is open to all JUR token holders and driven by game theoretic principles;
    - the "Community Layer", a DDRS meant for medium value disputes and derived from the Open Layer, where only experts who are members of the

[9]The parties signed a traditional car sale and purchase agreement under Austrian laws. Then they used the Jur Beta Platform to manage proof of car's delivery and payment of the price. First, the parties established that evidence of car delivery would have been delivery of documents and car keys. Then, the purchaser transferred Jur tokens worthy USD 10.000,00 to an escrow smart contract on Jur technology. Once evidence of documents and keys delivery was given by uploading pictures to the blockchain through the Jur Beta Platform, the escrow smart contract transferred the purchase price to the seller's wallet.

community selected by the parties can participate in the decision-making process.

3 The JUR Token

As previously mentioned, the JUR token is the crypto-asset required to use the Jur Beta Platform. It is the token[10] to be staked and spent to use the features of the Jur Platform.

In legal terms, according to the non-action letter issued by FINMA,[11] the Swiss authority for financial markets, the JUR token is a hybrid token that has both utility token characteristics and payment token characteristics. Practically speaking, parties to a contractual relationship and/or to a dispute, voters, and any other kind of participants to Jur ecosystem need JUR tokens for many purposes, including interacting with the Open Layer, the Community Layer, and the Court Layer; purchasing smart (legal) contracts templates, and depositing escrows. On Jur's end, having its own token whose value is a reflection of the value of the Jur Platform itself makes sense for the purpose of creating a sustainable business model suitable for a decentralized application.

JUR token's sale plan is fully compliant with Swiss Guidelines on ICO and Anti-Money Laundering Regulations.[12]

On August 28th, 2019, Jur completed the public phase of its funding with the conclusion of their initial exchange offering of JUR tokens on the "OceanEx GO!" platform.[13] Participation numbers exceeded the target hard cap, as the community completed the 100 million JUR token target using only 25 min from the 4 h allotted.[14] At the same time, Jur launched the Jur Beta Platform. This event marked the first launch on the market of a legal tech decentralized application by means of an initial exchange offering, in contrast to models such as initial token offerings and security token offerings.

---

[10]A token is a representation of value in digital form. It is based on cryptography and blockchain technology. Tokens are usually divided in three main categories according to their function: payment tokens are utilized as means of exchange, utility tokens are those required to access a digital platform and security tokens incorporate or represent voting rights, profit rights or assets.

[11]The Swiss Financial Market Supervisory Authority (FINMA) is in charge of supervising the financial market in Switzerland. On 16 February 2018, FINMA disseminated "Guidelines" on initial coin offerings. Companies willing to issue tokens in Switzerland are required to liaise with FINMA in order to properly qualify the legal nature of the tokens to be issued. In the event of payment and utility tokens, it is usually suggested to obtain a so-called "no-action letter" from FINMA stating that the token is not a security tokens subject to regulated offering.

[12]In particular, Anti-Money Laundering Act of 10 October 1997.

[13]Learn more at https://medium.com/jur-io/jur-grand-opening-a-complete-success-for-jurs-ieo-on-oceanex-go-4c48a1c98ddc.

[14]Learn more at https://medium.com/jur-io/jur-grand-opening-a-complete-success-for-jurs-ieo-on-oceanex-go-4c48a1c98ddc.

4 The Open Layer

In this section, we will address the functioning of the Open Layer and, most of all, the principles of game theory applied to this system. We will not discuss the legal nature and validity of the decisions obtained through the Open Layer: this matter will be examined in a dedicated future paper.

4.1 Purpose of the Open Layer

As previously mentioned, the Open Layer aims to work as a blockchain-based decentralized dispute resolution mechanism accessible through the Jur Platform. This system has been developed having in mind micro-claims up to a value of USD 500,00 but the parties may use it for larger disputes as well. Also, this system can be used for paper-based contracts as well as for smart (legal) contracts created on the Jur Platform or elsewhere. The Open Layer can also be used as an outsourced dispute resolution infrastructure for digital platforms that involve micro-transactions. Currently, Jur is testing fake disputes with international Universities.

In any case, the dispute resolution process relies on:

- the open community of users of the Jur ecosystem, meaning anyone who owns JUR tokens;
- economic incentives based on an application of game theory in order to give stability to the system.

In order to avoid possible misinterpretations, it is worth stressing that the Open Layer is not a democratic voting system where each person has one vote but uses economic incentives to motivate persons to voluntarily participate in choosing fair outcomes, where each voter has influence in proportion to the willingness to stake JUR tokens.

We can summaries the main conceptual differences with respect to a democratic voting system as follows:

- vote is not per capita but per token;
- voters must stake tokens to participate;
- staked tokens are forfeited if the voter fails to select the position that is supported by the majority of voted tokens when voting ends;
- staked tokens will be matched with reward tokens if the voter chooses the side that is supported by the majority when voting ends and votes early enough to be instrumental in establishing the majority.

4.2 Functioning of the Open Layer

In order to briefly explain how the Open Layer works, we will use a very simple case.

Alice and Bob enter into a freelancer agreement whereby Bob undertakes to draft three articles for Alice's new blog. Alice and Bob agree on details such as deadline, remuneration and topics.

Alice and Bob then load a digital print, called "hash", of that freelancer agreement into a smart contract. Alice deposits 300 JUR in escrow (attached to the smart contract) that will be transferred to Bob if he finishes the work.

Let us assume that the relationship does not unfold as expected: Bob is able to deliver only one article. Alice feels she has been harmed by Bob's failure to deliver the other two articles and only wants to pay 50 JUR, but Bob wants to be paid 100 JUR. Since they cannot agree, Bob opens a dispute on the Open Layer, staking 3 JUR on his proposal. Alice uploads her proposal as well. Then any JUR token holder can act as a voter and stake their tokens for either proposal. If at the end of the period of voting Alice's proposal gets the most votes, the smart contract will refund her 250 JUR and deliver 50 JUR to Bob. If Bob's proposal gets the most votes, the smart contract will deliver to Bob 100 JUR and refund 200 JUR to Alice. Either way, both parties pay nothing to the voters to have their dispute solved, other than possibly forfeiting voted tokens if they participated in the voting process.

Holders of JUR who voted for the minority side forfeit the JUR that they voted. Holders of JUR voted for the majority side are compensated for their efforts with the JUR of those who voted for the minority side, until those tokens are exhausted. Matching reward tokens are allocated only to those JUR tokens that were voted soon enough to have been required to establish the majority.

It should be noted that, to open a dispute, the claimant party must stake 1% or more of the contract value on their proposal. This commitment is a vote like any other. As such, if the proposition it supports receives a majority of the vote, it will be refunded and, if tokens were voted in opposition, matched with a reward. If the proposition it supports receives a minority of the vote, the amount voted will be forfeited as a penalty for ruling incorrectly. A party who submits a fair proposal will pay nothing for dispute resolution and may even earn reward tokens.

It is worth mentioning that JUR token holder may express also a "reject" vote. Considering that the Open Layer and the entire Jur ecosystem are based on decentralization and that two parties could use it for an illegal contract or something manifestly contrary to their own individual rights, Jur is interested in preserving a proper and licit use of the Open Layer. Therefore, the Open Layer offers this third type of vote: "Reject." A reject vote indicates the voters believe the contract is too unethical or outright illegal to receive any ruling. If reject votes prevail, the reject voters earn the tokens of the voters who selected either of the two proposed solutions and the escrow amounts are simply returned to whoever paid them in. If reject voters do not prevail, they forfeit their tokens to those who voted for the winning proposal.

4.3 Game Theory Applied to the Open Layer

After describing the Open Layer purpose and functioning, it is possible to address the principles of game theory and the incentives behind the mechanism.

In order to do so, it is necessary to briefly mention the "Schelling Point" or "Focal Point" as per the work of Thomas Schelling.[15] In a Schelling Point game, participants faced with a question must try to guess the answer of other participants. If such persons have proper incentive, in the form of a reward, and are unable to communicate with each other, they will provide the proper answer to the question because there is no incentive in behaving otherwise. As Schelling clarifies, the "Focal Point" is a solution of the game that persons will tend to use in the absence of communication, because it seems natural, special, or relevant to them. Focal points have been ever since a matter of further studies in game theory,[16] but also in law,[17] and psychology.[18]

The Open Layer works on this very principle. JUR token holders are asked to select the fairest proposal and, if they predict the majority's position, they will be rewarded. The best strategy to gain the reward is to predict what other JUR token holders think is fair. The possible token reward provides an incentive to predict correctly. Voters know they will lose tokens if they predict incorrectly, so they also have a disincentive to predict incorrectly.

The focal point within the Open Layer ought to be the fairest solution between the two proposals according to what the parties established in their agreement. Having to predict the behavior of the other voters, they will all vote for the party that they believe will be chosen by the majority. The payoff to stake ratio will be the same for both propositions; there is no difference that could affect voter behavior. Having no reason to assume the other voters are ignoring the instruction to choose the fairest proposition, an individual voter will try to predict which proposal the other voters will consider fairer.

The above so clarified, it is possible to move forward and discuss the incentive mechanisms for voters which have been envisioned to ensure that each of them seeks to understand and anticipate the behavior of the majority.

A voter knows that:

- all voters have exactly the same system of incentives;
- voters cannot directly communicate with each other;
- all voters have access to the same information;
- payoffs (i.e. gains and losses) are equal for each voter.

---

[15] Schelling (1958).

[16] Sugden (1995).

[17] McAdams (2000).

[18] De Freitas et al. (2019).

It is worth noting that the scenario for the Open Layer is slightly different from the hypothetical conditions under which Shelling explains the focal point because, within the Open Layer:

- voters do not act simultaneously;
- each voter is able to see how prior votes have been allocated.

However, there are counterbalances to these deviations.

First of all, the system does not accept votes that would make one position more than 100% larger than the other.

As a matter of fact, it may happen that one large token holder (called "whale" in the crypto-world jargon), would try to corrupt a dispute by staking a large amount of tokens with the aim to purchase an unfair verdict, conspire with one of the parties, win tokens of the losing side, or nullify the Open Layer.

The "100% limit" has been devised to avoid this kind of risk: users can stake votes in favor of a proposition up to the point where it has a 100% of votes more than the other proposal.

Hence if Bob's proposal has 100 and Alice's proposal has 199, only one more vote can be cast for Alice until Bob receives more votes. This limit ensures that the gap between the majority and the minority is never too wide.

Consequently, the whale cannot discourage minority voters by creating a vast margin of victory to overcome.

Secondly, only voters whose votes are necessary to create and maintain the majority are rewarded with the tokens of the minority side. This means that the voter and the voters comprising the majority must vote early enough so that their votes are required to determine the majority. The system provides that reward tokens are matched to majority-side votes in the chronological order they were received, providing a reward for each token up to the point where a lasting majority is established. For instance, if Bob's proposal has 200.1 votes and Alice's proposal has 100 when voting ends, the owners of the first 100.1 tokens voted in favor of Bob will be rewarded with the 100 tokens voted for Alice. The owners of the next 100 tokens voted for Bob will only get a refund of their tokens with no matching reward.

This means that, in case of an early majority being established, there is an incentive to vote *against* it and not in its *favor*. In other words, voters are not only incentivized to vote according to the fairness as perceived by the majority, but also to vote quickly to be relevant to that majority.

So the best strategy for average voters is to study the dispute, carefully choose the proposition that seems to be the fairest, and vote as soon as possible to maximize the possibility of a reward. Although counterintuitive, theoretically the "early voting" strategy is one that relies more heavily on the information that the player can get from the dispute itself, as opposed to information coming from the behaviour of other voters. This makes the early voters fit better the profile of a player as imagined by Schelling.

Another important counterbalance concerns the time period for voting. The Open Layer is meant to solve disputes within a minimum of 24 h, but parties can choose their own time limit. Whatever the case, in the event that an unusually high number of votes are received in the final 30 min of voting, the time limit is extended automatically until volume subsides. If the majority position changes again due to an unusually high number of votes being received in the final hour, the voting will be extended again, repeatedly if necessary, until a majority prevails throughout the final hour of voting.

Further, it is worth pointing out that a voter can not retrieve the vote: this measure is to avoid misuse of the system.

Finally, the last rule is called "Safety Clause". Both during the regular duration of the dispute and during one or more extensions of time, the amount of tokens staked could reach an abnormally high number. This could be a reflection of the presence of one or more whales among the voters, or of voters strongly oriented to speculation. If this happens, and specifically if the total value of the tokens staked as votes exceeds "x" times the value of the agreement under dispute, the Open Layer will automatically refer the dispute to the Court Layer in order to ensure the recognition and enforceability of issued decisions before national courts. As a matter of fact, the Court Layer is a digitized commercial arbitration procedure based on blockchain technology, and that reflects the principles of the New York Convention and the UNCITRAL Model Law, the most important legal cornerstone in international arbitration.

As such, its activation is legitimate provided that the parties to the agreement have expressed their consent to arbitration in a specific arbitration clause. And 50% of the tokens staked by voters will be used to pay the arbitrator.

This mechanism of escalation of the dispute from the Open Layer to the Court Layer ensures the parties will receive in any case a decision not based on speculation. Also, it serves as a deterrent against speculators and whale attacks.

The Safety Clause is therefore meant to discourage or correct any improper *manoeuvre* carried out by voters holding a large amount of JUR tokens, eliminating the chances of a dispute ending in a corrupt ruling.

4.4 Reward and Not "Game of Chance"

Having so clarified the principles of game theory behind the Open Layer, it is possible to state that voters earn JUR tokens for studying the case and delivering a just verdict rather than say that voters win tokens for participating in a "game of chance".

As a matter of fact, there is no incentive to try to earn JUR tokens by voting unjustly or randomly. When a voter notes that someone has voted on the wrong side, she can easily vote against and earn the matching JUR tokens.

In other words, the reward to stake ratio is the same for both proposals: this render the Open Layer different from games of chance and betting markets where low probability events carry higher reward to stake ratios.

Since the reward to stake ratio (in the case of winning) is the same for both propositions, voters will select the proposition with the highest perceived probability of being supported by the majority: they will choose the side that they believe most persons will perceive as fair.

Therefore, it is possible to state that, within the Open Layer, the rational person will choose the more likely event that coincides with the highest probability of success because there is no incentive to vote on an unlikely event. Voting on low probability outcomes does not lead to a higher return.

4.5 Voters and Competence

Given the game theoretic rules applied to the Open Layer, we can infer that poorly-qualified voters will tend to stop voting in order to avoid forfeiting tokens, incurring an economic loss.

In addition, we can further infer that, to some degree, voters will self-select for competence. A voter with good competence on the subject to be addressed may be very motivated to vote due to confidence in his or her ability to predict which outcome will receive the most support and earn tokens.

However, while rational voters will choose to vote when they are confident that they can predict the majority position, the attitude of some voters may ultimately prove to be irrational: such voters may be referred to as "weak voters". Meaning those who cannot accurately predict what the majority believes is fair.

The best strategy for weak voters will be to abstain from voting otherwise they risk losing their tokens to the prevailing voters.

In summary, the weak voter will have two choices:

- continue to lose tokens in favor of those who vote wisely: weak voters will eventually not be in a position to purchase more JUR tokens;
- sell their remaining JUR tokens to other persons who want to start or increase their voting activity within the Open Layer.

The above leads to a natural selection mechanism within the Open Layer which will result in the prevalence of competent voters.

4.6 Open Layer and Disputants' Approach

Getting back to the example, both Alice and Bob propose a solution to the dispute.

Knowing that an impartial group of voters will be selecting the proposal that they believe is the fairer of the two, rational parties will be careful to make reasonable proposals. Parties can certainly propose unfair solutions, but they do so at their own risk. As a matter of fact, it is not practical or rational for a party to the contract to knowingly make an unfair proposal and vote for it, hoping to gain by buying an unfair result with votes made in bad faith. The amount in dispute that could be potentially gained by "buying" an unfair verdict is tiny in comparison to the total potential vote (especially when taking into account the 100% limit rule). It would be irrational to attempt to buy an unjust outcome knowing the size of the possible loss far exceeds the size of the possible gain.

A disputant which deliberately submit an unfair proposal and attempts to buy a biased result by voting unfairly is simply offering their money to the distributed voters, who collectively control much greater wealth than any individual. The fair majority will enjoy the forfeit tokens of the self interested voter, and Jur will function better for their unwittingly generous contribution that creates an incentive for attentive voting.

Therefore, this form of corruption by one of the parties to the dispute is theoretically possible but practically inconvenient and easily counterable. Voting for one's own unfair proposition or conspiring to gain by voting for an unfair result in exchange for sharing the proceeds of an unfair result is just giving away tokens to voters eager to gain by delivering a fair verdict.

When the two parties are negotiating with each other privately, in direct conflict, their proposals may tend to diverge as a result of positional bargaining. On the Open Layer, the parties must submit their proposals for impartial consideration, so their solutions will tend to converge, approximating a solution that lies somewhere in between, since each party strives to appear to be the most reasonable.

It is possible to state that the Open Layer encourages the parties to make fair self-assessment and to request a reasonable sum, because unreasonable proposals are unlikely to win.

This is the opposite of what happens in judgments before national courts, where the parties usually ask for the maximum possible amount, in a positional bargaining strategy, because they are aware of the fact that the judge has broad discretionary powers and can opt for an allocation of sums different from those proposed by the parties. This may seem like an advantage, but it ends up making the verdict of the judgments highly uncertain and unpredictable.

Within the Open Layer, voters cannot depart from the parties' proposals, therefore the risk of an alternative and unpredictable outcome is completely eliminated.

If the disputants propose two solutions with a very small margin of difference, one might be concerned that the dispute is difficult to resolve fairly. It is indeed true that, when the proposals are very similar, it is more difficult to predict what other persons will find fairer, increasing the risk involved in voting. But this is not a major issue. As far as the disputant are concerned, when proposals converge, we can see that the system is creating fairer behaviors in relationships. As far as voters are concerned, the outcome will approximate a relatively fair solution, since the claims of the parties are nearly the same to begin with.

5 Conclusions

The Open Layer is an attempt to offer a new tool to solve disputes that otherwise may remain with no affordable dispute resolution mechanism. The Open Layer should be seen as a tool aimed at solving the problem of inefficient and expensive management of micro-claims.

The described process is based on game theory, economic incentives and disincentives, measures to ensure resilience of the system, wisdom of the crowd.

Thus, the result is a voting system rather than a proper legal judgement system.

As already mentioned, the Open Layer is not suitable for deciding complex commercial disputes; for instance, where examining a lot of documentation or structuring a complex legal reasoning is needed in order to arrive at a valid decision, and in general involving decisions other than or in addition to the mere transfer of sums of money.

It is also important to point out that the Open Layer works best under a particular set of optimal conditions. In particular, disputes concerning clear agreements such as those with objective key performance indicators. A dispute involving subjective evaluations only deliver the majority's subjective opinion of fairness which, by its very nature, is apt to be more controversial than a decision based on objective factors.

Finally, we want to stress the fact that the Open Layer is not a legally binding solution. As such, it is plausible that the Open Layer will encounter barriers in terms of recognition as an ADR mechanism enforceable before a national court.

But its strength relies on self-execution of decisions through smart contracts and almost no costs for disputants. The impossibility of obtaining enforcement before a court is not a problem because the Open Layer is designed for disputes concerning the transfer of sums so the parties to a contract know that they can count on the function of self-enforcement guaranteed by the smart contract.

We are also aware that any theoretical model, even if apparently effective and incorruptible, can be seriously stressed by concrete use cases, to the point of revealing behaviors by actors that had never occurred in another system based on the same theoretical models. Tests will be necessary, with the aim to optimize the parameters that control the Open Layer dynamics (incentives and disincentives distribution, minimal stake, duration), and suggestions from the academic world will be welcome.

And this is the aim of this chapter: fostering discussions within the academic world about new ways of solving disputes based on cutting-edge technologies and socio-economic theoretical rules.

References

De Freitas J, Thomas K, DeScioli P, Pinker S (2019) Common knowledge, coordination, and strategic mentalizing in human social life. Proc Natl Acad Sci 116:13751–13758
Grigg I (2004) The Ricardian contract. In: Proceedings. First IEEE International Workshop on Electronic Contracting, 2004. IEEE, pp 25–31
McAdams RH (2000) A focal point theory of expressive law. Va Law Rev:1649–1729
Schelling TC (1958) The strategy of conflict. Prospectus for a reorientation of game theory. J Confl Resolut 2:203–264
Sugden R (1995) A theory of focal points. Econ J 105:533–550

Blockchain and the GDPR: New Challenges for Privacy and Security

Marco Tullio Giordano

Contents

1 GDPR and Blockchain

Identifying the applicable rules under the General Data Protection Regulation (GDPR) is certainly a challenging task when such rules are confronted with the heterogeneity of solutions in the field of distributed ledgers. The GDPR was, indeed, designed and shaped in the light of pre-existing and completely different systems.

Against this background, it is important to bear in mind that the preparatory work for the GDPR began in 2012, when the blockchain technology was still unknown to many. Above all, in 2012, this technology was not so widespread to represent a state of affairs that the legislator should have necessarily taken into account when drafting the new European Union (EU) provisions on the protection of personal data.

At that time, the only application of blockchain was Bitcoin, which was launched a few years earlier by Satoshi Nakamoto and in which only a small number of users and nodes was participating. Back then, only a few additional information—including personal data—was uploaded on the chain of blocks. More recently, several and heterogenous projects based on blockchain have started to emerge, also thanks to the

M. T. Giordano (✉)
Legal Tech, LT42, Milan, Italy
e-mail: m.giordano@lt42.it

B. Cappiello, G. Carullo (eds.), *Blockchain, Law and Governance*,
https://doi.org/10.1007/978-3-030-52722-8_20

so called-Initial Coin Offering (ICO). As a result, this technology has spread widely and the first services specifically designed to make information (potentially including personal and sensitive data) transit through the blocks have started to emerge.

The GDPR responds to the need to translate into more detailed rules the principle of protection of personal data laid down in Article 8(1) of the Charter of Fundamental Rights of the European Union and in Article 16(1) of the Treaty on the Functioning of the European Union. Moreover, the choice of resorting to a regulation (instead of a directive) was mainly driven by the need to overcome the fragmented application of Directive 95/46/EC in the different national legal systems.

It is worth stressing, once again, that the technological paradigm that was taken into account by legislators and stakeholders involved in the consultation and evaluation processes at the time of the preparatory work (2012–2016) did not include the blockchain technology.

As it clearly emerges from the analysis of the preparatory work, the philosophy underpinning the GDPR refers to a centralised—rather than a decentralised—ecosystem. Indeed, the whole Regulation assumes, and almost takes for granted, the existence of a data controller which determines the purposes and means of the data processing and which is able to identify, authorise and constantly monitor its data processors. Therefore, there seems to be no room for a decentralised and permissionless approach to data processing in a distributed framework.

This original sin has an impact on the application of the principles set out under GDPR to these new decentralised systems. These inherent limitations that affect the rules set out under the GDPR should hence be duly considered.

In this regard, we should probably wait until the first Commission's report on the evaluation and review of the Regulation which is expected in May 2020. This report will give the EU legislators the chance to take into account blockchain technology, and its peculiarities, when revising the existing regulation on the protection of personal data.

What is sure is that, given the decentralized nature of the most important and widespread permissionless blockchain technologies, it is hard to imagine that non-compliance with the existing data protection rules may lead to an outright ban on or limitation to the use of these technologies. The hope is that the EU legislator will soon become aware of the widespread use of this instrument and of the undeniable benefits it brings about and that it will find a way to flatten the possible frictions with the existing regulatory system thus enabling its more fruitful mass adoption.

In any case, this "mismatch" between the blockchain technology and the GDPR leads to an initial conceptual difficulty when one questions whether these rules are effectively applicable to this technology and, if so, how they should be applied.

GDPR compliance is not about technology,[1] it is about how technology is deployed. It is important to note that there is no GDPR-compliant Internet or

[1]The European Union Blockchain Observatory & Forum, *Blockchain and the GDPR*, 16 October 2018.

GDPR-compliant artificial intelligence algorithm and there is also no GDPR-compliant blockchain technology. After all, the GDPR does not aim to prohibit *tout-court* any processing of data, but it requires that the data controller carries out an assessment of the processing of data, even if the processing is only envisaged, and makes efforts to minimize the risks that may derive from that processing. From this point of view, the processing of data that involves a risk that cannot be prevented should not necessarily be considered prohibited. However, it will be important to assess the likelihood of such risks, to balance it with the specific interests at stake that may be connected to the processing of data (data subjects' interests on the one hand and data controller's interests on the other) and, if necessary, to implement corrective measures that minimize the risk to the extent possible or provide for compensation for any damage that may be caused by the processing in question.[2]

Perhaps, only a private blockchain, managed by a central body entrusted with the power to grant and revoke permissions, as well as to rewrite the content of transactions included in closed and certified blocks in the chain, could be virtually compliant with the GDPR. However, rather than a proper blockchain technology, private blockchain is closer to a centralized database disguised as a distributed tool. As mentioned, blockchain technology is not (il)legal as such. GDPR compliance should rather be assessed in the light of specific use cases and applications of a given technology the impact of which vary depending on the technology used and the controllability of the data concerned.

On a purely theoretical level, the main tensions between GDPR and blockchain revolve around the following topics, which should be analyzed in greater details:

- Identification and attribution of the roles foreseen by the GDPR to the actors of the Distributed Ledger Technology (DLT) ecosystem: although there are many cases in which controllers and processors can be immediately identified, there are also cases where it is difficult, and perhaps impossible, to identify with certainty who covers these roles, especially when transactions are written by data subjects themselves.
- Identification and attribution of the respective responsibilities to the actors of the system: in the DLT environment, a node of the blockchain could be regarded as a controller or a joint controller for some of the data it processes, or as a processor in relation to other data. In this framework, it is hence hard to attribute in an unequivocal manner the responsibilities that derive from this classification (as data controller or as data processor) of the nodes.
- Anonymisation of personal data: as of today, there is no consensus on the rules that should be followed to anonymise personal data when such data are stored in a public network. It follows from this that the potential re-identification of the

[2]The GDPR, indeed, provides that where a type of processing in particular using new technologies, is likely to result in a high risk to the rights and freedoms of natural persons, the controller shall, prior to the processing, carry out an assessment of the impact of the envisaged processing operations on the protection of personal data (art. 35 e 36). Such assessment would be required every time blockchain is deployed to process personal data.

subject to whom data relates generates serious concerns in relation to the large number of third parties who might access those data. This appears to be in contrast both with the principles of necessity and minimization of the processing of data, and with the principles of privacy by design and privacy by default that have been introduced by the GDPR.

– The exercise of data subjects' rights under the GDPR: there is no doubt that in some solutions (the most orthodox ones in terms of DLT) the rectification or deletion of data is practically impossible. This appears to be in stark contrast to some of the new rights that the GDPR grants to data subjects.

After all, the GDPR seems to be unequivocally aimed at regulating centralized roles in the processing of data, without considering any possible alternative. No alternative paradigm was, indeed, envisaged.

Problems inevitably arise when trying to implement such rules to systems that neither follow nor are aligned with that conceptual paradigm. The absence of a central body in permissionless systems and the development of an organized system without an organizer leads to a short circuit that could significantly hamper the diffusion of this technology. Indeed, the GDPR distributes responsibilities on the basis of the roles played by the different actors involved. These roles have been designed considering the scenario where an entity collects personal data that are then subject to a specific processing.

Once again, it is worth recalling that such regulation does not seem to have taken the slightest account of other possible data management methods such as the one on which the blockchain technology is based and which has introduced the idea of a shared and egalitarian participation of the nodes in the processing of data.

2 Difficulties in Identifying Subjects and Roles

Technology is usually neutral and self-determined and, consequently, is not affected by the normative framework: it is the people who use technology who must verify the applicability of rules. At a theoretical level, however, the classification made by the existing normative framework become useful for the identification of the actors and their level of involvement.

Centralised systems are characterized by the presence of an intermediary, i.e., an entity holding the data to which the GDPR applies in its entirety. In this context, the intermediary itself assumes the role of data controller and no issues of difficult interpretation seem to arise.

From a practical point of view, greater uncertainties arise when trying to define who is the data controller in a distributed system, like the one underlying blockchain technology. The GDPR, indeed, defines data controller as "the natural or legal person, public authority, agency or other body which, alone or jointly with others, determines the purposes and means of the processing of personal data".[3] With reference to the blockchain, the role of data controller seems to be distributed among the various participants in the network. Each node can therefore be considered as a data controller while acting as data processers on behalf of the other nodes.

In the blockchain ecosystem, every actor has his own digital identity represented by a public address or "wallet address". Such wallet address includes some attributes that can be reconnected to a specific individual. It can be argued that this may have an avalanche effect: all those who process data could hypothetically take on the role of data controllers, with the automatic attribution of the related responsibilities to them.

Decentralized systems (so-called permissionless) do not have this possibility: it is necessary to make a distinction between necessary and accessory (and hence not indispensable) subjects. Blockchain can, by definition, be managed by several participants, making it difficult to identify the different roles with certainty.

On the other hand, in "permissioned" systems, the identification of certain roles may be easier. In a small community where the parties decide on data validation rules, such parties may be joint controllers[4] while if the "validators" did not actually participate in the determination of the rules, they could assume the role of data processors. Lastly, in systems subject to "controlled" access and where the identities of participants are known, it would even be possible to theorize the creation of contracts and privacy notices consistent with legal provisions, as it is the case today in centralized ecosystems.

All this is impossible in permissionless blockchain, where the roles identified above fade away: the subjects involved cannot be identified *a priori* and those who process the data do so without any permission, as these data are irreparably public. A distributed and permissionless blockchain is, indeed, accessible to all, open source and transparent by default; there are neither corrective measures nor distinctions in what the different nodes can do; in the absence of trust between the parties, there are no limitations on the rights to read and write; trust only rests upon the platform and encryption, thus enabling the so-called trustless validations. The interpreter is hence bound to struggle when trying to apply and adapt the GDPR to such a different paradigm.

In order to solve these problems, the *Commission nationale de l'informatique et des libertés* (CNIL, the French Data Protection Authority), in its explanatory document issued in November 2018 and entitled "*Blockchain and the GDPR: Solutions for a responsible use of the blockchain in the context of personal data*",[5] has considered the exception set out under Article 2(2)(c) GDPR for purely personal and household activities applicable in most of the cases. The applicability of this exemption entails that the processing carried out by private parties do not fall under

[3]Article 4, para. 1, n. 7, Regulation 2016/679/EU.

[4]Article 26, Regulation 2016/679/EU.

[5]CNIL (Commission National Informatique et liberté), *Premiers éléments d'analyse de la Blockchain*, September 2018.

the strict provisions of the GDPR. The nodes (where managed by non-professional users) would hence not be considered as data controllers. The same reasoning would also apply to the so-called miners, which, following this interpretation, are merely validating other people's transactions and, as such, are unable to determine the purposes and the means of the processing. Miners would hence have no responsibility under the GDPR.

3 Anonymisation of Personal Data

The possibility to trace the data back to an identified or identifiable individual is a central aspect in the regulatory context. Article 4 paragraph 1 lett. a), indeed, provides for a definition of personal data: only those data relating to natural persons are taken into account. It is hence clear that concepts such as anonymisation and pseudonymisation become extremely relevant, especially in a context such as the DLT and blockchain context where a wallet, a transaction, a public key cannot immediately be referred with certainty to a given natural person.

In order to set out under what conditions personal data falls outside the scope of the Regulation, it is first essential to clarify the meaning of anonymisation and pseudonymisation.

Even before the entry into force of the GDPR, the Article 29 Working Party (A29WP),[6] in its opinion 5/2014 on anonymisation techniques,[7] has tried to establish some principles, which are still relevant under the current framework.

First of all, anonymisation shall be understood as the result of processing of personal data with the aim of irreversibly preventing identification of the data subject through an anonymisation technique. Second of all, the outcome of anonymisation should be, in the current state of technology, as permanent as erasure, thus making it impossible to further process personal data. Differently, pseudonymisation should not be equated to an anonymization technique. Pseudonymisation reduces the linkability of a dataset with the original identity of a data subject which makes it a useful security measure. At the same time, however, pseudonymised data, unlike anonymized data, stays within the scope of the data protection regulation.

Under the current normative framework where the concept of "pseudonymisation" has been specifically codified, it is useful, in order to identify the scope of application of the GDPR in the context of the blockchain, to draw a line between the meaning of "anonymisation" and "pseudonymisation".[8]

[6]The Article 29 Working Party is a consultative and independent body established under Directive 95/46/EC: it does not have legislative and coercive powers, but its Guidelines and Opinions are an important instrument for interpreting the EU data protection legislation.

[7]Article 29 Data Protection Working Party, Opinion 05/2014 on Anonymisation Techniques, adopted on 10 April 2014, https://ec.europa.eu/justice/article-29/documentation/opinion-recommendation/files/2014/wp216_en.pdf.

[8]Article 4 n.5 Regulation 2016/679/EU.

Pseudonymisation is defined under Article 4 GDPR as "the processing of personal data in such a manner that the personal data can no longer be attributed to a specific data subject without the use of additional information, provided that such additional information is kept separately and is subject to technical and organisational measures to ensure that the personal data are not attributed to an identified or identifiable natural person". On the other hand, anonymisation seems to entail a more radical and irreversible transformation of the information in question: anonymous information is defined as "information which does not relate to an identified or identifiable natural person or to personal data rendered anonymous in such a manner that the data subject is not or no longer identifiable".[9]

If data that have undergone a pseudonymisation process (e.g. encryption through hash algorithm, as in blockchain technology) can still be attributed to a natural person by the use of additional information that are stored separately by the data controller (e.g., by linking a given wallet to its user), those data cannot be considered anonymous or anonymised since they can still be traced back to an identifiable natural person and, as such, subject to the provisions of the GDPR.

Now, in relation to DLT technology, it may be difficult to establish without any residual doubt when an information flow can be considered "effectively" anonymised rather than pseudonymised, and which techniques ensure effective anonymisation of the data.[10]

The reasoning of the "Article 29 Working Party"[11] in Opinion 5/2014 also refers to the centralized paradigm described in the premises of this work and does not take into account the fact that in the blockchain ecosystem there is no central party which has access to the private key. Even if the private key is potentially able to decipher the hash algorithm and lead back to the original data and to its author/controller, this information usually remains in the exclusive ownership of the user himself, without any other public evidence that leads back to his identity.

---

[9]Recital n. 26 Regulation 2016/679/EU: "The principles of data protection should apply to any information concerning an identified or identifiable natural person. Personal data which have undergone pseudonymisation, which could be attributed to a natural person by the use of additional information should be considered to be information on an identifiable natural person. To determine whether a natural person is identifiable, account should be taken of all the means reasonably likely to be used, such as singling out, either by the controller or by another person to identify the natural person directly or indirectly. To ascertain whether means are reasonably likely to be used to identify the natural person, account should be taken of all objective factors, such as the costs of and the amount of time required for identification, taking into consideration the available technology at the time of the processing and technological developments. The principles of data protection should therefore not apply to anonymous information, namely information which does not relate to an identified or identifiable natural person or to personal data rendered anonymous in such a manner that the data subject is not or no longer identifiable. This Regulation does not therefore concern the processing of such anonymous information, including for statistical or research purposes".

[10]As a general rule, obfuscation, generalization, randomization and encryption are considered adequate in this regard.

[11]The Article 29 Working Party (Art. 29 WP) was an advisory body composed by one representative from the data protection authority of each Member State, the European Data Protection Supervisor and the European Commission.

In other words, in the permissionless blockchain, the private key is exclusively owned by and is under the responsibility of the natural person: under ordinary conditions, no intermediary nor central body has knowledge of the link between the said key and its user, not even in the form of digital identity.

In any case, just as it happened in the past with regard to other disruptive and innovative technologies—think of the TCP/IP protocol and the lengthy debate on the nature of the IP address as personal data which was finally solved after about ten years and thanks to the European Court of Justice's judgment delivered on 19/10/2016 by its second section in case no. C-582/14—it seems that a definitive interpretation about the nature of the information and of data flows affected by blockchain technology is still far from being defined.

4 Difficulties in the Exercise of Data Subjects' Rights

There is no doubt that one of the most relevant and distinctive aspects of the GDPR is the codification of some new data subjects' rights (i.e., the natural persons to which data refer). The need to codify these rights has emerged as a result of the changes in our lives brought about by the spread of technology and the development of the Internet. For example, we could think of the right to be forgotten which arose from the increasing amount of personal information indexed on search engines and which have been debated by both national and supranational judicial authorities.[12] The jurisprudential experience that arose from the impossibility of deleting some information from the Internet has finally led to the codification in Article 17 GDPR of the right to erasure, as a fundamental data subjects' right.

In the light if this, the technology of distributed ledger seems, to some extent, to run counter to the GDPR: due to the decentralised structure of the blockchain, it would be technically impossible to satisfy data subjects' requests to rectify and delete personal data without destroying the chain itself. Indeed, since the various blocks are interconnected, in order to comply with such requests, it would be necessary to operate on the whole chain. As a further element of complexity, it should be noted that data stored in a blockchain are tamper-proof. This entails that the deletion of these data will not be possible once they are entered into the distributed chain. After all, persistence and immutability are two of the most fundamental features of this technology and, more generally, of its decentralised application.[13]

[12]Both EU and national courts have recently delivered several judgments with reference to the "right to be forgotten", starting from 2014 with the Costeja Gonzales case dealt with by the European Court of Justice in C-131/12 *Google vs Spain*, and Corte di Cassazione (Court of Cassation) judgment n. 13161 of 24.06.2016. For an in-depth analysis, see Finocchiaro, *Il diritto all'oblio nel quadro dei diritti della personalità*, in *Internet e Diritto civile*, Napoli, Edizioni Scientifiche Italiane, 2015.

[13]See on this point the definition of "Distributed Ledger Technology" under the Italian legislation and, in particular, under Article 8-ter of Law no. 12 of 11/02/2019: "technologies and informatic protocols which use a ledger which is shared, distributed, replicable, simultaneously accessible,

Some possible solutions have been suggested by experts, such as the possibility of intervening on the blocks by modifying/deleting their content. Others have suggested the possibility of separating data from the hash values by using separate databases on so-called side-chains, which would allow to retain control over the information entered in the chain. Another option could be the creation of off-line copies of data. However, at this stage, all these proposals still have many disadvantages and unresolved issues. Only a judicial intervention in a practical case may eventually provide a conclusive interpretation.

It should also be recalled that, although the right to erasure is codified under Article 17 GDPR, data subjects' requests pursuant to the said Article may be left unsatisfied if the technology available does not allow the data controller to erase the personal data in question. Article 17 paragraph 2 GDPR, indeed, provides the following: "Where the controller has made the personal data public and is obliged pursuant to paragraph 1 to erase the personal data, the controller, taking account of available technology and the cost of implementation, shall take reasonable steps, including technical measures, to inform controllers which are processing the personal data that the data subject has requested the erasure by such controllers of any links to, or copy or replication of, those personal data". It is hence reasonable to argue that, where the erasure of personal data is not technically feasible or would require disproportionate efforts, data controllers should not be obliged to a result they cannot realistically guarantee. Under these circumstances, in accordance with the principles set out in the GDPR, data subjects would still be entitled to receive compensation for any damage they may have suffered.

In addition, with reference to the so-called "right of access" (which, pursuant to Article 15 GDPR gives the data subject the right to obtain confirmation from the data controller as to whether or not personal data concerning him/her are being processed and, if so, to obtain access to such data), in public networks based on permissionless blockchain, identifying the data controller to which access to data can be requested may be a challenging task. Moreover, even if it is possible to identify the specific node to which the right of access can be addressed, that node may not have the requested information.

5 Principles of Data Minimization, Necessity and Storage Limitation

The GDPR has formalized some general principles (which were already established under the pre-existing legislation, i.e., Directives of the European Parliament and the Council 1995/46/EC and 2002/58/EC) so as to provide greater and more complete

architecturally decentralised with cryptography, insomuch as it enables the registration, the validation, the update and the storage of data, both unencrypted and further encrypted, verifiable by each participant, not alterable nor changeable".

protection to the processing of personal data of data subjects in the European Union. Such principles are laid out under Article 5 GDPR, which includes, among others, the data minimization principle. The said principle prescribes that personal data shall be "adequate, relevant and limited to what is necessary in relation to the purposes for which they are processed".[14] Along the same lines, under the "storage limitation" principle, personal data shall be "kept in a form which permits identification of data subjects for no longer than is necessary for the purposes for which the personal data are processed".[15] It is immediately evident that the very architecture of the blockchain technology and, above all, of blockchain itself is ontologically structured in such a way that once data is entered into the chain of blocks, the data will remain unchanged and permanently on the platform. It is precisely the transparency and the immutability of the ledger which, on the one hand, guarantee the ledger itself and make it a disruptive technology and, on the other, create friction with the above-mentioned principles. Blockchain, at least in read-only mode and by deploying any block explorer, offers anyone indiscriminate access to the data stored in transactions and blocks. Likewise, no retention time is set and, potentially, data may be stored on the blockchain forever.[16] Although alternative solutions have been discussed so as to allow data to be moved off-chain, or to hide its content from the public, it is clear that these issues need to be urgently addressed by the European legislator, by Data Protection Authorities and interpreters. Potential frictions between blockchain technology and the GDPR may indeed hinder the adoption of the technology itself.

6 Questions of Jurisdictions and Transfer of Data to Third Countries

The GDPR requires that the competent jurisdiction for any disputes on data processing is identified *ab origine* and in a predetermined manner. Such activity seems to be almost impossible in a fully distributed system.

This regulatory approach can, in fact, be pursued in purely centralized ecosystems of networks and services. The distributed nature of the blockchain requires additional efforts, given that the subjects to be regulated cannot be easily distinguished and compelled with enforcement actions: such subjects operate globally and, at the same time, anonymously. Each node shall, in fact, be entitled to refer to its own jurisdiction in case of disputes and each data subjects may refer the matter to the local authority or to the competent authority in case the nodes violate the principles set out in the Regulation.

[14] Art. 5 lett. c) Regulation 2016/679/EU.

[15] Art. 5 lett. d) Regulation 2016/679/EU.

[16] Think of the Eternity Wall service, which uses part of the bitcoin algorithm to insert a personalized text message during the transaction, available at https://eternitywall.it/.

With regard to international data transfers, the GDPR provides that, where data are shared with entities established in non-EU territories, the level of protection afforded to the data shall not be undermined. Just like the internet has challenged traditional geographical boundaries and hence also the applicability of data transfer rules, blockchain is a virtual space which disregards borders and jurisdictions and which is populated by actors that have voluntarily decided to become part of it, thus accepting to abide by its rules. This also in the event that, as it is expected and as is already happening, non-EU countries adopt GDPR-like data protection rules or other mechanisms that guarantee that data are processed consistently with the EU data protection principles.

7 Concluding Remarks

DLT technologies, including blockchain, are a set of heterogeneous systems with, sometimes, radically different qualities and features. This chapter is certainly far from providing a comprehensive analysis of the opportunities offered and the challenges raised by blockchain but, at the same time, it aims to set the ground for further discussions that should be addressed by the stakeholders that revolves around this innovative and disruptive technological solution. Identifying who qualifies as data controller or as data processors and the exercise of data subject's rights are some of the major concerns that have been identified in this chapter and that should be subject to an in-depth analysis. Data protection rules should be interpreted on a case-by-case basis, also in the light of the principles that have been highlighted above.

More and more blockchain-based solutions will be offered on the market thus raising new questions which will need to be answered. Instead of transposing to a decentralized environment concepts and rules specifically designed for a centralized framework, the intimate nature of this new technology should be understood so as to ensure the effective implementation of the GDPR principles, and hence, of the right to protection of personal data as a fundamental right under the EU Charter of Fundamental Rights.

The analysis and the provision of privacy notices and procedures for the processing and the protection of personal data in compliance with the applicable data protection rules will be the real challenge, especially when it comes to reconciling the needs of the parties involved and the peculiarities of new technologies. Such peculiarities will need to be taken into due account. Specific attention should, in particular, be focused on permissioned or authorized networks in relation to which, under the current framework, there seem to be more problems than solutions.

Reference

Finocchiaro G (2015) Il diritto all'oblio nel quadro dei diritti della personalità. In: Perlingieri C, Ruggeri L (eds) Internet e Diritto civile. Edizioni Scientifiche Italiane, Napoli

Part V
Conclusions

Blockchain, Law and Governance: General Conclusion

Tony Lai

Contents

1 Introduction: A Multi-Disciplinary Perspective on Law

This volume allows us to draw in and consider multiple perspectives, including from regulators, miners, blockchain lawyers, privacy advocates, financial system architects, smart contract analysts, sustainability developers, technologists, transparency advocates, and beyond. This diversity of perspectives is no surprise: there is no doubt that law can no longer be taught in the same way, and that law professors must be supported in de-siloing themselves from other disciplines and perspectives.

The task we have set ourselves is to consider how to seek and channel the multiple perspectives raised by these new technologies; legal, economic and

---

This chapter covers the presentation given by Tony Lai to conclude the conference on Blockchain Law and Governance – Good for All: Towards a Paradigm Shift, at the University of Milan, on October 26th, 2019. The presentation slides can be found at https://www.slideshare.net/TonyLai7/blockchain-law-and-governance-general-conclusion-milan-october-2019.

T. Lai (✉)
Stanford University, Blockchain Group Stanford CodeX, San Francisco, CA, USA
e-mail: tony@codex.stanford.edu

B. Cappiello, G. Carullo (eds.), *Blockchain, Law and Governance*,
https://doi.org/10.1007/978-3-030-52722-8_21

sociological. The parallel task is to consider what story we tell about this interweaving of perspectives.

The story I will tell is of being in community with legal experts who are not afraid to innovate. I will tell stories of lawyers who embrace the idea of entrepreneurship and empowerment, who are comfortable with change, and seek to reduce inequalities in society. A common story we have been listening to is the prediction that we are entering a period of rapid innovation in the systems we design and operate across our societies: Systems of power, systems of trust, and systems of transparency into abuses of power. Analogously, the original promise of the Internet was to be a system designed by idealist Internet pioneers to be a free, diverse, and open digital commons; a thriving forest rather than a series of walled gardens.

Today again, new technologies offer the chance of a 'paradigm shift': The prospect of widespread deployment of blockchain technologies and a return to stories that are not carefully curated in these centralizing walled gardens, but rather emerge from a diversity of perspectives through a return to decentralization. Understanding how this deployment of blockchain technologies is governed, but also how blockchain technologies themselves can be a tool of governance in a more complex, decentralized world, will be instrumental to how artificial intelligence and other technology advances can be applied in a socially conscious way.

This process of both governing technologies, and also the use of technology to support governance, raises serious legal questions, including around the authority and power of states to enforce laws. There are legal issues around, for example, how blockchain-based legal instruments can be used in smart contracts, online dispute resolution, 'predictive' justice, or to monitor and support the flow and exchange of financial assets. These issues all raise new challenges for policymakers and regulators, in particular, the question of how to coordinate governance and regulations to reach common agreed-upon frameworks.

2 The Prospects Offered by This Volume

From public administrative law, to private international law and the application of contract law scholarship, a number of chapters consider the question of how to integrate and regulate the emergence of self-enforcing code-based law that enables 'new relationships entirely based on trust'. Thus, when blockchain advocates speak of 'trustless' systems, they refer to the ability to disintermediate middle-men from transactions and interactions when they are coordinated and processed through these systems. Where once, the middle-man would act as the guarantor of trust between the parties to the transaction, blockchain-based systems rely on economic incentives and transparency, such that the middle-men are substituted by the encoded 'blocks' of the blockchain, and trust is notionally guaranteed through the economically predictable actions of the block 'miners'.

In looking at these interactions between existing legal systems and these new code-based systems, through exposition on the governance of blockchain systems and infrastructure, one might ask what constitutes 'legitimate action' with respect to such governance. The discussions around 'on-chain governance' speak to this notion of using blockchain technology as a tool for governance. Where 'blockchain maximalists' argue for complete on-chain governance wherever possible, it will be possible to argue that 'no blockchain is an island', and that some 'off-chain governance' is essential to fulfilling the potential of blockchain technologies as part of a system of governance. Introducing the concept of 'functional equivalence', Cappiello highlights in her chapter how technology has the potential to guarantee and achieve specific regulatory or policy objectives, and where it can do so, it should be considered as an alternative to current regulatory processes that rely on the existing, but fraying fabric of stable, legitimate institutions. By using technology to increase confidence in the way technology operates, important challenges such as how to govern the protection and sharing of data can be addressed more easily. And while it is interesting to design private law systems based on the application of contract law that can be more efficient and less costly to administer, these systems cannot be abstracted out of a public law framework.

The chapter also address the issue of integrating new legal instruments into existing legal frameworks, by covering some of the public and private law responses to a new class of decentralized, autonomous (blockchain-based) organizations (often referred to as 'DAOs'). Showing us how these DAOs represent a new layer of innovation in legal systems, Cappiello notes that membership of these organizations can be fluid and even anonymous, that they transparently account for participation, rights, and responsibilities, allow for distributed decision-making and the direct distribution of proceeds, and are often operated using flat, non-hierarchical structures. One key takeaway is that DAOs can be seen as making the 'plumbing' of an organization reliable against manipulation: Transparency into the operation of the rules of the organization allows for the monitoring of others' behavior, which in turn acts to support self-regulation by members of the organization.

Carullo's chapter leads us to understanding how new technologies may be usefully exploited in the public sector, and how an efficient and trusted public sector increases the overall pivotal role of each nation state in addressing and guaranteeing people's needs.

This volume also offers us the chance to gain the perspectives of a regulator keen to promote their willingness to listen: Martina Tambucci, as the Head of the Regulation Office of the Italian Companies and Exchange Commission (CONSOB), describes in her chapter her office's work in creating opt-in, sandbox-style experiments around reducing the burdens of regulation, as part of an ongoing process of engagement. In looking to platform managers, for example, the operators of crowdfunding platforms, Ms. Tambucci showcases a new model of cooperation not just between nation states, but also with subsidiary players within a regulatory ecosystem.

This new model of cooperation is picked up also in the chapter written by Gino Giambelluca, who shares his central banker's rationale for supporting such a model: to support stability, efficiency, and reliability in financial services. This approach reflects the shift from a traditional bilateral relationship to a more multi-lateral, platform-based approach to service provision, with reference to the sharing economy, and the digital economy, and the new models of intermediation offered by digital technology. From a technical perspective, devices, applications, and network infrastructure are operating together in a more fragmented, decentralized, and complex environment; from a legal perspective it becomes harder to know who is behind a particular event or process that should be subject to regulation. At heart, regulations and their enforcement are based on a need to preserve users' confidence in the system and services. The challenge is to look beyond traditional players in a more complex environment and recognize the potential for 'good for all' as part of a redistribution of power away from these more traditional players.

In their discussion on smart (legal) contracts, Professors Rühl, Bertoli, Poncibò and Goodenough look to existing legal systems as a point of reference. A common position is that smart contracts can only have legal effect if applicable law allows for this effect. This harks back to the *lex mercatoria* discussion of the 1980s and 1990s, which held that while practical dynamics might be detached from domestic legal systems, the creation and existence of these dynamics is fully dependent on those domestic systems and the ability to have them enforced through the monopoly of coercive powers that rest with the state. Contrary to this position is the notion that smart contracts have an enforcement capacity that exists independent of the state. The concept of 'functional equivalence' should be seen as supporting this notion, where code is effectively replacing some of the regulatory and enforcement capacity of the state. Yet this concept also supports the assumption that parts of any regulatory or legal function cannot or should not be coded, for example, where concepts of good faith or reasonableness allow for the application of uniquely 'human' intelligence into our social and economic systems of coordination. This approach plays out through the concept of Ricardian contracts, where parts of the contract are coded, and parts rely on traditional legal application and enforcement.

In addition, Santosuosso, Ortolani and Palombo-Battaglini's chapters show that new technologies might be of help in delivering justice to all. Along with larger claims, smaller 'micro-claims' too might be heard by competent judges or arbitrators and be solved according to an agreed set of rules. Of note, the new arbitral procedure developed on these blockchain-based platforms provide for procedures combining principles based on the rule of law and game theory. The challenges and opportunities ahead in this space are well worth following.

The volume also teaches us how it is possible to use blockchain to achieve the Sustainable Development Goals ('SDGs'), premised on coordinating activity around the world to achieve these global goals. At the heart of this coordination is the ability to use blockchain along with other technologies to better track and create a shared record of the impact of different activities. For example, as explained in Burzykowska's chapter, by using sensors and cameras, with artificial intelligence, the components of pollution can be better detected and tracked. Yet the challenge remains: How should we feed these capabilities into policy? In parallel, Coppi has shown how new technologies might be helpful in ensuring humanitarian aid.

Lastly, the Zwitter, Giordano and Nastri chapters explore how technologies can pose a risk to our privacy: To reach the ultimate end of shaping a fairer, more resilient, sustainable and prosperous society based on trusted relationships, we must recognize how privacy can be embedded by design as part of opening space for a diversity of interdisciplinary, intergenerational, and cross-cultural relationships, voices and perspectives.

3 Enabling Hard Tech Through Human Connections

The power of relationships to drive innovation is a story I am intimately familiar with from my time in Silicon Valley. For the fifth year running, Reuters in their list of The World's Most Innovative Universities, ranks Stanford University at the top, noting that 'Stanford holds onto its top spot year after year because it produces a steady stream of innovations that are cited by other researchers in academia and private industry'. These innovations are nurtured in an environment where investors are rewarded for taking risks and entrepreneurs are steeped in a culture of embracing and learning from failure. Of greater import, though, in driving innovation, is the diversity of perspectives that comes from operating within and around the Stanford and Silicon Valley ecosystem.

Stanford's alumni network has been mapped by some colleagues of mine and compared to the networks of other major US academic institutions, and it is one of the world's most connected:

In my personal experience, it is the social technology of how we connect as humans that helps and enables the harder tech. As part of the founding team of Stanford's StartX accelerator,[1] I helped build a community of over 1300 founders who have built companies with a combined valuation of over US$19 Billion, partly by relying upon this network. Critical to the success of their disruptive innovations was the diverse network, the community of other founders, mentors, experts, and community supporters who are all focused on collaboration and accelerating each other's development. By opening our hearts, minds, and wills, to one another within the community, by being able to listen and to get feedback from men and women, from every race and creed; having this community to sustain and inspire us has been the difference in success versus failure for so many innovations that our founders have created to solve complex problems. In my experience, it is through such collectives of diverse perspectives, through their collective power, and through the processes around gathering and sharing collective intelligence, that the greatest impact can be achieved.

Another important collective I have been grateful to help nurture is the community around CodeX, the Stanford Center for Legal Informatics, and around the FutureLaw conference hosted by CodeX at Stanford Law School each year (this year, we held our first blockchain-specific day of discussions as part of the FutureLaw conference). At CodeX, our mission is to create and promote research

[1]See www.startx.com.

into technologies that improve our legal systems. We also hold that laws governing technology must include an understanding of how that technology works. Thus we believe that blockchain developers, economists, financial engineers, and many others, as well as lawyers, must be brought into and engaged within our community. And in keeping with our location at the heart of Silicon Valley, we believe that engaging with the mindset of an entrepreneur is also a critical factor in the impact of our approach: This mindset is founded on a willingness to experiment, to have a stake in the outcome, and to hold multiple truths.

Thus, at CodeX we look to both the law of technology and the technology of law. We address issues around regulating and governing technology, as well as the use of technology as a governance tool. Through the lens of informatics, we see law and governance as information systems.

4 Blockchain as a Tool to Define and Signal Agreed Normative Principles

As technology lawyers, for example, looking at terms of service for websites and online platforms, or as financial services lawyers looking at the stock-exchange rules, we understand that laws operate at many levels. So we understand that what we value can be defined at many levels of collective organization.

Where there is a marketplace of rulesets, people (however defined, including corporations and other institutions) can choose which rulesets to exist or operate under. Where regulators take a polycentric approach to governance, the regulated can seek to set their own standards with self-regulatory bodies and associations: Thus, information shared by an association that a particular certification is granted, or revoked, subject to the meeting of certain standards, can be a highly-effective regulatory mechanism in a market where people recognize the value of such a certification.

At the same time, as technology lawyers, we ask questions about the future of automation. We consider the potential impacts on human dislocation and displacement. We face a moment of fundamental crisis that threatens the legitimacy and stability of our values and institutions. A major part of this crisis in legitimacy is the sense of not being able to see the rules, and how they are made and operate. We are not able to participate. Automation and technological change seem to be amplifying this effect. With increasingly complex and unpredictable webs of connections and interdependencies, opaque rules and interactions enable a system to be silently influenced; opaque institutions get gamed. Complex rules or rules detached from the actual interactions they govern have the same effect, the institutions get gamed.

Blockchain technologies (understood as, or through the lens of, computational law) flip things around. Rules and interactions can be transparent and open, when they need to be. This can radically reduce the costs of coordination and cooperation, both within and between institutions.

Blockchain technologies have an inherently regulatory potential and represent a new way of governing ourselves, as collective interest groups, and ultimately as institutions. Code acts as law to define (and signal) the options of possible behavior and therefore what is collectively valued (the agreed normative principles).

To further investigate this potential, I established the Blockchain Group at CodeX to research and publish; track, guide and influence policy coordination; and to be an inclusive, neutral, learning and discussion forum, around the legal issues and opportunities presented by: blockchain technologies and their intersection with existing legal and regulatory frameworks; smart contracts and governance design for decentralized ecosystems; and legal empowerment and legal services use cases for blockchain technologies and computational law. Through the Blockchain Group, we founded the Stanford Journal of Blockchain Law & Policy, a first-of-its-kind academic law journal edited by Stanford and Stanford-affiliated scholars and practitioners, available in print and online at stanford-jblp.pubpub.org to enable optimized timeliness, agile peer review & commentary, and cross-publication interactivity.

As a neutral, reputable platform for peer-reviewed articles and essays, the journal has covered to date a range of issues, including comparative ICO regulation, blockchain and GDPR, governance around hard forks, cryptocurrency and digital asset taxation issues and enforcement, citizen central banking, digital asset taxonomies, decentralized exchanges, and the interaction of blockchain technologies with intellectual property law. While this conference has covered a similarly wide range of material, some of which we have looked into through our group and the journal, I would like to draw out some particular aspects of our research, which build on existing approaches where systems and processes have integrated law and technology.

5 Regulating Blockchain

5.1 How to Regulate the Unknown

Harking to the progressive approach of the regulators expressed in this volume, one member of our group and of the journal's editorial board, Michèle Finck, has shared a particularly pertinent set of typologies and principles for regulating blockchain technologies informed by broader, existing considerations around regulating the unknown. The eight principles are: (1) balance public interest and stimulating innovation; (2) regulatory stability, (3) engage early, (4) have regulatory conversations, (5) polycentric co-regulation, (6) experimentation, (7) focus on use cases not the tech, and (8) engage in transnational conversations. The five typologies are:

(1) wait and see; (2) offer guidance; (3) sandboxing; (4) new legislation; and (5) use blockchain as a regulatory tool.[2]

Similarly, by looking to the broader issues around platform and data governance, we can reference and be informed by the existing legal and technical work on governing multi-party systems and information flows.

Project Callisto[3] is an example of a pre-blockchain system for governing information flow that operates on analogous principles around transparency and accountability in the context of a loss of trust in institutions. Survivors of sexual assault within institutions, from universities to corporations, often face stigma in standing up alone against an assailant. Existing paths for reporting them (e.g. university administration, or HR) are often misaligned in terms of their interest in having such activity come to light. By using methods based on the work of Ayers and Unkovic around information escrow,[4] Project Callisto works with the institutions to offer their members a hotline, staffed by lawyers acting as 'options counsellors', where survivors are given a variety of options beyond making a report up the traditional, institutional chain of information custody, such as the opportunity to speak to their own lawyer, speak to the press, or speak with a therapist. Critically, they are given the chance to speak with another victim—this is the information escrow component: If the victim is the first to report an assailant, this is logged in escrow, and each time a subsequent victim reports the same actor, each victim is given the opportunity to be in touch with the other, and to decide together if, now no longer alone, they wish to take an option together. This approach creates a competitive marketplace around reporting ethical or unethical behavior and has potential applications in other areas of corporate and public-sector whistleblowing. Like good mechanism-design in blockchain-based systems, Project Callisto's approach also changes the game-theoretic dynamics for assailants within an institution or ecosystem that has adopted their system: Assailants need to now assume that their survivors *will* collaborate and communicate to out them as defectors in the now repeated game of following the rules (and behaving ethically). What Project Callisto also reveals is the residual importance of human (off-chain) governance within a functioning system of information governance, particularly where sensitive issues and information are at involved. When the idea for a blockchain-based project purporting to offer a similar escrow system for outing sexual assailants was floated, valid criticisms were levelled around the potential abuse of such a decentralized system that lacked human-governance safeguards. Nevertheless, the potential remains for designing mechanisms that incentivize normatively desirable behavior and collaboration as part of decentralized and scalable information governance systems that can reinforce systems of trust and expose abuses of power.

---

[2]Finck (2018).

[3]https://www.projectcallisto.org.

[4]Ayres and Unkovic (2012).

Multi-party systems have also existed in various ways prior to blockchain,[5] and their governance can also inform the design of blockchain governance mechanisms. Credit card systems (Visa, Mastercard), payment systems (SWIFT, ACH), identity systems (IdenTrust, eIDAS), social media networks and online marketplaces (Facevolume, Alibaba), are all examples of pre-blockchain systems that operate based on (i) rules; (ii) a governance mechanism to make, amend, and maintain the rules; and (iii) a mechanism to make the rules enforceable on the participants. Each participant in these multi-party systems agrees once to a common set of rules that is binding on all participants. With the same rules applied to everyone, this can form the basis of overall trust in the system, in that each participant knows how each other participant is obliged to act. In addition, these multi-party systems work by identifying and aligning the separate business, legal, and technical rules of the system. The business rules define who can or should do what, what roles exist, and what their duties and responsibilities are. Legal rules set compliance requirements and allocate risk and loss, for example through warranties and limitations on liability. The technical rules govern how the data is structured, formatted, communicated, secured, verified, etc., and the technical processes to be used. Where blockchain-based systems can bring about a paradigm shift in the design and operation of these multi-party systems is through the application of identity standards around parties, documents, and other identifiable elements and resources as part of self-enforcing, smart legal contracts, which could remove the need for an intermediary or platform operator with the technical power (though not necessarily the legal right) to manipulate or otherwise control the flow of information and resources through the system.

5.2 *Self-Organizing Capabilities of Blockchain-Based Communities*

Robust models of social and economic interaction have described emerging patterns of order and "self-organizing capabilities": Markets are widely recognized as generating social order through both price signals and social rules. Yet in practice, public services are provided and shared resources managed through a variety institutional arrangements, both formal and informal.

Through studying how these resources and risks are co-managed, design principles for collective governance of these 'Common Pool Resources' can be articulated. Any group whose members must work together to achieve a common goal is vulnerable to self-serving behaviors, and so should benefit from applying the same principles.

In a time of decreasing trust in institutions, states, and corporations, with concerns over the loss of community bonds and people expressing worries over a lack of control and stake in their communities, their work, and their future, the application of

[5] Smedinghoff (2018).

theories for governing Common Pool Resources to collective goals increases in importance, especially where those resources relate to knowledge and data, which are not only non-rivalrous, but can be seen to increase in value the more they are used and engaged with.

I have been referencing here the work of Elinor Ostrom and other economists, mathematicians and sociologists engaging in commons scholarship, who have been studying how humans can coordinate and take collective action. Ostrom was the first and so far only woman to win the Nobel Economics Prize in 2009 and her empirical research into collective governance of the commons represents a major opportunity for the development of blockchain-based systems of computational law. Computational law concerns the flow of data and trust, indeed one of the core purposes of law itself is to provide answers to the question of 'How do we build trust?' Ostrom notes that "building trust in one another and developing institutional rules that are well matched to the ecological systems being used are of central importance for solving social dilemmas,"[6] and that "the surprising but repeated finding is that users of resources that are in relatively good or even improving condition are willing to invest in various ways of monitoring one another", which relates to the core problem of building trust.

The eight design principles referenced in her Nobel Economics Prize speech and updated by her colleagues[7] are as follows: 1A. User Boundaries: Clear and locally understood boundaries between legitimate users and nonusers are present. 1B. Resource Boundaries: Clear boundaries that separate a specific common-pool resource from a larger social-ecological system are present. 2A. Congruence with Local Conditions: Appropriation and provision rules are congruent with local social and environmental conditions. 2B. Appropriation and Provision: Appropriation rules are congruent with provision rules; the distribution of costs is proportional to the distribution of benefits. 3. Collective Choice Arrangements: Most individuals affected by a resource regime are authorized to participate in making and modifying its rules. 4A. Monitoring Users: Individuals who are accountable to or are the users monitor the appropriation and provision levels of the users. 4B. Monitoring the Resource: Individuals who are accountable to or are the users monitor the condition of the resource. 5. Graduated Sanctions: Sanctions for rule violations start very low but become stronger if a user repeatedly violates a rule. 6. Conflict Resolution Mechanisms: Rapid, low cost, local arenas exist for resolving conflicts among users or with officials. 7. Minimal Recognition of Rights: The rights of local users to make their own rules are recognized by the government. 8. Nested Enterprises: When a common-pool resource is closely connected to a larger social-ecological system, governance activities are organized in multiple nested layers.

Without going into detail on each design principle, the last principle relates to governance of groups that are part of larger social systems, where there must be appropriate coordination among relevant groups. Large scale governance requires

[6]Ostrom (2010).

[7]Cox et al. (2009).

finding the optimal scale for each sphere of activity and appropriately coordinating the activities, a concept called polycentric governance. In polycentric governance, multiple governing bodies interact to make and enforce rules within a specific policy arena or location, or around a specific set of shared resources. Most cases of natural resource governance are complex and cross-level in character and most human–environment interactions concerning natural resources take place at multiple scales. Similarly, where we anticipate blockchains being used as part of governance, as we have seen, we will often need to consider how such a system is nested within, and interacts with local, state-level and international legal frameworks. With the use of blockchains, we open the potential for greater transparency and accountability between the different levels, and more emergent coordination, particularly as these complex systems adapt.[8]

A related concept is subsidiarity, which assigns governance tasks by default to the lowest jurisdiction, unless this is explicitly determined to be ineffective. Designing institutions and multi-party systems to force (or nudge) entirely self-interested individuals to achieve better outcomes has been the major goal of law and governance for the last few decades. Ostrom argues that, instead, a core goal of law and policy should be to facilitate the development of institutions that 'bring out the best in humans'.[9] In applying Ostrom's theories to blockchain-based systems, we need to ask how diverse systems and institutions based on polycentric governance help or hinder the building of trust and bringing out the best in humans: Innovativeness, learning, adaptiveness, trustworthiness, levels of cooperation between humans, and also between human and AI-agent participants, and the achievement of more effective, equitable, and sustainable outcomes at different scales can all be optimized for.

5.3 *Tokens as Digital Assets Representing the Collective Value of Coordinated Markets*

Turning to the blockchain technology use case of creating tokens as digital assets on a blockchain ledger: Token economies indicate collectively defined and accepted values.

One accepts the values and rules of the system by buying or accepting the token. Tokens themselves can act to enable different measurements of what we consider of value. The opportunity to have coordinated markets for collective value is based on the idea that free, open and competitive markets are a force that can emancipate societies from feudal prejudices and privileges. As a global collective of humanity, we recently agreed some high-level definitions for what we collectively value, the SDGs, along with targets and indicators—each a set of vectors around which we can collectively measure this collective value. Tokens can thus be a key component of

[8] Lewis (2017).

[9] Ostrom (2010).

the paradigm shift in international coordination of human activities that are increasingly interconnected at the national and global level on account of technological advancements, changes in governance systems, and the growth of capital markets. Computational law as applied through the judicious use of tokens to create transparently well-regulated markets and commons, with interoperable governance, will allow collaboration across institutions and scales, improving connectivity and learning across scales and cultures.

Well-connected, interoperable governance structures can swiftly deal with change and disturbance because these changes and disturbances can be addressed by the right people at the right time.

By incorporating the feedback of data from Internet-of-Things systems, with pricing data based on markets and commons running on token systems, voluntary data contributions, and those from corporations mandated by laws, the rules of the system as a whole can also be set up to be adaptive. Blockchain technologies have the potential to support adaptive policymaking that is responsive to the outcomes of those policies.

One example of this is in New Zealand, where a data commons project[10] is coordinating data at multiple levels, from multiple contributors, working over a twelve-year window to prevent runaway climate change by making it possible to take coordinated, effective and informed environmental action (in New Zealand), by measuring the impact of everyone's contribution to the environment. The project, including a token aspect, allows for learning from the collective data, and making measurement of environmental action economically valuable. What we can measure, we can manage or change. This involves developing a broad-based data-commons, where data flows between different systems under legal agreements and associated market mechanisms to encourage responsible collection, use and management of data.

6 How Blockchain Can Be "Good for All" and Represent a "Paradigm Shift"

In considering the notion of "Good for All", and what blockchain technologies could represent in terms of a paradigm shift, I would like to consider now some of the questions being asked more broadly around technology platforms and their governance. In May 2019, San Francisco, the beating heart of Silicon Valley, became the first city in the United States to ban the use of facial recognition technologies by local agencies. Legislators and policy-makers around the world are grappling with the correct approach to regulating technology platform companies that have been gathering unprecedented levels of data about users. This data gathering feeds into

[10]http://datacommons.org.nz.

business models that have propelled them to become the most valuable companies in the world.

Today, they increasingly look to encompass roles, like the creation of currencies, that were once the exclusive domain of sovereign states. Facebook announced earlier this year their intent to work with a consortium of organizations to create Libra, a 'stablecoin'. Beyond the standard concerns over money laundering and terrorist financing, the broader question is: 'Do you trust a tech company with your money?' Private stablecoin providers could unseat banks, which generally face strict consumer protection rules, as the main intermediaries between central banks and consumers.

A greater concern for privacy advocates is the prospect of technology companies using their networks to shut out competitors and monetize information, using their proprietary access to data on customer transactions.

In August 2019, a distributed 'world legal summit' was held in 33 countries around the world to simultaneously discuss a series of common legal and policy questions with experts and commentators from around the world. I had the pleasure of kicking off Singapore's contribution, alongside the Dean of NUS Law, Professor Simon Chesterman, counsel for Singapore's personal data protection commission, and the director of an emerging technologies thinktank, where our session sought to address the topic of personal identity in a time of rapid technological change. Using the issues covered in his earlier article, 'We, the Robots?',[11] Chesterman, set some of the context for the session, and we took the opportunity to address some of the recent issues raised by the increased focus, particularly in Silicon Valley, on A.I. and Ethics, and algorithmic bias, in the wake of a wider focus upon privacy.

Among the engineers and designers who have been exhorted to "move fast and break things" as part of the market and venture-capital driven push to grow at all costs, philosophers of technology, like Tristan Harris, have emerged to critique the 'weaponization' of data to control billions of minds.[12] Shoshana Zuboff has popularized the term 'surveillance capitalism' to call attention to the digital threat posed by technology platforms that have been commodifying personal information for profit and the regulation of user behavior.[13]

As we consider whether A.I. and robots might deserve rights and legal personhood in some version of the future, others have recalled that women, slaves, or African Americans, were once rightless, and that "until the rightless thing receives its rights, we cannot see it as anything but a thing for the 'use' of those who are holding rights at the time."[14] Might we humans, data subjects, be in danger of becoming robot-like automatons for the profitable use of our A.I.-wielding, data-controlling overlords? This perceived danger helps square the paradox of how

[11]Chesterman (2019).

[12]https://www.wired.com/story/tristan-harris-tech-is-downgrading-humans-time-to-fight-back/.

[13]Zuboff (2019).

[14]Stone (1972).

Silicon Valley's shining city upon a hill came to ban facial recognition based on the perceived specter of a disempowered citizenry.

In the fictional futures presented on the one hand by Aldous Huxley in Brave New World, and on the other hand by George Orwell in 1984, we see Huxley imagining humanity controlled by that we desire, and Orwell imagining us controlled by that we fear. Coming back to our all-too-real present, on the one hand, we have the Facebooks of the world targeting us ever more precisely to control our spending and cravings, while on the other hand we have sovereign states, like China, empowered with technology and creating all-encompassing surveillance networks with social credit systems that govern one's access to critical societal functions.

Against this set of competing visions, I would like to bring us back to the prospects and potential solutions offered by Computational Law—the emerging field of research I've been discussing, of which blockchain technologies are a subset, that offers a path towards embedding considered, ethical oversight of these complex data-driven, human-machine systems and platforms, on which increasingly large portions of social and economic activity operate. Traditional laws and regulations can be seen as algorithms executed by humans towards collective goals. As these algorithms are increasingly executed by machines, designing systems to include the guardrails of human judgement and interpretation will be of critical importance to maintain fairness, inclusion, and legitimacy, as well as effectiveness—the ability to promote common goals and sanction bad actors. Through adopting pattern languages and methodologies common to the software development world—such as design, testing, continuous audit, modular systems, and responsive instrumenting—regulators, courts, counsel, and legislators can monitor the performance of laws and policies and make responsive revisions to specific modules or to the overall system architecture.

Privacy as a 'common good' speaks to the benefits of trust in these larger systems, and a corollary willingness to share data, collaborate and coordinate based upon perceptions of safety. Data governance as a related field of research addresses the business, legal, and technical systems put in place by institutions—both public and private—that can enable these notions of trust and safety. The fear of innovators and regulators alike is that an overly restrictive focus on protection will stifle the potential social and individual benefits of A.I. when powered by large, representative datasets. How might, for example, patients with valuable medical data to share as part of larger research studies feel safe and rewarded in doing so? 'Data Trust' proposals[15] could bring the best of both worlds, supporting both privacy and innovation, by separating out the functions of data custody and data aggregation, while borrowing from the collective bargaining approaches of trade unions. With computational law and human-centered design frameworks, these approaches to data governance architecture could overcome the current complexity of delivering end-user aligned value, while managing consent, using a combination of legal and

[15] See e.g. https://www.centerfordigitalcommons.org/.

technological tools, in more informed and legitimate ways than the current click-wrap approach of privacy policies.

Emerging technology solutions for managing data in line with these principles, such as homomorphic encryption, a form of encryption that allows for computation to be conducted on data that is held in privacy-preserving, outsourced storage, may also offer answers. Technology companies working with blockchain-based systems are developing approaches that offer alternatives to the default impulse to aggregate personal data under centralized custody and control.[16]

With the recent Singapore Convention on Mediation, the 'missing third piece in the international dispute resolution enforcement framework', we are making further steps towards a multilateral world of international rules. As we look, through blockchain and computational law, to opportunities to coordinate governmental and commercial activity on a transnational basis, many questions remain to be researched and understood.

In the spirit of taking these developments and building collective intelligence and capacity around the challenges and potential solutions, in 2018, I helped found a global effort featuring over 50 cities, focusing on these questions at the intersection of Computational Law and Blockchain, which continued in 2019 in its second edition.[17] In considering next steps for the future of legal practice, we will need interdisciplinary collaboration between lawyers, engineers, and many others, to develop the blockchain ecosystems of DAOs and other open platforms, the secure, tested smart contract templates that will form the backbone of a new legal and economic infrastructure, and the multi-party governance frameworks that will support the new extended enterprise frameworks and cross-organizational data- and work-flows. We will need to develop out use cases around reducing the costs of dispute resolution and compliance, reducing the costs of collaboration, and efficiently managing supply chains, digital rights, identity, payments, trade finance, asset management lifecycles, and more.

If we do this, future lawyers will be fulfilling their potential: as counsel to companies in making ethical decisions (even as they pursue profit); as peace re-makers; as stewards of trust, confidences, and private data stores; as creative designers of non-zero sum games and liberating structures; as smart contract platform administrators; as masters of the arts of dispute resolution and governance of multi-stakeholder systems; and as guides to our legislators on the moral limits of markets.

---

[16]See e.g. http://points.org/.

[17]http://legalhackers.org/clbfest2019/.

7 Conclusion

Together, we can be the keystones, the catalysts, welcoming dialog and exchange, change, at every level, local and international, and everything in between. Together, we can restore law to its place as the people's collective conscience, as a flexible and adaptive discipline, bringing together other disciplines: combining the best of self-disciplined markets and collective intention. Human-Agent Collectives will collect and reuse data in a fluid form of pervasive edge-based computing. And these agents will act in our interests, as people. We can establish polycentric rules-based governance to coordinate activity at every level around common goals and purposes, sowing the seeds for a future of scientific brotherhood and common humanity.

References

Ayres I, Unkovic C (2012) Information escrows. Mich Law Rev 111:145

Chesterman S (2019) We, the Robots? SSRN. https://doi.org/10.2139/ssrn.3428441

Cox M, Arnold G, Tomás SV (2009) A review and reassessment of design principles for community-based natural resource management. Ecol Soc 15:234–262

Finck M (2018) Blockchains: regulating the unknown. German Law J 19:665–692. https://doi.org/10.1017/S2071832200022847

Lewis P (2017) The Ostroms and Hayek as theorists of complex adaptive systems: commonality and complementarity. Adv Austrian Econ 22

Ostrom E (2010) Beyond markets and states: polycentric governance of complex economic systems. Am Econ Rev 100:641–672

Smedinghoff TJ (2018) Multiparty system governance and the shared signals use-case. In: Open Identity Exchange Blockchain, Identity, Trust, and Governance (BITGov) Workshop. Stanford

Stone CD (1972) Should trees have standing–toward legal rights for natural objects. South Calif Law Rev 45:450

Zuboff S (2019) The age of surveillance capitalism: the fight for a human future at the new frontier of power: Barack Obama's Books of 2019. Profile Books, New York

The manufacturer's authorised representative in the EU is Springer Nature Customer Service Centre GmbH, Europaplatz 3, 69115 Heidelberg, Germany. If you have any concerns regarding our products, please contact ProductSafety@springernature.com

Printed and bound by CPI Group (UK) Ltd, Croydon, CR0 4YY
28/09/2026
02224074-0014